The Major International
Treaties 1914–1945. *A*
history and guide
with texts

The Major International Treaties 1914–1945. *A history and guide with texts*

J. A. S. Grenville

Methuen
London and New York

EE

First published in 1974 as The Major International
Treaties 1914–1973 *by Methuen & Co. Ltd*
11 New Fetter Lane, London EC4P 4EE

Published in the USA by
Methuen & Co.
in association with Methuen, Inc.
29 West 35th Street, New York, NY 10001

Chapters I to IX and part of chapter XII reprinted
1987 with a new introduction

Introduction © *1987 J. A. S. Grenville*

Printed in Great Britain

British Library Cataloguing in Publication Data
Grenville, J.A.S.
The major international treaties, 1914–1945:
a history and guide with texts.
1. Treaties — Collections
I. Title   II. Grenville, J.A.S. Major
international treaties, 1914–1973
341'.026   JX171

ISBN 0-416-08092-8

Library of Congress Cataloging in Publication Data
Grenville, J. A. S. (John Ashley Soames), 1928–
The major international treaties, 1914–1945.

Rev. ed. of: The major international treaties,
1914–1973. 1974.
Continued by: The major international treaties since
1945/J.A.S. Grenville and Bernard Wasserstein. 1987.
Bibliography: p.
Includes index.
1. Treaties — Collections.   2. World politics — 20th century.
I. Grenville, J. A. S. (John Ashley Soames), 1928–
Major international treaties, 1914–1973.
II. Title.
JX171.G736   1987   341'.026   87-14091

ISBN 0-416-08092-8

Contents

Page references in *italic* lettering refer to the commentary,
and those in **bold** to the texts of the treaties

Maps

Preface

This book is intended for students and the general reader concerned with international affairs. It provides a short history and analysis of the major treaties and agreements since 1914, together with the texts of the most important of them. A firm grasp of the major international treaties is fundamental to an understanding of international affairs and recent history. Most monographs and general books on diplomatic history assume their knowledge, although the treaties themselves are not easily available to students. They are scattered through many volumes; few libraries possess even the most important collections and only a handful would be able to trace the text of every treaty in this book.

Many years of teaching modern international history have convinced me of the urgent need to provide a *usable* collection of such treaties in one volume. It proved a formidable task that has taken several years to complete. A selection had to be made from the more than 20,000 treaties and agreements concluded since 1914. From the point of view of the historian seeking to understand the course of events, the distinction made by international lawyers between multi-national and bilateral treaties is not relevant. Nevertheless Manley O. Hudson's *International Legislation. A Collection of Texts of Multipartite International Instruments of General Interest*, in nine volumes covering the period from 1920 to 1945 (Washington, D.C., Carnegie Endowment for International Peace, 1931–50), and the Harvard *Index to Multilateral Treaties . . . from the Sixteenth Century through 1963 . . .* (ed. Vaclav Mostecky and Francis R. Doyle, Cambridge, Mass., 1965) will remain landmarks in the indexing and assembly of multilateral treaties. The great collection of *Documents* and the *Survey* of the Royal Institute of International Affairs is another useful tool, though some caution has to be exercised since the volumes were generally written close to the events described. Even treaties 'change' as subsequent secret clauses come to light and the records of the negotiations leading to them are revealed.

There exist already a number of exceptionally good collections of treaties each dealing with a specific aspect of international relations. L. Shapiro's *Soviet Treaties, 1917–1939* (Washington, D.C., Georgetown University Press, 1950–5, 2 vols.) is a model of its kind; J. C. Hurewitz, *Diplomacy in the Near and Middle East. A Documentary Record* (Princeton, N.J., Van Nostrand, and London, Macmillan, 1956, 2 vols.) is another masterly survey; Keesing's *Treaties and Alliances of the World* (Bristol, Keesing's Publications Ltd, 1968) provides an excellent analysis of international treaties actually in force in the year 1968, though in the last five years a number of important treaties have been concluded; Ian Brownlie has edited treaties and documents on African affairs and other important subjects. These are only a few of the lawyers, political scientists and historians who since 1945 have made important specialist contributions. Government collections also exist on various international problems. But for the student who does not intend to specialize in a short period or in any one region, but who wishes to gain a general grasp, the task of studying all available specialist volumes and relating them to each other is formidable and usually beyond practical realization. It is also entirely beyond a student's financial means.

There is no one volume which can be referred to where the period 1914 to 1973 is treated as a whole. The basic research for this volume had to be done by patiently working through the many hundred volumes of the *League of Nations Treaty Series* and the *United Nations Treaty Series*. I would like to express my especial thanks to J. K. Nielsen and to the staff of the Dag Hammarskjöld Library of the United Nations in New York who in so many ways assisted this work. The treaties not to be found in these two great series may be discovered in national treaty series or specialist works. I found them partly in the United Nations Library in New York, also in the Library of the Royal Institute of International Affairs, in the Library of the Institute of Historical Research (University of London) and in the London Library. To the staff of these libraries I am much indebted for their expert and courteous assistance. I am grateful to Her Majesty's Stationery Office for permission to reprint treaties, and also to the National Archives, Washington.

The actual selection and editing of these treaties has been undertaken in the light of our present understanding of the diplomatic history of the last fifty years. The question may be asked, why edit the treaties at all? A study of the actual texts soon reveals that they contain much formal material which can be dispensed with. Secondly, to make the treaties usable it is helpful to focus attention on the important articles and where necessary to summarize the remainder.

Finally, even in their edited form, the major treaties fill a sizeable volume. To have printed all the treaties discussed in this book in full would have required at least twenty volumes and would have defeated my purpose, which is to high-light the significant and to bring the major treaties within one manageable volume. In editing these treaties I have kept in mind the student whose time for studying the subject is limited, but the references to the original printed texts of the treaties at the end of the book will guide those researchers who may require a particular treaty in full. The choice of treaties is difficult and bound to be subjective; I have kept in mind the use to which such a volume may be put.

This work is not meant to be a diplomatic history; it is intended for use with such histories. The treaties and introductions have been arranged to provide an historical framework to clarify their relationship to each other. I am most grateful to Methuen & Co., especially Peter Wait, and to Stein & Day for their general support while I was preparing the manuscript for publication. To my third year 'special subject' students I am also much indebted for their kind additional help in checking for errors at a time when they were very busy with their own work. For any faults or slips I alone must take responsibility; for constant encouragement and patience beyond the call of duty I have to thank Betty Anne, my wife.

December 1973

Preface to the 1987 reprint

There has been a growing demand for a reissue of the original work, *The Major International Treaties, 1914–1973*. The opportunity has been taken to bring it up to date (1986); but so much new material has been added that to produce the work in one volume would have made it rather unwieldy. Furthermore, for reference purposes, and also for use in courses, 1945 appears to be the obvious dividing line. There is, however, an overlap. The years 1944 to 1945 mark the end of one period, but also the foundations of contemporary international relations. So that both the volumes of international treaties, *1914–1945* and *Since 1945* can be used independently, there is a small amount of duplication for the years 1944 to 1945; the same is true of technical information in the introduction to each volume. Otherwise, apart from a new introduction and a new revised chapter X, *The Major International Treaties 1914–1945* is a reprint of the original book. I hope it will continue to prove useful to students and the enquiring readers who use it for reference.

March 1987

J. A. S. Grenville
Birmingham University

Introduction: International treaties

The role of the treaties 1914–1945

The Great War of 1914–18 was the first conflict involving armies drawn from five continents, whilst fighting actually took place on three of them – in Asia, Europe and Africa. It was the First World War, and the civilized, developed nations of Europe began the conflict. Alliances and alignments dividing Europe into hostile camps before 1914 had kept the great powers at peace with each other for forty-three years, but finally involved them all in the bloody confrontations of 1914–18. And when the war was over, and the statesmen were searching for better ways of managing conflicts between States, was not suspicion bound to fall on the 'treaties' themselves? President Woodrow Wilson condemned the *secret* treaties of pre-war Europe as the cause of tension, of miscalculation, even of war, especially treaties with clauses that could not be openly avowed. There should now be an entirely new start, he declared, open diplomacy; not a rejection of all treaties, but an overarching global treaty. The purpose of such a treaty was not only to provide security, that is collective security, with its signatories undertaking to come to the assistance of any signatory which was the victim of aggression, but also to create an organization which would offer a means of mediation, a diplomatic forum for the settlement of disputes, and provide institutional support for economic and social cooperation. The solemnity of the undertakings and their fundamentally moral intent was underlined by calling the agreement not a 'treaty', but a covenant, the Covenant of the League of Nations. Thus the bad reputation which had attached itself to many of the pre-war treaties was to be replaced by a new compact which would reinforce positive endeavours for peace and for the betterment of all mankind.

I

How would this idealistic view of the new purpose of treaties survive the consolidation of the Soviet Union? The revolutionary State was not willing at first to accept the premise of the sanctity of treaties concluded by its 'capitalist', Tsarist predecessor with other capitalist nations. The Soviet Union viewed the West as implacably hostile. How could treaties be concluded with an open enemy? The doctrine of world revolutions, of a life and death struggle between the first communist State and the capitalist West could not easily be reconciled either with Western concepts of a stable world of sovereign States whose conflicts could be peacefully resolved, and if that failed, would be settled through the collective pressure of the most powerful nations of the world. Yet in the 1920s the U.S.S.R. found it could not further its own national interests without resort to treaties and soon began, in 1921, to conclude formal treaties, just like any traditional State, with Iran, Turkey, Afghanistan and Britain. In September 1934 the Soviet Union joined the world community by becoming a member of the League of Nations. Egypt was the last country to join the League in May 1937. Perhaps this was symbolic. Egypt was not a genuinely independent country and was being admitted to a not very genuine League that could no longer fulfil its most important obligations, a pale shadow of the hopes placed in it by its founders.

The history of the League mirrors the extraordinary change in the role of treaties and their public and professional perception during the decade of the 1920s and the decade of the 1930s. Treaties did appear powerfully to work for peace in the 1920s. The League of Nations was seen to be functioning and showed itself capable of settling disputes. It is true that the United States Senate had repudiated American membership and the United States held aloof in the 1920s, but the United States did not repudiate international agreements or international involvement, or the value of international treaties. Faith in treaties prevailed and one of the most significant international treaties of the 1920s was signed in the capital of the United States. At the Washington Conference in February 1922 an effective naval disarmament treaty was concluded by the world's principal naval powers, which succeeded in reducing the number of powerful battleships threatening the oceans and settled the proportion to be allowed to each one of the five signatory nations, the U.S., France, Italy, Britain and Japan. Three years later, in October 1925, peace and security in Europe was reinforced by the five treaties making up the Locarno Pact, with their provisions for arbitration in the event of disputes between Germany and her western and eastern neighbours. The western treaties were further guaranteed by Britain and Italy, and the principal architect of these imposing treaties, Sir Austen Chamberlain, was honoured with the Nobel Peace Prize. The 'Locarno spirit' of reconciliation was fostered by the French

Foreign Minister, Aristide Briand, and the German Foreign Minister, Gustav Stresemann, who shared the Peace Prize a year later – in 1926. The faith in the ability of treaties to uphold peace, to set a moral standard and settle disputes by arbitration, reached its peak with the conclusion of the Pact of Paris in August 1928, negotiated by Briand and the American Secretary of State, Kellogg, which renounced war altogether as the method to settle conflicts between nations; differences of whatever nature were to be settled by pacific means alone.

If treaties could guarantee peace, there were a plethora of them now each overlapping the other with that purpose in mind. But the suspicion that they just might not is evidenced in the 1920s by the conclusion of many old-fashioned alliances and ententes as well. Defensive treaties between France and Czechoslovakia, between the 'Little Entente States' of the Balkans and so on. Still, by 1933, the very year Adolf Hitler came to power, sixty-five nations had also promised to renounce war as the Pact of Paris required.

What a contrast the 1930s were to the previous decade. Faith in the League faltered when Japanese aggression was not halted in 1931–3. As the United States increasingly cooperated with the weakened League, other great powers left it as soon as their aggressions were condemned. China, the first victim of aggression, was not defended; Japan, a founding member, left in March 1933; Germany, brought in with so much fanfare after Locarno, walked out in October 1933; Italy, having swallowed up Abyssinia four years later, departed in December 1937; Austria, a member of the League, was occupied by Germany in the following year. Haiti was the last member to leave the League in April 1942, by which time it did not matter any more; diplomacy had long by-passed Geneva, the headquarters of the League, which had become an irrelevance except for the germ of the idea, to be revived later in the United Nations.

Would national self-interest still ensure the observance of some treaties even if no longer for humanitarian or moral reasons? Would alliances prove effective? Such was still the hope of those in the 1930s who wished to settle conflicts peacefully. The Munich Agreement of 29 September 1938, partitioning Czechoslovakia, was possibly the last occasion when the peacemakers still expected a treaty to be observed by the dictator. Neville Chamberlain even secured Hitler's signature to an 'Anglo-German Declaration', expressing the desire 'of our two peoples never to go to war with one another again'. That was the famous paper he waved in the air at Heston echoing another 'scrap of paper' relating to Belgian neutrality in 1914. Hitler had already planned to break the Munich Agreement, and proceeded to do so when he occupied Prague in March 1939, and later that year he accepted the risk of a major European war when he invaded Poland on 1 September.

The Second World War had begun. Britain and France went to war with Germany on the principle of the defence of Poland. This appeared very moral but Britain had, by secret treaty with Poland, carefully excluded the commitment to go to war with the Soviet Union if it also invaded Poland, which it did soon after by arrangement with the Germans. Diplomacy and treaties in wartime with their cynical bargaining, their need to lure or keep military allies, repeated the pattern of the secret treaties of the First World War. But Wilsonian idealism also found its expression when Winston Churchill and Franklin Delano Roosevelt put their signatures to the Atlantic Charter in August 1941. The foundation and organization of the United Nations sought to avoid the mistakes of the League.

Why did treaties continue to be concluded after the disillusionment of the 1930s? Even if democratic Western countries felt they could rely on treaty commitments they had undertaken towards each other could the Soviet dictator be trusted any more than Hitler? And if the question is reversed, could Stalin trust the 'capitalist' Western powers? Yet treaties, as a means of regulating international relations, continued unabated whether between the Axis enemies or the Allied nations. That this was so was not due to blindness or unwarranted faith in the morality of all the signatories. Treaty observance does not depend on good faith alone. There are solid reasons for treaty observance.

Treaties reduce uncertainties and promote reciprocal relationships. No country can afford to cut itself off entirely from international contact and such contacts, economic, cultural and political, need to be regulated in many ways. A treaty is concluded because at the time it provides for reciprocal advantages. If a country violates a treaty, or is found out doing so, it will risk losing the advantages it enjoys under the treaty. Of course, a treaty may be concluded for a very short-term reason only; it suited Hitler to conclude a non-aggression treaty with Poland in 1934, which he totally disregarded five years later. There is no guarantee a treaty will be observed even before the ink is dry, but these are the exceptions rather than the rule. As long as it remains in the interests of the parties to it to benefit from the advantages of the treaty, it will at least appear to be observed. When one signatory no longer regards the treaty as providing a balance of advantage, the treaty will not be renewed (if renewal is provided for), renegotiated if that is possible, but in the last resort, despite 'international law' it will be broken. In such cases efforts may be made to obscure the breach as Hitler did when he accused France of breaking the Locarno treaties, when he himself broke treaties to march into the demilitarized Rhineland.

In the real world the practice of diplomacy has long recognized that when those who control foreign relations in one country regard a particular treaty as against the national interests in changed circumstances, its provisions will be broken or hollowed out. One option is not to conclude such treaties. Lord Salisbury at the turn of the century was opposed to the conclusion of an Anglo–German alliance because: 'the British Government cannot undertake to declare war, for any purpose, unless it is a purpose of which the electors of this country would approve. . . . I do not see how, in conscious honesty, we could invite other nations to rely upon our aid in a struggle, which must be formidable and probably supreme, when we have no means whatsoever of knowing what may be the humour of our people in circumstances which cannot be foreseen.' Yet a year later the Prime Minister's advice was ignored when Britain concluded an alliance with Japan in 1902 on the grounds of Britain's strategic and national interests. The refusal to conclude a treaty because in years to come it might be expedient to abandon it, has not generally inhibited diplomats. Rather, there is a recognition that no treaty automatically settles all future relationships between its signatories in perpetuity. The treaty marks no more than a new starting point of a relationship. It may be strengthened by strict observance and further cooperation, and agreements based on the principles of the original treaty. Or the reverse may occur. The terms of a treaty may prove less important than the relationship that follows on its signature.

A sense of realism has not lessened a desire for setting standards by treaty, whether of human rights or national behaviour. Some treaties continue to divide the world into hostile confrontational groups. Other treaties make relationships between nations that face each other less tense. This is especially true of successful attempts to agree to disarm. Treaties between nations friendly with each other further their cooperation in many spheres and so ultimately benefit their citizens. Treaties as such are neither 'good' nor 'bad'; they are not 'traps' as some political scientists have labelled them; they serve many purposes from the most modest postal agreement to supreme issues of national defence. The interdependence of nations continues to make them an indispensable feature of the conduct of international relations.

Clearly a study of treaties is not, by itself, sufficient to explain and understand international relationships over a period of time. At the same time, treaties as important as those discussed and printed here are essential for an adequate study of international relations.

The form and structure of treaties

The technical and legal aspects of treaties have, over the years, received much scholarly attention. Here it may be useful to summarize those points, especially important in international relations. But there are no hard and fast rules.

Before the conclusion of the *Vienna Convention on the Law of Treaties* in 1969, which established a generally agreed framework for treaty making, treaty forms and structure and practices were based on custom and precedents, but left considerable freedom of choice to the signatories.

DEFINITION

International treaties are concluded between sovereign States and presuppose their existence. There have been a few exceptions to this simple working definition: States under the suzerainty of another State have sometimes concluded international treaties; the degree of a State's sovereignty may be in dispute, as for instance in the case of the two Boer Republics, the Transvaal and the Orange Free State, which in 1899 went to war with Britain to assert their complete independence. There are other exceptions, but the overwhelming number of treaties are concluded between sovereign States; in the twentieth century they are also concluded between an organization of States such as the European Economic Community and another State. Here the organization of States acts in a collective capacity as one party to a treaty.

The treaties of main concern to the international historian are those which are intended to create legal rights and obligations between the countries which are party to them. Whether there can be 'treaties' properly so called which do not create such rights and obligations depends on definition. The Atlantic Charter of 14 August 1941 was a 'Joint Declaration' by Roosevelt and Churchill setting out certain agreed principles of policy; no legal obligations were incurred by Britain and the United States, though Churchill's signature as Prime Minister had been approved by the War Cabinet. Was it a genuine treaty or a press communiqué? On rare occasions an agreement on a minor matter can prove of major importance. One of the most bizarre examples occurred in 1971 when an agreement between the United States and the People's Republic of China for a U.S. table tennis team to visit China proved the prelude for President Nixon's visit in the following year and agreements (the Shanghai communiqué) which fundamentally altered U.S.–Chinese relations. Still, the treaties discussed and printed in this volume are of the more conventional kind.

In the nineteenth century and earlier, treaties were always concluded between the Heads of State, whether Monarchs or Presidents. This still remains true for many treaties. But equally important treaties may be concluded between Governments rather than Heads of State, as was the North Atlantic Treaty of 4 April 1949 and the Peace Treaty with Italy of 10 February 1947. Treaties are generally drawn up in the languages of the countries party to a treaty, more than one text often being declared authentic. The Treaty of Versailles of 1919 was declared authentic both in the English and French texts, though not in German.

It is generally accepted that unless there are contrary provisions laid down by the signatories of a treaty not inconsistent with overriding principles of international law, all questions concerning the interpretation and execution of treaties, their validity and how they may be ended, are governed by international custom and where appropriate by general principles of law recognized by civilized nations.

FORM

What is in a name? Less when it comes to a treaty than in almost anything else. What a treaty is called may be a matter of chance or design but it is not significant by itself. The obligations and rights have to be studied in each case with equal care: for example, an 'alliance' may not create the relationship and obligations which the common meaning of the word would lead one to expect. The Alliance for Progress of 1961 is quite a different kind of treaty to the Austro-Hungarian–German Alliance of 1879. It is therefore not possible to distinguish treaties or the rights or obligations arising from them, or their relative importance, by their particular form or heading. One has to work from 'the other end' and disentangle from the contents of the treaty the precise obligations and rights. This is a point of great importance in the understanding of international relations. The historian, for instance, will be especially concerned to discover whether a treaty contains commitments to go to war, or merely promises support in more general terms avoiding any automatic commitment to go to war in conditions specified by the treaty. Whether the treaty is called an 'Alliance Treaty' or a 'Declaration' makes no difference. Treaties have been called by many other names and each type of treaty is usually cast in its own conventional form. Some of the more common types of treaties are headed Convention, *Acte Final*, Pact, Agreement, Protocol, Exchange of Notes, *Modus Vivendi*, or Understanding, as well as Treaty, with some prefix such as alliance, boundary, etc.; and this list is not comprehensive. It also has to be noted that until the actual contents of a document are examined it cannot be assumed that any legal rights or obligations do in fact arise, and so the document may not be a treaty at all despite appearances. The historian thus has to exercise extreme caution in distinguishing between the 'content' and the 'form' or 'packaging' of diplomatic agreements.

THE VALIDITY OF TREATIES AND THEIR RATIFICATION

There is a wide range of choice as to the means by which a country may assume treaty obligations. There is no one answer to the question of what needs to be done before a treaty becomes binding and precisely when this moment occurs.

If the treaty is in the form of an exchange of notes it usually comes into force as soon as the documents have been signed, and only rarely is additional ratification provided for. The number of treaty agreements under this heading has become large. In Britain during the years 1951–2 about half the treaties signed were in this form. Such treaties are not necessarily confined to questions of a technical nature or of minor importance. Exchanges of notes may deal with questions of major importance, as was the case in the Anglo-German Treaty of 18 June 1935 concerning limitations of naval armaments.

Treaties may always be concluded which expressly stipulate that they come into force at the moment of signature and require no ratification; an important example is the Anglo-Polish Treaty of Alliance of 25 August 1939; the same was true of many treaties concluded during the Second World War.

A Government in practice has to choose how it will assume treaty obligations. Even where a country has a written constitution which requires the submission and consent of a representative assembly to a treaty, as is the case in the United States where Senate is required to approve treaties by a two-thirds majority, means may be found to circumvent the powers of such assemblies. Senator William Fulbright, the Chairman of the Senate Foreign Relations Committee, has observed that since 1940, 'the beginning of this age of crisis', 'the Senate's constitutional powers of advice and consent have atrophied into what is widely regarded as, though never asserted to be, a duty to give prompt consent with a minimum of advice'. Presidents have resorted to executive agreements at times when the consent of Senate to a treaty appeared doubtful. The important Anglo-American Agreement embodying the destroyers bases deal of September 1940 was concluded in this form. In the United States the Senate may ratify a treaty but can only do so with amendments; this in effect changes the treaty into a new one which may not be acceptable to the other signatories.

A treaty is concluded when signed, but where ratification is necessary becomes binding when ratified. Traditionally ratification signified the consent of the Sovereign to a treaty negotiated by the Sovereign's plenipotentiary, who might have no means of consulting the Sovereign when negotiating in distant countries. In modern times speed of communication has made it possible to submit the actual text of a treaty to the Government before it is signed. The practical importance of ratification now lies in the need to secure the consent of a Parliament or other elected assembly before the Government is ready to advise ratification of a treaty. In Britain, though treaty-making powers are vested in the Sovereign, the real decision lies with the Government and, where legislation is required to adapt British law to bring it into line with that required by the treaty, also with Parliament, for the necessary enabling legislation must first be passed by Parliament before the treaty can be ratified 'by the Sovereign' on the advice of the Government. The legislative and treaty-making process of Britain's adhesion to the European Economic Community provides a good example. It is the practice in Britain for the texts of all treaties requiring ratification to lie on the Table of the House of Commons for twenty-one days before ratification by the Sovereign. In France, the 1946 constitution, though vesting in the President treaty-making power, required that a wide range of treaties did not become valid unless embodied in a law passed by the French Parliament. The precise powers of representative assemblies differ widely and the constitution and practice of each country has to be considered separately.

Ratification is therefore not always a formality; important treaties by one means or another may be submitted to the approval of elected assemblies before the Government of the State concerned is able to give its consent to the treaty becoming binding. This may be due to constitutional custom or constitutional requirement, or to a Government's desire to retain the support of a majority of the elected representatives in order to continue in power.

The drafting of treaties

By this stage it will have become clear that there are no hard and fast rules as to how a treaty has to be drawn up. This is entirely a question on which the participants have free choice. But it is possible to speak of some widely adopted conventions which tend to give treaties certain common forms. Many diplomats in the world's various Foreign Ministries are employed in treaty drafting: their task is to put the intentions of the parties of a treaty in acceptable professional legal phraseology, which can at times strike the reader as rather stylized and even archaic. By way of example, a treaty between Heads of State is here considered.

Such a treaty commences with a *descriptive title*, as for instance the 'Treaty of Mutual Cooperation and Security between the United States of America and Japan'. Then follows the *preamble*, beginning with the names or description of the High Contracting Parties as 'The United States of America and Japan'; next the general purpose is set out, 'Desiring to strengthen the bonds of peace and friendship traditionally existing between them etc. . . . Having resolved to conclude a treaty of mutual cooperation and security, therefore agree as follows. . . .' The preamble often includes also, though not in the particular treaty here cited, the names and designation of the plenipotentiaries who have produced their full powers, which have been found in good order, and have agreed as follows. . . . Next follow the substantive articles each with a numeral, I, II, III, etc. which constitute the objectives, the obligations and the rights of the signatories; these articles are frequently arranged beginning with the more general and leading to the more specific. Where appropriate, an article follows which sets out the provisions for other States who may wish to accede to the treaty. Next follows an article (or articles) concerning ratification where this is provided for, the duration of the treaty and provisions for its renewal. Finally a clause is added stating 'in witness whereof' the undersigned plenipotentiaries have signed this treaty; the place where the treaty is signed is given, together with a statement as to the authentic languages of the treaty texts; and last the date is written in, followed by the seals and the signatures of the plenipotentiaries. *Conventions*, *Protocols* and other types of treaties each have their own customary form.

The vocabulary of treaties

Some terms used in treaty-making – a few of them in French and Latin – have special meanings.

Accession or *adhesion*: these terms are interchangeably used to describe the practice where a State which is not a party to a treaty later on joins such a treaty. No State has a right to accede to a treaty; the possibility and method of accession are often contained in a clause of the treaty as signed by the original parties to it.

Aggression: the common meaning of the term is an unjustified attack, and efforts have been made to define aggression by means of treaties. For example, a convention was signed in July 1933 between Russia, Afghanistan, Estonia, Poland, Rumania and Turkey which defined aggression as having been committed by the State which first (*a*) declares war on another State, (*b*) invades with its armed forces another State, (*c*) attacks with its armed forces the territory, naval vessels or aircraft of another State, (*d*) initiates a naval blockade of coasts or ports of another State; and (*e*), most interestingly of all, aggression was defined as 'aid to armed bands formed on the territory of a State and invading the territory of another State, or refusal, despite demands on the part of the State subjected to attack, to take all possible measures on its own territory to deprivate said bands of any aid and protection'. Despite the existence of such treaties, however, in the last resort each State or international tribunal has to judge on the merits of the facts before it whether particular actions constitute aggression or not.

Bilateral treaties are those between two States; *multilateral* treaties are concluded between three or more States.

Casus foederis is literally the case contemplated by the treaty, usually one of alliance; it is the event which when it occurs imposes the duty on one or more of the allies to render the assistance promised in the treaty to the other; *casus belli* has a slightly different meaning though frequently confused with *casus foederis*; *casus belli* is the provocative action by one State, which in the opinion of the injured State justifies it in declaring war.

Compromis in diplomacy has a meaning different from the everyday modern meaning of compromise. Deriving from the Latin word, *compromissum*, meaning 'mutual promise', a *compromis* in diplomacy is an agreement to abide by an arbitrator's award.

Denunciation is the giving of notice by a State of its intention to terminate a treaty. Some treaties provide for terminating by one of the parties on giving a certain period of notice. Others contain no such provision but are nevertheless denounced. Denunciation of treaties is a common occurrence after revolutionary changes in government, where the incoming regime adopts a different diplomatic stance from its predecessor. But international law recognizes no automatic right to such unilateral denunciation.

Delimitation and *demarcation* of boundaries: boundaries of State territories are the lines drawn to divide the sovereignties of adjoining States. They form the frontiers of each respective country. Concern for frontiers is the basis of many political treaties and the cause of many conflicts and wars. When a boundary can be drawn on a map and it is accepted by the States which are divided by it, even though the boundary has not actually been physically marked out on the ground by frontier posts, then it is said to have been *delimited*. The frontier is also *demarcated* when it actually has been physically set out on the ground and not only marked on a map. European frontiers have all been both delimited and demarcated. The same is not true of all boundary lines in the world especially in difficult and unpopulated regions. The distinction between delimitation and demarcation is an important one. There are no settled principles of demarcation though there are certain common practices such as to draw boundary lines through the middle of land-locked seas and rivers where they lie between two States. Estuaries and mountain ranges, however, cause more difficulty. In the absence of specific agreements the demarcation of an actual frontier based on a general boundary treaty signed much earlier – quite possibly when the state of geographical knowledge was imperfect – can become a matter of serious dispute. To avoid such disputes countries sometimes sign treaties setting out how a boundary is to be demarcated; an example is the boundary treaty between Great Britain and the United States of 11 April 1908 respecting the demarcation of the boundary between Canada and the United States. In other cases of dispute the two nations may resort to arbitration by a third party; finally a commission of two States or an international commission may have the power to demarcate boundaries. It is, however, helpful to be reminded by Professor Alistair Lamb that there are still boundaries which have been neither delimited nor demarcated; instead there is a *de facto* line. This is true of many stretches of boundaries in Asia, for example much of the Sino-Indian border, and the western end of the boundary between Chinese Sinkiang and the Soviet Union. Sometimes boundaries have been arbitrarily drawn by cartographers over country so difficult that it has not been surveyed and mapped with complete accuracy.

Demilitarization is an agreement between two or more States by treaty not to fortify or station troops in a particular zone of territory; such zones are known as *demilitarized zones*.

High Contracting Parties or *Contracting Parties:* when treaties are concluded between Heads of States they are referred to as the High Contracting Parties; when treaties are concluded between States or Governments the phrase used to describe them is usually Contracting Parties.

Internationalization refers to the placing under multilateral control of land or sea areas. Rivers (such as the Danube) have also often been the subject of such agreements.

Modus vivendi: usually refers to a temporary or provisional agreement which it is intended shall later be replaced by a more permanent and detailed treaty.

Most-favoured-nation clause: many commercial treaties between countries contain this clause, the effect of which is that any commercial advantages either State has granted in the past to other nations, or may grant in the future, have to be granted also to the signatories of a treaty which contains a most-favoured-nation clause. The intent is therefore that the commercial advantages of two States who have signed a treaty with this provision shall never be less than those of any third State which is not a signatory. The United States has not recognized quite so unconditional an operation of this clause.

Procès-verbal: is the official record or minutes of the daily proceedings of a conference and of any conclusions arrived at, and is frequently signed by the participants; a *Protocol* is sometimes used in the same sense but more accurately is a document which constitutes an international agreement.

Revision of treaties (save where the treaty itself specifically provides for subsequent changes) is generally permissable only by agreement of the parties.

Sine qua non: describes a condition or conditions that have to be accepted by another party to a proposed agreement; it implies that without such acceptance the agreement cannot be proceeded with.

Status quo: the common meaning is the state of affairs existing, but an agreement can refer specifically to a previous state of affairs as for instance in the phrase *status quo ante bellum* which means the state existing before the war began, for example as relating to frontiers.

Treaties imposed by force

How can any system of law admit that right is based on might? This is what is involved if in the relations between States international law accepts that the stronger nation may impose its terms on the weaker nation by war or by threat of force.

Before 1914, war and the use of force were accepted as legitimate means of securing national interests when diplomacy failed to achieve the desired objects. Two Great Powers of Europe, Germany and Italy, owed their very unity and existence to war. Indeed, the 1914 frontiers of the continental States of Europe were based on treaties concluded by the victorious Powers. The colonial empires of Britain and other Powers, moreover, had all been acquired mainly by conquest. Might was right in the sense that the mighty rarely admit to wrongdoing.

The League of Nations was to usher in a new era of international relations, based on the acceptance of the League Covenant which limited the right to go to war. Henceforth there would be two kinds of war, illegal wars waged in breach of the League Covenant and 'legal' wars which were not in breach of treaty engagements. The Pact of Paris of 1928 and the United Nations Charter extended the limitations of the signatories to threaten or to use force. International lawyers since then have wrestled with the problem of whether treaties imposed by countries who have used force in breach of their treaty engagements are valid. In the 1930s there evolved the principle of 'non-recognition' whereby other States refused to recognize the rights of States derived from the illegal use of force. But, as one distinguished international lawyer put it, the attitude of other States 'may, after a prolonged period of time, be adjusted to the requirements of international peace and stability'. More recently, the United Nations' *Vienna Conference on the Law of Treaties* in 1969 declared, after some seventeen years of preparatory work, that 'A treaty is void if its conclusion has been procured by the threat of force in violation of the principles of international law embodied in the Charter of the United Nations' (Article 52). But even this clear statement was made conditional; Article 75 of the same Convention appears to mean that an aggressor State cannot claim this safeguard if other States acting in conformity with the Charter use force against the aggressor and then impose a treaty related to the aggression. The *Vienna Convention* in any case will only apply when thirty-five States have ratified it, and then usually only to treaties signed after it has come into force.

As long as individual States or international organizations of States apply and interpret the law, political considerations will remain a strong, even a predominant influence. Progress in the codification of international law is made. Yet today we are far from a position where international and general agreement on how to apply it regulates international conduct on issues where nations wish to use force. Important national interests will induce States to recognize many rights 'illegally' secured, and this will remain true so long as it is believed that legal and moral precepts cannot alone determine foreign policy.

I · Secret agreements and treaties of the First World War

The outbreak of the First World War in August 1914 violated more than Belgian neutrality. The majority of the great territorial settlements of the nineteenth century, embodied in international treaties since 1815, were jeopardized. During the war international treaties ceased to be respected and the belligerents engaged in fierce bargaining to gain allies and to assure for themselves a favourable territorial settlement when the war was won. Each of the Powers at war had vague and shifting 'war aims' often motivated by immediate military needs. Diplomacy in wartime was designed to support the military effort, to strengthen existing alliances and to make new allies. Secret agreements and undertakings between several allies or between one State and another were made throughout the war. They were sometimes inconsistent and could not all be reconciled with each other when the war ended, leaving a bitter legacy of dispute to the post-war world. Nor did any one State have full knowledge of the secret bargains that had been struck.

In the actual declaration of war (as opposed to mobilizations) the Central Powers took the initiative. Austria-Hungary declared war on Serbia on 28 July 1914. Germany declared war on Russia on 1 August, and on France on 3 August. The German invasion of Belgium on 4 August was followed by a British ultimatum and a British declaration of war on Germany on 4 August 1914.

Austria-Hungary remained at peace with Russia after Germany's declaration of war and was only prevailed upon to declare war on Russia on 6 August 1914. It was France and Britain who declared war on Austria-Hungary on 12 August 1914. Portugal declared its adherence to the British alliance in the autumn of 1914 and commenced military operations against Germany. Thus only in mid-August were the Central Powers – Austria-Hungary and Germany – at war with all the Allied Entente Powers – France, Britain and Russia.

1 Europe, 1914

Japan did not join the Grand Alliance of Russia, Britain and France. It sent its own ultimatum to Germany on 15 August 1914 and declared war when it expired, basing its action on the Anglo-Japanese alliance. Japan did share one treaty in common with all the Allied Entente Powers when the Japanese Government on 19 October 1915 signed the *Declaration of London*, which had been concluded between Russia, France and Britain on 5 September 1914. This declaration stipulated that none of the signatories would conclude peace separately or demand conditions of peace without the previous agreement of the other signatories.

Italy, with Germany and Austria-Hungary, was a member of the Triple Alliance (last renewed in 1912) but declared its neutrality on 3 August 1914. Italy's obligations according to Articles 2 and 3 of the Triple Alliance required Italy to fight in case of unprovoked aggression by France on Germany. This, the Italian Government concluded, had not occurred. Moreover, in August 1914 the Italian Government claimed that Austria-Hungary had not acted in accordance with Article 7 of the Triple Alliance treaty when deciding to attack Serbia, for this article required previous consultation and agreement between Italy and Austria-Hungary based on reciprocal compensations.

The Central Powers, 1914–18

Germany secured a hasty secret alliance with *Turkey on 2 August 1914* (p. 24). It stipulated that the two Powers would remain neutral in the conflict between Austria-Hungary and Serbia; but that if Russia intervened with active military measures Germany would intervene on the side of Austria-Hungary and the alliance with Turkey would become active. The German military mission was to exercise in the event of war an 'effective influence' over the Turkish army, and Germany undertook to defend Ottoman territory if it were threatened. Turkey did not enter the war straight away but took a number of steps against the Entente Powers: two German warships were sheltered and transferred to the Turkish navy in August, and on 26 September the Straits were closed thus cutting the supply route to Russia. By the end of October 1914 Turkey actively entered the war on the side of Germany and Austria-Hungary and began operations against Russia. A new alliance was signed by Turkey and Germany in January 1915 and Austria-Hungary adhered to it in March 1915.

Bulgaria was induced in September 1915 to join the war on the side of Germany and Austria-Hungary by the promise of large territorial gains including Serbian Macedonia and a substantial grant of money. On *6 September 1915*

Bulgaria signed a military agreement and an alliance treaty with Germany and Austria-Hungary to join in a military offensive against Serbia, and in mid-October 1915 Bulgaria started fighting in accordance with this treaty.

The Allied and Associated Powers, 1914–18

Despite Italy's treaty engagement as a member of the Triple Alliance to remain benevolently neutral and not make alliances with the enemies of Germany and Austria-Hungary, Italy accepted the inducements of the Allies to join the war on their side. The promises of territorial expansion after the war held out to Italy were contained in the secret *Treaty of London, 26 April 1915* (p. 24). Italy was promised territory at the expense of the Austrian-Hungarian Empire, the Trentino, the South Tyrol, Istria and a third of Dalmatia, the sovereignty of the Dodecanese Islands which Italy already occupied, as well as a 'just share' of the Ottoman Empire in Asia in the event of its partial or total partition, taking into account Italy's special position in the province of Adalia. Italy was also promised compensation for British and French gains at the expense of Germany's colonies. On 23 May 1915 Italy declared war on Austria-Hungary.

Rumania, despite its treaty relations with Germany and Austria-Hungary before the war, also changed sides and abandoned neutrality in favour of joining the Allies. By *a secret treaty between Rumania, Britain, France, Italy and Russia signed on 17 August 1916* Rumania undertook to declare war and to attack Austria-Hungary and not to conclude a separate peace. Rumania was promised portions of Austria-Hungary, Transylvania, the Bukovina and Banat. But the value of these promises was made doubtful by a secret exchange of notes between Russia, Italy, France and Britain that Rumania's promised territorial gains would be granted only so far as the general situation at the end of the war allowed. In the event, the Allies were spared embarrassment for by Rumania's separate peace signed at Bucharest on 7 May 1917 Rumania forfeited alliance claims.

The most important of the 'Associated Powers' entering the war during the first week of April 1917, side by side with the Allied Powers, was the United States. Germany resumed unrestricted submarine warfare on 1 February 1917. President Wilson asked Congress on 2 April 1917 to formally recognize that a state of war existed between the United States and Germany. The House of Representatives passed a resolution for war and the Senate also on 6 April 1917. The United States declared war on Austria-Hungary several months later on 7 December 1917. In Europe, Greece was finally brought into the war by the Allies on their side on 2 July 1917 after they had blockaded the Greek coast and forced the abdication of King Constantine. China declared a state of war with Germany and Austria-Hungary in August 1917, thus complicating the intended settlement of Japanese claims at the expense of China.

The Ottoman Empire

The Allied Powers jointly and individually concluded a number of wartime treaties, agreements and understandings concerning the future of the Ottoman Empire. They proved impossible to reconcile when the war ended. Russia was promised Constantinople and the Straits at the time of the negotiations with Italy which had led to the *Treaty of London, 26 April 1915* (p. 24). An exchange of several diplomatic notes between Russia, Britain and France during March and April 1915 set out the attitude of the Allies: a Russian note in the *Russian Circular Telegram to France and Britain, 4 March 1915* (p. 27) contained extensive Russian demands for the annexation by Russia of Constantinople, the Straits, part of southern Thrace and part of the Adriatic shore. British replies in two *aides-mémoire*, both dated 12 March 1915, agreed in principle to the Russian acquisition of Constantinople and the Straits but made this dependent on a number of conditions, including some counter-concessions to Britain in the Ottoman Empire and Persia. The French reply in a note on 10 April 1915 agreed to the Russian proposal 'relating to Constantinople and the Straits', provided war was fought until victory and France and Britain realized their plans in the East and elsewhere. These conditional promises to Russia lapsed as Allied obligations when Russia concluded a separate armistice and peace with Germany in December 1917 and March 1918.

In the Ottoman Empire in Asia and the Middle East the Allies had made a number of promises to various factions, and came to agreements with each other which laid Britain and France open to charges of bad faith when engaged in peace-making from 1919 to 1923 (pp. 48, 51). Irreconcilable claims were embittered further when each party attempted to rely on wartime promises and undertakings. In April 1915 the secret *Treaty of London* between Italy, France, Russia and Britain (pp. 25–6), as it applied to the Ottoman Empire, promised Italy the Dodecanese Islands and a share of the Mediterranean region of Anatolia adjacent to and including the province of Adalia. From *July 1915 to March 1916, Sir Henry McMahon, High Commissioner in Egypt, exchanged ten letters with the Sherif of Mecca* (p. 29) to encourage an Arab revolt against Ottoman rule; in return McMahon promised that the British would recognize and support the independence of the Arabs in all regions demanded by the Sherif of Mecca, with some major reservations – the Mediterranean coastal strip west of Damascus, Hama, Homs and Aleppo (later Lebanon and the coastal region of

French-mandated Syria) – and only in those areas where Britain was free to act without detriment to the interests of her ally, France. British interests required the Arabs to recognize Britain's special position in the provinces of Baghdad and Basra. The correspondence left the political area of Arab independence indefinite and ambiguous. Certain regions were excluded with some precision by their special mention, but Palestine was not specifically mentioned. In other regions the Arabs could assume support for independence, but the proviso that French interests would be taken into account by Britain left a very elastic loophole. Since Palestine did not become a region of French interest, the correspondence would lead the Arabs to suppose that Palestine would form part of the territory of Arab independence. But the promise to the Zionists contained in the *Balfour Declaration, 2 November 1917* (p. 34) of a 'national home for the Jewish people' could not easily be reconciled with Arab sovereignty in Palestine.

A tripartite agreement for the partition of the Ottoman Empire in Asia was worked out between France, Britain and Russia in exchanges of notes from April to October 1916, and is known as the *Sykes–Picot Agreement* (p. 30). The agreement created French and British spheres of interest; an 'independent' Arab State was foreseen as falling within French and British spheres of interest. In other specified regions more direct French and British administration was foreseen. Palestine became an international sphere of interest. The Russians sanctioned the Anglo-French partition, and in return France and Britain permitted Russian annexation in Turkish Armenia and Kurdistan. The secret Sykes–Picot Agreement was published by the Bolshevik Government after the Revolution. The tripartite British, French, Italian *Agreement at St Jean de Maurienne, 19–21 April 1917* (p. 33) assigned to Italy a large region including Adalia and Smyrna for Italian administration, and a further zone of Italian influence to the north. This agreement, subject to Russia's consent, could only have been enforced on a completely prostrate Turkey and was incompatible with Greek and French ambitions in Asia Minor (p. 49). In fact no effort was made to enforce it after 1919.

China, Japan and the Pacific

In August 1914 British policy vacillated on the desirability of invoking the Anglo-Japanese alliance and so ensuring Japan's entry into the war. Japan was expected to press its claims to take over the German lease of the port of Kiaochow and rights in the province of Shantung. Japan also sought possession of the German island colonies in the Pacific. Their future was of especial concern to two British Dominions, Australia and New Zealand, as well as to the

United States. Japan decided the issue by declaring war on Germany after the expiration of its ultimatum of 15 August 1914. *Agreement between Japan and Britain was not finally reached until February 1917*, when Britain secretly agreed to support Japanese claims to those German islands which lay north of the Equator, the Marianas, Carolines and Marshalls, as well as to German concessions in Shantung; whilst Japan promised to support British claims south of the Equator, that is, for German Samoa, German New Guinea and Nauru. The French and Italian Governments shortly after entered into similar agreements with Japan.

Japan was determined to strengthen and extend her interests and influence in China. Following the military occupation of Kiaochow Bay, Japan on 18 January 1915 presented to China *Twenty-One Demands*. They included the following: China was to give full assent to any agreement Japan might eventually make with Germany about the lease of Kiaochow and German rights in the province of Shantung; the Japanese were to be allowed to build an additional railway in the province and no land in it was to be alienated to any other country; an extension for a further ninety-nine years of the Japanese lease of Port Arthur and Dairen was to be granted; certain towns were to be opened to foreign trade; Japan demanded a recognition of her predominant position in southern Manchuria and eastern Inner Mongolia; China was not to cede or lease to any other Power any harbour, bay or island along the China coast; finally, 'seven wishes' comprised group V of the demands, including the proposal that the Chinese Government should employ Japanese political, military and financial advisers. After delivery of an ultimatum by Japan, *China and Japan signed two treaties and thirteen notes on 25 May 1915* based on the Twenty-One Demands, but the 'wishes' comprising group V were dropped. China, who had declared war on Germany in August 1917, later at the peace conference refused to accept the validity of the agreements, declaring they had been signed under threat of coercion, and left without signing the Treaty of Versailles.

Japan's ally, Britain, and the neutral United States attempted to exercise a moderating influence on Japan in 1915. The United States was still committed to upholding the 'Open Door' and China's political and territorial integrity, but the U.S. Secretary of State, Bryan, in a note to the Japanese Ambassador in Washington of 13 March 1915, had stated that the 'United States frankly recognizes that territorial contiguity creates special relations between Japan' with regard to Shantung, south Manchuria and east Mongolia. This attitude was confirmed by the *Lansing–Ishii Agreement, 2 November 1917*. The United States tried to reconcile a recognition of Japan's special interests in China with China's territorial and political integrity.

In pursuing a forceful Chinese policy, Japan had acted in concert with

Russia. Russia and Japan concluded four secret treaties and conventions between 1907 and 1916. The last of the treaties was the most extensive in scope. The *Russo-Japanese Treaty, 3 July 1916*, of two articles made public and an additional secret convention, stated that the two signatories had 'vital interests in China' and that they would cooperate to prevent China falling under the political influence of a 'third power which entertains a hostile feeling against Japan and Russia'. The secret treaty was published and repudiated some eighteen months later by the Soviet Russian leaders after the Revolution. The secret treaty is notable for extending the interest of Japan to the whole of China and for being presumably directed against the United States.

The Treaty of Brest-Litovsk: Eastern and Central Europe, 1917–18

The Europe of the inter-war years began to take shape in the spring of 1918 with the victory of the Central Powers over Russia and Rumania. The signature on *3 March 1918 of the Treaty of Brest-Litovsk* (p. 34) was of lasting importance, even though the treaty itself was formally abrogated after the defeat of the Central Powers (the abandonment of Brest-Litovsk had been one of the conditions of the Allied armistice on 11 November 1918).

The peace of Brest-Litovsk marked the break-up of the Russian Empire, the first of the three pre-war multinational empires to collapse (the Hapsburg Monarchy and the Ottoman Empire were the others). During the war the Germans had encouraged nationalism as a weapon against the Tsarist Russian Empire and had supported non-Russian ethnic groups as a means of limiting Soviet Russian power. The Ukraine was recognized as an independent State by the Central Powers in February 1918, but German and Austro-Hungarian armies under the Supreme Command remained in occupation of the 'border' territories from the Baltic to the Caucasus, and occupied the Ukraine defeating the advancing Bolshevik forces. At the request of the Finnish Government, German armed forces in April and May 1918 helped the White Finns achieve victory over the Bolsheviks in the Finnish Civil War. Towards the independence of the Baltic States and Poland, Germany maintained a reserved and equivocal attitude. The defeat of Tsarist Russia had been the first condition of the independence of the Russian borderlands; the subsequent defeat of Germany was the second condition; and before some of these States attained independence during the inter-war years, the defeat of Soviet Russia in 1919 and 1920 had become just as necessary (see pp. 129–30).

Rumania also accepted defeat and concluded the *Peace of Bucharest on 7 May 1918* with the Central Powers. The treaty deprived Rumania of the southern part of the Dobruja which was incorporated in Bulgaria; Rumania also lost territory to Hungary but retained Bessarabia. Bessarabia had only been incorporated in Rumania in April 1918, a month before the Peace of Bucharest. Bessarabia was beyond the control of the Bolsheviks in 1917 and 1918; it had been proclaimed by its leaders independent and later voted for incorporation with Rumania on 8 April 1918. This was recognized by the Central Powers but not by Soviet Russia. With the Allied victory, Rumania regained the southern Dobruja and much more than the territory lost to Hungary; Rumania also kept Bessarabia (p. 114).

For Lenin and the Bolshevik leaders, Brest-Litovsk was a bitter peace. Russia was deprived of one-third of her population and her expansion during the last three centuries was lost. But what was far more important, as Lenin understood, was that Bolshevik power had survived and was consolidated in the heart of Russia. The Bolsheviks survived by only a narrow margin and could not have withstood Germany's determination to destroy them. But the Germans, desiring peace with some established Government and fearing that the opponents of the Bolsheviks might fight on, had been keen to preserve Bolshevik control in Petrograd. Lenin had bought time. Russia's losses he regarded as temporary. They would last until the war among the imperialist Powers had been turned into an international class war with the spread of revolution outward from Russia.

The armistice and peace negotiations of Brest-Litovsk lasted from December 1917 to March 1918 and were conducted at the German headquarters of the Eastern Front. Broken off by Trotsky early in February 1918, the Russian Soviets found themselves in an even more disastrous position when they were resumed as *the Germans had by then signed a separate peace with the Ukraine on 9 February 1918*. A week later the German and Austrian armies resumed the military offensive and penetrated deeply into Russia. Eventually, on 3 March 1918, the Russians signed the treaty of peace with Germany and Lenin secured its ratification. Thereby imperial Germany became the first State to accord *de jure* recognition to the Russian Soviet Government.

The Russians had broken their undertaking to their Allies not to conclude a separate peace. From this undertaking they had not been released. Yet their sacrifices for the Allied cause had exceeded that of any other single nation. During the armistice negotiations a vain attempt had also been made by the Russians to stipulate that no German troops should be transferred to the Western Front; but the Russians were powerless to prevent such transfers. Even so, a large German army remained in the East until November 1918, regarded by the German High Command as too unreliable or ill-equipped for use on the Western Front.

Secret Treaty of Alliance between Germany and the Ottoman Empire, 2 August 1914

Article 1. The two Contracting Powers undertake to observe strict neutrality in the present conflict between Austria-Hungary and Serbia.

Article 2. In the event that Russia should intervene with active military measures and thus should create for Germany a *casus foederis* with respect to Austria-Hungary, this *casus foederis* would also come into force for Turkey.

Article 3. In the event of war, Germany will leave its Military Mission at the disposal of Turkey.

The latter, for its part, assures the said Military Mission effective influence over the general conduct of the army, in conformity with what has been agreed upon directly by His Excellency the Minister of War and His Excellency the Chief of the Military Mission.

Article 4. Germany obligates itself, by force of arms if need be, to defend Ottoman territory in case it should be threatened.

Article 5. This Agreement, which has been concluded with a view to protecting the two Empires from the international complications which may result from the present conflict, enters into force at the time of its signing by the above-mentioned plenipotentiaries and shall remain valid, with any analogous mutual agreements, until 31 December 1918.

• • •

[*Article 8.* The treaty to be secret unless signatories agree otherwise.]

Agreement between France, Russia, Britain and Italy (Treaty of London), 26 April 1915

Article 1. A military convention shall be immediately concluded between the General Staffs of France, Great Britain, Italy and Russia. This convention shall settle the minimum number of military forces to be employed by Russia against Austria-Hungary in order to prevent that Power from concentrating all its strength against Italy, in the event of Russia deciding to direct her principal effort against Germany.

This military convention shall settle question of armistices, which necessarily comes within the scope of the Commanders-in-chief of the Armies.

Article 2. On her part, Italy undertakes to use her entire resources for the purpose of waging war jointly with France, Great Britain and Russia against all their enemies.

Article 3. The French and British fleets shall render active and permanent assistance to Italy until such time as the Austro-Hungarian fleet shall have been destroyed or until peace shall have been concluded.

A naval convention shall be immediately concluded to this effect between France, Great Britain and Italy.

Article 4. Under the Treaty of Peace, Italy shall obtain the Trentino, Cisalpine Tyrol with its geographical and natural frontier (the Brenner frontier), as well as Trieste, the counties of Gorizia and

Gradisca, all Istria as far as the Quarnero and including Volosca and the Istrian islands of Cherso and Lussin, as well as the small islands of Plavnik, Unie, Canidole, Palazzuoli, San Pietro di Nembi, Asinello, Gruica, and the neighbouring islets. . . . [frontier details]

Article 5. Italy shall also be given the province of Dalmatia within its present administrative boundaries, including to the north . . . [frontier details]

NOTE: The following Adriatic territory shall be assigned by the four Allied Powers to Croatia, Serbia and Montenegro:

In the Upper Adriatic, the whole coast from the bay of Volosca on the borders of Istria as far as the northern frontier of Dalmatia, including the coast which is at present Hungarian and all the coast of Croatia, with the port of Fiume and the small ports of Novi and Carlopago, as well as the islands of Veglia, Pervichio, Gregorio, Goli and Arbe. And, in the Lower Adriatic (in the region interesting Serbia and Montenegro) the whole coast from Cape Planka as far as the River Drin, with the important harbours of Spalato, Ragusa, Cattaro, Antivari, Dulcigno and St Jean de Medua and the islands of Greater and Lesser Zirona, Bua, Solta, Brazza, Jaclian and Calamotta. The port of Durazzo to be assigned to the independent Moslem State of Albania.

Article 6. Italy shall receive full sovereignty over Valona, the island of Saseno and surrounding territory of sufficient extent to assure defence of these points . . . [frontier details]

Article 7. Should Italy obtain the Trentino and Istria in accordance with the provisions of Article 4, together with Dalmatia and the Adriatic islands within the limits specified in Article 5, and the Bay of Valona (Article 6), and if the central portion of Albania is reserved for the establishment of a small autonomous neutralized State, Italy shall not oppose the division of Northern and Southern Albania between Montenegro, Serbia and

Greece, should France, Great Britain and Russia so desire. The coast from the southern boundary of the Italian territory of Valona (see Article 6) up to Cape Stylos shall be neutralized.

Italy shall be charged with the representation of the State of Albania in its relations with foreign Powers.

Italy agrees, moreover, to leave sufficient territory in any event to the east of Albania to ensure the existence of a frontier line between Greece and Serbia to the west of Lake Ochrida.

Article 8. Italy shall receive entire sovereignty over the Dodecanese Islands which she is at present occupying.

Article 9. Generally speaking, France, Great Britain and Russia recognize that Italy is interested in the maintenance of the balance of power in the Mediterranean and that, in the event of the total or partial partition of Turkey in Asia, she ought to obtain a just share of the Mediterranean region adjacent to the province of Adalia, where Italy has already acquired rights and interests which formed the subject of an Italo-British convention. The zone which shall eventually be allotted to Italy shall be delimited, at the proper time, due account being taken of the existing interests of France and Great Britain.

The interests of Italy shall also be taken into consideration in the event of the territorial integrity of the Turkish Empire being maintained and of alterations being made in the zones of interest of the Powers.

If France, Great Britain and Russia occupy any territories in Turkey in Asia during the course of the war, the Mediterranean region bordering on the Province of Adalia within the limits indicated above shall be reserved to Italy, who shall be entitled to occupy it.

Article 10. All rights and privileges in Libya at present belonging to the Sultan by virtue of the Treaty of Lausanne are transferred to Italy.

Article 11. Italy shall receive a share of any eventual war indemnity corresponding to her efforts and her sacrifices.

Article 12. Italy declares that she associates herself in the declaration made by France, Great Britain and Russia to the effect that Arabia and the Moslem Holy Places in Arabia shall be left under the authority of an independent Moslem Power.

Article 13. In the event of France and Great Britain increasing their colonial territories in Africa at the expense of Germany, those two Powers agree in principle that Italy may claim some equitable compensation, particularly as regards the settlement in her favour of the questions relative to the frontiers of the Italian colonies of Eritrea, Somaliland and Libya and the neighbouring colonies belonging to France and Great Britain.

Article 14. Great Britain undertakes to facilitate the immediate conclusion, under equitable conditions, of a loan of at least £50,000,000, to be issued on the London market.

Article 15. France, Great Britain and Russia shall support such opposition as Italy may make to any proposal in the direction of introducing a representative of the Holy See in any peace negotiations or negotiations for the settlement of questions raised by the present war.

Article 16. The present arrangement shall be held secret. The adherence of Italy to the Declaration of the 5th September 1914 shall alone be made public, immediately upon declaration of war by or against Italy.

After having taken act of the foregoing memorandum the representatives of France, Great Britain and Russia, duly authorized to that effect, have concluded the following agreement with the representative of Italy, also duly authorized by his Government:

France, Great Britain and Russia give their full assent to the memorandum presented by the Italian Government.

With reference to Articles 1, 2, and 3 of the memorandum which provide for military and naval cooperation between the four Powers, Italy declares that she will take the field at the earliest possible date and within a period not exceeding one month from the signature of these present ...

[Signed] E. GREY, IMPERIALI, BENCKENDORFF, PAUL CAMBON.

Declaration by which France, Great Britain, Italy and Russia undertake not to conclude a separate peace during the course of the present European war

The Italian Government, having decided to participate in the present war with the French, British and Russian Governments, and to accede to the Declaration made at London, the 5th September 1914, by the three above-named Governments,

The undersigned, being duly authorized by their respective Governments, make the following declaration:

The French, British, Italian and Russian Governments mutually undertake not to conclude a separate peace during the course of the present war.

The four Governments agree that, whenever there may be occasion to discuss the terms of peace, none of the Allied Powers shall lay down any conditions of peace without previous agreement with each of the other Allies.

Declaration

The Declaration of the 26th April 1915, whereby France, Great Britain, Italy and Russia undertake not to conclude a separate peace during the present European war, shall remain secret.

After the declaration of war by or against Italy, the four Powers shall sign a new declaration in identical terms, which shall thereupon be made public.

Secret Agreements between Russia, France and Britain concerning the Straits and Constantinople, 4 March–10 April 1915

Russian Memorandum to French and British Governments, 4 March 1915

The course of recent events leads His Majesty Emperor Nicholas to think that the question of Constantinople and of the Straits must be definitively solved, according to the time-honoured aspirations of Russia.

Every solution will be inadequate and precarious if the city of Constantinople, the western bank of the Bosphorus, of the Sea of Marmara and of the Dardanelles, as well as southern Thrace to the Enez-Midye line, should henceforth not be incorporated into the Russian Empire.

Similarly, and by strategic necessity, that part of the Asiatic shore that lies between the Bosphorus, the Sakarya River and a point to be determined on the Gulf of Izmit, and the islands of the Sea of Marmara, the Imbros Islands and the Tenedos Islands must be incorporated into the [Russian] Empire.

The special interests of France and of Great Britain in the above region will be scrupulously respected.

The Imperial Government entertains the hope that the above considerations will be sympathetically received by the two Allied Governments. The said Allied Governments are assured similar understanding on the part of the Imperial Government for the realization of plans which they may frame with reference to other regions of the Ottoman Empire or elsewhere.

British Memorandum to Russian Government, 12 March 1915

Subject to the war being carried on and brought to a successful conclusion, and to the desiderata of Great Britain and France in the Ottoman Empire and elsewhere being realized, as indicated in the Russian communication herein referred to, His Majesty's Government will agree to the Russian Government's *aide-mémoire* relative to Constantinople and the Straits, the text of which was communicated to His Britannic Majesty's Ambassador by his Excellency M. Sazonof on February 19th/March 4th instant.

British Memorandum (a comment on earlier memorandum) to Russian Government, 12 March 1915

His Majesty's Ambassador has been instructed to make the following observations with reference to the *aide-mémoire* which this Embassy had the honour of addressing to the Imperial Government on February 27/March 12, 1915.

The claim made by the Imperial Government in their *aide-mémoire* of February 19/March 4, 1915, considerably exceeds the desiderata which were foreshadowed by M. Sazonof as probable a few weeks ago. Before His Majesty's Government have had time to take into consideration what their own desiderata elsewhere would be in the final terms of peace, Russia is asking for a definite promise that her wishes shall be satisfied with regard to what is in fact the richest prize of the entire war. Sir Edward Grey accordingly hopes that M. Sazonof will realize that it is not in the power of His Majesty's Government to give a greater proof of friendship than that which is afforded by the terms of the above-mentioned *aide-mémoire*. That document involves a complete reversal of the traditional policy of His Majesty's Government, and is in direct opposition to the opinions and sentiments at one time universally held in England and which have still by no means died out. Sir Edward Grey therefore trusts that the Imperial Government will recognize that the recent general assurances given to M. Sazonof have been most loyally and amply fulfilled. In presenting the *aide-mémoire* now, His Majesty's Government believe and hope that a lasting friendship between Russia and Great Britain will be assured as soon as the proposed settlement is realized.

From the British *aide-mémoire* it follows that the desiderata of His Majesty's Government, however important they may be to British interests in other parts of the world, will contain no condition which could impair Russia's control over the territories described in the Russian *aide-mémoire* of February 19/March 4, 1915.

In view of the fact that Constantinople will always remain a trade *entrepôt* for South-Eastern Europe and Asia Minor, His Majesty's Government will ask that Russia shall, when she comes into possession of it, arrange for a free port for goods in transit to and from non-Russian territory. His Majesty's Government will also ask that there shall be commercial freedom for merchant ships passing through the Straits, as M. Sazonof has already promised.

Except in so far as the naval and military operations on which His Majesty's Government are now engaged in the Dardanelles may contribute to the common cause of the Allies, it is now clear that these operations, however successful, cannot be of any advantage to His Majesty's Government in the final terms of peace. Russia alone will, if the war is successful, gather the direct fruits of these operations. Russia should therefore, in the opinion of His Majesty's Government, not now put difficulties in the way of any Power which may, on reasonable terms, offer to cooperate with the Allies. The only Power likely to participate in the operations in the Straits is Greece. Admiral Carden has asked the Admiralty to send him more destroyers, but they have none to spare. The assistance of a Greek flotilla, if it could have been secured, would thus have been of inestimable value to His Majesty's Government.

To induce the neutral Balkan States to join the Allies was one of the main objects which His Majesty's Government had in view when they undertook the operations in the Dardanelles. His Majesty's Government hope that Russia will spare no pains to calm the apprehensions of Bulgaria and Roumania as to Russia's possession of the Straits and Constantinople being to their disadvantage. His Majesty's Government also hope that Russia will do everything in her power to render the cooperation of these two States an attractive prospect to them.

Sir E. Grey points out that it will obviously be necessary to take into consideration the whole question of the future interests of France and Great Britain in what is now Asiatic Turkey; and, in formulating the desiderata of His Majesty's Government with regard to the Ottoman Empire, he must consult the French as well as the Russian Government. As soon, however, as it becomes known that Russia is to have Constantinople at the conclusion of the war, Sir E. Grey will wish to state that throughout the negotiations, His Majesty's Government have stipulated that the Mussulman Holy Places and Arabia shall under all circumstances remain under independent Mussulman dominion.

Sir E. Grey is as yet unable to make any definite proposal on any point of the British desiderata; but one of the points of the latter will be the revision of the Persian portion of the Anglo-Russian Agreement of 1907 so as to recognize the present neutral sphere as a British sphere.

Until the Allies are in a position to give to the Balkan States, and especially to Bulgaria and Roumania, some satisfactory assurance as to their prospects and general position with regard to the territories contiguous to their frontiers to the possession of which they are known to aspire; and until a more advanced stage of the agreement as to the French and British desiderata in the final peace terms is reached, Sir E. Grey points out that it is most desirable that the understanding now arrived at between the Russian,

French, and British Governments should remain secret.

French *Note Verbal* to Russian Government, 10 April 1915

The Government of the [French] Republic will give its agreement to the Russian *aide-mémoire* addressed by M. Isvolsky to M. Delcassé on 6 March last, relating to Constantinople and the Straits, on condition that war shall be prosecuted until victory and that France and Great Britain realize their plans in the Orient as elsewhere, as it is stated in the Russian *aide-mémoire*.

Correspondence between Sir Henry McMahon and Sherif Hussayn: letter to Hussayn, 24 October 1915

... I regret that you should have received from my last letter the impression that I regarded the question of the limits and boundaries with coldness and hesitation; such was not the case ... I have realized, however, from your last letter that you regard this question as one of vital and urgent importance. I have, therefore, lost no time in informing the Government of Great Britain of the contents of your letter, and it is with great pleasure that I communicate to you on their behalf [i.e. that of the British Government] the following statement, which I am confident you will receive with satisfaction:

The two districts of Mersina and Alexandretta and portions of Syria lying to the west of the districts of Damascus, Homs, Hama and Aleppo cannot be said to be purely Arab, and should be excluded from the limits demanded.

With the above modification, and without prejudice to our existing treaties with Arab chiefs, we accept those limits.

As for those regions lying within those frontiers wherein Great Britain is free to act without detriment to the interests of her ally, France, I am empowered in the name of the Government of Great Britain to give the following assurances and make the following reply to your letter:

1. Subject to the above modifications, Great Britain is prepared to recognize and support the independence of the Arabs in all the regions within the limits demanded by the Sherif of Mecca.

2. Great Britain will guarantee the Holy Places against all external aggression and will recognize their inviolability.

3. When the situation admits, Great Britain will give to the Arabs her advice and will assist them to establish what may appear to be the most suitable forms of government in those various territories.

4. On the other hand, it is understood that the Arabs have decided to seek the advice and guidance of Great Britain only, and that such European advisers and officials as may be required for the formation of a sound form of administration will be British.

5. With regard to the *vilayets* of Baghdad and Basra, the Arabs will recognize that the established position and interests of Great Britain necessitate special administrative arrangements in order to secure these territories from foreign aggression, to promote the welfare of the local populations and to safeguard our mutual economic interests.

I am convinced that this declaration will assure you beyond all possible doubt of the sympathy of Great Britain towards the aspirations of her friends the Arabs and will result in a firm and lasting alliance, the immediate results of which will be the expulsion of the Turks from the Arab countries and the freeing of the Arab peoples from the Turkish yoke, which for so many years has pressed heavily upon them. . . .

Tripartite (Sykes–Picot) Agreement for the partition of the Ottoman Empire by Britain, France and Russia, 26 April–23 October 1916

Grey to Cambon, French Ambassador in London, 16 May 1916

I have the honour to acknowledge the receipt of your Excellency's note of the 9th instant, stating that the French Government accept the limits of a future Arab State, or Confederation of States, and of those parts of Syria where French interests predominate, together with certain conditions attached thereto, such as they result from recent discussions in London and Petrograd on the subject.

I have the honour to inform your Excellency in reply that the acceptance of the whole project, as it now stands, will involve the abdication of considerable British interests, but, since His Majesty's Government recognize the advantage to the general cause of the Allies entailed in producing a more favourable internal political situation in Turkey, they are ready to accept the arrangement now arrived at, provided that the cooperation of the Arabs is secured, and that the Arabs fulfil the conditions and obtain the towns of Homs, Hama, Damascus, and Aleppo.

It is accordingly understood between the French and British Governments:

1. That France and Great Britain are prepared to recognize and protect ['protect' changed in August 1916 to 'uphold'] an independent Arab State or a Confederation of Arab States in the areas (A) and (B) marked on the annexed map, under the suzerainty of an Arab chief. That in area (A) France, and in area (B) Great Britain, shall have priority of right of enterprise and local loans. That in area (A) France, and in area (B) Great Britain, shall alone supply advisers or foreign functionaries at the request of the Arab State or Confederation of Arab States.

2. That in the blue area France, and in the red area Great Britain, shall be allowed to establish such direct or indirect administration or control as they desire and as they may think fit to arrange with the Arab State or Confederation of Arab States.

3. That in the brown area there shall be established an international administration, the form of which is to be decided upon after consultation with Russia, and subsequently in consultation with the other Allies, and the representatives of the Shereef of Mecca.

4. That Great Britain be accorded (1) the ports of Haifa and Acre, (2) guarantee of a given supply of water from the Tigris and Euphrates in area (A) for area (B). His Majesty's Government, on their part, undertake that they will at no time enter into negotiations for the cession of Cyprus to any third Power without the previous consent of the French Government.

5. That Alexandretta shall be a free port as regards the trade of the British Empire, and that there shall be no discrimination in port charges or facilities as regards British shipping and British goods; that there shall be freedom of transit for British goods through Alexandretta and by railway through the blue

area, whether those goods are intended for or originate in the red area, or (B) area, or area (A); and there shall be no discrimination, direct or indirect, against British goods on any railway or against British goods or ships at any port serving the areas mentioned.

That Haifa shall be a free port as regards the trade of France, her dominions and protectorates, and there shall be no discrimination in port charges or facilities as regards French shipping and French goods. There shall be freedom of transit for French goods through Haifa and by the British railway through the brown area, whether those goods are intended for or originate in the blue area, area (A), or area (B), and there shall be no discrimination, direct or indirect, against French goods on any railway, or against French goods or ships at any port serving the areas mentioned.

6. That in area (A) the Bagdad Railway shall not be extended southwards beyond Mosul, and in area (B) northwards beyond Samarra, until a railway connecting Bagdad with Aleppo via the Euphrates Valley has been completed, and then only with the concurrence of the two Governments.

7. That Great Britain has the right to build, administer, and be sole owner of a railway connecting Haifa with area (B), and shall have a perpetual right to transport troops along such a line at all times.

It is to be understood by both Governments that this railway is to facilitate the connection of Bagdad with Haifa by rail, and it is further understood that, if the engineering difficulties and expense entailed by keeping this connecting line in the brown area only make the project unfeasible, the French Government shall be prepared to consider that the line in question may also traverse the polygon Banias-Keis Marib-Salkhad Tell Otsda-Mesmie before reaching area (B).

8. For a period of twenty years the existing Turkish customs tariff shall remain in force throughout the whole of the blue and red areas, as well as in areas (A) and (B), and no increase in the rates of duty or conversion from *ad valorem* to specific rates shall be made except by agreement between the two powers.

There shall be no interior custom barriers between any of the above-mentioned areas. The customs duties leviable on goods destined for the interior shall be collected at the port of entry and handed over to the administration of the area of destination.

9. It shall be agreed that the French Government will at no time enter into any negotiations for the cession of their rights and will not cede such rights in the blue area to any third Power, except the Arab State or Confederation of Arab States, without the previous agreement of His Majesty's Government, who, on their part, will give a similar undertaking to the French Government regarding the red area.

10. The British and French Governments, as the protectors of the Arab State ['protectors of the Arab State' deleted August 1916], shall agree that they will not themselves acquire and will not consent to a third Power acquiring territorial possessions in the Arabian peninsula, or consent to a third Power installing a naval base either on the east coast, or on the islands, of the Red Sea. This, however, shall not prevent such ádjustment of the Aden frontier as may be necessary in consequence of recent Turkish aggression.

11. The negotiations with the Arabs as to the boundaries of the Arab State or Confederation of Arab States shall be continued through the same channel as heretofore on behalf of the two Powers.

12. It is agreed that measures to control the importation of arms into the Arab territories will be considered by the two Governments.

I have further the honour to state that, in order to make the agreement complete, His Majesty's Government are proposing to the Russian Government to exchange notes analogous to those exchanged by the latter and your Excellency's Government on the 26th April last. Copies of these notes will be communicated to your Excellency as soon as exchanged.

I would also venture to remind your Excellency that the conclusion of the present agreement raises, for practical consideration, the question of the claims of Italy to a share in any partition or rearrangement of Turkey in Asia, as formulated in Article 9 of the agreement of the 26th April, 1915, between Italy and the Allies.

His Majesty's Government further consider that the Japanese Government should be informed of the arrangements now concluded.

Grey to Benckendorff, Russian Ambassador in London, 23 May 1916

I have received from the French Ambassador in London copies of the notes exchanged between the Russian and French Governments on the 26th ultimo, by which your Excellency's Government recognize, subject to certain conditions, the arrangement made between Great Britain and France, relative to the constitution of an Arab State or a Confederation of Arab States, and to the partition of the territories of Syria, Cilicia, and Mesopotamia, provided that the cooperation of the Arabs is secured.

His Majesty's Government take act with satisfaction that your Excellency's Government concur in the limits set forth in that arrangement, and I have now the honour to inform your Excellency that His Majesty's Government, on their part, in order to make the arrangement complete, are also prepared to recognize the conditions formulated by the Russian Government and accepted by the French Government in the notes exchanged at Petrograd on the 26th ultimo.

In so far, then, as these arrangements directly affect the relations of Russia and Great Britain, I have the honour to invite the acquiescence of your Excellency's Government in an agreement on the following terms:

1. That Russia shall annex the regions of Erzeroum, Trebizond, Van, and Bitlis, up to a point subsequently to be determined on the littoral of the Black Sea to the west of Trebizond.

2. That the region of Kurdistan to the south of Van and of Bitlis between Mush, Sert, the course of the Tigris, Jezireh-ben-Omar, the crest-line of the mountains which dominate Amadia, and the region of Merga Var, shall be ceded to Russia; and that starting from the region of Merga Var, the frontier of the Arab State shall follow the crest-line of the mountains which at present divide the Ottoman and Persian Dominions. These boundaries are indicated in a general manner and are subject to modifications of detail to be proposed later by the Delimitation Commission which shall meet on the spot.

3. That the Russian Government undertake that, in all parts of the Ottoman territories thus ceded to Russia, any concessions accorded to British subjects by the Ottoman Government shall be maintained. If the Russian Government express the desire that such concessions should later be modified in order to bring them into harmony with the laws of the Russian Empire, this modification shall only take place in agreement with the British Government.

4. That in all parts of the Ottoman territories thus ceded to Russia, existing British rights of navigation and development, and the rights and privileges of any British religious, scholastic, or medical institutions shall be maintained. His Majesty's Government, on their part, undertake that similar Russian rights and privileges shall be maintained in those regions which, under the conditions of this agreement, become entirely British, or in which British interests are recognized as predominant.

5. The two Governments admit in principle that every State which annexes any part of the Ottoman Empire is called upon to participate in the service of the Ottoman Debt.

Tripartite (St Jean de Maurienne) Agreement for the partition of the Ottoman Empire by Britain, France and Italy, 19 April–27 September 1917

**The Agreement, London,
18 August 1917**

Subject to Russia's assent.

1. The Italian Government adheres to the stipulations contained in Articles 1 and 2 of the Franco-British [Sykes–Picot] agreements of 9 and 16 May 1916. For their part, the Governments of France and of Great Britain cede to Italy, under the same conditions of administration and of interests, the green and 'C' zones as marked on the attached map . . .

2. Italy undertakes to make Smyrna a free port for the commerce of France, its colonies and its protectorates, and for the commerce of the British Empire and its dependencies. Italy shall enjoy the rights and privileges that France and Great Britain have reciprocally granted themselves in the ports of Alexandretta, of Haifa, and of St Jean d'Acre, in accordance with Article 5 of the said agreements. Mersina shall be a free port for the commerce of Italy, its colonies and its protectorates, and there shall be neither difference of treatment nor advantages in port rights which may be refused to the navy or the merchandise of Italy. There shall be free transit through Mersina, and by railroad across the *vilayet* of Adana, for Italian merchandise bound to and from the Italian zone. There shall be no difference of treatment, direct or indirect, at the expense of Italian merchandise or ships in any port along the coast of Cilicia serving the Italian zone.

3. The form of international administration in the yellow zone [same as Sykes–Picot brown zone] mentioned in Article 3 of the said agreements of 9 and 16 May shall be decided together with Italy.

4. Italy, in so far as she is concerned, approves the provisions on the ports of Haifa and of Acre contained in Article 4 of the same agreements.

5. Italy adheres, in that which relates to the green zone and zone 'C', to the two paragraphs of Article 8 of the Franco-British agreements concerning the customs régime that shall be maintained in the blue and red zones, and in zones 'A' and 'B'.

6. It is understood that the interests that each Power possesses in the zones controlled by the other Powers shall be scrupulously respected, but that the Powers concerned with these interests shall not use them as means for political action.

7. The provisions contained in Articles 10, 11 and 12 of the Franco-English agreements, concerning the Arabian Peninsula and the Red Sea, shall be considered as fully binding on Italy as if that Power were named in the articles with France and Great Britain as a Contracting Party.

8. It is understood that if, at the conclusion of peace, the advantages embodied in the agreements contracted among the allied Powers regarding the allocation to each of a part of the Ottoman Empire cannot be entirely assured to one or more of the said Powers, then in whatever alteration or arrangement of provinces of the Ottoman Empire resulting from the war the maintenance of equilibrium in the Mediterranean shall be given equitable consideration, in conformity with Article 9 of the London agreement of 26 April 1915.

9. It has been agreed that the present memorandum shall be communicated to the Russian Government, in order to permit it to make its views known.

The Balfour Declaration (letter from Balfour to Lord Rothschild), 2 November 1917

I have much pleasure in conveying to you, on behalf of His Majesty's Government, the following declaration of sympathy with Jewish Zionist aspirations which has been submitted to, and approved by, the Cabinet:

His Majesty's Government view with favour the establishment in Palestine of a national home for the Jewish people, and will use their best endeavours to facilitate the achievement of this object, it being clearly understood that nothing shall be done which may prejudice the civil and religious rights of existing non-Jewish communities in Palestine, or the rights and political status enjoyed by Jews in any other country.

I should be grateful if you would bring this declaration to the knowledge of the Zionist Federation.

Peace Treaty between Russia and Germany, Austria-Hungary, Bulgaria and Turkey (Treaty of Brest-Litovsk), 3 March 1918

Article I. Germany, Austria-Hungary, Bulgaria, and Turkey, for the one part, and Russia for the other part, declare that the state of war between them has ceased. They are resolved to live henceforth in peace and amity with one another.

Article II. The Contracting Parties will refrain from any agitation or propaganda against the Government or the public and military institutions of the other party. In so far as this obligation devolves upon Russia, it holds good also for the territories occupied by the Powers of the Quadruple Alliance.

Article III. The territories lying to the west of the line agreed upon by the Contracting Parties which formerly belonged to Russia, will no longer be subject to Russian sovereignty; the line agreed upon is traced on the map submitted as an essential part of this Treaty of Peace (Annex I). The exact fixation of the line will be established by a Russo-German Commission.

No obligations whatever toward Russia shall devolve upon the territories referred to, arising from the fact that they formerly belonged to Russia.

Russia refrains from all interference in the internal relations of these territories. Germany and Austria-Hungary purpose to determine the future status of these territories in agreement with their population.

Article IV. As soon as a general peace is concluded and Russian demobilization is carried out completely, Germany will evacuate the territory lying to the east of the line designated in paragraph 1 of Article III in so far as Article VI does not determine otherwise.

Russia will do all within her power to ensure the immediate evacuation of the provinces of Eastern Anatolia and their lawful return to Turkey.

The districts of Ardahan, Kars, and Batum will likewise and without delay be cleared of Russian troops. Russia will not interfere in the reorganization of the national and international relations of these districts, but leave it to the population of these districts to carry out this reorganization in agreement with the neighbouring States, especially with Turkey.

Article V. Russia will, without delay, carry out the full demobilization of her army inclusive of those units recently organized by the present Government.

Furthermore, Russia will either bring her warships into Russian ports and there detain them until the day of the conclusion of a general peace, or disarm them forthwith. Warships of the States which continue in a state of war with the Powers of the Quadruple Alliance, in so far as they are within Russian sovereignty, will be treated as Russian warships....

Article VI. Russia obligates herself to conclude peace at once with the Ukrainian People's Republic and to recognize the treaty of peace between that State and the Powers of the Quadruple Alliance. The Ukrainian territory will, without delay, be cleared of Russian troops and the Russian Red Guard. Russia is to put an end to all agitation or propaganda against the Government or the public institutions of the Ukrainian People's Republic.

Estonia and Livonia will likewise, without delay, be cleared of Russian troops and the Russian Red Guard. The eastern boundary of Estonia runs, in general, along the river Narva. The eastern boundary of Livonia crosses, in general, lakes Peipus and Pskov, to the south-western corner of the latter, then across Lake Luban in the direction of Livenhof on the Dvina. Estonia and Livonia will be occupied by a German police force until security is ensured by proper national institutions and until public order has been established. Russia will liberate at once all arrested or deported inhabitants of Estonia and Livonia, and ensures the safe return of all deported Estonians and Livonians.

Finland and the Aaland Islands will immediately be cleared of Russian troops and the Russian Red Guard, and the Finnish ports of the Russian fleet and of the Russian naval forces. So long as the ice prevents the transfer of warships into Russian ports, only limited forces will remain on board the warships. Russia is to put an end to all agitation or propaganda against the Government or the public institutions of Finland.

The fortresses built on the Aaland Islands are to be removed as soon as possible. As regards the permanent non-fortification of these islands as well as their further treatment in respect to military and technical navigation matters, a special agreement is to be concluded between Germany, Finland, Russia, and Sweden; there exists an understanding to the effect that, upon Germany's desire, still other countries bordering upon the Baltic Sea would be consulted in this matter.

Article VII. In view of the fact that Persia and Afghanistan are free and independent States, the Contracting Parties obligate themselves to respect the political and economic independence and the territorial integrity of these States.

Article VIII. The prisoners of war of both parties will be released to return to their homeland. The settlement of the questions connected therewith will be effected through the special treaties provided for in Article XII.

Article IX. The Contracting Parties mutually renounce compensation for their war expenses, i.e. of the public expenditures for the conduct of the war, as well as compensation for war losses, i.e. such losses as were caused them and their nationals within the war zones by military measures, inclusive of all requisitions effected in enemy country.

Article X. Diplomatic and consular relations between the Contracting Parties will be resumed immediately upon the ratification of the Treaty of Peace. As regards the reciprocal admission of consuls, separate agreements are reserved.

Article XI. As regards the economic relations between the Powers of the Quadruple Alliance and Russia the regulations

contained in Appendices II–V are deter-
minative, namely Appendix II for the
Russo-German, Appendix III for the
Russo-Austro-Hungarian, Appendix IV
for the Russo-Bulgarian, and Appendix
V for the Russo-Turkish relations.

Supplementary Treaty of Peace between Russia and the Central Powers, Berlin, 27 August 1918

Guided by the wish to solve certain political questions which have arisen in connection with the Peace Treaty of March
3–7, 1918, between Germany, Austria-
Hungary, Bulgaria, and Turkey, for the
one part, and Russia, for the other part,
in the spirit of friendly understanding
and mutual conciliation, and, in so doing,
to promote the restoration of good and
confidential relations between the two
Empires, for which a way was paved by
the conclusion of peace, the German Imperial Government and the Government
of the Russian Socialist Federal Soviet
Republic have agreed to conclude a supplementary treaty to the Peace Treaty
with this object, and have ... agreed to
the following provisions:

[*Article 1*. Demarcation of frontiers.]

[*Article 2*. Frontier commission.]

Article 3. Germany will evacuate the territory occupied by her east of Beresina, even
before the conclusion of general peace, in
proportion as Russia makes the cash payments stipulated in Article 2 of the Russo-
German Financial Agreement of this
date; further provisions as to this, particularly the fixing of the individual sec-
tors to be evacuated, are left to the Commission referred to in Article 2, paragraph
1, of this Supplementary Treaty.

The Contracting Parties reserve the
right to make further agreements with regard to the effecting of the evacuation of
the occupied territory west of the Beresina
before the conclusion of general peace, in
accordance with the fulfilment by Russia

of the remaining financial obligations
undertaken by her.

Part II · Separatist movements in the Russian Empire

Article 4. In so far as is not otherwise
prescribed in the Peace Treaty or in this
Supplementary Treaty, Germany will in
no wise interfere in the relations between
the Russian Empire and parts of its territory, and will thus in particular neither
cause nor support the formation of independent States in those territories.

Part III · North Russian territory

Article 5. Russia will at once employ all
the means at her disposal to expel the
Entente forces from North Russian territory in observance of her neutrality.

Germany guarantees that during these
operations there shall be no Finnish attack
of any kind on Russian territory, particularly on St Petersburg.

Article 6. When the Entente forces shall
have evacuated North Russian territory,
the local Russian coast shipping within
the three-mile limit from the north coast,
and the fishing boats within a stretch of
thirty miles along this coast shall be re-
lieved of the barred zone menace. The
German naval command shall have an
opportunity, in a way to be further agreed
upon, of convincing itself that this concession shall not be taken advantage of to
forward contraband goods.

Part IV · Estonia, Livonia, Courland, and Lithuania

Article 7. Russia, taking account of the condition at present existing in Estonia and Livonia, renounces sovereignty over these regions, as well as all interference in their internal affairs. Their future fate shall be decided in agreement with their inhabitants. . . .

[*Article 13.* Recognition of Georgia's independence.]

[In a Financial Agreement concluded at the same time, Russia agreed to pay Germany 6,000 million marks as compensation for losses to Germany caused by Russian measures.]

Decree of the All-Russian Central Executive Committee of the Soviets on the cancellation of the Brest-Litovsk Treaty, 13 November 1918

To all peoples of Russia, to the population of all occupied regions and territories:

The All-Russian Central Executive Committee of the Soviets hereby declares solemnly that the conditions of peace with Germany signed at Brest on March 3, 1918, are null and void. The Brest-Litovsk treaty (and equally the annexed agreement signed at Berlin on August 27, and ratified by the All-Russian Central Executive Committee on September 6, 1918), in their entirety and in all their articles, are herewith declared as annulled. All obligations assumed under the Brest-Litovsk treaty and dealing with the payment of contributions or the cession of territory or regions, are declared void. . . .

II · The peace settlements and the League of Nations, 1919–23

The armed conflict of the First World War came to an end with the separate signatures of armistices between the belligerents. Turkey signed an armistice at Mudros on 30 October 1918, Austria-Hungary on 3 November 1918 and Germany on 11 November 1918.

In the West the armistice conditions of 11 November 1918 between the Allies and Germany provided for an orderly withdrawal of the German army from occupied territories and also from the right and left banks of the Rhine. But the conditions of the German armistice did not provide for the German evacuation of all occupied Tsarist territory. Territories in Central and Eastern Europe that had once formed part of the Tsarist Russian Empire of 1914 were not to be evacuated by German troops, according to Article 12 of the armistice, until 'the Allies think the moment suitable, having regard to the internal situation of these territories'. Thus the Allies enlisted German help to prevent the spread of Bolshevism until they were ready to intervene; Article 16 reserved to the Allies 'free access to the territories evacuated by the Germans on their eastern frontier, either through Danzig or by the Vistula, in order to convey supplies to the population of these territories or for the purpose of maintaining order'. Similarly anti-Bolshevik terms had been included in the Austro-Hungarian armistice of 3 November 1918. In the Turkish armistice the Allies assured themselves of strategic access to the Black Sea; they asserted their right to occupy the forts of the Dardanelles and Bosphorus and provided for an Allied occupation of Batum and Baku; they also claimed the general right to occupy any strategic point 'in the event of a situation arising which threatens the security of the Allies'. In December 1918 and January 1919 the Allies, referring to Article 12 of the German armistice, strenuously objected to German withdrawals in southern Russia, the Ukraine and from Estonia.

2 The peace settlements, 1919–23

'Livonia and Courland' (Latvia, Lithuania). The Allies feared that they would not be able to reinforce German and anti-Bolshevik forces fast enough to maintain their *cordon sanitaire*. During the course of 1918 the provisional independent Governments of Estonia and Latvia were reorganized by the Allies though under foreign occupation. The Allies attempted to stop the Bolshevik advance in the Baltic and in Central Europe, and as the peace conference opened in January 1919 the Germans assisted by despatching the *Free Corps* troops to the Baltic.

During the *Paris Peace Conference* four of the five Great Powers, Britain, France, Italy and the United States (but not Japan) in their negotiations and discussions ranged over the international problems of the whole world, but did not settle all the world's problems; only the Covenant of the League of Nations was intended to be of universal application. The frontiers and peace treaties settled by the peace conference were those that concerned the Allied and Associated Powers on the one hand and the defeated enemy States, Germany, Austria, Hungary, Bulgaria and Turkey, on the other. Excluded from the territorial peace settlements were Russia and the frontiers of Russia and its neighbours. The failure of Allied intervention and the outcome of the Civil War determined the fate of Russia. Russia's frontiers were dealt with separately in negotiations and treaties between Russia on the one hand, and Finland, Estonia, Latvia, Lithuania, Poland and Turkey on the other, after continued fighting in Eastern and Central Europe during 1919 and 1920. Thus the territorial peace settlements of the Allied and Associated Powers did not cover the whole of Europe.

THE ORGANIZATION OF THE PARIS PEACE CONFERENCE

The Peace Conference of Paris opened on 18 January 1919 and officially ended on 21 January 1920. Thirty-two nations, enemies of Germany or one of its allies, sent plenipotentiaries; included were five Latin American States which had severed diplomatic relations with Germany. The following States were represented: United States; Britain; Canada; Australia; South Africa; New Zealand; India; France; Italy; Japan; Belgium; Bolivia; Brazil; China; Cuba; Czechoslovakia; Ecuador; Greece; Guatemala; Haiti; the Hejaz; Honduras; Liberia; Nicaragua; Panama; Peru; Portugal; Poland; Rumania; Kingdom of the Serbs, Croats and Slovenes (Yugoslavia); Siam; Uruguay. The Council of Ten (see below) accepted separate representation for the Dominions, Canada, South Africa, Australia, New Zealand and India. Much expert research had been undertaken on the subjects with which the peace conference would have to deal, but little thought had been given to the actual organization and procedure of the conference itself. The order in which issues were to be raised and resolved was never settled, or rather the approach adopted was pragmatic; issues were decided as and when they should prove ready for discussion. Consequently the major political settlements were reached in detail by a piecemeal process and not according to an overall design and plan. The second Plenary Session of the conference established the main special commissions to examine specific issues. The crucial bargaining, however, was not conducted by all the participating nations, but only by the 'Big Five', Britain, France, Italy, Japan and the United States, which with two plenipotentiaries each formed the Council of Ten. This Great Power directorate promised to consult the smaller States when their interests were affected and established a large number of expert territorial commissions to deal with frontier questions.

After 24 March 1919 the Council of Ten gave way to a smaller, more informal, Council of Four of Wilson, Lloyd George, Clemenceau and Orlando. In the fourth week of April when Fiume was not awarded to Italy, Orlando left the Council of Four in protest, so the decisions were then left to the remaining three. The Treaty of Versailles, 28 June 1919, formally concluded the League of Nations and the German aspects of the peace settlements, and Wilson returned to the United States. Negotiations continued on the other peace treaties, with the United States playing a decreasing role after the rejection of them by the Senate on 19 November 1919 and 19 March 1920. The United States concluded separate peace treaties with Germany, Austria and Hungary in August 1921.

The Treaty of Versailles: the peace settlement with Germany

THE ARMISTICE

Germany did not 'surrender unconditionally' in November 1918. On 4 October 1918 Prime Minister Max von Baden, the German Chancellor, sought an armistice on the basis of the Fourteen Points in an appeal to President Wilson. Only after exchanging three notes with the German Government did Wilson, on 23 October, formally consult the Allies, who meantime were alarmed at the prospect of bilateral US–German negotiations for peace. The biggest obstacle did not prove to be the Fourteen Points as far as they applied to Germany, but American insistence of 'absolute freedom of navigation upon the seas, outside territorial waters' in time of peace and war. Britain strenuously resisted and maintained her national right to blockade and interruption in 1918 as she had done in 1812. Agreement was finally reached between the United States and the Allies on 4 November which accepted peace on the Fourteen Points, together with Wilson's subsequent addresses and pronouncements of principles and two further provisos, one concerning reparations, the other leaving open the question of the freedom of the seas for the peace conference. This marked the first official acceptance of Wilson's unilateral proclamation of war aims in *the Fourteen Points, 8 January 1918* (p. 57) which he had delivered in his address to a joint session of Congress. Independently, in a speech three days earlier on 5 January 1918, Lloyd George had defined British war aims, which were closely similar to all but one of Wilson's Fourteen Points, namely the second point on the freedom of the seas. Germany accepted the terms agreed by the Allies and the United States together with the military terms decided upon by the commander in the field; the armistice was signed on 11 November 1918.

THE TERRITORIAL TERMS

In the West, Alsace-Lorraine was returned to France and Germany's request for a plebiscite was rejected; the Saar was placed under an International Commission of the League and it was agreed that a plebiscite would be held at the end of fifteen years (in 1935 the Saar opted for Germany with Germany then able to repurchase mines); the mines of the Saar passed into French ownership as part of the reparations for damage to French mines; three small territories became Belgian – Moresnet, Eupen and Malmedy.

French demands for the strategic frontier of the Rhine caused a crisis among the Big Four in March and April 1919. France only acquiesced to German sovereignty continuing over the territories of both banks of the Rhine on two conditions agreed to by the Allies and the United States. Firstly, Allied troops were to occupy German territory west of the Rhine and some bridgeheads across the Rhine in three zones, to be evacuated at five-year intervals provided Germany fulfilled the treaty conditions of Versailles. In June 1919, a concession was made to Germany that if it gave proof of goodwill and satisfactory guarantees of fulfilling its obligations, the projected fifteen-year occupation might be shortened; the German territory west of the Rhine, moreover, was demilitarized (no troops or fortifications permitted in the demilitarized zone) as well as a strip of territory running 50 kilometres east of the Rhine. Secondly, France received a *Treaty of Guarantee* from the United States and Britain of military support if Germany attacked France. The *Treaties of Guarantee were signed on 28 June 1919* (p. 71), at the same time as the Treaty of Versailles, but the coming into force of the British treaty depended on the prior ratification by the Senate of the United States. Thus when Senate rejected the Versailles Treaty, the U.S. Treaty of Guarantee with France and the British Treaty of Guarantee with France lapsed also.

In the North, on the Danish–German frontier, it was agreed that a new frontier would be fixed according to a plebiscite of the population of Schleswig; the predominantly Danish-speaking northern part of Schleswig chose to join Denmark in 1920, and southern Schleswig stayed in Germany.

In the East, Germany lost large territories to the new Polish State. To allow Poland an outlet to the sea the Polish 'corridor' was created which separated Germany from the east Prussian territories. The province of Posen (Poznan) was also placed under Polish sovereignty together with Upper Silesia; the German-speaking town of Danzig was made a Free City under the supervision of the League, but with Poland enjoying special rights, a customs union and control of foreign affairs. German protests in June 1919 modified the final terms of the German eastern frontier significantly in that the final disposition of Upper Silesia was to be dependent on plebiscites held in that region. In July 1920 the territory of East Prussia was considerably enlarged southwards as a result of plebiscites in the Allenstein and Marienwerder zones; in March 1921 about two-thirds of the area of Upper Silesia voted for Germany, and only about one-third became Polish though it contained the greater mineral wealth. The settlement of the Polish–German frontier in 1920 and 1921 left a German minority of more than one million in Poland and a Polish minority in excess of half a million in Germany. Germany lost Memel and its district with its half German-speaking and half Lithuanian population, which Lithuania seized in 1923. Germany also lost a small piece of Silesian territory to Czechoslovakia.

Germany was obliged to give up all her colonies. The African colonies were divided in the form of different classes of mandates under the League of Nations between Britain, South Africa, France and Belgium (except for some small areas annexed by France and Portugal); Australia, New Zealand, Britain and Japan took over the Pacific territories. Japanese insistence on acquiring Germany's special privileges in the Chinese province of Shantung caused great difficulty at the peace conference as China was an ally that had declared war on Germany; but secret British, French and Italian wartime promises secured Japan the necessary support at the peace conference. China thereupon refused to sign the Treaty of Versailles.

REPARATIONS

The question of reparations proved among the most contentious issues of the peace conference. Too large a sum might lead the Germans to refuse to sign the treaty, and a sum likely to prove within Germany's reasonable capacity to pay would not satisfy public opinion in France and Britain, on which the British and French Prime Ministers negotiating in Paris were dependent. No total sum was stated in the treaty nor any limit to the years of payment; instead a Reparations Commission was set up to determine by 1 May 1921 the total of Germany's obligations. The inability to fix a relatively moderate sum made the earlier hard-won agreement secured by Wilson that Germany should only pay for civilian damage, not the whole of the war costs, of little practical importance. The famous War Guilt clause (Article 231) came to symbolize the injustices of the Treaty of Versailles. The wording was ill-considered and in subsequent years helped to undermine credibility in the treaty. It was not intended to be considered by itself, but was the first article in the reparations section; in Article 232 German liability was limited and 'complete reparation for all such loss and damage', that is the whole of the war costs, would not be demanded. To make the concession of requiring reparations only for civilian damage (and pensions) more palatable, it was agreed that the Allies should assert, and Germany should be obliged to accept, German responsibility with its allies for 'all the loss and damage . . . as a consequence of the war imposed upon them by the aggression of Germany and her allies'.

FOOD SUPPLIES AND THE BLOCKADE

A loosely coordinated Allied relief effort under Herbert Hoover as Director-General began to function early in 1919, and brought food and relief to the peoples of Eastern Europe facing starvation. The bulk of food supplies and services came from the United States, and Britain also made a major contribution, but Germany was excluded from the relief grants. The blockade was maintained against Germany, a later potent propaganda plank used by the Nazis to discredit all the proceedings of Versailles. The French demanded immediate reparations payments and the handing over of the German merchant fleet. This was made an additional condition of renewing the armistice on 16 January 1919. At first Germany refused, but Allied agreement was eventually reached, in Brussels on 14 March 1919, on German payments in foreign securities for food and the surrender of the German merchant fleet; before the end of the month food supplies began to reach the Germans. The blockade was relaxed but not finally raised until 12 July 1919, after the German ratification of the peace treaty.

MILITARY LIMITATIONS

The provisions of the treaty made Germany virtually defenceless; her armed forces were sufficient only for the internal preservation of law and order. The German army was limited to 100,000 men, and to prevent the training of more men a conscript army was forbidden; the period of service was set for twelve years for all but officers, who would have to serve twenty-five years. The German navy was limited and permitted no submarines; Germany was permitted no military air force, and the armaments industry was placed under the severest restraint and Allied control and inspection. The demilitarization and occupation of the Rhineland completed Germany's military impotence in facing French military strength. To make these clauses more palatable to Germany, the intention of general disarmament among all the Powers was expressed in the treaty.

OTHER PROVISIONS

Among the many other provisions of the treaty the more important were those concerning Russia; Germany had to renounce the Treaty of Brest-Litovsk and the Treaty of Bucharest, and acknowledge the right to independence of all the territories of the Russian Empire as it existed on 1 August 1914; Russia retained rights to reparations from Germany. Germany also had to recognize the frontiers and accept all treaties the Allies might conclude with present and future States, existing or coming into existence, whose territories had once formed part of the Russian Empire of 1914 (Articles 116 and 117). But the provisions for the trial of 'war criminals', including the Kaiser, proved largely inoperative. The rights of the German minority in Poland were safeguarded not in the Treaty of Versailles itself but in a treaty signed the same day, *the Minorities Treaty between the Allied and Associated Powers and Poland, 28 June 1919* (p. 72). It served as the model for treaties dealing with German and other minorities in Czechoslovakia, Yugoslavia, Rumania and Greece.

The draft peace treaty was presented to the German representatives, who were summoned for this purpose to the Trianon Palace, on 7 May 1919. After German written protests had been considered, and a few amendments made, the most significant being the plebiscite in Upper Silesia, *the Treaty of Peace was signed at Versailles on 28 June 1919* (p. 59).

Peace treaties with Austria, Bulgaria and Hungary, 1919–20

The crucial decisions affecting the territorial distributions of Central and Eastern Europe had been taken before the signature of the Versailles Treaty, indeed in many cases before the peace conference opened in Paris. Thus the Allies and the United States were committed to confirming the new multinational succession States of the Austro-Hungarian Empire, which had broken up in the aftermath of defeat: these were Czechoslovakia and Yugoslavia. Military action too, either against the defeated forces of Austria and Hungary or to fill the vacuum left by their departure, created a number of situations by force which later proved completely or partially irrevocable and were recognized by the Allies. The Hungarian *Banat* was occupied after the armistice with Hungary by Serbian troops in November 1918, and Rumania claimed the whole region at the peace conference in vain. The Rumanians in turn occupied the whole of Transylvania and even Budapest during the spring and summer of 1919. The Italians seized disputed Fiume in September 1919, and the Czechoslovaks in the previous autumn occupied the whole of historic Bohemia and Moravia, including large German-speaking minorities. The Poles and Czechs clashed in the district of Teschen and the Poles occupied the mainly Ukrainian–Ruthenian ethnic region of eastern Galicia, which had formed part of Austria. The actual boundaries contained in the peace treaties with Austria, Hungary and Bulgaria were thus drawn largely as a result of territorial awards eventually made to the neighbouring States, of territory for the most part already occupied by them, after investigation by the Territorial Claims Commissions set up by the Council of Ten.

The Treaty of St Germain with Austria, 10 September 1919, was modelled on the Treaty of Versailles, as were the other peace treaties. The Covenant of the League of Nations was integrally included in the peace treaties, and the war responsibility and reparations clauses were similar in form to the German treaty. Austria was limited militarily and permitted a conscript army of no more than 30,000 officers and men. Austria was expressly forbidden union with Germany. The South Tyrol, with a German-speaking population of some 240,000, was handed over to Italy, giving Italy the Brenner pass frontier promised in the Allied *Treaty of London, April 1915* (p. 24); Bohemia and Moravia merged into Czechoslovakia; Bukovina was acquired by Rumania. Owing to disputes among the Allies, other areas were ceded by Austria to the Allies for disposition by them; these regions included the northern Adriatic and Galicia. In the Klagenfurth district of Carinthia a plebiscite in October 1920 decided for Austria against Yugoslavia. Austria received a small area from Hungary, and most of the 'Burgenland', but in a smaller part of 'Burgenland' a plebiscite favoured Hungary. Apart from these small areas, populations were transferred and frontiers redrawn without benefit of plebiscites. These cessions of territory left independent Austria with little more than a quarter of the territory that had formed the Austrian half of the pre-war Dual Monarchy.

The Treaty of Trianon with Hungary, 4 June 1920, was only signed several months after the formal end of the Paris Peace Conference. Peacemaking was in part delayed by the revolution and setting up of the Bolshevik Government of Béla Kun from March 1919 to August 1919. The Kun régime collapsed after attacking and being defeated by the Rumanians who were occupying western Hungary (Transylvania) and now advanced to occupy Budapest; the

Rumanians could not be induced to withdraw from some of the territory until the autumn of 1919. Historic Hungary had in practice been dismembered before the presentation of the peace treaty to the Hungarian delegates. Almost one-third of the Hungary of 1918, Transylvania and two-thirds of Banat, was ceded to Rumania, and this demarcation left about two million Magyars, mainly in south-east Transylvania, as a minority in post-war Rumania; Croatia–Slavonia and one-third of the Banat were ceded to Yugoslavia; Slovakia, Ruthenia and the region of Pressburg (Bratislava) with some 700,000 Magyars to Czechoslovakia; Fiume eventually to Italy; the greater part of the Burgenland to Austria; and finally to Poland and Czechoslovakia the small areas of Ostrava and Spis in northern Slovakia. Altogether Hungary lost rather more than two-thirds of its territory. Apart from the plebiscites permitted in two small regions, the transfer of population in Hungary was also decided upon without plebiscites. Hungary was limited to a professional army of 35,000 officers and men, and in common with the other peace treaties, the League Covenant and other clauses such as war responsibility and reparations were included. An unusual feature of the treaty was an accompanying letter from the French Prime Minister, Millerand, promising that if the Treaty contained any injustice which it would be in the general interest to remove, the Frontier Delimitation Commission might suggest revisions to the League of Nations. This as it turned out raised Hungarian hopes in vain.

The Treaty of Neuilly with Bulgaria, 27 November 1919. By the armistice terms Bulgaria had to withdraw its troops to the pre-war frontier. The territorial terms required Bulgaria to return the southern Dobruja to Rumania regardless of ethnic considerations; and to cede to Yugoslavia most of the four small regions occupied by Serbia in 1918. To the Allies, Bulgaria had to cede nearly the whole of western Thrace thus losing Bulgaria's Aegean littoral; the Allies transferred this territory to Greece by treaty on 10 August 1920, and at the same time a treaty was signed with Turkey. Reparations were required and the Bulgarian army was limited to 33,000 professionals.

Allied disputes and settlements

The peace treaties of St Germain, Neuilly and Trianon, whilst they settled the reduced frontiers of Austria, Bulgaria and Hungary, did not determine the final division of all the ceded territories among the various Allies. The principal disputes occurred over:

1. FIUME

Italy was scarcely reconciled to a compact Yugoslav State along the Adriatic which would prove an obstacle to Italian Balkan ambitions. In addition to the

Italian-speaking Trieste region, a part of Austrian domains of the Dual Monarchy, Italy also claimed Fiume, once part of Hungary, which the Yugoslavs desired as their major seaport. Italy had been excluded from Fiume in the Treaty of London, and Orlando's claim was resisted by the others in the Council of Four, causing an Allies crisis in April 1919 and the departure for a time of the Italians from the Peace Conference of Paris. In September 1919 d'Annuncio with Italian 'volunteers' seized the city and drove out the inter-Allied force of occupation. Allied efforts secured no agreement. Eventually by the *Yugoslav–Italian Treaty of Rapallo, 12 November 1920*, the Italian–Yugoslav frontier dispute was settled and Fiume made a Free City; Italy finally acquired Fiume together with a small strip of territory so that Fiume and the rest of Italy were contiguous.

2. THE BANAT

This territory ceded by Hungary had been promised by the Allies in a secret treaty to Rumania in 1916, but Rumania's separate peace treaty with the Central Powers at Bucharest in 1918 had voided the Allied promise. In November 1918 the Serbians occupied the Banat. The Allied decision in June 1919 to partition the Banat between Yugoslavia and Rumania was rejected by Rumania until Allied pressure forced Rumania to give way in December 1919.

3. ALBANIA

Italy and Greece desired Albanian territory and planned its partition in 1919 and 1920. Yugoslavia too made territorial claims. Long drawn-out negotiations ended in the recognition of Albanian independence, though Albania's frontiers were not finally agreed until 1926.

4. TESCHEN

The *Teschen* dispute was resolved largely in Czechoslovakia's favour, the incorporation of Galicia in Poland was finally acknowledged and the still uncertain frontier between Austria and Hungary settled by plebiscites.

The Allies, Turkey and Greece, 1920–3

The Allies planned the partition of Turkey at the peace conference. Not only were the subject national groups to be taken from the Ottoman Empire, but Turkey proper was to be placed under the tutelage of the Western Powers. In the Middle East, the wartime inter-Allied agreements and promises to the Arabs and Zionists made the disposition of this part of the Ottoman Empire the subject of protracted negotiations. The problems of Asia Minor were only considered intermittently at Paris during the spring of 1919. It was decided at Paris to internationalize the Straits and to assist and encourage autonomous

Governments among the liberated subject peoples. The mandate system was devised to reconcile autonomous national development and Great Power influence and supervision both in the Middle East and in respect to the German colonies. France claimed the mandate for the whole of Syria. Lloyd George wished to restrict the French mandate to the coastal region as determined in the *Sykes–Picot Agreement* of 1916 (p. 30). A mandate for Armenia and the Straits was offered at Paris to the United States, but Wilson could give no decision before his return to Washington in June 1919, and Congress did not formally refuse the mandate until a year later. The peace settlement was further delayed by the claims of Italy and Greece. In April 1919, the Italians had landed troops in Antalya (Adalia) in Asia Minor, and in May 1919 the Greeks landed troops in Izmir (Smyrna). An Allied force had been in occupation of the Straits in accordance with the terms of the Armistice of Mudros, 30 October 1918, and in March 1920 occupied Constantinople. The peace terms were presented to the practically captive Sultan's Government in May 1920 and the Sultan's Government concluded the *Treaty of Sèvres with the Allies on 10 August 1920*. In European Turkey, eastern Thrace was ceded to Greece and most of the Aegean islands; the Straits were left under nominal Turkish sovereignty, but the waterway was internationalized, demilitarized and was to be open to all merchant ships and warships in peace and in war (a reversal of the régime established by the Straits Convention of 1841); it was to be run by a Commission of ten Powers under the League of Nations framework. Smyrna and district in western Anatolia was to be administered by Greece for five years, followed by a plebiscite. In eastern Anatolia, Armenia was granted independence and its frontiers were to be decided later; Kurdistan was permitted autonomy; Turkey lost Syria which became a French mandate, Palestine and Mesopotamia which became British mandates, and the Arabian peninsula which was granted independence as the Kingdom of Hejaz. Turkish finances were placed under British, French and Italian supervision.

These onerous terms were signed by the Sultan's Government which was increasingly losing control of the country to the Turkish Nationalists led by Mustafa Kemal. Kemal and the Nationalist Assembly in Ankara rejected the terms. Kemal and the reorganized Turkish army concluded *a treaty with Bolshevik Russia on 16 March 1921* (p. 77), and crushed Armenia. The Moscow treaty with Soviet Russia settled Turkey's eastern frontier without reference to the Allies and rejected the validity of any treaty imposed on Turkey.

Kemal's growing strength decided the Allies against attempting to enforce the Treaty of Sèvres by force. The United States had withdrawn its support altogether. In June 1921 Italy began to evacuate Asia Minor. France and Turkey concluded the *Treaty of Ankara, 20 October 1921*. Hostilities between

France and Kemal's troops ceased; a new frontier was drawn between Syria and Turkey more favourable to Turkey than that of Sèvres. France recognized Kemal's Government of the Grand National Assembly. By the treaty Allied unity and the Treaty of Sèvres was shattered as France concluded a separate peace.

The Greek army in Asia Minor was decisively defeated in August 1922 and Kemal's troops entered Izmir on 9 September. In the Straits Allied unity had crumbled when French and Italian garrisons were withdrawn in September 1922. The British remained alone guarding the Straits at Chanak with the Turks in October 1922 determined to regain control. The consequent Chanak crisis was resolved by negotiation and the *Armistice of Mudanya* between Turkey, Italy, France and Britain on *11 October 1922* (on 14 October the Greeks acceded to it): by the terms of the armistice eastern Thrace as far as the Maritsa river and Adrianople was handed by the Greeks to the Nationalist Turks, and Turkish sovereignty over Istanbul (Constantinople) and the Straits was recognized.

The final settlement was worked out at the *Conference of Lausanne, 21 November 1922–4 February 1923 and 23 April–24 July 1923*. The ambiguous position of the Turkish Nationalists and the Sultan was resolved by the abolition of the Sultanate on 1 November 1922. During the course of the conference agreement was reached in January 1923 on a compulsory exchange of Greek and Turkish minorities and a convention signed to this effect by *Greece and Turkey, 30 January 1923*. After protracted negotiations the conference ended with the signature by Turkey of the *Treaty of Lausanne, 24 July 1923* (p. 79). Many of the onerous terms of the Treaty of Sèvres were abandoned. Turkey alone among ex-enemy States was not required to pay reparations. The special legal privileges which the 'civilized' Western nations had enjoyed in their dealings with the Ottoman Empire, known as the capitulations, were abolished. Few restrictions on national Turkish sovereignty remained. The treaty settled the boundaries of Turkey, and, with the restoration of eastern Thrace, Turkey's frontier in Europe was restored to what it had been in 1914 (with the exception of a small piece of territory ceded to Bulgaria). Greece retained all but two of the former Turkish Aegean islands, which were near the mouth of the Dardanelles and which were returned to Turkey. (The Dodecanese Islands were retained by Italy.) British sovereignty over Cyprus was confirmed. The frontier between British-mandated Iraq and Turkey was not finally settled; the key region of Mosul had been left for later settlement, eventually reached in 1926 when Mosul was given to Iraq.

The question of the Straits was settled by the *Straits Convention* (p. 80) which formed an annex to the treaty. A demilitarized zone was established on both the Asian and European shores, but the Turks were permitted to garrison

Istanbul; the security of the Straits and the demilitarized zones and free navigation was guaranteed by the signatories of the convention and more especially by France, Britain, Italy and Japan; the Soviet Union signed but did not ratify the convention. The passage of merchant vessels was guaranteed through the Straits in time of peace or war, and if Turkey itself was at war; the passage of warships in time of peace was limited by tonnage and number, and to a maximum force for each country not exceeding 'the most powerful fleet of the littoral Powers of the Black Sea', at such a time. In time of war, Turkey being neutral, warships of belligerents could pass the Straits without practical limitations (this marked the great change of rule from that established by the Straits Convention of 1841). In time of war, *Turkey being a belligerent*, the passage of neutral warships was permitted, limited by the same provision as for warships in time of peace.

The rule of the Straits established by the Treaty of Lausanne lasted until 1936 when it was replaced by the *Montreux Convention, 20 July 1936* (p. 83). This treaty restored Turkish sovereignty over the Straits, subject to certain conditions. It permitted the Black Sea powers *in time of peace* to send warships through the Straits subject to certain restrictions (Articles 11–14); other naval Powers could pay courtesy visits to Turkish ports in the Straits (Article 17). The total tonnage any Black Sea Power could have in the Black Sea was limited by Article 18, but the limitations were only relative and flexible. Thus the Black Sea States, including the Soviet Union, enjoyed considerable advantages of egress denied to the other Powers desiring to enter the Black Sea. In time of war, Turkey being neutral, warships of belligerents were *not* permitted to pass through the Straits unless assisting the victim of aggression within the framework of the League of Nations (Article 19). If Turkey itself were at war, or threatened with war, the passage of warships was left to its discretion (Articles 20 and 21). Turkish control of the Straits was restored; the International Straits Commission's work was handed over to the Turkish Government (Article 24) and the demilitarized zones abolished, allowing Turkey to guard the Straits (this was done by omitting the relevant articles of the Treaty of Lausanne).

The settlement in the Middle East

The settlement of the territories of the former Ottoman Empire outside the Asian frontiers of Turkey was modified by the *Treaty of Lausanne in 1923* (p. 79) which made the full application of the secret inter-Allied wartime agreements of Italian, French and British spheres of influence in Anatolia and Asia Minor impossible to fulfil. At the *Conference of San Remo, April 1920*, the

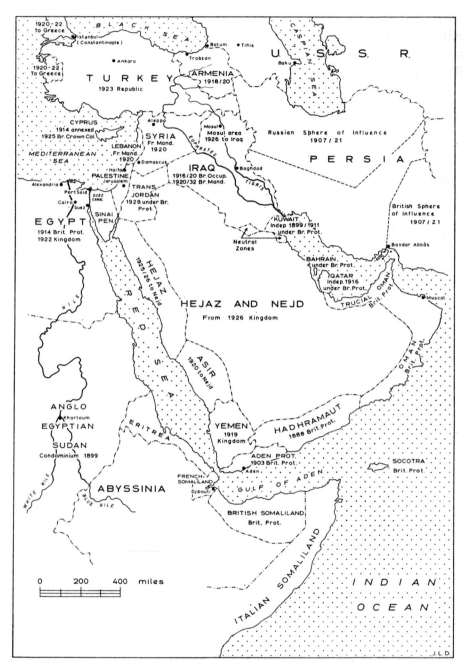

3 The Middle East, 1926

former Ottoman province of Syria was divided between French and British mandates and the Arabian peninsula proper permitted independent Arab government. The outcome of the various Allied decisions and actions for the Middle East was as follows.

1. *Under British influence and/or jurisdiction.* Palestine, where Britain was given full control by the mandate; Transjordan granted its own government by a treaty with Britain in 1928, with British influence over finance, foreign policy and defence. Britain received the mandate for Mesopotamia, renamed Iraq; Iraq became a kingdom in 1921, and gained independence by the *Anglo-Iraq Alliance Treaty, 30 June 1930*, which terminated the British mandate; but Britain retained special rights for the defence of Iraq as well as air bases. Iraq was admitted to the League of Nations in October 1932. Egypt was pronounced independent by Britain on 1 March 1922, but here too Britain retained special rights including the presence of British troops to defend Egypt and the Suez Canal; Britain also reserved to itself the continuing control of the Sudan. A new *Anglo-Egyptian Alliance Treaty, 26 August 1936*, brought the British military occupation of Egypt to an end, but Britain was permitted to continue stationing forces in 'Egyptian territory in the vicinity of the Canal' to defend the Canal. Iran (Persia) was an independent State, but British influence was exerted through controlling interests in the oil industry. Britain had special treaty arrangements with Sheiks in the Persian Gulf. Britain also concluded the *Jedda Treaty, 20 May 1927*, with the independent kingdom of Hejaz and Nejd (renamed Saudi Arabia after 1932). Aden was a Crown colony and British influence predominated over the Aden Protectorate.

2. *Under French influence.* The history of these territories before 1939 is in this sense simpler in that the French mandate was maintained. France had received the mandate of Syria, which the French did not confine to the coastal regions but extended to the interior by military action in July 1920. The French divided their mandate into the State of Syria (1924) and the Lebanon (1920). Draft alliance treaties between France and Syria, 9 September 1936, making provisions for the ending of the mandates but preserving special French rights were not signed owing to the fall of the French Government that had negotiated the treaty. The independent States of Syria and Lebanon were proclaimed by the 'Free French' in 1941 after replacing the Vichy Authorities during the Second World War. The admission of Syria and Lebanon to the U.N., at the foundation of the organization, internationally confirmed the end of the French mandates, and French troops withdrew in 1946.

China, Japan and the Pacific: the Washington Conference, 1921-2

The Paris Peace Conference had assigned to Japan mandates of Germany's Pacific island colonies north of the Equator; Japan had also secured German rights in Shantung. Apart from thus disposing of German assets, no general settlement between the Powers concerning their future relationships in China and the Pacific was reached in Paris. These problems were the subject of the negotiations at the *Washington Conference, November 1921-February 1922*. Of the Powers with interests in the Pacific only Soviet Russia was not invited. Three major treaties were concluded. A treaty on the *limitation of naval armaments, 6 February 1922, between the British Empire, France, Italy, Japan and the United States* (p. 87) limited and set proportions between the signatories of warships of the largest tonnage, mainly battleships, as follows: Britain – 5, United States – 5, Japan – 3, France – 1·7, and Italy – 1·7. A ten-year 'naval holiday' on the construction of capital ships apart from specific exceptions was to be followed by only limited construction until 1936. The disadvantage of the proportions to Japan was counterbalanced by an agreement in the treaty limiting the construction of new naval bases or the expansion of existing bases in the Pacific, but excluding Hawaii. A *Nine Power Treaty concerning China was signed on 6 February 1922 by the British Empire, France, Italy, Japan, the United States, China, Netherlands, Belgium and Portugal* (p. 90). Its purpose was to bolster up the integrity and independence of China, particularly threatened by the special rights demanded by Japan during the First World War. Japan made some concessions in Shantung and the signatories promised to respect the sovereignty and integrity of China and the 'Open Door', but China did not secure the withdrawal of Japanese troops from Manchuria or the recognition of Chinese sovereignty over Manchuria. Nor was China's unequal status abolished. The foreign Powers maintained special rights; by a separate treaty the Chinese were permitted to raise their customs tariff over whose rates the foreign Powers retained control. The Powers were unwilling to give up their existing rights, and only promised not to extend them. The third treaty to be signed was the *Four Power Treaty relating to insular possessions and insular dominions in the Pacific Ocean between the British Empire, France, the United States and Japan, 13 December 1921* (p. 91). This Four Power Treaty replaced the alliance relationship between Britain and Japan (last renewed in 1911). The four Powers undertook to respect the rights of each other in their 'insular possessions and insular dominions in the region of the Pacific Ocean', whereby any American recognition of Japan's position in China and Siberia was avoided. The treaty also contained provision for conferences between the signatories to resolve disputes and frank exchanges if the rights of the signatories were threatened by other Powers.

The League of Nations

The devastation of two great European wars encouraged the victors on both occasions to try to find a better way of conducting diplomacy. After the Napo- leonic Wars, the Vienna settlement of 1815 was accompanied by the coopera- tion of the Great Powers known as the 'Concert of Europe', and the First World War led in 1920 to the *League of Nations* (p. 59) whose aim it was to allow States great and small to find security with justice. Within ten years of the foundation of the League it could be seen that these high hopes were unlikely to be fulfilled. Britain, France and the United States were not willing to check aggression by risking war in the 1930s; no one else could. The League had been weakened at the outset by the Senate's rejection of the peace treaties which meant that the United States could not become a member. But this was not the cause of its failure since the U.S. was frequently ready to cooperate.

The League provided both the rules of conduct between nations and new diplomatic machinery intended to ensure that these rules would be observed. The strength of the League ultimately depended on its members and not on the procedures written into the Covenant. But the will to uphold and strengthen the purposes of the League was lacking when the State to be disciplined was a Great Power. The sacrifices required of the other Great Powers in such a situation were not made. Support for the principles and rules of the League came second when weighed against individual national interests.

The immediate origins of the League are to be found in the advocacy of English and American statesmen, notably the former President Taft, President Wilson, Lord Robert Cecil and Sir Edward Grey. Organized groups of private citizens advocating a new international order after the war were influential in persuading the British and American leaders at Paris that the creation of an international organization was likely to win strong political support in their own countries.

Various drafts reflecting the French, American and British points of view on how to best 'organize' peace were considered at Paris in January and February 1919 by the League Commission, and the text of a completed draft of the Covenant was submitted to the Plenary Session of the peace conference on 14 February 1919. President Wilson then explained to the members of that session that *the Covenant* was based on two principles: (1) that 'no nation shall go to war with any other nation until every other possible means of settling the dispute shall have been full and fairly tried'; and (2) that 'under no circum- stances shall any nation seek forcibly to disturb the territorial settlement to be arrived at as the consequence of this peace or to interfere with the political independence of any of the States of the world'.

The League came into existence when the Treaty of Versailles entered into force on 10 January 1920, and was an association of States each retaining its sovereignty. The institutions of the League provided the machinery for working out agreed policies. Its two major purposes were the achievement of international security through collective action, and international cooperation for social and economic welfare. The following articles of the Covenant should be especially noted. In Article 10 members subscribed to a mutual guarantee of the political independence and territorial integrity of all Member States. This was really no more than a declaration of intent, a moral commitment; military support for a victim of aggression was not automatic. The drafting of Article 10 was ambiguous. Any military obligations which might have arisen were in any case made optional when in 1923 an interpretive resolution of Article 10 was adopted by the League which left it to each State to decide how far it was bound to contribute military force to fulfil its obligations.

Articles 12 to 17 provided the League with fact-finding and some arbitral functions. Here too are to be found the sanctions which could be adopted against the aggressor. These sanctions emphasized economic pressure which it was believed would be effective and left the ultimate military obligations of Member States obscure.

The Geneva Protocol of 1924 attempted to strengthen the League by filling in the 'gaps' of the existing Covenant. The Covenant as it stood did not cover all possible situations of aggression and victimization. If the Council of the League, for instance, should fail to reach unanimous agreement on its report on a dispute, or if for any reason that seemed sufficient to it the Council did not report on a dispute, then League sanctions could not be invoked and one State could make war on another with impunity. In any case an individual State desiring to go to war was obliged only to observe a three-month cooling-off period; thereafter the Council was not bound to impose sanctions if the two States involved in a conflict refused to accept the report of the Council, or the decision of the Court of Arbitrators. The Geneva Protocol sought to ensure that all disputes would be settled by some means other than war. Sanctions would, according to the Geneva Protocol, be imposed on any State resorting to war. Without the adoption of the Protocol sanctions could only be imposed when a State was found to be at war in breach of the Covenant. Although the Geneva Protocol was agreed to and recommended to members by the League, the British Conservative Government in 1925 rejected it as it was unwilling to accept a widening of obligations.

The League was ineffective during the decade of aggression 1931–41, but its record of promoting international and social collaboration through such bodies as the Health Organization, World Economic Conferences and the International Labour Organizations was notable. Through the League was devised the mandate system for providing a period of European 'tutelage' over emerging non-European nations or former colonies. The League also sought to ensure the rights of minorities and to carry out humanitarian work for refugees.

By November 1920 there were forty-two members of the League, ten more than the Allied States originally signatories of the treaties of peace. But the United States never became a member. Germany was admitted in 1926 and the U.S.S.R. in 1934. Those Great Powers who planned or carried out aggression left the League one by one in the 1930s: Nazi Germany in 1933, Japan in the same year, Italy in 1937 and the U.S.S.R. was expelled in December 1939 after its attack on Finland. In April 1946, after the establishment of the United Nations, the League was dissolved by resolution of the U.N. Assembly which, however, provided for the continuation of some of its functions.

President Wilson's Fourteen Points, 8 January 1918

We entered this war because violations of right had occurred which touched us to the quick and made the life of our own people impossible unless they were corrected and the world secure once for all against their recurrence. What we demand in this war, therefore, is nothing peculiar to ourselves. It is that the world be made fit and safe to live in; and particularly that it be made safe for every peace-loving nation which, like our own, wishes to live its own life, determine its own institutions, be assured of justice and fair dealing by the other peoples of the world as against force and selfish aggression. All the peoples of the world are in effect partners in this interest, and for our own part we see very clearly that unless justice be done to others it will not be done to us. The programme of the world's peace, therefore, is our programme; and that programme, the only possible programme, as we see it, is this:

I. Open covenants of peace, openly arrived at, after which there shall be no private international understandings of any kind but diplomacy shall proceed always frankly and in the public view.

II. Absolute freedom of navigation upon the seas, outside territorial waters, alike in peace and in war, except as the seas may be closed in whole or in part by international action for the enforcement of international covenants.

III. The removal, so far as possible, of all economic barriers, and the establishment of an equality of trade conditions among all the nations consenting to the peace and associating themselves for its maintenance.

IV. Adequate guarantees given and taken that national armaments will be reduced to the lowest point consistent with domestic safety.

V. A free, open-minded, and absolutely impartial adjustment of all colonial claims, based upon a strict observance of the principle that in determining all such questions of sovereignty the interests of the populations concerned must have equal weight with the equitable claims of the Government whose title is to be determined.

VI. The evacuation of all Russian territory and such a settlement of all questions affecting Russia as will secure the best and freest cooperation of the other nations of the world in obtaining for her an unhampered and unembarrassed opportunity for the independent determination of her own political development and national policy and assure her of a sincere welcome into the society of free nations under institutions of her own choosing; and, more than a welcome, assistance also of every kind that she may need and may herself desire. The treatment accorded Russia by her sister nations in the months to come will be the acid test of their good will, of their comprehension of her needs as distinguished from their own interests, and of their intelligent and unselfish sympathy.

VII. Belgium, the whole world will agree, must be evacuated and restored, without any attempt to limit the sovereignty which she enjoys in common with all other free nations. No other single act will serve as this will serve to restore confidence among the nations in the laws which they have themselves set and determined for the government of their relations with one another. Without this healing act the whole structure and validity of international law is forever impaired.

VIII. All French territory should be freed and the invaded portions restored, and the wrong done to France by Prussia in 1871 in the matter of Alsace-Lorraine, which has unsettled the peace of the world for nearly fifty years, should be righted, in order that peace may once more be made secure in the interest of all.

IX. A readjustment of the frontiers of Italy should be effected along clearly recognizable lines of nationality.

X. The peoples of Austria-Hungary, whose place among the nations we wish to see safeguarded and assured, should be accorded the freest opportunity of autonomous development.

XI. Rumania, Serbia, and Montenegro should be evacuated; occupied territories restored; Serbia accorded free and secure access to the sea; and the relations of the several Balkan States to one another determined by friendly counsel along historically established lines of allegiance and nationality; and international guarantees of the political and economic independence and territorial integrity of the several Balkan States should be entered into.

XII. The Turkish portions of the present Ottoman Empire should be assured a secure sovereignty, but the other nationalities which are now under Turkish rule should be assured an undoubted security of life and an absolutely unmolested opportunity of autonomous development, and the Dardanelles should be permanently opened as a free passage to the ships and commerce of all nations under international guarantees.

XIII. An independent Polish State should be erected which should include the territories inhabited by indisputably Polish populations, which should be assured a free and secure access to the sea, and whose political and economic independence and territorial integrity should be guaranteed by international covenant.

XIV. A general association of nations must be formed under specific covenants for the purpose of affording mutual guarantees of political independence and territorial integrity to great and small States alike.

In regard to these essential rectifications of wrong and assertions of right we feel ourselves to be intimate partners of all the Governments and peoples associated together against the Imperialists. We cannot be separated in interest or divided in purpose. We stand together until the end. . . .

Treaty of Peace between the Allied and Associated Powers and Germany (Treaty of Versailles), 28 June 1919

Part I · The Covenant of the League of Nations

THE HIGH CONTRACTING PARTIES,

In order to promote international co-operation and to achieve international peace and security

by the acceptance of obligations not to resort to war,

by the prescription of open, just and honourable relations between nations,

by the firm establishment of the under-standings of international law as the actual rule of conduct among Governments, and

by the maintenance of justice and a scrupulous respect for all treaty obligations in the dealings of organ-ized peoples with one another,

Agree to this Covenant of the League of Nations.

Article 1. The original Members of the League of Nations shall be those of the Signatories which are named in the Annex to this Covenant and also such of those other States named in the Annex as shall accede without reservation to this Covenant. Such accession shall be effected by a declaration deposited with the Sec-retariat within two months of the com-ing into force of the Covenant. Notice thereof shall be sent to all other Members of the League.

Any fully self-governing State, Dom-inion or Colony not named in the Annex may become a Member of the League if its admission is agreed to by two-thirds of the Assembly, provided that it shall give effective guarantees of its sincere in-tention to observe its international obli-gations, and shall accept such regulations as may be prescribed by the League in regard to its military, naval and air forces and armaments.

Any Member of the League may, after two years' notice of its intention so to do, withdraw from the League, provided that all its international obligations and all its obligations under this Covenant shall have been fulfilled at the time of its with-drawal.

Article 2. The action of the League under this Covenant shall be effected through the instrumentality of an Assembly and of a Council, with a permanent Secre-tariat.

Article 3. The Assembly shall consist of Representatives of the Members of the League.

The Assembly shall meet at stated inter-vals and from time to time as occasion may require at the Seat of the League or at such other place as may be decided upon.

The Assembly may deal at its meetings with any matter within the sphere of action of the League or affecting the peace of the world.

At meetings of the Assembly each Member of the League shall have one vote, and may have not more than three Representatives.

Article 4. The Council shall consist of Representatives of the Principal Allied and Associated Powers, together with Representatives of four other Members of the League. These four Members of the League shall be selected by the Assembly from time to time in its discretion. Until the appointment of the Representatives of the four Members of the League first selected by the Assembly, Representatives of Belgium, Brazil, Spain and Greece shall be members of the Council.

With the approval of the majority of the Assembly, the Council may name additional Members of the League whose Representatives shall always be members of the Council; the Council with like approval may increase the number of

Members of the League to be selected by the Assembly for representation on the Council.

The Council shall meet from time to time as occasion may require, and at least once a year, at the Seat of the League, or at such other place as may be decided upon.

The Council may deal at its meetings with any matter within the sphere of action of the League or affecting the peace of the world.

Any Member of the League not represented on the Council shall be invited to send a Representative to sit as a member at any meeting of the Council during the consideration of matters specially affecting the interests of that Member of the League.

At meetings of the Council, each Member of the League represented on the Council shall have one vote, and may have not more than one Representative.

Article 5. Except where otherwise expressly provided in this Covenant or by the terms of the present Treaty, decisions at any meeting of the Assembly or of the Council shall require the agreement of all the Members of the League represented at the meeting.

All matters of procedure at meetings of the Assembly or of the council, including the appointment of Committees to investigate particular matters, shall be regulated by the Assembly or by the Council and may be decided by a majority of the Members of the League represented at the meeting.

The first meeting of the Assembly and the first meeting of the Council shall be summoned by the President of the United States of America.

Article 6. The permanent Secretariat shall be established at the Seat of the League. The Secretariat shall comprise a Secretary-General and such secretaries and staff as may be required.

The first Secretary-General shall be the person named in the Annex; thereafter the Secretary-General shall be appointed by the Council with the approval of the majority of the Assembly.

The secretaries and staff of the Secretariat shall be appointed by the Secretary-General with the approval of the Council.

The Secretary-General shall act in that capacity at all meetings of the Assembly and of the Council.

The expenses of the Secretariat shall be borne by the Members of the League in accordance with the apportionment of the expenses of the International Bureau of the Universal Postal Union.

Article 7. The Seat of the League is established at Geneva.

The Council may at any time decide that the Seat of the League shall be established elsewhere.

Article 8. The Members of the League recognize that the maintenance of peace requires the reduction of national armaments to the lowest point consistent with national safety and the enforcement by common action of international obligations.

The Council, taking account of the geographical situation and circumstances of each State, shall formulate plans for such reduction for the consideration and action of the several Governments . . .

[*Article 9.* Permanent Commission to be set up to advise Council on the execution of Articles 1–8.]

Article 10. The Members of the League undertake to respect and preserve as against external aggression the territorial integrity and existing political independence of all Members of the League. In case of any such aggression or in case of any threat or danger of such aggression the Council shall advise upon the means by which this obligation shall be fulfilled.

Article 11. Any war or threat of war, whether immediately affecting any of the Members of the League or not, is hereby declared a matter of concern to the whole League, and the League shall take any action that may be deemed wise and effectual to safeguard the peace of nations. In case any such emergency should arise the Secretary-General shall on the request of any Member of the League forthwith summon a meeting of the Council.

It is also declared to be the friendly right of each Member of the League to bring to the attention of the Assembly or of the Council any circumstance whatever affecting international relations which threatens to disturb international peace or the good understanding between nations upon which peace depends.

Article 12. The Members of the League agree that if there should arise between them any dispute likely to lead to a rupture, they will submit the matter either to arbitration or to inquiry by the Council, and they agree in no case to resort to war until three months after the award by the arbitrators or the report by the Council.

In any case under this Article the award of the arbitrators shall be made within a reasonable time, and the report of the Council shall be made within six months after the submission of the dispute.

Article 13. The Members of the League agree that whenever any dispute shall arise between them which they recognize to be suitable for submission to arbitration and which cannot be satisfactorily settled by diplomacy, they will submit the whole subject-matter to arbitration.

Disputes as to the interpretation of a treaty, as to any question of international law, as to the existence of any fact which if established would constitute a breach of any international obligation, or as to the extent and nature of the reparation to be made for any such breach, are declared to be among those which are generally suitable for submission to arbitration.

For the consideration of any such dispute the court of arbitration to which the case is referred shall be the court agreed on by the parties to the dispute or stipulated in any convention existing between them.

The Members of the League agree that they will carry out in full good faith any award that may be rendered, and that they will not resort to war against a Member of the League which complies therewith. In the event of any failure to carry out such an award, the Council shall propose what steps should be taken to give effect thereto.

Article 14. The Council shall formulate and submit to the Members of the League for adoption plans for the establishment of a Permanent Court of International Justice. The Court shall be competent to hear and determine any dispute of an international character which the parties thereto submit to it. The Court may also give an advisory opinion upon any dispute or question referred to it by the Council or by the Assembly.

Article 15. If there should arise between Members of the League any dispute likely to lead to a rupture, which is not submitted to arbitration in accordance with Article 13, the Members of the League agree that they will submit the matter to the Council. Any party to the dispute may effect such submission by giving notice of the existence of the dispute to the Secretary-General, who will make all necessary arrangements for a full investigation and consideration thereof.

For this purpose the parties to the dispute will communicate to the Secretary-General, as promptly as possible, statements of their case, with all the relevant facts and papers, and the Council may forthwith direct the publication thereof.

The Council shall endeavour to effect a settlement of the dispute, and if such efforts are successful, a statement shall be made public giving such facts and explanations regarding the dispute and the terms of settlement thereof as the Council may deem appropriate.

If the dispute is not thus settled, the Council either unanimously or by a majority vote shall make and publish a report containing a statement of the facts of the dispute and the recommendations which are deemed just and proper in regard thereto.

Any Member of the League represented on the Council may make public a statement of the facts of the dispute and of its conclusions regarding the same.

If a report by the Council is unanimously agreed to by the members thereof other than the Representatives of one or more of the parties to the dispute, the Members of the League agree that they will not go to war with any party to the dispute which complies with the recommendations of the report.

If the Council fails to reach a report which is unanimously agreed to by the members thereof, other than the Representatives of one or more of the parties to the dispute, the Members of the League reserve to themselves the right to take such action as they shall consider necessary for the maintenance of right and justice.

If the dispute between the parties is claimed by one of them, and is found by the Council, to arise out of a matter which by international law is solely within the domestic jurisdiction of that party, the Council shall so report, and shall make no recommendation as to its settlement.

The Council may in any case under this Article refer the dispute to the Assembly. The dispute shall be so referred at the request of either party to the dispute, provided that such request be made within fourteen days after the submission of the dispute to the Council.

In any case referred to the Assembly, all the provisions of this Article and of Article 12 relating to the action and powers of the Council shall apply to the action and powers of the Assembly, provided that a report made by the Assembly, if concurred in by the Representatives of those Members of the League represented on the Council and of a majority of the other Members of the League, exclusive in each case of the Representatives of the parties to the dispute, shall have the same force as a report by the Council concurred in by all the members thereof other than the Representatives of one or more of the parties to the dispute.

Article 16. Should any Member of the League resort to war in disregard of its covenants under Articles 12, 13 or 15, it shall *ipso facto* be deemed to have committed an act of war against all other Members of the League, which hereby undertake immediately to subject it to the severance of all trade or financial relations, the prohibition of all intercourse between their nationals and the nationals of the covenant-breaking State, and the prevention of all financial, commercial or personal intercourse between the nationals of the covenant-breaking State and the nationals of any other State, whether a Member of the League or not.

It shall be the duty of the Council in such case to recommend to the several Governments concerned what effective military, naval or air force the Members of the League shall severally contribute to the armed forces to be used to protect the covenants of the League.

The Members of the League agree, further, that they will mutually support one another in the financial and economic measures which are taken under this Article, in order to minimize the loss and inconvenience resulting from the above measures, and that they will mutually support one another in resisting any special measures aimed at one of their number by the covenant-breaking State, and that they will take the necessary steps to afford passage through their territory to the forces of any of the Members of the League which are cooperating to protect the covenants of the League.

Any Member of the League which has violated any covenant of the League may be declared to be no longer a Member of the League by a vote of the Council concurred in by the Representatives of all the other Members of the League represented thereon.

Article 17. In the event of a dispute between a Member of the League and a State which is not a Member of the League, or between States not Members of the League, the State or States not Members of the League shall be invited to accept the obligations of Membership in the League for the purposes of such dispute, upon such conditions as the Council may deem just. If such invitation is accepted, the provisions of Articles 12 to 16 inclusive shall be applied . . .

Article 18. Every treaty or international engagement entered into hereafter by any Member of the League shall be forthwith registered with the Secretariat and shall as soon as possible be published by it. No such treaty or international engagement shall be binding until so registered.

Article 19. The Assembly may from time to time advise the reconsideration by Members of the League of treaties which have become inapplicable and the consideration of international conditions whose continuance might endanger the peace of the world.

Article 20. The Members of the League severally agree that this Covenant is accepted as abrogating all obligations or understandings *inter se* which are inconsistent with the terms thereof, and solemnly undertake that they will not hereafter enter into any engagements inconsistent with the terms thereof.

In case any Member of the League shall, before becoming a Member of the League, have undertaken any obligations inconsistent with the terms of this Covenant, it shall be the duty of such Member to take immediate steps to procure its release from such obligations.

Article 21. Nothing in this Covenant shall be deemed to affect the validity of international engagements, such as treaties of arbitration or regional understandings like the Monroe Doctrine, for securing the maintenance of peace.

Article 22. To those colonies and territories which as a consequence of the late war have ceased to be under the sovereignty of the States which formerly governed them and which are inhabited by peoples not yet able to stand by themselves under the strenuous conditions of the modern world, there should be applied the principle that the well-being and development of such peoples form a sacred trust of civilization and that

securities for the performance of this trust should be embodied in this Covenant.

The best method of giving practical effect to this principle is that the tutelage of such peoples should be entrusted to advanced nations who by reason of their resources, their experience or their geographical position can best undertake this responsibility, and who are willing to accept it, and that this tutelage should be exercised by them as Mandatories on behalf of the League.

The character of the mandate must differ according to the stage of the development of the people, the geographical situation of the territory, its economic conditions and other similar circumstances.

Certain communities formerly belonging to the Turkish Empire have reached a stage of development where their existence as independent nations can be provisionally recognized subject to the rendering of administrative advice and assistance by a Mandatory until such time as they are able to stand alone. The wishes of these communities must be a principal consideration in the selection of the Mandatory.

Other peoples, especially those of Central Africa, are at such a stage that the Mandatory must be responsible for the administration of the territory under conditions which will guarantee freedom of conscience and religion, subject only to the maintenance of public order and morals, the prohibition of abuses such as the slave trade, the arms traffic and the liquor traffic, and the prevention of the establishment of fortifications or military and naval bases and of military training of the natives for other than police purposes and the defence of territory, and will also secure equal opportunities for the trade and commerce of other Members of the League.

There are territories, such as Southwest Africa and certain of the South Pacific Islands, which, owing to the sparseness of their population, or their small size, or their remoteness from the centres of civilization, or their geographical contiguity to the territory of the Mandatory, and other circumstances, can be best administered under the laws of the Mandatory as integral portions of its territory, subject to the safeguards above mentioned in the interests of the indigenous population.

In every case of mandate, the Mandatory shall render to the Council an annual report in reference to the territory committed to its charge.

The degree of authority, control, or administration to be exercised by the Mandatory shall, if not previously agreed upon by the Members of the League, be explicitly defined in each case by the Council.

A permanent Commission shall be constituted to receive and examine the annual reports of the Mandatories and to advise the Council on all matters relating to the observance of the mandates.

Article 23. Subject to and in accordance with the provisions of international conventions existing or hereafter to be agreed upon, the Members of the League:

(*a*) will endeavour to secure and maintain fair and humane conditions of labour for men, women, and children, both in their own countries and in all countries to which their commercial and industrial relations extend, and for that purpose will establish and maintain the necessary international organizations;

(*b*) undertake to secure just treatment of the native inhabitants of territories under their control;

(*c*) will entrust the League with the general supervision over the execution of agreements with regard to the traffic in women and children, and the traffic in opium and other dangerous drugs;

(*d*) will entrust the League with the general supervision of the trade in arms and ammunition with the countries in which the control of this traffic is necessary in the common interest;

(*e*) will make provision to secure and maintain freedom of communications and of transit and equitable treatment for the commerce of all Members of the League. In this connection, the special necessities of the regions devastated during the war of 1914–1918 shall be borne in mind;

(*f*) will endeavour to take steps in matters of international concern for the prevention and control of disease.

[*Article 24.* International bureaux to be placed under League if parties consent.]

[*Article 25.* Encouragement of Red Cross.]

Article 26. Amendments to this Covenant will take effect when ratified by the Members of the League whose Representatives compose the Council and by a majority of the Members of the League whose Representatives compose the Assembly.

No such amendment shall bind any Member of the League which signifies its dissent therefrom, but in that case it shall cease to be a Member of the League.

Part II · Boundaries of Germany

Article 27. The boundaries of Germany will be determined as follows ... [see map on p. 39]

Part III · Political clauses for Europe

SECTION I · BELGIUM

Article 31. Germany, recognizing that the Treaties of April 19, 1839, which established the status of Belgium before the war, no longer conform to the requirements of the situation, consents to the abrogation of the said treaties and undertakes immediately to recognize and to observe whatever conventions may be entered into by the Principal Allied and Associated Powers, or by any of them, in concert with the Governments of Belgium and of the Netherlands, to replace the said Treaties of 1839. If her formal adhesion should be required to such conventions or to any of their stipulations, Germany undertakes immediately to give it.

Article 32. Germany recognizes the full sovereignty of Belgium over the whole of the contested territory of Moresnet (called *Moresnet neutre*).

. . .

[*Article 40.* Germany renounces all rights in Luxembourg.]

SECTION III · LEFT BANK OF THE RHINE

Article 42. Germany is forbidden to maintain or construct any fortifications either on the left bank of the Rhine or on the right bank to the west of a line drawn 50 kilometres to the east of the Rhine.

Article 43. In the area defined above the maintenance and the assembly of armed forces, either permanently or temporarily, and military manœuvres of any kind, as well as the upkeep of all permanent works for mobilization, are in the same way forbidden.

Article 44. In case Germany violates in any manner whatever the provisions of Articles 42 and 43, she shall be regarded as committing a hostile act against the Powers signatory of the present Treaty and as calculated to disturb the peace of the world.

SECTION IV · SAAR BASIN

Article 45. As compensation for the destruction of the coal mines in the north of France and as part payment towards the total reparation due from Germany for the damage resulting from the war, Germany cedes to France in full and absolute possession, with exclusive rights of exploitation, unencumbered and free from all debts and charges of any kind, the coal mines situated in the Saar Basin as defined in Article 48.

. . .

Article 49. Germany renounces in favour of the League of Nations, in the capacity of trustee, the government of the territory defined above.

At the end of fifteen years from the coming into force of the present Treaty the inhabitants of the said territory shall be called upon to indicate the sovereignty under which they desire to be placed.

SECTION V · ALSACE-LORRAINE

The HIGH CONTRACTING PARTIES, recognizing the moral obligation to redress the wrong done by Germany in 1871 both to the rights of France and to the wishes of the population of Alsace and Lorraine, which were separated from their country in spite of the solemn protest of their representatives at the Assembly of Bordeaux,

Agree upon the following Articles:

Article 51. The territories which were ceded to Germany in accordance with the Preliminaries of Peace signed at Versailles on February 26, 1871, and the Treaty of Frankfurt of May 10, 1871, are restored to French sovereignty as from the date of the Armistice of November 11, 1918.

The provisions of the Treaties establishing the delimitation of the frontiers before 1871 shall be restored.

. . .

SECTION VI · AUSTRIA

Article 80. Germany acknowledges and will respect strictly the independence of Austria, within the frontiers which may be fixed in a Treaty between that State and the Principal Allied and Associated Powers; she agrees that this independence shall be inalienable, except with the consent of the Council of the League of Nations.

SECTION VII · CZECHO-SLOVAK STATE

Article 81. Germany, in conformity with the action already taken by the Allied and Associated Powers, recognizes the complete independence of the Czecho-Slovak State which will include the autonomous territory of the Ruthenians to the south of the Carpathians. Germany hereby recognizes the frontiers of this State as determined by the Principal Allied and Associated Powers and the other interested States.

. . .

SECTION VIII · POLAND

Article 87. Germany, in conformity with the action already taken by the Allied and Associated Powers, recognizes the complete independence of Poland, and renounces in her favour all rights and title over the territory bounded by the Baltic Sea, the eastern frontier of Germany as laid down in Article 27 of Part II (Boundaries of Germany) of the present Treaty up to a point situated about 2 kilometres to the east of Lorzendorf, then a line to the acute angle which the northern boundary of Upper Silesia makes about 3 kilometres north-west of Simmenau, then the boundary of Upper Silesia to its meeting point with the old frontier between Germany and Russia, then this frontier to the point where it crosses the course of the Niemen, and then the northern frontier of East Prussia as laid down in Article 28 of Part II aforesaid.

The provisions of this Article do not, however, apply to the territories of East Prussia and the Free City of Danzig, as defined in Article 28 of Part II (Boundaries of Germany) and in Article 100 of Section XI (Danzig) of this Part.

The boundaries of Poland not laid down in the present Treaty will be subsequently determined by the Principal Allied and Associated Powers. . . .

Article 89. Poland undertakes to accord freedom of transit to persons, goods, vessels, carriages, wagons and mails in transit between East Prussia and the rest of Germany over Polish territory, including territorial waters, and to treat them at least as favourably as the persons, goods, vessels, carriages, wagons and mails respectively of Polish or of any other more favoured nationality, origin, importation, starting point, or ownership as regards facilities, restrictions and all other matters.

Goods in transit shall be exempt from all customs or other similar duties.

Freedom of transit will extend to telegraphic and telephonic services under the conditions laid down by the conventions referred to in Article 98.

. . .

Article 93. Poland accepts and agrees to embody in a Treaty with the Principal Allied and Associated Powers such provisions as may be deemed necessary by the said Powers to protect the interests of inhabitants of Poland who differ from the majority of the population in race, language or religion.

Poland further accepts and agrees to embody in a Treaty with the said Powers such provisions as they may deem necessary to protect freedom of transit and equitable treatment of the commerce of other nations.

SECTION IX · EAST PRUSSIA

Article 94. In the area between the southern frontier of East Prussia, as described in Article 28 of Part II (Boundaries of Germany) of the present Treaty, and the line described below, the inhabitants will be called upon to indicate by a vote the State to which they wish to belong. . . .

SECTION X · MEMEL

Article 99. Germany renounces in favour of the Principal Allied and Associated Powers all rights and title over the territories included between the Baltic, the north-eastern frontier of East Prussia as defined in Article 28 of Part II (Boundaries of Germany) of the present Treaty and the former frontier between Germany and Russia.

Germany undertakes to accept the settlement made by the Principal Allied and Associated Powers in regard to these territories, particularly in so far as concerns the nationality of the inhabitants.

SECTION XI · FREE CITY OF DANZIG

Article 100. Germany renounces in favour of the Principal Allied and Associated Powers all rights and title over the territory comprised within the following limits. . . .

Article 102. The Principal Allied and Associated Powers undertake to establish the town of Danzig, together with the rest of the territory described in Article 100, as a Free City. It will be placed under the protection of the League of Nations.

Article 103. A constitution for the Free City of Danzig shall be drawn up by the duly appointed representatives of the Free City in agreement with a High Commissioner to be appointed by the League of Nations. This constitution shall be placed under the guarantee of the League of Nations.

The High Commissioner will also be entrusted with the duty of dealing in the first instance with all differences arising beween Poland and the Free City of Danzig in regard to this Treaty or any arrangements or agreements made thereunder.

The High Commissioner shall reside at Danzig.

Article 104. The Principal Allied and Associated Powers undertake to negotiate a Treaty between the Polish Government and the Free City of Danzig, which shall come into force at the same time as the establishment of the said Free City, with the following objects:

(1) To effect the inclusion of the Free City of Danzig within the Polish customs frontiers, and to establish a free area in the port;

(2) To ensure to Poland without any restriction the free use and service of all waterways, docks, basins, wharves and other works within the territory of the Free City necessary for Polish imports and exports;

(3) To ensure to Poland the control and administration of the Vistula and of the whole railway system within the Free City, except such street and other railways as serve primarily the needs of the Free City, and of postal, telegraphic and telephonic communication between Poland and the port of Danzig;

(4) To ensure to Poland the right to develop and improve the waterways, docks, basins, wharves, railways and other works and means of communication mentioned in this Article, as well as to lease or purchase through appropriate processes such land and other property as may be necessary for these purposes;

(5) To provide against any discrimination within the Free City of Danzig to the detriment of citizens of Poland and other persons of Polish origin or speech;

(6) To provide that the Polish Government shall undertake the conduct of the foreign relations of the Free City of Danzig as well as the diplomatic protection of citizens of that city when abroad.

SECTION XIV · RUSSIA AND RUSSIAN STATES

Article 116. Germany acknowledges and agrees to respect as permanent and inalienable the independence of all the territories which were part of the former Russian Empire on August 1, 1914.

In accordance with the provisions of Article 259 of Part IX (Financial Clauses) and Article 292 of Part X (Economic Clauses) Germany accepts definitely the abrogation of the Brest-Litovsk Treaties and of all other treaties, conventions and agreements entered into by her with the Maximalist Government in Russia.

The Allied and Associated Powers formally reserve the rights of Russia to obtain from Germany restitution and reparation based on the principles of the present Treaty.

Article 117. Germany undertakes to recognize the full force of all treaties or agreements which may be entered into by the Allied and Associated Powers with States now existing or coming into existence in future in the whole or part of the former Empire of Russia as it existed on August 1, 1914, and to recognize the frontiers of any such States as determined therein.

Part IV · German rights and interests outside Germany

Article 118. In territory outside her European frontiers as fixed by the present Treaty, Germany renounces all rights, titles and privileges whatever in or over territory which belonged to her or to her allies, and all rights, titles and privileges whatever their origin which she held as against the Allied and Associated Powers.

Germany hereby undertakes to recognize and to conform to the measures which may be taken now or in the future by the Principal Allied and Associated Powers, in agreement where necessary with third Powers, in order to carry the above stipulation into effect.

In particular Germany declares her acceptance of the following Articles relating to certain special subjects.

SECTION I · GERMAN COLONIES

Article 119. Germany renounces in favour of the Principal Allied and Associated Powers all her rights and titles over her oversea possessions. . . .

[*Article 128.* Germany renounces all rights acquired in 1901 in China.]

[*Article 138.* Germany renounces all rights in Liberia.]

[*Article 141.* Germany renounces all rights in Morocco.]

[*Article 147.* Germany renounces all rights in Egypt.]

SECTION VIII · SHANTUNG

Article 156. Germany renounces, in favour of Japan, all her rights, title and privileges – particularly those concerning the territory of Kiaochow, railways, mines and submarine cables – which she acquired in virtue of the Treaty concluded by her with China on March 6, 1898, and of all other arrangements relative to the Province of Shantung. . . .

Part V · Military, naval and air clauses

In order to render possible the initiation of a general limitation of the armaments of all nations, Germany undertakes strictly to observe the military, naval and air clauses which follow.

SECTION I · MILITARY CLAUSES

Chapter I: Effectives and cadres of the German army

Article 159. The German military forces shall be demobilized and reduced as prescribed hereinafter.

Article 160. 1. By a date which must not be later than March 31, 1920, the German army must not comprise more than seven divisions of infantry and three divisions of cavalry.

After that date the total number of effectives in the army of the States constituting Germany must not exceed one hundred thousand men, including officers and establishments of depots. The army shall be devoted exclusively to the maintenance of order within the territory and to the control of the frontiers.

. . .

Chapter II: Armament, munitions and material

Article 164. Up till the time at which Germany is admitted as a member of the League of Nations the German army must not possess an armament greater than the amounts fixed in Table No. II annexed to this Section. . . .

Article 173. Universal compulsory military service shall be abolished in Germany.

The German army may only be constituted and recruited by means of voluntary enlistment.

Article 174. The period of enlistment for non-commissioned officers and privates must be twelve consecutive years. . . .

Article 175. The officers who are retained in the army must undertake the obligation to serve in it up to the age of forty-five years at least. . . .

Chapter IV: Fortifications

Article 180. All fortified works, fortresses and field works situated in German territory to the west of a line drawn 50 kilometres to the east of the Rhine shall be disarmed and dismantled. . . .

[*Article 181.* Naval limitation to six battleships and thirty smaller warships; no submarines.]

[*Article 198.* No military or naval air force.]

SECTION IV · INTER-ALLIED COMMISSIONS OF CONTROL

Article 203. All the military, naval and air clauses contained in the present Treaty, for the execution of which a time limit is prescribed, shall be executed by Germany under the control of Inter-Allied Commissions specially appointed for this purpose by the Principal Allied and Associated Powers. . . .

Part VIII · Reparation

SECTION I · GENERAL PROVISIONS

Article 231. The Allied and Associated Governments affirm and Germany accepts the responsibility of Germany and her allies for causing all the loss and damage to which the Allied and Associated Governments and their nationals have been subjected as a consequence of the war imposed upon them by the aggression of Germany and her allies.

Article 232. The Allied and Associated Governments recognize that the resources of Germany are not adequate, after taking into account permanent diminutions of such resources which will result from other provisions of the present Treaty, to make complete reparation for all such loss and damage.

The Allied and Associated Governments, however, require, and Germany undertakes, that she will make compensation for all damage done to the civilian population of the Allied and Associated Powers and to their property during the period of the belligerency of each as an Allied or Associated Power against Germany by such aggression by land, by sea and from the air, and in general all damage as defined in Annex I hereto.

In accordance with Germany's pledges, already given, as to complete restoration for Belgium, Germany undertakes, in addition to the compensation for damage elsewhere in this Part provided for, as a consequence of the violation of the Treaty of 1839, to make reimbursement of all sums which Belgium has borrowed from the Allied and Associated Governments up to November 11, 1918, together with interest at the rate of five per cent (5%) per annum on such sums. This amount shall be determined by the Reparation Commission. . . .

Article 233. The amount of the above damage for which compensation is to be made by Germany shall be determined by an Inter-Allied Commission, to be called the *Reparation Commission* and constituted in the form and with the powers set forth hereunder and in Annexes II to VII inclusive hereto.

This Commission shall consider the claims and give to the German Government a just opportunity to be heard.

The findings of the Commission as to the amount of damage defined as above shall be concluded and notified to the German Government on or before May 1, 1921, as representing the extent of that Government's obligations.

The Commission shall concurrently draw up a schedule of payments prescribing the time and manner for securing and discharging the entire obligation within a period of thirty years from May 1, 1921. If, however, within the period mentioned, Germany fails to discharge her obligations, any balance remaining unpaid may, within the discretion of the Commission, be postponed for settlement in subsequent years, or may be handled otherwise in such manner as the Allied and Associated Governments, acting in accordance with the procedure laid down in this Part of the present Treaty, shall determine.

Part IX · Financial clauses

Article 248. Subject to such exceptions as the Reparation Commission may approve, a first charge upon all the assets and revenues of the German Empire and its constituent States shall be the cost of reparation and all other costs arising under the present Treaty or any treaties or agreements supplementary thereto or under arrangements concluded between

Germany and the Allied and Associated Powers during the Armistice or its extensions. . . .

Article 249. There shall be paid by the German Government the total cost of all armies of the Allied and Associated Governments in occupied German territory from the date of the signature of the Armistice of November 11, 1918, including the keep of men and beasts, lodging and billeting, pay and allowances, salaries and wages, bedding, heating, lighting, clothing, equipment, harness and saddlery, armament and rolling stock, air services, treatment of sick and wounded, veterinary and remount services, transport service of all sorts (such as by rail, sea or river, motor lorries), communications and correspondence, and in general the cost of all administrative or technical services the working of which is necessary for the training of troops and for keeping their numbers up to strength and preserving their military efficiency.

The cost of such liabilities under the above heads so far as they relate to purchases or requisitions by the Allied and Associated Governments in the occupied territories shall be paid by the German Government to the Allied and Associated Governments in marks at the current or agreed rate of exchange. All other of the above costs shall be paid in gold marks.

Part XIV · Guarantees

SECTION I · WESTERN EUROPE

Article 428. As a guarantee for the execution of the present Treaty by Germany, the German territory situated to the west of the Rhine, together with the bridgeheads, will be occupied by Allied and Associated troops for a period of fifteen years from the coming into force of the present Treaty.

Article 429. If the conditions of the present Treaty are faithfully carried out by Germany, the occupation referred to in Article 428 will be successively restricted as follows:

(i) At the expiration of five years there will be evacuated: the bridgehead of Cologne and the territories north of a line running along the Ruhr, then along the railway Jülich, Düren, Euskirchen, Rheinbach, thence along the road Rheinbach to Sinzig, and reaching the Rhine at the confluence with the Ahr; the roads, railways and places mentioned above being excluded from the area evacuated.

(ii) At the expiration of ten years there will be evacuated: the bridgehead of Coblenz and the territories north of a line to be drawn from the intersection between the frontiers of Belgium, Germany and Holland, running about 4 kilometres south of Aix-la-Chapelle, then to and following the crest of Forst Gemünd, then east of the railway of the Urft Valley, then along Blankenheim, Valdorf, Dreis, Ulmen to and following the Moselle from Bremm to Nehren, then passing by Kappel and Simmern, then following the ridge of the heights between Simmern and the Rhine and reaching this river at Bacharach; all the places, valleys, roads and railways mentioned above being excluded from the area evacuated.

(iii) At the expiration of fifteen years there will be evacuated: the bridgehead of Mainz, the bridgehead of Kehl and the remainder of the German territory under occupation.

If at that date the guarantees against unprovoked aggression by Germany are not considered sufficient by the Allied and Associated Governments, the evacuation of the occupying troops may be delayed to the extent regarded as necessary for the purpose of obtaining the required guarantees.

Article 430. In case either during the occupation or after the expiration of the fifteen years referred to above the Reparation Commission finds that Germany refuses to observe the whole or part of her obligations under the present Treaty with regard to reparation, the whole or part of the areas specified in Article 429 will be reoccupied immediately by the Allied and Associated forces.

Article 431. If before the expiration of the period of fifteen years Germany complies with all the undertakings resulting from the present Treaty, the occupying forces will be withdrawn immediately.

Article 432. All matters relating to the occupation and not provided for by the present Treaty shall be regulated by subsequent agreements, which Germany hereby undertakes to observe.

SECTION II · EASTERN EUROPE

Article 433. As a guarantee for the execution of the provisions of the present Treaty, by which Germany accepts definitely the abrogation of the Brest-Litovsk Treaty, and of all treaties, conventions and agreements entered into by her with the Maximalist Government in Russia, and in order to ensure the restoration of peace and good government in the Baltic Provinces and Lithuania, all German troops at present in the said territories shall return to within the frontiers of Germany as soon as the Governments of the Principal Allied and Associated Powers shall think the moment suitable, having regard to the internal situation of these territories. These troops shall abstain from all requisitions and seizures and from any other coercive measures, with a view to obtaining supplies intended for Germany, and shall in no way interfere with such measures for national defence as may be adopted by the Provisional Governments of Estonia, Latvia and Lithuania.

No other German troops shall, pending the evacuation or after the evacuation is complete, be admitted to the said territories.

Part XV · Miscellaneous provisions

Article 434. Germany undertakes to recognize the full force of the Treaties of Peace and Additional Conventions which may be concluded by the Allied and Associated Powers with the Powers who fought on the side of Germany and to recognize whatever dispositions may be made concerning the territories of the former Austro-Hungarian Monarchy, of the Kingdom of Bulgaria and of the Ottoman Empire, and to recognize the new States within their frontiers as there laid down.

Treaty between France and Great Britain (Treaty of Guarantee), 28 June 1919

Assistance to France in the event of unprovoked aggression by Germany

Article 1. In case the following stipulations relating to the Left Bank of the Rhine contained in the Treaty of Peace with Germany signed at Versailles the 28th day of June, 1919, by the British Empire, the French Republic, and the United States of America among other Powers:

ARTICLE 42. Germany is forbidden to maintain or construct any fortifications either on the left bank of the Rhine or on the right bank to the west of a line drawn 50 kilometres to the east of the Rhine.

ARTICLE 43. In the area defined above the maintenance and assembly of armed forces, either permanently, or temporarily, and military manœuvres of any kind, as well as the upkeep of all permanent works for mobilization, are in the same way forbidden.

ARTICLE 44. In case Germany violates in any manner whatsoever the provisions of Articles 42 and 43, she shall be regarded as committing a hostile act against the Powers signatory of the present Treaty and as calculated to disturb the peace of the world.

may not at first provide adequate security and protection to France, Great Britain agrees to come immediately to her assistance in the event of any unprovoked movement of aggression against her being made by Germany.

Article 2. The present Treaty, in similar terms with the Treaty of even date for the same purpose concluded between the French Republic and the United States of America, a copy of which Treaty is annexed hereto, will only come into force when the latter is ratified.

Article 3. The present Treaty must be submitted to the Council of the League of Nations and must be recognized by the Council, acting if need be by a majority, as an engagement which is consistent with the Covenant of the League; it will continue in force until on the application of one of the Parties to it the Council, acting if need be by a majority, agree that

the League itself affords sufficient protection.

Article 4. The present Treaty shall before ratification by His Majesty be submitted to Parliament for approval.

It shall before ratification by the President of the French Republic be submitted to the French Chambers for approval.

Article 5. The present Treaty shall impose no obligation upon any of the Dominions of the British Empire unless and until it is approved by the Parliament of the Dominion concerned.

The present Treaty shall be ratified, and shall, subject to Articles 2 and 4, come into force at the same time as the Treaty of Peace with Germany of even date comes into force for the British Empire and the French Republic.

In Faith Whereof the above-named plenipotentiaries have signed the present Treaty, drawn up in the English and French languages.

Done in duplicate at Versailles, on the twenty-eighth day of June, 1919.

(Seal) D. LLOYD GEORGE
(Seal) ARTHUR JAMES BALFOUR
(Seal) G. CLEMENCEAU
(Seal) S. PICHON

Treaty between the Allied and Associated Powers and Poland on the protection of minorities, 28 June 1919

Article 2. Poland undertakes to assure full and complete protection of life and liberty to all inhabitants of Poland without distinction of birth, nationality, language, race or religion.

All inhabitants of Poland shall be entitled to the free exercise, whether public or private, of any creed, religion or belief, whose practices are not inconsistent with public order or public morals.

Article 3. Poland admits and declares to be Polish nationals *ipso facto* and with-

out the requirement of any formality German, Austrian, Hungarian or Russian nationals habitually resident at the date of the coming into force of the present Treaty in territory which is or may be recognized as forming part of Poland, but subject to any provisions in the Treaties of Peace with Germany or Austria respectively relating to persons who became resident in such territory after a specified date.

Nevertheless, the persons referred to above, who are over eighteen years of age will be entitled under the conditions contained in the said Treaties to opt for any other nationality which may be open to them. Option by a husband will cover his wife and option by parents will cover their children under eighteen years of age. . . .

Article 7. All Polish nationals shall be equal before the law and shall enjoy the same civil and political rights without distinction as to race, language or religion.

Differences of religion, creed or confession shall not prejudice any Polish national in matters relating to the enjoyment of civil or political rights, as for instance admission to public employments, functions and honours, or exercise of professions and industries.

No restriction shall be imposed on the free use by any Polish national of any language in private intercourse, in commerce, in religion, in the press or in publications of any kind, or at public meetings. . . .

Article 8. Polish nationals who belong to racial, religious or linguistic minorities shall enjoy the same treatment and security in law and in fact as the other Polish nationals. In particular they shall have an equal right to establish, manage and control at their own expense charitable, religious and social institutions, schools and other educational establishments, with the right to use their own language and to exercise their religion freely therein.

Article 9. Poland will provide in the public educational system in towns and districts in which a considerable proportion of Polish nationals of other than Polish speech are residents adequate facilities for ensuring that in the primary schools the instruction shall be given to the children of such Polish nationals through the medium of their own language. This provision shall not prevent the Polish Government from making the teaching of the Polish language obligatory in the said schools.

. . .

Article 11. Jews shall not be compelled to perform any act which constitutes a violation of their Sabbath, nor shall they be placed under any disability by reason of their refusal to attend courts of law or to perform any legal business on their Sabbath. This provision however shall not exempt Jews from such obligations as shall be imposed upon all other Polish citizens for the necessary purposes of military service, national defence or the preservation of public order. . . .

Treaty of Peace between the Allied and Associated Powers and Turkey (Treaty of Sèvres), 10 August 1920

[Part I · Covenant of the League of Nations]

Part II · Frontiers of Turkey

Article 27. I. In Europe, the frontiers of Turkey will be laid down as follows:

1. *The Black Sea:* From the entrance of the Bosphorus to the point described below.

2. *With Greece:* From a point to be chosen on the Black Sea near the mouth of the Biyuk Dere, situated about 7 kilometres north-west of Podima, south-westwards to the most north-westerly point of the limit of the basin of the Istranja Dere (about 8 kilometres north-west of Istranja),

a line to be fixed on the ground passing through Kapilja Dagh and Uchbunar Tepe;

thence south-south-eastwards to a point to be chosen on the railway from Chorlu to Chatalja about 1 kilometre west of the railway station of Sinekli,

a line following as far as possible the western limit of the basin of the Istranja Dere;

thence south-eastwards to a point to be chosen between Fener and Kurfali on the watershed between the basins of those rivers which flow into Biyuk Chekmeje Geul, on the north-east, and the basin of those rivers which flow direct into the Sea of Marmora on the south-west,

a line to be fixed on the ground passing south of Sinekli;

thence south-eastwards to a point to be chosen on the Sea of Marmora about 1 kilometre south-west of Kalikratia,

a line following as far as possible this watershed.

3. *The Sea of Marmora:* From the point defined above to the entrance of the Bosphorus.

II. In Asia, the frontier of Turkey will be laid down as follows:

1. *On the West and South:* From the entrance of the Bosphorus into the Sea of Marmora to a point described below, situated in the eastern Mediterranean Sea in the neighbourhood of the Gulf of Alexandretta near Karatash Burun,

the Sea of Marmora, the Dardanelles, and the Eastern Mediterranean Sea; the islands of the Sea of Marmora, and those which are situated within a distance of 3 miles from the coast, remaining Turkish, subject to the provisions of Section IV and Articles 84 and 122, Part III (Political Clauses).

2. *With Syria:* From a point to be chosen on the eastern bank of the outlet of the Hassan Dede, about 3 kilometres north-west of Karatash Burun, north-eastwards to a point to be chosen on the Djaihun Irmak about 1 kilometre north of Babeli,

a line to be fixed on the ground passing north of Karatash;

thence to Kesik Kale,

the course of the Djaihun Irmak upstream;

thence north-eastwards to a point to be chosen on the Djaihun Irmak about 15 kilometres east-southeast of Karsbazar,

a line to be fixed on the ground passing north of Kara Tepe;

thence to the bend in the Djaihun Irmak situated west of Duldul Dagh,

the course of the Djaihun Irmak upstream;

thence in a general south-easterly direction to a point to be chosen on Emir Musi Dagh about 15 kilometres south-south-west of Giaour Geul,

a line to be fixed on the ground at a distance of about 18 kilometres from the railway, and leaving Duldul Dagh to Syria;

thence eastwards to a point to be chosen about 5 kilometres north of Urfa,

a generally straight line from west to east to be fixed on the ground passing north of the roads connecting the towns of Baghche, Aintab, Biridjik, and Urfa and leaving the last three named towns to Syria;

thence eastwards to the south-western extremity of the bend in the Tigris about 6 kilometres north of Azekh (27 kilometres west to Djezire-ibn-Omar),

a generally straight line from west to east to be fixed on the ground leaving the town of Mardin to Syria;

thence to a point to be chosen on the Tigris between the point of confluence of the Khabur Su with the Tigris and the bend in the Tigris situated about 10 kilometres north of this point,

the course of the Tigris downstream, leaving the island on which is situated the town of Djezire-ibn-Omar to Syria.

3. *With Mesopotamia:* Thence in a general easterly direction to a point to be chosen on the northern boundary of the *vilayet* of Mosul,

a line to be fixed on the ground;

thence eastwards to the point where it meets the frontier between Turkey and Persia,

the northern boundary of the *vilayet*

of Mosul, modified, however, so as to pass south of Amadia.

4. *On the East and the North-east:* From the point above defined to the Black Sea, the existing frontier between Turkey and Persia, then the former frontier between Turkey and Russia, subject to the provisions of Article 89.

5. *The Black Sea.*

Part III · Political clauses

Section I · Constantinople

Article 36. Subject to the provisions of the present Treaty, the High Contracting Parties agree that the rights and title of the Turkish Government over Constantinople shall not be affected, and that the said Government and His Majesty the Sultan shall be entitled to reside there and to maintain there the capital of the Turkish State.

Nevertheless, in the event of Turkey failing to observe faithfully the provisions of the present Treaty, or of any treaties or conventions supplementary thereto, particularly as regards the protection of the rights of racial, religious or linguistic minorities, the Allied Powers expressly reserve the right to modify the above provisions, and Turkey hereby agrees to accept any dispositions which may be taken in this connection.

Section II · Straits

Article 37. The navigation of the Straits, including the Dardanelles, the Sea of Marmora and the Bosphorus, shall in future be open, both in peace and war, to every vessel of commerce or of war and to military and commercial aircraft, without distinction of flag.

These waters shall not be subject to blockade, nor shall any belligerent right be exercised nor any act of hostility be committed within them, unless in pursuance of a decision of the Council of the League of Nations.

Article 38. The Turkish Government recognizes that it is necessary to take further measures to ensure the freedom of navigation provided for in Article 37, and accordingly delegates, so far as it is concerned, to a Commission to be called the 'Commission of the Straits', and hereinafter referred to as 'the Commission', the control of the waters specified in Article 39.

The Greek Government, so far as it is concerned, delegates to the Commission the same powers and undertakes to give it in all respects the same facilities.

Such control shall be exercised in the name of the Turkish and Greek Governments respectively, and in the manner provided in this Section.

Article 39. The authority of the Commission will extend to all the waters between the Mediterranean mouth of the Dardanelles and the Black Sea mouth of the Bosphorus, and to the waters within three miles of each of these mouths.

This authority may be exercised on shore to such extent as may be necessary for the execution of the provisions of this Section.

Article 40. The Commission shall be composed of representatives appointed respectively by the United States of America (if and when that Government is willing to participate), the British Empire, France, Italy, Japan, Russia (if and when Russia becomes a member of the League of Nations), Greece, Roumania, and Bulgaria and Turkey (if and when the two latter States become members of the League of Nations). Each Power shall appoint one representative. The representatives of the United States of America, the British Empire, France, Italy, Japan and Russia shall each have two votes. The representatives of Greece, Roumania, and Bulgaria and Turkey shall each have one vote. Each Commissioner shall be removable only by the Government which appointed him.

Article 42. The Commission will exercise the powers conferred on it by the present Treaty in complete independence of the local authority. It will have its own flag, its own budget and its separate organization.

Article 43. Within the limits of its jurisdiction as laid down in Article 39 the Commission will be charged with the following duties:

(*a*) the execution of any works considered necessary for the improvement of the channels or the approaches to harbours;

(*b*) the lighting and buoying of the channels;

(*c*) the control of pilotage and towage;

(*d*) the control of anchorages;

(*e*) the control necessary to assure the application in the ports of Constantinople and Haidar Pasha of the régime prescribed in Articles 335 to 344, Part XI (Ports, Waterways and Railways) of the present Treaty;

(*f*) the control of all matters relating to wrecks and salvage;

(*g*) the control of lighterage.

Article 44. In the event of the Commission finding that the liberty of passage is being interfered with, it will inform the representatives at Constantinople of the Allied Powers providing the occupying forces provided for in Article 178. These representatives will thereupon concert with the naval and military commanders of the said forces such measures as may be deemed necessary to preserve the freedom of the Straits. Similar action shall be taken by the said representatives in the event of any external action threatening the liberty of passage of the Straits.

. . .

Article 48. In order to facilitate the execution of the duties with which it is entrusted by this Section, the Commission shall have power to organize such a force of special police as may be necessary. This force shall be drawn so far as possible from the native population of the zone of the Straits and islands referred to in Article 178, Part V (Military, Naval and Air Clauses), excluding the islands of Lemnos, Imbros, Samothrace, Tenedos and Mitylene. The said force shall be commanded by foreign police officers appointed by the Commission.

[Provision for autonomy, and later on, if people were considered ready, independence.]

SECTION IV · SMYRNA

Article 65. The provisions of this Section will apply to the city of Smyrna and the adjacent territory defined in Article 66, until the determination of their final status in accordance with Article 83.

Article 66. The geographical limits of the territory adjacent to the city of Smyrna will be laid down as follows. . . .

[*Articles 69–71.* The city of Smyrna and territory defined in Article 66 to remain under Turkish sovereignty. Turkey however transfers to the Greek Government the exercise of her rights over these territories. Greek Government will be responsible for administration and will maintain such military forces necessary for order and public security.]

[*Article 72.* A local parliament to be set up; electoral system to ensure proportional representation of all sections of the population including linguistic, racial and religious minorities.]

. . .

Article 83. When a period of five years shall have elapsed after the coming into force of the present Treaty the local parliament referred to in Article 72 may, by a majority of votes, ask the Council of the League of Nations for the definitive incorporation in the Kingdom of Greece of the city of Smyrna and the territory defined in Article 66. The Council may require, as a preliminary, a plebiscite under conditions which it will lay down.

In the event of such incorporation as a result of the application of the foregoing paragraph, the Turkish sovereignty referred to in Article 69 shall cease. Turkey hereby renounces in that event in favour of Greece all rights and title over the city of Smyrna and the territory defined in Article 66.

Section V · Greece

Article 84. Without prejudice to the frontiers of Bulgaria laid down by the Treaty of Peace signed at Neuilly-sur-Seine on November 27, 1919, Turkey renounces in favour of Greece all rights and title over the territories of the former Turkish Empire in Europe situated outside the frontiers of Turkey as laid down by the present Treaty.

The islands of the Sea of Marmora are not included in the transfer of sovereignty effected by the above paragraph.

Turkey further renounces in favour of Greece all her rights and title over the islands of Imbros and Tenedos. . . .

Treaty of Friendship between Russia and Turkey, 16 March 1921

The Government of the Russian Socialist Federal Soviet Republic and the Government of the Grand National Assembly of Turkey, sharing as they do the principles of the liberty of nations, and the right of each nation to determine its own fate, and taking into consideration, moreover, the common struggle undertaken against imperialism, foreseeing that the difficulties arising for the one would render worse the position of the other, and inspired by the desire to bring about lasting good relations and uninterrupted sincere friendship between themselves, based on mutual interests, have decided to sign an agreement to assure amicable and fraternal relations between the two countries. . . .

Article I. Each of the Contracting Parties agrees not to recognize any peace treaty or other international agreement imposed upon the other against its will. The Government of the R.S.F.S.R. agrees not to recognize any international agreement relating to Turkey which is not recognized by the National Government of Turkey, at present represented by the Grand National Assembly.

The expression 'Turkey' in the present Treaty is understood to mean the territories included in the Turkish National Pact on the 28th January 1920, eleborated and proclaimed by the Ottoman Chamber of Deputies in Constantinople, and communicated to the press and to all foreign Governments.

The north-east frontier of Turkey is fixed as follows: [frontier definition]

Article II. Turkey agrees to cede to Georgia the right of suzerainty over the town and the port of Batum, and the territory situated to the north of the frontier mentioned in Article I, which formed a part of the district of Batum, on the following conditions:

(a) The population of the localities specified in the present Article shall enjoy a generous measure of autonomy, assuring to each community its cultural and religious rights, and allowing them to enact agrarian laws in accordance with the wishes of the population of the said districts.

(b) Turkey will be granted free transit for all Turkish imports and exports through the port of Batum, without payment of taxes and customs duties and without delays. The right of making use of the port of Batum without special expenses is assured to Turkey.

Article III. Both Contracting Parties agree that the Nakhichevan district, with the boundaries shown in Annex 1 (C) to the present Treaty, shall form an autonomous territory under the protection of Azerbaijan, on condition that the latter cannot transfer this protectorate to any third State. . . .

Article IV. The Contracting Parties, establishing contact between the national movement for the liberation of the Eastern peoples and the struggle of the workers of Russia for a new social order, solemnly recognize the right of these nations to freedom and independence, also their right to choose a form of government according to their own wishes.

Article V. In order to assure the opening of the Straits to the commerce of all nations, the Contracting Parties agree to entrust the final elaboration of an international agreement concerning the Black Sea to a conference composed of delegates of the littoral States, on condition that the decisions of the above-mentioned conference shall not be of such a nature as to diminish the full sovereignty of Turkey or the security of Constantinople, her capital.

Article VI. The Contracting Parties agree that the treaties concluded heretofore between the two countries do not correspond with their mutual interests, and therefore agree that the said treaties shall be considered as annulled and abrogated.

The Government of the R.S.F.S.R. declares that it considers Turkey to be liberated from all financial and other liabilities based on agreements concluded between Turkey and the Tsarist Government.

Article VII. The Government of the R.S.F.S.R., holding that the Capitulations régime is incompatible with the full exercise of sovereign rights and the national development of any country, declares this régime and any rights connected therewith to be null and void.

Article VIII. The Contracting Parties undertake not to tolerate in their respective territories the formation and stay of organizations or associations claiming to be the Government of the other country or of a part of its territory and organizations whose aim is to wage warfare against the other State.

Russia and Turkey mutually accept the same obligation with regard to the Soviet Republic of the Caucasus.

'Turkish territory', within the meaning of this Article, is understood to be territory under the direct civil and military administration of the Government of the Grand National Assembly of Turkey.

Article IX. To secure uninterrupted communication between the two countries, both Contracting Parties undertake to carry out urgently, and in agreement one with the other, all necessary measures for the security and development of the railway lines, telegraph and other means of communication, and to assure free movement of persons and goods between the two countries. It is agreed that the regulations in force in each country shall be applied as regards the movement, entry and exit of travellers and goods.

Article X. The nationals of the Contracting Parties residing on the territory of the other shall be treated in accordance with the laws in force in the country of their residence, with the exception of those connected with national defence, from which they are exempt. . . .

Article XI. The Contracting Parties agree to treat the nationals of one of the parties residing in the territory of the other in accordance with the most-favoured-nation principles.

This Article will not be applied to citizens of the Soviet Republics allied with Russia, nor to nationals of Mussulman States allied with Turkey.

Article XII. Any inhabitant of the territories forming part of Russia prior to 1918, and over which Turkish sovereignty has been acknowledged by the Government of the R.S.F.S.R., in the present Treaty, shall be free to leave Turkey and to take with him all his goods and possessions or the proceeds of their sale. The population of the territory of Batum, sovereignty over which has been granted to Georgia by Turkey, shall enjoy the same right.

Article XIII. Russia undertakes to return, at her own expense within three months, to the north-east frontier of Turkey all

Turkish prisoners of war and interned civilians in the Caucasus and in European Russia, and those in Asiatic Russia within six months, dating from the signature of the present Treaty. . . .

Article XIV. The Contracting Parties agree to conclude in as short a time as possible a consular agreement and other arrangements regulating all economic, financial and other questions which are necessary for the establishment of friendly relations between the two countries, as set forth in the preamble to the present Treaty.

Article XV. Russia undertakes to take the necessary steps with the Transcaucasian Republics with a view to securing the recognition by the latter, in their agreement with Turkey, of the provisions of the present Treaty which directly concern them.

[*Article XVI.* Ratification.]

Treaty of Peace with Turkey (Treaty of Lausanne), 24 July 1923

The British Empire, France, Italy, Japan, Greece, Roumania and the Serb-Croat-Slovene State,

of the one part,

and Turkey,

of the other part;

Being united in the desire to bring to a final close the state of war which has existed in the East since 1914 . . . have agreed as follows:

Part I · Political clauses

Article 1. From the coming into force of the present Treaty, the state of peace will be definitely re-established between the British Empire, France, Italy, Japan, Greece, Roumania and the Serb-Croat-Slovene State of the one part, and Turkey of the other part, as well as between their respective nationals. . . .

Section I · Territorial clauses

Article 2. From the Black Sea to the Ægean the frontier of Turkey is laid down as follows. . . .

[*Article 3.* The frontier from the Mediterranean to the frontier of Persia.]

[*Articles 4–11.* Frontier delimitation, work of the Boundary Commission.]

[*Article 12.* Greek sovereignty over islands in Eastern Mediterranean confirmed. Unless provision to contrary, Turkey to retain sovereignty over islands less than 3 miles from Asiatic coast.]

[*Article 13.* Greece undertakes not to fortify Mytilene, Chios, Samos and Nikaria.]

. . .

Article 15. Turkey renounces in favour of Italy all rights and title over the following islands: Stampalia (Astrapalia), Rhodes (Rhodos), Calki (Kharki), Scarpanto, Casos (Casso), Piscopis (Tilos), Misiros (Nisyros), Calimnos (Kalymnos), Leros, Patmos, Lipsos (Lipso), Simi (Symi), and Cos (Kos), which are now occupied by Italy, and the islets dependent thereon, and also over the island of Castellorizzo. . . .

Article 16. Turkey hereby renounces all rights and title whatsoever over or respecting the territories situated outside the frontiers laid down in the present Treaty and the islands other than those over which her sovereignty is recognized by the said Treaty, the future of these territories and islands being settled or to be settled by the parties concerned.

The provisions of the present Article do

not prejudice any special arrangements arising from neighbourly relations which have been or may be concluded between Turkey and any limitrophe countries.

Article 17. The renunciation by Turkey of all rights and titles over Egypt and over the Soudan will take effect as from the 5th November 1914.

...

Article 20. Turkey hereby recognizes the annexation of Cyprus proclaimed by the British Government on the 5th November 1914.

...

[*Article 22.* Turkey renounces rights in Libya.]

...

[*Article 28.* Abolition of Capitulations is accepted.]

SECTION III · PROTECTION OF MINORITIES

Article 37. Turkey undertakes that the stipulations contained in Articles 38 to 44 shall be recognized as fundamental laws, and that no law, no regulation, nor

official action shall conflict or interfere with these stipulations, nor shall any law, regulation, nor official action prevail over them.

Article 38. The Turkish Government undertakes to assure full and complete protection of life and liberty to all inhabitants of Turkey without distinction of birth, nationality, language, race or religion.

[*Articles 39–44.* Non-Moslem Turkish citizens to enjoy equal political and civil rights as Moslem Turkish citizens.]

[*Article 45.* The same rights as in Articles 39 to 44 to be enjoyed by Moslem majority in Greece.]

Part II · Financial clauses

[*Articles 46–58.* These deal with the Ottoman Public Debt. Article 58 states that Turkey and the Allied Powers, except Greece, renounce all financial claims arising from war and conflict since 1 August 1914.]

Convention regarding the régime of the Straits (Lausanne Convention), 24 July 1923

Article 1. The High Contracting Parties agree to recognize and declare the principle of freedom of transit and of navigation by sea and by air in the Strait of the Dardanelles, the Sea of Marmora and the Bosphorus, hereinafter comprised under the general term of the 'Straits'.

Article 2. The transit and navigation of commercial vessels and aircraft, and of war vessels and aircraft in the Straits in time of peace and in time of war shall henceforth be regulated by the provisions of the attached Annex.

Annex · *Rules for the Passage of Commercial Vessels and Aircraft, and of War Vessels and Aircraft through the Straits...*

1. MERCHANT VESSELS, INCLUDING HOSPITAL SHIPS, YACHTS AND FISHING VESSELS AND NON-MILITARY AIRCRAFT

[In time of peace: freedom of passage. In time of war, Turkey being neutral: freedom of passage. In time of war, Turkey being belligerent: freedom of passage for neutrals, Turkey being permitted the right of search of contraband. Turkey may take whatever measures regarded as necessary to prevent use of Straits by enemy ships.]

2. WARSHIPS, INCLUDING FLEET AUXILIARIES, TROOPSHIPS, AIRCRAFT CARRIERS AND MILITARY AIRCRAFT

(a) *In time of peace.* Complete freedom of passage by day and by night under any flag, without any formalities, or tax, or charge whatever, but subject to the following restrictions as to the total force:

The maximum force which any one Power may send through the Straits into the Black Sea is not to be greater than that of the most powerful fleet of the littoral Powers of the Black Sea existing in that sea at the time of passage; but with the proviso that the Powers reserve to themselves the right to send into the Black Sea, at all times and under all circumstances, a force of not more than three ships, of which no individual ship shall exceed 10,000 tons.

Turkey has no responsibility in regard to the number of war vessels which pass through the Straits.

In order to enable the above rule to be observed, the Straits Commission provided for in Article 10 will, on the 1st January and 1st July of each year, enquire of each Black Sea littoral Power the number of each of the following classes of vessel which such Power possesses in the Black Sea: battleships, battle-cruisers, aircraft carriers, cruisers, destroyers, submarines, or other types of vessels as well as naval aircraft; distinguishing between the ships which are in active commission and the ships with reduced complements, the ships in reserve and the ships undergoing repairs or alterations.

The Straits Commission will then inform the Powers concerned that the strongest naval force in the Black Sea comprise: battleships, battle-cruisers, aircraft carriers, cruisers, destroyers, submarines, aircraft and units of other types which may exist. The Straits Commission will also immediately inform the Powers concerned when, owing to the passage into or out of the Black Sea of any ship of the strongest Black Sea force, any alteration in that force has taken place.

The naval force that may be sent through the Straits into the Black Sea will be calculated on the number and type of the ships of war in active commission only.

(b) *In time of war, Turkey being neutral.* Complete freedom of passage by day and by night under any flag, without any formalities, or tax, or charge whatever, under the same limitations as in paragraph 2 (a).

However, these limitations will not be applicable to any belligerent Power to the prejudice of its belligerent rights in the Black Sea.

The rights and duties of Turkey as a neutral Power cannot authorize her to take any measures liable to interfere with navigation through the Straits, the waters of which, and the air above which, must remain entirely free in time of war, Turkey being neutral, just as in time of peace.

Warships and military aircraft of belligerents will be forbidden to make any capture, to exercise the right of visit and search, or to carry out any other hostile act in the Straits.

As regards revictualling and carrying out repairs, war vessels will be subject to the terms of the Thirteenth Hague Convention of 1907, dealing with maritime neutrality.

Military aircraft will receive in the Straits similar treatment to that accorded under the Thirteenth Hague Convention of 1907 to warships, pending the conclusion of an international convention establishing the rules of neutrality for aircraft.

(c) *In time of war, Turkey being belligerent.* Complete freedom of passage for neutral warships, without any formalities, or tax, or charge whatever, but under the same limitations as in paragraph 2 (a).

The measures taken by Turkey to prevent enemy ships and aircraft from using the Straits are not to be of such a nature as to prevent the free passage of neutral ships and aircraft, and Turkey agrees to provide the said ships and aircraft with either the necessary instructions or pilots for the above purpose.

Neutral military aircraft will make the passage of the Straits at their own risk and peril, and will submit to investigation as to their character. For this purpose aircraft are to alight on the ground or on the sea in such areas as are specified and prepared for this purpose by Turkey.

3. (a) The passage of the Straits by submarines of the Powers at peace with Turkey must be made on the surface....

(c) The right of military and non-military aircraft to fly over the Straits, under the conditions laid down in the present rules, necessitates for aircraft:

(i) Freedom to fly over a strip of territory of 5 kilometres wide on each side of the narrow parts of the Straits;
(ii) Liberty, in the event of a forced landing, to alight on the coast or on the sea in the territorial waters of Turkey.

...

Article 3. With a view to maintaining the Straits free from any obstacle to free passage and navigation, the provisions contained in Articles 4 to 9 will be applied to the waters and shores thereof as well as to the islands situated therein, or in the vicinity.

Article 4. The zones and islands indicated below shall be demilitarized:

1. Both shores of the Straits of the Dardanelles and the Bosphorus over the extent of the zones delimited below [*Dardanelles; Bosphorus*].
2. All the islands in the Sea of Marmora, with the exception of the island of Emir Ali Adasi.
3. In the Ægean Sea, the islands of Samothrace, Lemnos, Imbros, Tenedos and Rabbit Islands.

Article 5. A Commission composed of four representatives appointed respectively by the Governments of France, Great Britain, Italy and Turkey shall meet within 15 days of the coming into force of the present Convention to determine on the spot the boundaries of the zone laid down in Article 4 (1)....

Article 6. Subject to the provisions of Article 8 concerning Constantinople, there shall exist, in the demilitarized zones and islands, no fortifications, no permanent artillery organization, no submarine engines of war other than submarine vessels, no military aerial organization, and no naval base.

No armed forces shall be stationed in the demilitarized zones and islands except the police and *gendarmerie* forces necessary for the maintenance of order....

Article 7. No submarine engines of war other than submarine vessels shall be installed in the waters of the Sea of Marmora.

The Turkish Government shall not install any permanent battery or torpedo tubes, capable of interfering with the passage of the Straits, in the coastal zone of the European shore of the Sea of Marmora or in the coastal zone on the Anatolian shore situated to the east of the demilitarized zone of the Bosphorus as far as Darije.

Article 8. At Constantinople, ... there may be maintained for the requirements of the capital, a garrison with maximum strength of 12,000 men....

Article 9. If, in case of war, Turkey, or Greece, in pursuance of their belligerent rights, should modify in any way the provisions of demilitarization prescribed above, they will be bound to re-establish as soon as peace is concluded the régime laid down in the present Convention.

Article 10. There shall be constituted at Constantinople an International Commission composed in accordance with Article 12 and called the 'Straits Commission'.

Article 11. The Commission will exercise its functions over the waters of the Straits.

Article 12. The Commission shall be composed of a representative of Turkey, who shall be President, and representatives of France, Great Britain, Italy, Japan, Bulgaria, Greece, Roumania, Russia, and the Serb-Croat-Slovene State, in so far as these Powers are signatories of the present Convention, each of these Powers being entitled to representation as from its ratification of the said Convention.

The United States of America, in the event of their acceding to the present Convention, will also be entitled to have one representative on the Commission.

Under the same conditions any independent littoral States of the Black Sea which are not mentioned in the first paragraph of the present Article will possess the same right.

[*Articles 14–16.* Duties of Commission to see provisions of treaties are observed.]

Article 17. The terms of the present Convention will not infringe the right of Turkey to move her fleet freely in Turkish waters.

Article 18. The High Contracting Parties, desiring to secure that the demilitariza-tion of the Straits and of the contiguous zones shall not constitute an unjustifiable danger to the military security of Turkey, and that no act of war should imperil the freedom of the Straits or the safety of the demilitarized zones, agree as follows:

Should the freedom of navigation of the Straits or the security of the demilitarized zones be imperilled by a violation of the provisions relating to freedom of passage, or by a surprise attack or some act of war or threat of war, the High Contracting Parties, and in any case France, Great Britain, Italy and Japan, acting in conjunction, will meet such violation, attack, or other act of war or threat of war, by all the means that the Council of the League of Nations may decide for this purpose.

So soon as the circumstance which may have necessitated the action provided for in the preceding paragraph shall have ended, the régime of the Straits as laid down by the terms of the present Convention shall again be strictly applied.

The present provision, which forms an integral part of those relating to the demilitarization and to the freedom of the Straits, does not prejudice the rights and obligations of the High Contracting Parties under the Covenant of the League of Nations.

Convention regarding the régime of the Straits (Montreux Convention), 20 July 1936

Article 1. The High Contracting Parties recognize and affirm the principle of freedom of transit and navigation by sea in the Straits.

The exercise of this freedom shall henceforth be regulated by the provisions of the present Convention.

SECTION I · MERCHANT VESSELS

Article 2. In time of peace, merchant vessels shall enjoy complete freedom of transit and navigation in the Straits, by day and by night, under any flag and with any kind of cargo, without any formalities, except as provided in Article 3 below. No taxes or charges other than those authorized by Annex I to the present Convention shall be levied by the Turkish authorities on these vessels when passing in transit without calling at a port in the Straits. . . .

[*Article 3.* Sanitary regulations.]

Article 4. In time of war, Turkey not being belligerent, merchant vessels, under any flag or with any kind of cargo, shall enjoy freedom of transit and navigation in the Straits subject to the provisions of Articles 2 and 3.

Pilotage and towage remain optional.

Article 5. In time of war, Turkey being belligerent, merchant vessels not belonging to a country at war with Turkey shall enjoy freedom of transit and navigation in the Straits on condition that they do not in any way assist the enemy.

Such vessels shall enter the Straits by day and their transit shall be effected by the route which shall in each case be indicated by the Turkish authorities.

Article 6. Should Turkey consider herself to be threatened with imminent danger of war, the provisions of Article 2 shall nevertheless continue to be applied except that vessels must enter the Straits by day and that their transit must be effected by the route which shall, in each case, be indicated by the Turkish authorities. . . .

SECTION II · VESSELS OF WAR

Article 11. Black Sea Powers may send through the Straits capital ships of a tonnage greater than that laid down in the first paragraph of Article 14, on condition that these vessels pass through the Straits singly, escorted by not more than two destroyers.

Article 12. Black Sea Powers shall have the right to send through the Straits, for the purpose of rejoining their base, submarines constructed or purchased outside the Black Sea, provided that adequate notice of the laying down or purchase of such submarines shall have been given to Turkey.

Submarines belonging to the said Powers shall also be entitled to pass through the Straits to be repaired in dockyards outside the Black Sea on condition that detailed information on the matter is given to Turkey.

In either case, the said submarines must travel by day and on the surface, and must pass through the Straits singly.

[*Article 13.* Details of notification to Turkish authorities of transit of warships.]

Article 14. The maximum aggregate tonnage of all foreign naval forces which may be in course of transit through the Straits shall not exceed 15,000 tons, except in the cases provided for in Article 11 . . .

The forces specified in the preceding paragraph shall not, however, comprise more than nine vessels.

Vessels, whether belonging to Black Sea or non-Black Sea Powers, paying visits to a port in the Straits, in accordance with the provisions of Article 17, shall not be included in this tonnage.

Neither shall vessels of war which have suffered damage during their passage through the Straits be included in this tonnage; such vessels, while undergoing repair, shall be subject to any special provisions relating to security laid down by Turkey.

[*Article 15.* Prohibition against use of aircraft by warships in transit.]

[*Article 16.* Except in case of damage, transit to be accomplished without delay.]

Article 17. Nothing in the provisions of the preceding Articles shall prevent a naval force of any tonnage or composition from paying a courtesy visit of limited duration to a port in the Straits, at the invitation of the Turkish Government. Any such force must leave the Straits by the same route as that by which it entered, unless it fulfils the conditions required for passage in transit through the Straits as laid down by Articles 10, 14 and 18.

Article 18. 1. The aggregate tonnage which non-Black Sea Powers may have in that sea in time of peace shall be limited as follows:

(a) Except as provided in paragraph (b) below, the aggregate tonnage of the said Powers shall not exceed 30,000 tons;

(b) If at any time the tonnage of the

strongest fleet in the Black Sea shall exceed by at least 10,000 tons the tonnage of the strongest fleet in that sea at the date of the signature of the present Convention, the aggregate tonnage of 30,000 tons mentioned in paragraph (a) shall be increased by the same amount, up to a maximum of 45,000 tons. For this purpose, each Black Sea Power shall, in conformity with Annex IV to the present Convention, inform the Turkish Government, on the 1st January and the 1st July of each year, of the total tonnage of its fleet in the Black Sea; and the Turkish Government shall transmit this information to the other High Contracting Parties and to the Secretary General of the League of Nations;

(c) The tonnage which any one non-Black Sea Power may have in the Black Sea shall be limited to two-thirds of the aggregate tonnage provided for in paragraphs (a) and (b) above;

(d) In the event, however, of one or more non-Black Sea Powers desiring to send naval forces into the Black Sea, for a humanitarian purpose, the said forces, which shall in no case exceed 8,000 tons altogether, shall be allowed to enter the Black Sea without having to give the notification provided for in Article 13 of the present Convention, provided an authorization is obtained from the Turkish Government . . .

2. Vessels of war belonging to non-Black Sea Powers shall not remain in the Black Sea more than twenty-one days, whatever be the object of their presence there.

Article 19. In time of war, Turkey not being belligerent, warships shall enjoy complete freedom of transit and navigation through the Straits under the same conditions as those laid down in Articles 10 to 18.

Vessels of war belonging to belligerent Powers shall not, however, pass through the Straits except in cases arising out of the application of Article 25 of the present Convention, and in cases of assistance rendered to a State victim of aggression in virtue of a treaty of mutual assistance binding Turkey, concluded within the framework of the Covenant of the League of Nations, and registered and published in accordance with the provisions of Article 18 of the Covenant.

In the exceptional cases provided for in the preceding paragraph, the limitations laid down in Articles 10 to 18 of the present Convention shall not be applicable.

Notwithstanding the prohibition of passage laid down in paragraph 2 above, vessels of war belonging to belligerent Powers, whether they are Black Sea Powers or not, which have become separated from their bases, may return thereto.

Vessels of war belonging to belligerent Powers shall not make any capture, exercise the right of visit and search, or carry out any hostile act in the Straits.

Article 20. In time of war, Turkey being belligerent, the provisions of Articles 10 to 18 shall not be applicable; the passage of warships shall be left entirely to the discretion of the Turkish Government.

Article 21. Should Turkey consider herself to be threatened with imminent danger of war she shall have the right to apply the provisions of Article 20 of the present Convention.

Vessels which have passed through the Straits before Turkey has made use of the powers conferred upon her by the preceding paragraph, and which thus find themselves separated from their bases, may return thereto. It is, however, understood that Turkey may deny this right to vessels of war belonging to the State whose attitude has given rise to the application of the present Article.

Should the Turkish Government make use of the powers conferred by the first paragraph of the present Article, a notification to that effect shall be addressed to the High Contracting Parties and to the Secretary-General of the League of Nations.

If the Council of the League of Nations decide by a majority of two-thirds that the measures thus taken by Turkey are not justified, and if such should also be the opinion of the majority of the High Contracting Parties signatories to the present Convention, the Turkish Government undertakes to discontinue the measures in question as also any measures which may have been taken under Article 6 of the present Convention.

Protocol

At the moment of signing the Convention bearing this day's date, the undersigned plenipotentiaries declare for their respective Governments that they accept the following provisions:

1. Turkey may immediately remilitarize the zone of the Straits as defined in the Preamble to the said Convention.

2. As from the 15th August, 1936, the Turkish Government shall provisionally apply the régime specified in the said Convention.

3. The present Protocol shall enter into force as from this day's date.

SECTION III · AIRCRAFT

[*Article 23*. Turkish Government to indicate routes for civil aircraft between Mediterranean and Black Sea.]

Article 24. The functions of the International Commission set up under the Convention relating to the régime of the Straits of the 24th July 1923, are hereby transferred to the Turkish Government.

The Turkish Government undertake to collect statistics and furnish information concerning the application of Articles 11, 12, 14 and 18 of the present Convention.

They will supervise the execution of all the provisions of the present Convention relating to the passage of vessels of war through the Straits.

As soon as they have been notified of the intended passage through the Straits of a foreign naval force the Turkish Government shall inform the representatives at Angora of the High Contracting Parties of the composition of that force, its tonnage, the date fixed for its

entry into the Straits, and, if necessary, the probable date of its return.

The Turkish Government shall address to the Secretary-General of the League of Nations and to the High Contracting Parties an annual report giving details regarding the movements of foreign vessels of war through the Straits and furnishing all information which may be of service to commerce and navigation, both by sea and by air, for which provision is made in the present Convention.

Article 25. Nothing in the present Convention shall prejudice the rights and obligations of Turkey, or of any of the other High Contracting Parties members of the League of Nations, arising out of the Covenant of the League of Nations.

SECTION V · FINAL PROVISIONS

Article 26. The present Convention shall be ratified as soon as possible. . . .

[*Article 27*. After entry into force, Convention open to accession by any signatory of Treaty of Lausanne, 1923.]

Article 28. The present Convention shall remain in force for twenty years from the date of its entry into force.

The principle of freedom of transit and navigation affirmed in Article 1 of the present Convention shall however continue without limit of time.

If, two years prior to the expiry of the said period of twenty years, no High Contracting Party shall have given notice of denunciation to the French Government the present Convention shall continue in force until two years after such notice shall have been given. Any such notice shall be communicated by the French Government to the High Contracting Parties.

In the event of the present Convention being denounced in accordance with the provisions of the present Article, the High Contracting Parties agree to be represented at a conference for the purpose of concluding a new Convention.

Article 29. At the expiry of each period of five years from the date of the entry into force of the present Convention each of the High Contracting Parties shall be entitled to initiate a proposal for amending one or more of the provisions of the present Convention. . . .

Should it be found impossible to reach an agreement on these proposals through the diplomatic channel, the High Contracting Parties agree to be represented at a conference to be summoned for this purpose.

Such a conference may only take decisions by a unanimous vote, except as regards cases of revision involving Articles 14 and 18, for which a majority of three-quarters of the High Contracting Parties shall be sufficient.

The said majority shall include three-quarters of the High Contracting Parties which are Black Sea Powers, including Turkey. . . .

Treaty between the United States, the British Empire, France, Italy and Japan limiting naval armament, 6 February 1922

The United States of America, the British Empire, France, Italy and Japan;

Desiring to contribute to the maintenance of the general peace, and to reduce the burdens of competition in armament . . .

Have agreed as follows:

Chapter I: General provisions relating to the limitation of naval armament

Article I. The Contracting Powers agree to limit their respective naval armament as provided in the present Treaty.

Article II. The Contracting Powers may retain respectively the capital ships which are specified in Chapter II, Part 1. On the coming into force of the present Treaty, but subject to the following provisions of this Article, all other capital ships, built or building, of the United States, the British Empire and Japan shall be disposed of as prescribed in Chapter II, Part 2.

In addition to the capital ships specified in Chapter II, Part 1, the United States may complete and retain two ships of the *West Virginia* class now under construction. On the completion of these two ships the *North Dakota* and *Delaware* shall be disposed of as prescribed in Chapter II, Part 2.

The British Empire may, in accordance with the replacement table in Chapter II, Part 3, construct two new capital ships not exceeding 35,000 tons (35,560 metric tons) standard displacement each. On the completion of the said two ships the *Thunderer, King George V, Ajax* and *Centurion* shall be disposed of as prescribed in Chapter II, Part 2.

Article III. Subject to the provisions of Article II, the Contracting Powers shall abandon their respective capital ship building programmes, and no new capital ships shall be constructed or acquired by any of the Contracting Powers except replacement tonnage which may be constructed or acquired as specified in Chapter II, Part 3.

Ships which are replaced in accordance with Chapter II, Part 3, shall be disposed of as described in Part 2 of that Chapter.

Article IV. The total capital ship replacement tonnage of each of the Contracting Powers shall not exceed in standard displacement, for the United States 525,000 tons (533,400 metric tons); for the British Empire 525,000 tons (533,400 metric tons); for France 175,000 tons (177,800 metric tons); for Italy 175,000 tons (177,800 metric tons); for Japan 315,000 tons (320,040 metric tons).

Article V. No capital ship exceeding 35,000 tons (35,560 metric tons) standard displacement shall be acquired by, or constructed by, for, or within the jurisdiction of, any of the Contracting Powers.

Article VI. No capital ship of any of the Contracting Powers shall carry a gun with a calibre in excess of 16 inches (406 millimetres).

Article VII. The total tonnage for aircraft carriers of each of the Contracting Powers shall not exceed in standard displacement, for the United States 135,000 tons (137,160 metric tons); for the British Empire 135,000 tons (137,160 metric tons); for France 60,000 tons (60,960 metric tons); for Italy 60,000 tons (60,960 metric tons); for Japan 81,000 tons (82,296 metric tons).

Article VIII. The replacement of aircraft carriers shall be effected only as prescribed in Chapter II, Part 3, provided, however, that all aircraft carrier tonnage in existence or building on November 12, 1921, shall be considered experimental, and may be replaced, within the total tonnage limit prescribed in Article VII, without regard to its age.

Article IX. No aircraft carrier exceeding 27,000 tons (27,432 metric tons) standard displacement shall be acquired by, or constructed by, for or within the jurisdiction of, any of the Contracting Powers.

However, any of the Contracting Powers may, provided that its total tonnage allowance of aircraft carriers is not thereby exceeded, build not more than two aircraft carriers, each of a tonnage of not more than 33,000 tons (33,528 metric tons) standard displacement, and in order to effect economy any of the Contracting Powers may use for this purpose any two of their ships, whether constructed or in course of construction, which would otherwise be scrapped under the provisions of Article II ... [limitation on armament].

[*Article X.* Armament limitation : calibre of guns.]

Article XI. No vessel of war exceeding 10,000 tons (10,160 metric tons) standard displacement, other than a capital ship or aircraft carrier shall be acquired by, or constructed by, for, or within the jurisdiction of, any of the Contracting Powers. Vessels not specifically built as fighting ships nor taken in time of peace under government control ... shall not be within the limitations of this Article.

...

Article XV. No vessel of war constructed within the jurisdiction of any of the Contracting Powers for a non-Contracting Power shall exceed the limitations as to displacement and armament prescribed by the present Treaty for vessels of a similar type which may be constructed by or for any of the Contracting Powers; provided, however, that the displacement for aircraft carriers constructed for a non-Contracting Power shall in no case exceed 27,000 tons (27,432 metric tons) standard displacement.

Article XIX. The United States, the British Empire and Japan agree that the *status quo* at the time of the signing of the present Treaty, with regard to fortifications and naval bases, shall be maintained in their respective territories and possessions specified hereunder :

(1) The insular possessions which the United States now holds or may hereafter acquire in the Pacific Ocean, except (a) those adjacent to the coast of the United States, Alaska and the Panama Canal Zone, not including the Aleutian Islands, and (b) the Hawaiian Islands;

(2) Hongkong and the insular possessions which the British Empire now holds or may hereafter acquire in the Pacific Ocean, east of the meridian 110° east longitude, except (a) those adjacent to the coast of Canada, (b) the Commonwealth of Australia and its Territories, and (c) New Zealand;

(3) The following insular territories and possessions of Japan in the Pacific Ocean, to wit: the Kurile Islands, the Bonin Islands, Amami-Oshima, the Loochoo Islands, Formosa and the Pescadores,

and any insular territories or possessions in the Pacific Ocean which Japan may hereafter acquire.

The maintenance of the *status quo* under the foregoing provisions implies that no new fortifications or naval bases shall be established in the territories and possessions specified, that no measures shall be taken to increase the existing naval facilities for the repair and maintenance of naval forces, and that no increase shall be made in the coast defences of the territories and possessions above specified. This restriction, however, does not preclude such repair and replacement of worn-out weapons and equipment as is customary in naval and military establishments in time of peace.

Article XX. The rules for determining tonnage displacement prescribed in Chapter II, Part 4, shall apply to the ships of each of the Contracting Powers.

Chapter III: Miscellaneous provisions

Article XXI. If during the term of the present Treaty the requirements of the national security of any Contracting Power in respect of naval defence are, in the opinion of that Power, materially affected by any change of circumstances, the Contracting Powers will, at the request of such Power, meet in conference with a view to the reconsideration of the provisions of the Treaty and its amendment by mutual agreement.

In view of possible technical and scientific developments, the United States, after consultation with the other Contracting Powers, shall arrange for a conference of all the Contracting Powers which shall convene as soon as possible after the expiration of eight years from the coming into force of the present Treaty to consider what changes, if any, in the Treaty may be necessary to meet such developments.

Article XXII. Whenever any Contracting Power shall become engaged in a war which in its opinion affects the naval defence of its national security, such Power may after notice to the other Contracting Powers suspend for the period of hostilities its obligations under the present Treaty other than those under Articles XIII and XVII, provided that such Power shall notify the other Contracting Powers that the emergency is of such a character as to require such suspension.

The remaining Contracting Powers shall in such case consult together with a view to agreement as to what temporary modifications if any should be made in the Treaty as between themselves. Should such consultation not produce agreement, duly made in accordance with the constitutional methods of the respective Powers, any one of said Contracting Powers may, by giving notice to the other Contracting Powers, suspend for the period of hostilities its obligations under the present Treaty, other than those under Articles XIII and XVII.

On the cessation of hostilities the Contracting Powers will meet in conference to consider what modifications, if any, should be made in the provisions of the present Treaty.

Article XXIII. The present Treaty shall remain in force until December 31, 1936, and in case none of the Contracting Powers shall have given notice two years before that date of its intention to terminate the Treaty, it shall continue in force until the expiration of two years from the date on which notice of termination shall be given by one of the Contracting Powers, whereupon the Treaty shall terminate as regards all the Contracting Powers. . . .

[*Article XXIV*. Ratification.]

Treaty between the United States, Belgium, the British Empire, China, France, Italy, Japan, the Netherlands and Portugal (Nine Power Treaty) concerning China, 6 February 1922

The United States of America, Belgium, the British Empire, China, France, Italy, Japan, the Netherlands and Portugal:

Desiring to adopt a policy designed to stabilize conditions in the Far East, to safeguard the rights and interests of China, and to promote intercourse between China and the other Powers upon the basis of equality of opportunity . . .

Have agreed as follows:

Article I. The Contracting Powers, other than China, agree:

1. To respect the sovereignty, the independence, and the territorial and administrative integrity of China;

2. To provide the fullest and most unembarrassed opportunity to China to develop and maintain for herself an effective and stable government;

3. To use their influence for the purpose of effectually establishing and maintaining the principle of equal opportunity for the commerce and industry of all nations throughout the territory of China;

4. To refrain from taking advantage of conditions in China in order to seek special rights or privileges which would abridge the rights of subjects or citizens of friendly States, and from countenancing action inimical to the security of such States.

Article II. The Contracting Powers agree not to enter into any treaty, agreement, arrangement, or understanding, either with one another, or individually or collectively, with any Power or Powers, which would infringe or impair the principles stated in Article I.

Article III. With a view to applying more effectually the principles of the Open Door or equality of opportunity in China for the trade and industry of all nations, the Contracting Powers, other than China, agree that they will not seek, nor support their respective nationals in seeking:

(a) Any arrangement which might purport to establish in favour of their interests any general superiority of rights with respect to commercial or economic development in any designated region of China;

(b) Any such monopoly or preference as would deprive the nationals of any other Power of the right of undertaking any legitimate trade or industry in China, or of participating with the Chinese Government, or with any local authority, in any category of public enterprise, or which by reason of its scope, duration or geographical extent is calculated to frustrate the practical application of the principle of equal opportunity.

It is understood that the foregoing stipulations of this Article are not to be so construed as to prohibit the acquisition of such properties or rights as may be necessary to the conduct of a particular commercial, industrial, or financial undertaking or to the encouragement of invention and research.

China undertakes to be guided by the principles stated in the foregoing stipulations of this Article in dealing with applications for economic rights and privileges from Governments and nationals of all foreign countries, whether parties to the present Treaty or not.

Article IV. The Contracting Powers agree not to support any agreements by their respective nationals with each other designed to create Spheres of Influence or to provide for the enjoyment of mutually exclusive opportunities in designated parts of Chinese territory.

Article V. China agrees that, throughout the whole of the railways in China, she will not exercise or permit unfair discrimination of any kind. . . .

Article VI. The Contracting Powers, other than China, agree fully to respect China's rights as a neutral in time of war to which China is not a party; and China declares that when she is a neutral she will observe the obligations of neutrality.

Article VII. The Contracting Powers agree that, whenever a situation arises which in the opinion of any one of them involves the application of the stipulations of the present Treaty, and renders desirable discussion of such application, there shall be full and frank communication between the Contracting Powers concerned.

Article VIII. Powers not signatory to the present Treaty, which have Governments recognized by the signatory Powers and which have treaty relations with China, shall be invited to adhere to the present Treaty. To this end the Government of the United States will make the necessary communications to non-signatory Powers and will inform the Contracting Powers of the replies received. Adherence by any Power shall become effective on receipt of notice thereof by the Government of the United States.

[*Article IX.* Ratification.]

Declaration by China

China, upon her part, is prepared to give an undertaking not to alienate or lease any portion of her territory or littoral to any Power.

Treaty between the United States, the British Empire, France and Japan (Four Power Treaty) relating to their insular possessions and insular dominions in the Pacific Ocean, 13 December 1921

The United States of America, the British Empire, France and Japan,

With a view to the preservation of the general peace and the maintenance of their rights in relation to their insular possessions and insular dominions in the region of the Pacific Ocean, have determined to conclude a Treaty to this effect and have agreed as follows:

Article I. The High Contracting Parties agree as between themselves to respect their rights in relation to their insular possessions and insular dominions in the region of the Pacific Ocean.

If there should develop between any of the High Contracting Parties a controversy arising out of any Pacific question and involving their said rights which is not satisfactorily settled by diplomacy and is likely to affect the harmonious accord now happily subsisting between them, they shall invite the other High Contracting Parties to a joint conference to which the whole subject will be referred for consideration and adjustment.

Article II. If the said rights are threatened by the aggressive action of any other Power, the High Contracting Parties shall communicate with one another fully and frankly in order to arrive at an understanding as to the most efficient measures to be taken, jointly or separately, to meet the exigencies of the particular situation.

Article III. This Treaty shall remain in force for ten years from the time it shall take effect, and after the expiration of said period it shall continue to be in force subject to the right of any of the High Contracting Parties to terminate it upon twelve months' notice.

Article IV. This Treaty shall be ratified as soon as possible in accordance with the constitutional methods of the High Contracting Parties . . .
[In ratifying this Treaty the United States resolved . . . 'The United States understands that under the statement in the preamble or under the terms of this Treaty there is no commitment to armed force, no alliance, no obligation to join in any defense.']

Declaration accompanying the Treaty

In signing the Treaty this day between the United States of America, the British Empire, France and Japan, it is declared to be the understanding and intent of the signatory Powers:
  1. That the Treaty shall apply to the mandated islands in the Pacific Ocean; provided, however, that the making of the Treaty shall not be deemed to be an assent on the part of the United States of America to the mandates and shall not preclude agreements between the United States of America and the Mandatory Powers respectively in relation to the mandated islands.
  2. That the controversies to which the second paragraph of Article I refers shall not be taken to embrace questions which according to principles of international law lie exclusively within the domestic jurisdiction of the respective Powers.

Supplementary Agreement

. . . The term 'insular possessions and insular dominions' used in the aforesaid Treaty shall, in its application to Japan, include only Karafuto (or the southern portion of the island of Sakhalin), Formosa and the Pescadores, and the islands under the mandate of Japan . . .

III · France, Britain, Italy and Germany, 1921–33

Within six years of the signature of the Treaty of Versailles the relationship of Germany and the victorious Western Powers who had dictated the peace terms to Germany had profoundly changed. The terms imposed on Germany were being significantly changed and softened. The question of reparations bedevilled Germany's relations with the West. The huge total sum demanded in 1921 was progressively abandoned during the decade of the 1920s. The treaties of Locarno of 1925 established a new relationship and signified the practical abandonment of the policy of imposing the terms of Versailles by military sanction. The Rhineland was evacuated completely five years ahead of time in June 1930 and effective means of supervising German armaments by Allied control were abandoned in 1927. The Pact of Paris in 1928 symbolized the idealistic and optimistic side of Great Power diplomacy in this era, but the reservations added to it indicate an underlying sense of realism. By the end of the decade and the beginning of the 1930s disarmament had become largely a question of which powers were to disarm and which to *rearm*. The 1930s became increasingly dominated by Hitler, but the abandonment of parts of the Versailles settlement had already occurred before he came to power.

The reparations question

German 'reparations' in theory were intended to make good the civilian damage caused by Germany in France, Belgium, Britain and elsewhere and were expected to burden the German people for more than half a century. In the event the burden lasted only a decade and brought no benefit to those who received these sums. No sensible settlement of post-war finance was politically possible in the early 1920s. The debt the Allies owed each other was huge, as

93

was the debt of some 11,000 million dollars the Allied nations owed the United States. To be in a position to pay their debts the Allies created 'credits' by imposing reparations plans on the defeated Germans; France and Britain had to collect reparations if the debts to the United States were to be paid. But the Allied nations were not allowing Germany such conditions of international trade as would have permitted the Germans to make sustained large payments from surpluses earned by exports. Largely private loans to German industry and the German Government totalling more than 5,000 million dollars provided a means to pay the reparations of almost 4,700 million dollars, and these payments enabled the Allies to service the debts to the United States. (Note: to convert the dollar amount to pounds sterling divide by five.) The Allies' other 'creditor' was Soviet Russia whose leaders were pressed at the Genoa Conference and elsewhere to honour the debts of the Tsarist Empire. In turn the Soviet leaders were promised, as part of a deal, a share in German reparations according to Article 116 of the Treaty of Versailles. In the event the threats and counterthreats to collect debts and enforce reparations payments brought the Germans and Russians together and they concluded the *Treaty of Rapallo* (p. 139).

The Treaty of Versailles had empowered the Reparations Commission to collect 5,000 million dollars before 1 May 1921 and then to announce the total amount Germany would have to meet. Disputes on this liability led to an Allied ultimatum in March 1921 and an extension of Allied occupation to Düsseldorf and two other German towns, and subsequently the declaration that Germany was in default. The Reparations Commission finally worked out the German bill at about 33,000 million dollars, a huge and unrealistic sum. More important were the details of the annual payment plan worked out at the *Second London Conference, 30 April–5 May 1921*, involving reparations at an annual rate of about 500 million dollars, and in addition an amount equivalent to 26 per cent of German exports. A little over a year later, on 31 August 1922, Germany's inability to pay was recognized by the Allies. The policy of meeting Allied claims, the declared intention of the German Foreign Minister, Walter Rathenau, proved impossible to realize as far as reparations were concerned.

Under the London payment plan of 1921 Germany had paid a total of about 3,000 million gold marks in gold and goods (the Germans claimed that they had paid all that was due) and then made no further payment. The response of France and Belgium was to occupy the Ruhr, the centre of German industry, in January 1923. Some financial order was restored in 1924 by the *Dawes Plan* (p. 100) which began with a loan and called for payments rising annually to 2,500 million Reichsmarks. In May and June 1930, just after the *Young Plan* (p. 101) came into force, the occupation of the last zone of the Rhineland was ended prematurely. The Young Plan scaled down Germany's repayments to 1,900 million Reichsmarks. Under the Young Plan the ultimate total payment would have worked out to about a third of the original total fixed in 1921. In 1931, a year of deepening economic depression, President Hoover proposed and gained acceptance of a one-year moratorium of all inter-Government debts including Germany's reparation payments. Finally at the *Lausanne Conference, June–July 1932*, German reparations were reduced to a nominal sum, more important psychologically than financially.

Of the total reparations fixed by the Reparations Commission in 1921 as 132,000 million gold marks (33,000 million dollars) the Germans had 'paid' a little more than a tenth (the precise figures remain in dispute), and during the same period had obtained foreign loans attracted by a high interest rate well in excess of the payments made in reparation; the loans had been subscribed by American and Allied investors; Hitler in 1934 repudiated them. The huge total sum arrived at in 1921 was intended more as a political gesture to appease public opinion than as the kind of reparations the experts had the slightest expectations of ever collecting. Reality brought the reparations chapter to a virtual close in 1932–3 amid worldwide depression. Hitler's version of the history of reparations served Nazi propaganda in the years that followed.

The treaties of Locarno, 16 October 1925

France had emerged a victorious ally in 1918, but physically Germany remained potentially the preponderant Power in Europe. At the peace conference the French had only been prevailed upon to abandon plans of detaching large parts of Germany by the promise of a guarantee of security and the alliance offered to France by the United States and Britain. This treaty never came into force for the Senate repudiated Wilson's policy of global involvement (p. 41). Then the League of Nations' security procedures were hedged by so many qualifications that the French never placed undue faith in them. When the clarification and stiffening of measures against aggression embodied in the *Geneva Protocol of 1924* (p. 56) was abandoned in 1925, the writing was on the wall. In a Great Power conflict the League was unlikely to prove effective. What France desired above all was a British alliance, but British support could only be secured conditionally. This the French had to accept as better than nothing. The attraction to France of a German proposal for a security pact to cover the Rhine area was that Britain promised to support such a settlement. On French insistence the scope of the treaties was enlarged to include some arrangements for Eastern Europe. The British Government favoured the treaties signed at Locarno as they appeared to solve a number of problems simultaneously:

France would be promised support only conditionally on following a defensive policy in Europe; the reduction of Franco-German tension would contribute to general pacification, yet British commitments would remain strictly limited whilst allowing her the diplomatic initiative. But the Dominions were not bound and the British Government signed on behalf of the United Kingdom alone, not for the British Empire. In Anglo-French relations the Locarno relationship remained important until the eve of the Second World War. The architects of the Locarno complex of treaties were Aristide Briand, Austen Chamberlain and Gustav Stresemann.

For the German Government of the Weimar Republic, Locarno represented the exchange of a German undertaking to accept the Versailles territorial settlement in the West for the concrete advantages that a growing sense of French security would lead to the recovery of German sovereignty, to the relaxation of Allied control over German armaments, and above all, to the early evacuation of all the parts of the Rhineland occupied by the Allies. But Germany was not reconciled to the 1922 frontier with Poland. An alignment with Soviet Russia had been established at *Rapallo* (p. 139) and was maintained after the signature of the Locarno treaties, with the *Treaty of Berlin* (p. 142). Germany made it clear that when it entered the League of Nations and took its permanent seat on the Council as promised at Locarno, and achieved in the autumn of 1926, Article 16 would not bind Germany to fight Soviet Russia or oblige the German Government to permit armed forces passing across German territory to aid the victim of aggression. Germany had no intention of protecting 'Versailles' Poland. Nor would Germany guarantee its own eastern frontiers with Poland and Czechoslovakia as being permanent; only an arbitration agreement between these States and Germany in case of dispute was concluded. Its enforcement was not guaranteed by Britain and Italy; there was no reference in their preamble to the Treaty of Mutual Guarantee.

There were altogether five *Locarno treaties concluded on 16 October 1925* (p. 101): the Treaty of Mutual Guarantee and four arbitration treaties between Germany, Poland, Czechoslovakia, Belgium and France. The *Treaty of Mutual Guarantee* (p. 102) was signed by Britain, France, Germany, Belgium and Italy. These Powers guaranteed the territorial *status quo* resulting from the frontiers between France and Germany and Germany and Belgium. They also guaranteed the demilitarization of the Rhine as provided in Articles 42 and 43 of the Treaty of Versailles. Germany, France and Belgium mutually undertook not to invade each other or to resort to force (Article 2). But this stipulation did not apply 'to a flagrant breach of Articles 42 or 43 of the said Treaty of Versailles, if such breach constitutes an unprovoked act of aggression and by reason of the assembly of armed forces in the demilitarized zone immediate action is necessary': in such a case France could resort to force. If France, Belgium or Germany claimed a violation of the treaty had been committed, or a breach of Articles 42 or 43 of the Treaty of Versailles had been or was being committed, the question was to be brought to the League of Nations; and if the League found a violation to have been committed, the Guaranteeing Powers (Britain and Italy) would each come to the assistance of the victim. But the Guaranteeing Powers would anticipate the League decision and come to the immediate assistance of the victim in a case of 'flagrant violation' of Article 2, or if Germany 'flagrantly' violated Articles 42 and 43 concerning the demilitarized Rhineland, and the Guaranteeing Powers (Britain and Italy) were satisfied 'that this violation constitutes an unprovoked act of aggression and that by reason either of the crossing of the frontier or of the outbreak of hostilities or of the assembly of the armed forces in the demilitarized zone immediate action is necessary' (Article 4). Articles 2 and 4 had been very carefully worded and were the subject of lengthy negotiation. The actual commitment of Britain and Italy remained imprecise and would depend on their own decision whether the treaty had merely been violated or 'flagrantly' violated. There was thus no automatic commitment to go to war. There was no doubt Britain would do so if Germany actually invaded or attacked France. For French security the demilitarized Rhineland was of capital importance. The Versailles treaty regarded *any* violation as an 'hostile act'. The new treaty only promised the help of Britain and Italy if their view of the violation was flagrant. The diplomatic discussions preceding the Locarno treaty indicated that Britain would not regard Germany taking some military defensive measures as a 'flagrant violation' though they clearly were a violation of Versailles. Britain's view appears to have been that only if a German military build-up in the Rhineland was clearly an offensive step leading to the invasion of France or Belgium would the case of 'flagrant violation' be made out. The result for France was therefore a weakening of the terms imposed on Germany at Versailles, but also a strengthening of security in that military help was promised by Britain in certain circumstances without having to await the doubtful processes of the League of Nations. This undertaking was the substitute for the failed *Treaty of Guarantee of 1919* (p. 71). The French still retained another guarantee – the Allies remained in occupation of the three Rhineland zones, and would evacuate only one zone, the Cologne zone, towards the end of the year 1926.

Besides the Treaty of Mutual Guarantee, Germany signed *Arbitration Treaties with France and Belgium* (p. 104). These in turn were guaranteed by the Treaty of Mutual Guarantee. Germany also signed an *Arbitration Treaty with Poland and with Czechoslovakia* (p. 107) virtually identical in wording with the

German–French and German–Belgian arbitration treaties, but vitally different in that these two treaties were not related to or covered by the Treaty of Mutual Guarantee. This meant not only that Britain and Italy would not guarantee to come to the aid of the victim by reason of a violation of the arbitration clauses, but it also meant that there was no undertaking by Germany to accept the frontiers as settled in 1922, so that any violation of that frontier would not automatically place Germany in the wrong. Further, although Germany undertook not to resort to force from the start but to accept arbitration, the Germans made it clear at the time that this did not mean that under certain conditions force would not be employed eventually. France had been unable to secure an extension of a guarantee of the *status quo* in the East. France signed new alliance treaties with Czechoslovakia and Poland on the same day as the Locarno treaties, but it was clear that these alliances did not fall within the multinational framework of the latter. The French ability to fulfil its commitments to Poland and Czechoslovakia had in fact been weakened (p. 113).

The Pact of Paris, 27 August 1928

A treaty attempting to 'outlaw' war was first drafted by France and the United States on the initiative of Briand. This draft, the *Briand–Kellogg Pact*, fifteen nations were invited to sign on *27 August 1928* under its official title of the *Pact of Paris* (p. 108). Other nations quickly adhered and by 1933 sixty-five Governments had pledged themselves to observe its provisions.

During the course of negotiations the French Government, generally followed by other States, made four reservations: (1) the treaty was not to be effective unless it secured universal adherence or until some special further agreement had been reached; (2) each country retained the right of legitimate defence; (3) if one country violated its pledge then the others would be automatically released from theirs; (4) the treaty was not to interfere with French treaty obligations under the League, Locarno or her neutrality treaties. Specifically, in respect to Article 1 Britain reserved her right to act in the Empire and would not allow interference in these regions of the world. The U.S. Foreign Relations Committee understood that by the treaty the right of self defence was not curtailed nor the right to maintain the Monroe Doctrine. The Soviet Union sent a long protest at its exclusion from the discussions, but together with the Baltic States signed a declaration adhering to the treaty. The reservations undermined the credibility of the Pact of Paris.

The treaty was a self-denying undertaking containing no sanctions against countries in breach of it. The aggressors of the 1930s, Japan, Italy, Germany and the Soviet Union, were not restrained by it though they were all signatories. The treaty was based on the hope that the forces of moral diplomacy and the weight of world public opinion were powerful influences restraining the use of force. The events of the next two decades falsified that hope.

The Four Power Pact, 7 June 1933

In a speech at Turin in October 1932, Mussolini proposed a Four Power Pact between the four great European Powers, Italy, France, Germany and Britain. Its main purpose was to be the consideration of the revision of the peace treaties in a way agreed to by the four Powers, who would then 'induce' other countries to 'adopt the same policy of peace'. Germany would have been the principal beneficiary. It was intended that the revision of the treaties, such as gradual rearmament, would be brought about through agreement and not unilaterally by Hitler's Germany. The Little Entente Powers had most to lose from any revision of the peace treaties and they objected violently. The Four Power Pact was only signed on 7 June 1933 after France had secured substantial amendment to the original draft. The pact was never ratified and in its emasculated form proved of little influence even in the immediate months after its signature.

Disarmament

As an essential part of the general post-war settlement the Allies and Associated Powers worked for a reduction of armaments and the diminution of armament rivalries on land and on the sea. In accordance with Articles 8 and 9 of the Covenant a Permanent Advisory Commission of the League was set up in May 1920. In the following year the *Naval Limitation Treaty* was negotiated at the *Washington Conference, 1921–2* (p. 54). Little other progress was made, but with the signature of the Locarno treaties the Council of the League took a fresh initiative in setting up a Preparatory Commission in December 1925, which it was intended should be followed by a Disarmament Conference. Progress was frustrated by national assessments of security needs. Eventually in 1930 *the London Naval Conference led to a Naval Treaty, 22 April 1930*, which extended to other than capital ships the provisions of the naval limitations of the Washington treaty of 1922. But only three groups of Powers ratified the treaty: Britain and the Dominions, Japan, and the United States. Italian claims for parity with France frustrated the intention of including these two European States. The general Disarmament Conference sponsored by the Council of the League did not meet until February 1932. The various phases of the conference revealed the growing international conflicts and produced only one tangible result, the banning of chemical and bacteriological warfare. In October 1933 Nazi Germany withdrew from the conference; thereafter it dragged on a few months longer to its inevitable practical failure and adjournment in May 1934.

Japan gave notice of termination of the Washington treaty of 6 February 1922, and this treaty as well as provisions in the Naval Treaty of 22 April 1930 concerning naval limitation expired on 31 December 1936. A Naval Conference as provided by the treaty of 1930 met in London in December 1935, but Japan withdrew. A *Naval Treaty was signed between the United States, France, Great Britain and the Dominions on 25 March 1936* which provided for little more than consultation. In December 1938, subject to certain provisions, Italy acceded, but with the outbreak of war in September 1939 the treaty was suspended. In practice the naval conference of 1936 marked the end of the search for disarmament which had been pursued during the inter-war years.

Agreement between the Reparations Commission and the German Government (*Dawes Plan*), 9 August 1924

The Contracting Parties

Being desirous of carrying into effect the plan for the discharge of reparation obligations and other pecuniary liabilities of Germany under the Treaty of Versailles proposed to the Reparation Commission on April 9, 1924, by the First Committee of Experts appointed by the Commission (which plan is referred to in this agreement as the Experts' [Dawes] Plan) and of facilitating the working of the Experts' Plan by putting into operation such additional arrangements as may hereafter be made between the German Government and the Allied Governments at the Conference now being held in London, in so far as the same may lie within the respective spheres of action of the Reparation Commission and the German Government;

And the Reparation Commission acting in virtue not only of the powers conferred upon it by the said treaty but also of the authority given to it by the Allied Governments represented at the said Conference in respect of all payments by Germany dealt with in the Experts' Plan but not comprised in Part VIII of the said treaty;

Hereby agree as follows:

1. The German Government undertakes to take all appropriate measures for carrying into effect the Experts' Plan and for ensuring its permanent operation....

Protocol concerning approval in principle of Report of Experts on Reparations (Young Plan), 31 August 1929

The representatives of Germany, Belgium, France, Great Britain, Italy and Japan, meeting at Geneva on the 16 September 1928, expressed their determination to make a complete and final settlement of the question of reparations and, with a view to attaining this object, provided for the constitution of a Committee of Financial Experts.

With this object the Experts met at Paris and their report was made on the 7 June 1929. Approval in principle was given to this report by The Hague Protocol of the 31 August 1929....

Article 1. The Experts' Plan of the 7 June 1929, together with this present Agreement and the Protocol of the 31 August 1929 (all of which are hereinafter described as the New Plan) is definitely accepted as a complete and final settlement, so far as Germany is concerned, of the financial questions resulting from the war. By their acceptance the signatory Powers undertake the obligations and acquire the rights resulting for them respectively from the New Plan.

The German Government gives the creditor Powers the solemn undertaking to pay the annuities for which the New Plan provides in accordance with the stipulations contained therein.

...

Article 8. With a view to facilitating the successful working of the New Plan the German Government declares spontaneously that it is firmly determined to make every possible effort to avoid a declaration of postponement and not to have recourse thereto until it has come to the conclusion in good faith that Germany's exchange and economic life may be seriously endangered by the transfer in part or in full of the postponable portion of the annuities. It remains understood that Germany alone has authority to decide whether occasion has arisen for declaring a postponement as provided by the New Plan.

[In Annex III, Germany undertook to make annual payments beginning in 1929 and ending in 1988; these varied each year but averaged about 1,700 million Reichsmarks.]

Pact of Locarno, 16 October 1925

Final Protocol of the Locarno Conference, 1925

The representatives of the German, Belgian, British, French, Italian, Polish, and Czechoslovak Governments, who have met at Locarno from the 5th to 16th October 1925, in order to seek by common agreement means for preserving their respective nations from the scourge of war and for providing for the peaceful settlement of disputes of every nature which might eventually arise between them,

Have given their approval to the draft treaties and conventions which respectively affect them and which, framed in the course of the present conference, are mutually interdependent:

Treaty between Germany, Belgium, France, Great Britain, and Italy (Annex A).

Arbitration Convention between Germany and Belgium (Annex B).

Arbitration Convention between Germany and France (Annex C).

Arbitration Treaty between Germany and Poland (Annex D).

Arbitration Treaty between Germany and Czechoslovakia (Annex E).

These instruments, hereby initialed *ne varietur*, will bear today's date, the representatives of the interested parties agreeing to meet in London on the 1st December next, to proceed during the course of a single meeting to the formality of the signature of the instruments which affect them.

The Minister for Foreign Affairs of France states that as a result of the draft arbitration treaties mentioned above, France, Poland, and Czechoslovakia have also concluded at Locarno draft agreements in order reciprocally to assure to themselves the benefit of the said treaties. These agreements will be duly deposited at the League of Nations, but M. Briand holds copies forthwith at the disposal of the Powers represented here.

The Secretary of State for Foreign Affairs of Great Britain proposes that, in reply to certain requests for explanations concerning Article 16 of the Covenant of the League of Nations presented by the Chancellor and the Minister for Foreign Affairs of Germany, a letter, of which the draft is similarly attached (Annex F) should be addressed to them at the same time as the formality of signature of the above-mentioned instruments takes place. This proposal is agreed to.

The representatives of the Governments represented here declare their firm conviction that the entry into force of these treaties and conventions will contribute greatly to bring about a moral relaxation of the tension between nations, that it will help powerfully towards the solution of many political or economic problems in accordance with the interests and sentiments of peoples, and that, in strengthening peace and security in Europe, it will hasten on effectively the disarmament provided for in Article 8 of the Covenant of the League of Nations.

They undertake to give their sincere cooperation to the work relating to disarmament already undertaken by the League of Nations and to seek the realization thereof in a general agreement.

[Signed] Luther, Stresemann, Vandervelde, Briand, Chamberlain, Mussolini, Skrzynski, Benes.

Treaty of Mutual Guarantee between the United Kingdom, Belgium, France, Germany and Italy, Locarno, 16 October 1925

The Heads of State of Germany, Belgium, France, Britain, and Italy . . .

Anxious to satisfy the desire for security and protection which animates the peoples upon whom fell the scourge of the war of 1914–18;

Taking note of the abrogation of the treaties for the neutralization of Belgium, and conscious of the necessity of ensuring peace in the area which has so frequently been the scene of European conflicts;

Animated also with the sincere desire of giving to all the signatory Powers concerned supplementary guarantees within the framework of the Covenant of the League of Nations and the treaties in force between them;

Have determined to conclude a Treaty

with these objects, and have . . . agreed as follows:

Article 1. The High Contracting Parties collectively and severally guarantee, in the manner provided in the following Articles, the maintenance of the territorial *status quo* resulting from the frontiers between Germany and Belgium and between Germany and France and the inviolability of the said frontiers as fixed by or in pursuance of the Treaty of Peace signed at Versailles on the 28th June 1919, and also the observance of the stipulations of Articles 42 and 43 of the said treaty concerning the demilitarized zone.

Article 2. Germany and Belgium, and also Germany and France, mutually undertake that they will in no case attack or invade each other or resort to war against each other.

This stipulation shall not, however, apply in the case of:

1. The exercise of the right of legitimate defence, that is to say, resistance to a violation of the undertaking contained in the previous paragraph or to a flagrant breach of Articles 42 or 43 of the said Treaty of Versailles, if such breach constitutes an unprovoked act of aggression and by reason of the assembly of armed forces in the demilitarized zone immediate action is necessary.

2. Action in pursuance of Article 16 of the Covenant of the League of Nations.

3. Action as the result of a decision taken by the Assembly or by the Council of the League of Nations or in pursuance of Article 15, paragraph 7, of the Covenant of the League of Nations, provided that in this last event the action is directed against a State which was the first to attack.

Article 3. In view of the undertakings entered into in Article 2 of the present Treaty, Germany and Belgium and Germany and France undertake to settle by peaceful means and in the manner laid down herein all questions of every kind

which may arise between them and which it may not be possible to settle by the normal methods of diplomacy:

Any question with regard to which the parties are in conflict as to their respective rights shall be submitted to judicial decision, and the parties undertake to comply with such decision.

All other questions shall be submitted to a Conciliation Commission. If the proposals of this commission are not accepted by the two parties, the question shall be brought before the Council of the League of Nations, which will deal with it in accordance with Article 15 of the Covenant of the League.

The detailed arrangements for effecting such peaceful settlement are the subject of special agreements signed this day.

Article 4. 1. If one of the High Contracting Parties alleges that a violation of Article 2 of the present Treaty or a breach of Articles 42 or 43 of the Treaty of Versailles has been or is being committed, it shall bring the question at once before the Council of the League of Nations.

2. As soon as the Council of the League of Nations is satisfied that such violation or breach has been committed, it will notify its findings without delay to the Powers signatory of the present Treaty, who severally agree that in such case they will each of them come immediately to the assistance of the Power against whom the act complained of is directed.

3. In case of a flagrant violation of Article 2 of the present Treaty or of a flagrant breach of Articles 42 or 43 of the Treaty of Versailles by one of the High Contracting Parties, each of the other Contracting Parties hereby undertakes immediately to come to the help of the party against whom such a violation or breach has been directed as soon as the said Power has been able to satisfy itself that this violation constitutes an unprovoked act of aggression and that by reason either of the crossing of the frontier or of the outbreak of hostilities or of the assembly of armed forces in the demilitarized zone immediate action is necessary.

Nevertheless, the Council of the League of Nations, which will be seized of the question in accordance with the first paragraph of this Article, will issue its findings, and the High Contracting Parties undertake to act in accordance with the recommendations of the Council provided that they are concurred in by all the members other than the representatives of the parties which have engaged in hostilities.

Article 5. The provisions of Article 3 of the present Treaty are placed under the guarantee of the High Contracting Parties as provided by the following stipulations:

If one of the Powers referred to in Article 3 refuses to submit a dispute to peaceful settlement or to comply with an arbitral or judicial decision and commits a violation of Article 2 of the present Treaty or a breach of Articles 42 or 43 of the Treaty of Versailles, the provisions of Article 4 shall apply.

Where one of the Powers referred to in Article 3 without committing a violation of Article 2 of the present Treaty or a breach of Articles 42 or 43 of the Treaty of Versailles, refuses to submit a dispute to peaceful settlement or to comply with an arbitral or judicial decision, the other party shall bring the matter before the Council of the League of Nations, and the Council shall propose what steps shall be taken; the High Contracting Parties shall comply with these proposals.

Article 6. The provisions of the present Treaty do not affect the rights and obligations of the High Contracting Parties under the Treaty of Versailles or under arrangements supplementary thereto, including the agreements signed in London on the 30th August 1924.

Article 7. The present Treaty, which is designed to ensure the maintenance of peace, and is in conformity with the Covenant of the League of Nations, shall not be interpreted as restricting the duty of the League to take whatever action may be deemed wise and effectual to safeguard the peace of the world.

Article 8. The present Treaty shall be registered at the League of Nations in accordance with the Covenant of the League. It shall remain in force until the Council, acting on a request of one or other of the High Contracting Parties notified to the other signatory Powers three months in advance, and voting at least by a two-thirds majority, decides that the League of Nations ensures sufficient protection to the High Contracting Parties; the Treaty shall cease to have effect on the expiration of a period of one year from such decision.

Article 9. The present Treaty shall impose no obligation upon any of the British Dominions, or upon India, unless the Government of such Dominion, or of India, signifies its acceptance thereof.

Article 10. The present Treaty shall be ratified as soon as possible.

It shall enter into force as soon as all the ratifications have been deposited and Germany has become a member of the League of Nations....

Arbitration Convention between Germany and France, 16 October 1925

[An identical Arbitration Convention was concluded between Germany and Belgium.]

The undersigned duly authorized,

Charged by their respective Governments to determine the methods by which, as provided in Article 3 of the Treaty concluded this day between Germany, Belgium, France, Great Britain, and Italy, a peaceful solution shall be attained of all questions which cannot be settled amicably between Germany and Belgium,

Have agreed as follows:

Part I

Article 1. All disputes of every kind between Germany and France with regard to which the parties are in conflict as to their respective rights, and which it may not be possible to settle amicably by the normal methods of diplomacy, shall be submitted for decision either to an arbitral tribunal or to the Permanent Court of International Justice, as laid down hereafter. It is agreed that the disputes referred to above include in particular those mentioned in Article 13 of the Covenant of the League of Nations.

This provision does not apply to disputes arising out of events prior to the present Convention and belonging to the past.

Disputes for the settlement of which a special procedure is laid down in other conventions in force between Germany and France shall be settled in conformity with the provisions of those conventions.

Article 2. Before any resort is made to arbitral procedure or to procedure before the Permanent Court of International Justice, the dispute may, by agreement between the parties, be submitted, with a view to amicable settlement, to a permanent international commission styled the Permanent Conciliation Commission, constituted in accordance with the present Convention.

Article 3. In the case of a dispute the occasion of which, according to the municipal law of one of the parties, falls within the competence of the national courts of such party, the matter in dispute shall not be submitted to the procedure laid down in the present Convention until a judgement with final effect has been pronounced, within a reasonable time, by the competent national judicial authority.

Article 4. The Permanent Conciliation Commission mentioned in Article 2 shall be composed of five members, who shall be appointed as follows, that is to say: the German Government and the French Government shall each nominate a commissioner chosen from among their respective nationals, and shall appoint, by common agreement, the three other commissioners from among the nationals of third Powers; these three commissioners must be of different nationalities, and the German and French Governments shall appoint the president of the Commission from among them.

The commissioners are appointed for three years, and their mandate is renewable. Their appointment shall continue until their replacement and, in any case, until the termination of the work in hand at the moment of the expiry of their mandate. . . .

Article 5. The Permanent Conciliation Commission shall be constituted within three months from the entry into force of the present Convention. . . .

Article 6. The Permanent Conciliation Commission shall be informed by means of a request addressed to the president by the two parties acting in agreement or, in the absence of such agreement, by one or other of the parties.

The request, after having given a summary account of the subject of the dispute, shall contain the invitation to the Commission to take all necessary measures with a view to arrive at an amicable settlement.

If the request emanates from only one of the parties, notification thereof shall be made without delay to the other party.

Article 7. Within fifteen days from the date when the German Government or the French Government shall have brought a dispute before the Permanent Conciliation Commission either party may, for the examination of the particular dispute, replace its commissioner by a person possessing special competence in the matter. . . .

Article 8. The task of the Permanent Conciliation Commission shall be to elucidate questions in dispute, to collect with that-object all necessary information by means of inquiry or otherwise, and to endeavour to bring the parties to an agreement. It may, after the case has been examined, inform the parties of the terms of settlement which seem suitable to it, and lay down a period within which they are to make their decision.

At the close of its labours the Commission shall draw up a report stating, as the case may be, either that the parties have come to an agreement and, if need arises, the terms of the agreement, or that it has been impossible to effect a settlement.

The labours of the Commission must, unless the parties otherwise agree, be terminated within six months from the day on which the Commission shall have been notified of the dispute.

[*Article 9.* Commission shall lay down its own procedure failing any provision to the contrary.]

[*Article 10.* President chooses meeting place in absence of agreement by parties to the contrary.]

[*Article 11.* Work of Permanent Conciliation Commission not public unless agreement by parties to the contrary.]

[*Article 12.* The parties shall be represented by agents before the Commission; agents may be assisted by experts; Commission may obtain oral evidence from agents, experts and with the consent of their Government from any person they regard as useful.]

Article 13. Unless otherwise provided in the present Convention, the decisions of the Permanent Conciliation Commission shall be taken by a majority.

Article 14. The German and French Governments undertake to facilitate the labours of the Permanent Conciliation Commission ... to allow it to proceed in their territory and in accordance with their law to the summoning and hearing of witnesses or experts, and to visit the localities in question.

[*Article 15.* Salary of Commissioners.]

Article 16. In the event of no amicable agreement being reached before the Permanent Conciliation Commission the dispute shall be submitted by means of a special agreement either to the Permanent Court of International Justice under the conditions and according to the procedure laid down by its statute or to an arbitral tribunal under the conditions and according to the procedure laid down by the Hague Convention of the 18th October 1907, for the Pacific Settlement of International Disputes.

If the parties cannot agree on the terms of the special arrangement after a month's notice one or other of them may bring the dispute before the Permanent Court of International Justice by means of an application.

Part II

Article 17. All questions on which the German and French Governments shall differ without being able to reach an amicable solution by means of the normal methods of diplomacy the settlement of which cannot be attained by means of a judicial decision as provided in Article 1 of the present Convention, and for the settlement of which no procedure has been laid down by other conventions in force between the parties, shall be submitted to the Permanent Conciliation Commission, whose duty it shall be to propose to the parties an acceptable solution and in any case to present a report.

The procedure laid down in Articles 6–15 of the present Convention shall be applicable.

Article 18. If the two parties have not reached an agreement within a month from the termination of the labours of the Permanent Conciliation Commission the question shall, at the request of either party, be brought before the Council of the League of Nations, which shall deal with it in accordance with Article 15 of the Covenant of the League.

GENERAL PROVISION

Article 19. In any case, and particularly if the question on which the parties differ arises out of acts already committed or on the point of commission, the Conciliation Commission or, if the latter has not been notified thereof, the arbitral tribunal or the Permanent Court of International Justice, acting in accordance with Article 41 of its statute, shall lay down within the shortest possible time the provisional measures to be adopted. It shall similarly be the duty of the Council of the League of Nations, if the question is brought before it, to ensure that suitable provisional measures are taken. The German and French Governments undertake respectively to accept such measures, to abstain from all measures likely to have a reper-

cussion prejudicial to the execution of the decision or to the arrangements proposed by the Conciliation Commission or by the Council of the League of Nations, and in general to abstain from any sort of action whatsoever which may aggravate or extend the dispute.

Article 20. The present Convention continues applicable as between Germany and France even when other Powers are also interested in the dispute.

Article 21. The present Convention shall be ratified. Ratifications shall be deposited at Geneva with the League of Nations at the same time as the ratifications of the treaty concluded this day between Germany, Belgium, France, Great Britain, and Italy.

It shall enter into and remain in force under the same conditions as the said treaty. . . .

Arbitration Treaty between Germany and Poland, 16 October 1925

[An identical treaty was concluded between Germany and Czechoslovakia.

The terms of this treaty are the same as the Arbitration Convention with two exceptions. Article 22 states that the treaty is in conformity with the Covenant and does not affect the rights of members of the League. But the crucial difference lies in the preamble which does not refer to the Treaty of Mutual Guarantee. This link with the four Guaranteeing Powers is absent; compare with the preamble of the German–French Arbitration Convention.]

Preamble

The President of the German Empire and the President of the Polish Republic;

Equally resolved to maintain peace between Germany and Poland by assuring the peaceful settlement of differences

which might arise between the two countries;

Declaring that respect for the rights established by treaty or resulting from the law of nations is obligatory for international tribunals;

Agreeing to recognize that the rights of a State cannot be modified save with its consent;

And considering that sincere observance of the methods of peaceful settlement of international disputes permits of resolving, without recourse to force, questions which may become the cause of division between States;

Have decided to embody in a treaty their common intentions in this respect, and have named as their plenipotentiaries the following . . .

Who, having exchanged their full powers, found in due and good form, are agreed upon the following Articles . . .

Collective Note to Germany regarding Article 16 of the Covenant of the League of Nations

The German delegation has requested certain explanations in regard to Article 16 of the Covenant of the League of Nations.

We are not in a position to speak in the name of the League, but in view of the discussions which have already taken place in the Assembly and in the commissions of the League of Nations, and after the explanations which have been exchanged between ourselves, we do not hesitate to inform you of the interpretation which, in so far as we are concerned, we place upon Article 16.

In accordance with that interpretation the obligations resulting from the said Article on the Members of the League must be understood to mean that each State Member of the League is bound to cooperate loyally and effectively in support of the Covenant and in resistance to any act of aggression to an extent which is compatible with its military situation and takes its geographical position into account.

Pact of Paris (Briand–Kellogg Pact), 27 August 1928

[The Heads of State of the United States, Belgium, Czechoslovakia, Britain, Germany, Italy, Japan and Poland. . . .]

Deeply sensible of their solemn duty to promote the welfare of mankind; persuaded that the time has come when a frank renunciation of war as an instrument of national policy should be made, to the end that the peaceful and friendly relations now existing between their peoples may be perpetuated;

Convinced that all changes in their relations with one another should be sought only by pacific means and be the result of a peaceful and orderly process, and that any signatory Power which shall hereafter seek to promote its national interests by resort to war should be denied the benefits furnished by this Treaty;

Hopeful that, encouraged by their example, all the other nations of the world will join in this humane endeavour and, by adhering to the present Treaty as soon as it comes into force, bring their peoples within the scope of its beneficent provisions, thus uniting the civilized nations of the world in a common renunciation of war as an instrument of their national policy;

Have decided to conclude a treaty, . . . and . . . have agreed upon the following Articles:

Article I. The High Contracting Parties solemnly declare, in the names of their respective peoples, that they condemn recourse to war for the solution of international controversies and renounce it as an instrument of national policy in their relations with one another.

Article II. The High Contracting Parties agree that the settlement or solution of all disputes or conflicts, of whatever nature or of whatever origin they may be, which may arise among them, shall never be sought except by pacific means.

[*Article III.* Ratification] . . .

This Treaty shall, when it has come into effect as prescribed in the preceding paragraph, remain open as long as may be necessary for adherence by all the other Powers of the world. . . .

Protocol concluded between the Soviet Union, Estonia, Latvia, Poland and Rumania on 9 February 1929, giving effect to the treaty renouncing war

The Government of the Estonian Republic, the President of the Latvian Republic, the President of the Polish Republic, His Majesty the King of Rumania and the Central Executive Committee of U.S.S.R.; animated by the desire to contribute to the maintenance of the existing peace between their countries and for the purpose of putting into force without delay, between the peoples of those countries, the Treaty for the Renunciation of War as an Instrument of National Policy, signed at Paris on August 27, 1928; have decided to achieve this purpose by means of the present Protocol and have ... agreed as follows:

Article I. The Treaty for the Renunciation of War as an Instrument of National Policy, signed at Paris on August 27, 1928, a copy of which is attached to the present Protocol as an integral part of this instrument, shall come into force between the Contracting Parties after the ratification of the said Treaty of Paris of 1928 by the competent legislative bodies of the respective Contracting Parties.

Article II. The entry into force, in virtue of the present Protocol of the Treaty of Paris of 1928 in the reciprocal relations between the parties to the present Protocol shall be valid independently of the entry into force of the Treaty of Paris of 1928 as provided in Article III of the last-named Treaty.

Article III. The present Protocol shall be ratified by the competent legislative bodies of the Contracting Parties, in conformity with the requirements of their respective constitutions ...

Treaty between Britain and Dominions, France, Italy, Japan and the United States for the limitation and reduction of naval armament, London, 22 April 1930

...

Desiring to prevent the dangers and reduce the burdens inherent in competitive armaments, and

Desiring to carry forward the work begun by the Washington Naval Conference and to facilitate the progressive realization of general limitation and reduction of armaments,

Have resolved to conclude a Treaty for the limitation and reduction of naval armament, and have accordingly appointed as their plenipotentiaries ...

Part I

Article 1. The High Contracting Parties agree not to exercise their rights to lay down the keels of capital ship replacement tonnage during the years 1931–1936 inclusive as provided in Chapter II, Part 3, of the Treaty for the Limitation of Naval Armament signed between them at Washington on the 6th February 1922, and referred to in the present Treaty as the Washington Treaty.

This provision is without prejudice to the disposition relating to the replacement of ships accidentally lost or destroyed contained in Chapter II, Part 3, Section I, paragraph (c) of the said Treaty.

France and Italy may, however, build the replacement tonnage which they were entitled to lay down in 1927 and

1929 in accordance with the provisions of the said Treaty.

Article 2. 1. The United States, the United Kingdom of Great Britain and Northern Ireland and Japan shall dispose of the following capital ships as provided in this Article. . . .

[U.S. – 3, U.K. – 5, and Japan – 1 named ship.]

2. Subject to any disposal of capital ships which might be necessitated, in accordance with the Washington Treaty, by the building by France or Italy of the replacement tonnage referred to in Article 1 of the present Treaty, all existing capital ships mentioned in Chapter II, Part 3, Section II of the Washington Treaty and not designated above to be disposed of may be retained during the term of the present Treaty.

[*Articles 3 and 4.* Definition of aircraft carrier; no aircraft carrier to be constructed of less than 10,000 tons.]

[*Article 5.* Restriction on armament of aircraft carriers.]

[*Article 7.* Limitation on submarine construction.]

...

Part III

The President of the United States of America, His Majesty the King of Great Britain, Ireland and the British Dominions beyond the Seas, Emperor of India, and His Majesty the Emperor of Japan, have agreed as between themselves to the provisions of this Part III:

Article 14. The naval combatant vessels of the United States, the British Commonwealth of Nations and Japan, other than capital ships, aircraft carriers and all vessels exempt from limitation under Article 8, shall be limited during the term of the present Treaty as provided in this Part III, and, in the case of special vessels, as provided in Article 12.

Article 15. For the purpose of this Part III the definition of the cruiser and destroyer categories shall be as follows. . . .

Article 16. 1. The completed tonnage in the cruiser, destroyer and submarine categories which is not to be exceeded on the 31st December 1936, is given in the following table. . . .

2. Vessels which cause the total tonnage in any category to exceed the figures given . . . [*Cruisers:* U.S. tonnage, 323,500 tons; British Commonwealth, 339,000 tons; Japan, 208,850 tons. *Destroyers:* U.S. tonnage, 150,000 tons; British Commonwealth, 150,000 tons; Japan, 105,500 tons. *Submarines:* U.S. tonnage, 52,700 tons; British Commonwealth, 52,700 tons; Japan, 52,700 tons] shall be disposed of gradually during the period ending on the 31st December 1936.

3. The maximum number of cruisers of sub-category (a) shall be as follows: for the United States, 18; for the British Commonwealth of Nations, 15; for Japan, 12. . . .

Article 21. If, during the term of the present Treaty, the requirements of the national security of any High Contracting Party in respect of vessels of war limited by Part III of the present Treaty are in the opinion of that Party materially affected by new construction of any Power other than those who have joined in Part III of this Treaty, that High Contracting Party will notify the other Parties to Part III as to the increase required to be made in its tonnages within one or more of the categories of such vessels of war, . . . and shall be entitled to make such increase. Thereupon the other Parties to Part III of this Treaty shall be entitled to make a proportionate increase in the category or categories specified . . .

Part IV

[Accepted rules of international law.]

[*Article 23.* Treaty shall remain in force until 31 December 1936. New Conference to meet in 1935.]

Four Power Pact between Italy, Britain, France and Germany, Rome, 7 June 1933

[This was not ratified and did not enter into force.]

...

Article 1. The High Contracting Parties will consult together as regards all questions which appertain to them. They undertake to make every effort to pursue, within the framework of the League of Nations, a policy of effective cooperation between all Powers with a view to the maintenance of peace.

Article 2. In respect of the Covenant of the League of Nations, and particularly Articles 10, 16 and 19, the High Contracting Parties decide to examine between themselves and without prejudice to decisions which can only be taken by the regular organs of the League of Nations, all proposals relating to methods and procedure calculated to give due effect to these Articles.

Article 3. The High Contracting Parties undertake to make every effort to ensure the success of the Disarmament Conference and, should questions which particularly concern them remain in suspense on the conclusion of that Conference, they reserve the right to re-examine these questions between themselves in pursuance of the present Agreement with a view to ensuring their solution through the appropriate channels.

Article 4. The High Contracting Parties affirm their desire to consult together as regards all economic questions which have a common interest for Europe and particularly for its economic restoration, with a view to seeking a settlement within the framework of the League of Nations. . . .

[*Article 5.* Agreement concluded for ten years.]

[*Article 6.* Ratification.]

IV · France and her Eastern Allies, 1921–39

Even at the time of victory in January 1919, when the French Premier Georges Clemenceau became host to the peace conference and Paris was the centre of world diplomacy, the French never lost sight of the fact that France was in a position of fundamental weakness in post-war Europe. With more than 4 million dead and maimed and a huge debt of 34,000 million gold francs, as well as the physical destruction of much of northern France, French statesmen did not face the future with much confidence. The recovery of a Germany that contained 20 million more Germans than Frenchmen as well as the capacity of the industrial Ruhr basin could once more place France internationally on the defensive, contemplating the possibility of a third German invasion. French foreign policy was thus designed to fulfil two complementary objectives: to find a way of permanently reducing Germany's future power and to retain and gain new allies to ensure a preponderance of strength over a revived Germany. The League of Nations was the third prop, but successive French Governments were loath to place much reliance on it.

The search for firm alliances in the West, that is with Britain and the United States, proved elusive during the years 1919–24; only in the Locarno peace framework could France in 1925 secure British promises of help (p. 95). In the East the position had totally changed with Imperial Russia's defeat and the Bolshevik Revolution. At the end of the war the Czechs were in a good position to occupy and claim all the lands which were to become the Republic of Czechoslovakia.

French alliances with Czechoslovakia and Poland, 1921–5

The Czechs looked to the French as their allies. The position of the Polish frontiers, on the other hand, remained unsettled in the east and the west; what is more, the Poles were in bitter dispute over the Teschen territory with the Czechs. For the French there appeared to be the alternative policy of making a revived Russia France's major ally. As long as the Civil War continued in Russia and the overthrow of the Bolshevik Russian forces remained a possibility, France would not back Poland's policy of annexing more Russian territory as this would have earned France the enmity of the White Russians. And so Poland owed its national survival in the war with Bolshevik Russia (1920-1) to its own strength rather than to French help.

With the *Treaty of Riga, 18 March 1921* (p. 137) which settled the Russian-Polish frontier, and with the consolidation of Soviet power, the French reviewed their Eastern policy during the winter of 1920-1. The French Government now in 1921 concluded that a strong Poland linked in military alliance with France would prove a barrier to Bolshevik Russia and the best check on Germany. The alternative of attempting to gain the alliance of Soviet Russia was not adopted in the 1920s. Franco-Polish cooperation was seen by France as making an essential contribution to post-war European stability. *On 19 February 1921 Poland and France signed an Alliance Treaty, and on 21 February a secret Military Convention* (p. 116). These two agreements were coupled with a secret Polish-French economic agreement, not finally concluded until 6 February 1922, which provided that in return for a French loan of 400 million francs Poland would purchase all its war materials in France. The commercial agreements also gave France preferential treatment in bilateral trade, especially in the Polish oil industry.

At the time of concluding the alliance there remained widespread French misgivings on the extensive commitments assumed. By limiting the *casus foederis* to unprovoked aggression the French hoped to guard against an 'adventurous' Polish policy at the expense of Russia. The military commitment was nevertheless far reaching.

The Czechs felt themselves more secure than the Poles. When the *Franco-Czechoslovak Alliance was signed on 25 January 1924* (p. 117) it was the Czechs not the French who refused an additional secret military convention. The Czech Government wished to retain freedom of action and to follow an independent foreign policy in the Danubian regions. The Franco-Czech alliance was thus much more imprecise and flexible than the Franco-Polish treaties, and Franco-Czech military consultation and cooperation was provided for only by a secret exchange of letters and not by treaty.

Revised alliance treaties with Poland and Czechoslovakia were signed by France on 16 October 1925, at the time of the conclusion of the *Locarno Treaties* (p. 119). To reconcile French obligations under the Locarno treaties with commitments to Poland and Czechoslovakia, France's Eastern allies, was difficult even though the new alliance treaties did not supersede the old. France could no longer act in defence of Poland by invading Germany from the west. Poland and Czechoslovakia would first have to turn to the League of Nations. In practice France was tying its hands to the views taken by Britain and Italy, the Locarno guarantors of the Franco-German frontier. In practice too, Poland and Czechoslovakia followed, perhaps realistically, independent foreign policies and did not rely for sole support on the French alliance. In 1925, with the signature of the Locarno treaties, the French alliances and the Balkan alignments the European diplomatic pattern of the inter-war years was emerging from the uncertainties of the years immediately following Germany's collapse in 1918.

The Little Entente States and the Polish–Rumanian Alliance, 1920–39

The peace settlements did not mark an end to the frontier problems of the States of the Danube region. The diplomatic relations of the nations were largely influenced by three sometimes contradictory considerations.

1. The 'Successor States' carved out of the Austro-Hungarian Monarchy, namely Czechoslovakia and Yugoslavia together with Rumania, which had acquired much former Hungarian territory as well as Bulgarian territory, stood for the maintenance of the peace treaties, and tended to combine against Germany, Hungary, Austria and Bulgaria, countries that might desire to 'revise' these settlements. 2. Soviet Russia was not only feared by Rumania, which had received formerly Russian Bessarabia; for ideological reasons the spread of revolution was feared by all the States on its borders, and they tended to combine against the Bolsheviks. The Czechs were the most friendly to Soviet Russia. 3. Finally, just as before 1914 the smaller States of the Balkans were bound to react to the ambitions of those Great Powers who pursued an active Balkan policy during the inter-war period, especially France, Italy, and in the 1930s, Germany.

It was the uncertainty of French policy in the Balkans and French advances to Hungary in 1920 which first led some of the Balkan States to band together in a joint defence of their interests. Yugoslavia, Czechoslovakia and Rumania began in the summer of 1920 to negotiate the series of treaties which formed the *Little Entente: a defensive alliance between Czechoslovakia and Yugoslavia, 14 August 1920*, directed against Hungarian revisionist plans; a *treaty between Czechoslovakia and Rumania, 5 June 1921*, aimed at preventing Hungarian and Bulgarian revisionism, based on a *convention* directed only against Hungary of *23 April 1921*; finally a *treaty between Yugoslavia and Rumania, 7 June 1921*, directed against both Bulgaria and Hungary (pp. 121–2). Thus the basis of the

Little Entente was the determination to maintain the Treaty of Neuilly (p. 47) and the Treaty of Trianon (p. 46).

The Polish Government was not well disposed to the Little Entente, which tended to give diplomatic leadership to the Czechs. No lasting friendship and cooperation could be established between the Czechs and Poles during the inter-war years. The Rumanians, however, were not only afraid of Hungarian and Bulgarian irredentism (hence their partnership in the *Little Entente*) but also of Russian hostility over the loss of Bessarabia. As the Little Entente was not directed against Russia, *the Poles and Rumanians signed a separate Alliance Treaty, 3 March 1921* (p. 122), providing for help if either State was attacked by Russia. This treaty was renewed and extended by the *Treaty of Guarantee, 26 March 1926*, which stipulated immediate help to the ally in the event of unprovoked attack contrary to Articles 12, 13 and 15 of the Covenant of the League of Nations (p. 122).

The Little Entente States and Rumania and Poland wished by their alignments to create a stable and strong Central and Danubian Europe. They were prepared to make agreements with Great Power neighbours France, Italy, Germany and even the Soviet Union, in order to strengthen their security and independence. Thus the inter-war period saw the conclusion not only of treaties with France but also between *Italy and Yugoslavia* (January 1924), *Czechoslovakia and Italy* (July 1924), *France and Rumania* (January 1926), *Italy and Rumania* (September 1926) and *France and Yugoslavia* (November 1927).

These agreements had their effects on the relations of the Danubian States and Poland in the inter-war period, but from the moment of crisis in the autumn of 1938 onwards they counted for very little. Czechoslovakia was not preserved by the Little Entente in 1938-9, nor did Poland receive aid from Rumania in September 1939 when invaded by Germany and Russia. Yugoslavia was invaded by Germany in April 1941 and was left to fend for itself; Rumania, with Greece the recipient of a unilateral *Anglo-French Guarantee of March 1939* (p. 189), joined the Germans in their war against the Soviet Union in 1941. Though France had been the principal Great Power seeking allies in Eastern and Central Europe in the 1920s, the majority of French leaders came to look upon the Eastern connections in the 1930s as more of a liability and obstacle to effective 'appeasement' than a source of strength.

Political Agreement between France and Poland, 19 February 1921

The Polish Government and the French Government, both desirous of safeguarding, by the maintenance of the Treaties which both have signed or which may in future be recognized by both Parties, the peace of Europe, the security of their territories and their common political and economic interests, have agreed as follows:

1. In order to coordinate their endeavours towards peace, the two Governments undertake to consult each other on all questions of foreign policy which concern both States, so far as those questions affect the settlement of international relations in the spirit of the Treaties and in accordance with the Covenant of the League of Nations.

2. In view of the fact that economic restoration is the essential preliminary condition of the re-establishment of international order and peace in Europe, the two Governments shall come to an understanding in this regard, with a view to concerted action and mutual support.

They will endeavour to develop their economic relations, and for this purpose will conclude special agreements and a Commercial Treaty.

3. If, notwithstanding the sincerely peaceful views and intentions of the two Contracting States, either or both of them should be attacked without giving provocation, the two Governments shall take concerted measures for the defence of their territory and the protection of their legitimate interests, within the limits specified in the preamble.

4. The two Governments undertake to consult each other before concluding new agreements which will affect their policy in Central and Eastern Europe.

5. The present Agreement shall not come into force until the commercial agreements now in course of negotiation have been signed.

Secret Military Convention between France and Poland, 21 February 1921

[This summary is based on the reconstruction of this military treaty from manuscript sources by Piotr S. Wandycz, *France and her Eastern Allies 1919–1925*, Minneapolis, University of Minnesota Press, 1962, pp. 394–5.]

[*Article 1*. If the situation of Germany should become menacing to the extent that there is a threat of war against one of the two signatories, and especially if Germany mobilizes or if the maintenance of the Treaty of Versailles necessitates joint action by the signatories, then the two signatories undertake to strengthen their military preparations in such a way as to be in a position to provide effective and speedy assistance to each other and to act in common. If Germany attacks one of the two countries they are bound to afford assistance to each other following an agreement between them.

Article 2. If Poland is threatened or attacked by Soviet Russia, France undertakes to hold Germany in check by action as necessary on land and sea and to aid Poland in defence against the Soviet army as detailed below.

Article 3. If the eventualities foreseen in Articles 1 and 2 arise, direct French help to Poland will consist of sending to Poland war equipment and a technical mission, but not French troops, and securing the lines of sea communication between France and Poland.

...

Article 5. Poland undertakes with French help to develop its war indemnity according to a particular plan so as to be able to equip the Polish army as necessary.

Article 6. Provision for continuous consultations between the general staffs of the two countries to fulfil the provisions of this treaty.

Article 7. Measures to be taken to ensure the effectiveness of the French military mission in Poland.

Article 8. This Agreement will only come into force when the commercial agreement is concluded.]

Treaty of Alliance between France and Czechoslovakia, 25 January 1924

The President of the French Republic and the President of Czechoslovak Republic,

Being earnestly desirous of upholding the principle of international agreements which was solemnly confirmed by the Covenant of the League of Nations,

Being further desirous of guarding against any infraction of the peace, the maintenance of which is necessary for the political stability and economic restoration of Europe,

Being resolved for this purpose to ensure respect for the international juridical and political situation created by the Treaties of which they were both signatories,

And having regard to the fact that, in order to attain this object, certain mutual guarantees are indispensable for security against possible aggression and for the protection of their common interests,

Have appointed as their plenipotentiaries:

For the President of the French Republic:
  M. Raymond Poincaré, *President of the Council, Minister for Foreign Affairs*;

For the President of the Czechoslovak Republic:
  M. Edvard Benes, *Minister for Foreign Affairs,*

Who, after examining their full powers, which were found in good and due form, have agreed to the following provisions:

Article 1. The Governments of the French Republic and of the Czechoslovak Republic undertake to concert their action in all matters of foreign policy which may threaten their security or which may tend to subvert the situation created by the Treaties of Peace of which both parties are signatories.

Article 2. The High Contracting Parties shall agree together as to the measures to be adopted to safeguard their common interests in case the latter are threatened.

Article 3. The High Contracting Parties, being fully in agreement as to the importance, for the maintenance of the world's peace, of the political principles laid down in Article 88 of the Treaty of Peace of St Germain-en-Laye of September 10, 1919, and in the Protocols of Geneva dated October 4, 1922, of which instruments they both are signatories, undertake to consult each other as to the measures to be taken in case there should be any danger of an infraction of these principles.

Article 4. The High Contracting Parties, having special regard to the declarations made by the Conference of Ambassadors on February 3, 1920, and April 1, 1921, on which their policy will continue to be based, and to the declaration made on November 10, 1921, by the Hungarian Government to the Allied diplomatic representatives, undertake to consult each other in case their interests are threatened by a failure to observe the principles laid down in the aforesaid declarations.

Article 5. The High Contracting Parties solemnly declare that they are in complete agreement as to the necessity, for the maintenance of peace, of taking common action in the event of any attempt to restore the Hohenzollern dynasty in Germany, and they undertake to consult each other in such a contingency.

Article 6. In conformity with the principles laid down in the Covenant of the League of Nations, the High Contracting Parties agree that if in future any dispute should arise between them which cannot be settled by friendly agreement and through diplomatic channels, they will submit such dispute either to the Permanent Court of International Justice or to such other arbitrator or arbitrators as they may select.

Article 7. The High Contracting Parties undertake to communicate to each other all agreements affecting their policy in Central Europe which they may have previously concluded, and to consult one another before concluding any further agreements. They declare that, in this matter, nothing in the present Treaty is contrary to the above agreements, and in particular to the Treaty of Alliance between France and Poland, or to the Conventions and Agreements concluded by Czechoslovakia with the Federal Republic of Austria, Roumania, the Kingdom of the Serbs, Croats and Slovenes, or to the Agreement effected by an exchange of notes on February 8, 1921, between the Italian Government and the Czechoslovak Government.

Article 8. The present Treaty shall be communicated to the League of Nations in conformity with Article 18 of the Covenant.

The present Treaty shall be ratified and the instruments of ratification shall be exchanged at Paris as soon as possible.

In faith whereof the respective plenipotentiaries, being duly empowered for this purpose, have signed the present Treaty and have thereto affixed their seals.

Done at Paris, in duplicate, on January 25, 1924.

[Signed] R. POINCARÉ, DR EDVARD BENES

Treaty of Understanding between France and Yugoslavia, 11 November 1927

[This treaty is similar in text to the Treaty of Friendship between France and Rumania, 10 June 1926. Rumania also signed a Treaty of Friendship with Italy, 16 September 1926.]

. . .

Article 1. France and the Kingdom of the Serbs, Croats and Slovenes reciprocally undertake to refrain from all attacks or invasions directed against one another and in no circumstances to resort to war against one another . . . [unless in virtue of League obligations]

[*Article 2.* Pacific settlement of disputes.]

. . .

Article 5. The High Contracting Parties agree to take counsel together in the event of any modification, or attempted modification, of the political status of European countries and, subject to any resolutions which may be adopted in such case by the Council or Assembly of the League of Nations, to come to an understanding as to the attitude which they should respectively observe in such an eventuality.

Article 6. The High Contracting Parties declare that nothing in this Treaty is to be interpreted as contradicting the stipulations of the treaties at present in force which have been signed by France or the Kingdom of the Serbs, Croats and Slovenes, and which concern their policy in Europe. They undertake to exchange views on questions affecting European policy in order to coordinate their efforts in the cause of peace, and for this purpose to communicate to each other henceforward any treaties or agreements which they may conclude with third Powers on the same subject. Such treaties or agreements shall invariably be directed to aims which are compatible with the maintenance of peace.

Treaty of Mutual Guarantee between France and Poland, Locarno, 16 October 1925

[This treaty is identical in text to the Treaty of Mutual Guarantee between France and Czechoslovakia, 16 October 1925.]

The President of the French Republic and the President of the Polish Republic;

Equally desirous to see Europe spared from war by a sincere observance of the undertakings arrived at this day with a view to the maintenance of general peace,

Have resolved to guarantee their benefits to each other reciprocally by a treaty concluded within the framework of the Covenant of the League of Nations and of the treaties existing between them . . . and . . . have agreed on the following provisions:

Article 1. In the event of Poland or France being injured by a failure to observe the undertakings arrived at this day between them and Germany with a view to the maintenance of general peace, France, and reciprocally Poland, acting in application of Article 16 of the Covenant of the League of Nations, undertake to lend each other immediately aid and assistance, if such a failure is accompanied by an unprovoked resort to arms.

In the event of the Council of the League of Nations, when dealing with a question brought before it in accordance with the said undertakings, being unable to succeed in making its report accepted by all its members other than the representatives of the parties to the dispute, and in the event of Poland or France being attacked without provocation, France, or reciprocally Poland, acting in application of Article 15, paragraph 7, of the Covenant of the League of Nations, will immediately lend aid and assistance.

Article 2. Nothing in the present Treaty shall affect the rights and obligations of the High Contracting Parties as members of the League of Nations, or shall be interpreted as restricting the duty of the League to take whatever action may be deemed wise and effectual to safeguard the peace of the world.

Article 3. The present Treaty shall be registered with the League of Nations, in accordance with the Covenant.

Article 4. The present Treaty shall be ratified. The ratifications will be deposited at Geneva with the League of Nations at the same time as the ratification of the Treaty concluded this day between Germany, Belgium, France, Great Britain, and Italy, and the ratification of the Treaty concluded at the same time between Germany and Poland.

It will enter into force and remain in force under the same conditions as the said Treaties. . . .

Alliance between Yugoslavia and Czechoslovakia, 14 August 1920

Firmly resolved to maintain the peace obtained by so many sacrifices, and provided for by the Covenant of the League of Nations, as well as the situation created by the Treaty concluded at Trianon on June 4, 1920, between the Allied and Associated Powers on the one hand, and Hungary on the other, the President of the Czechoslovak Republic and His Majesty the King of the Serbs, Croats, and Slovenes have agreed to conclude a defensive Convention . . . and have agreed as follows:

Article 1. In case of an unprovoked attack on the part of Hungary against one of the High Contracting Parties, the other party agrees to assist in the defence of the party attacked, in the manner laid down by the arrangement provided for in Article 2 of the present Convention.

Article 2. The competent Technical Authorities of the Czechoslovak Republic and the Kingdom of the Serbs, Croats, and Slovenes shall decide, by mutual agreement, upon the provisions necessary for the execution of the present Convention.

Article 3. Neither of the High Contracting Parties shall conclude an alliance with a third Power without preliminary notice to the other.

Article 4. The present Convention shall be valid for two years from the date of the exchange of ratifications. On the expiration of this period, each of the Contracting Parties shall have the option of denouncing the present Convention. It shall, however, remain in force for six months after the date of denunciation.

Alliance between Rumania and Czechoslovakia, 23 April 1921

Firmly resolved to maintain the peace obtained by so many sacrifices, and provided for by the Covenant of the League of Nations, as well as the situation created by the Treaty concluded at Trianon on June 4, 1920, between the Allied and Associated Powers on the one hand, and Hungary on the other, the President of the Czechoslovak Republic and His Majesty the King of Rumania, have agreed to conclude a defensive Convention . . . and have agreed as follows:

Article 1. In case of an unprovoked attack on the part of Hungary against one of the High Contracting Parties, the other party agrees to assist in the defence of the party attacked, in the manner laid down by the arrangement provided for in Article 2 of the present Convention.

Article 2. The competent Technical Authorities of the Czechoslovak Republic and Rumania shall decide by mutual agreement and in a Military Convention to be concluded, upon the provisions necessary for the execution of the present Convention.

Article 3. Neither of the High Contracting Parties shall conclude an alliance with a third Power without preliminary notice to the other.

Article 4. For the purpose of coordinating their efforts to maintain peace, the two Governments undertake to consult together on questions of foreign policy concerning their relations with Hungary.

Article 5. The present Convention shall be valid for two years from the date of the exchange of ratifications. On the expiration of this period, each of the Contracting Parties shall have the option of denouncing the present Convention. It shall, however, remain in force for six months after the date of denunciation.

Alliance between Yugoslavia and Rumania, 7 June 1921

Firmly resolved to maintain the peace obtained by so many sacrifices, and the situation created by the Treaty concluded at Trianon on June 4, 1920, between the Allied and Associated Powers on the one hand, and Hungary on the other, as well as the Treaty concluded at Neuilly on November 27, 1919, between the same Powers and Bulgaria, His Majesty the King of the Serbs, Croats, and Slovenes and His Majesty the King of Rumania have agreed to conclude a defensive Convention . . . and have concluded the following Articles:

Article 1. In case of an unprovoked attack on the part of Hungary or of Bulgaria, or of these two Powers, against one of the two High Contracting Parties, with the object of destroying the situation created by the Treaty of Trianon or the Treaty of Neuilly, the other Party agrees to assist in the defence of the Party attacked, in the manner laid down by Article 2 of this Convention.

Article 2. The Technical Authorities of the Kingdom of the Serbs, Croats, and Slovenes and of the Kingdom of Rumania shall decide by mutual agreement, in a Military Convention to be concluded as soon as possible, upon the provisions necessary for the execution of the present Convention.

Article 3. Neither of the High Contracting Parties shall conclude an alliance with a third Power without preliminary notice to the other.

Article 4. With the object of associating their efforts to maintain peace, the two Governments bind themselves to consult together on questions of foreign policy concerning their relations with Hungary and Bulgaria.

Alliance between Poland and Rumania, 3 March 1921

Being firmly resolved to safeguard a peace which was gained at the price of so many sacrifices, the Chief of the State of the Polish Republic and His Majesty the King of Rumania have agreed to conclude a Convention for a defensive alliance....

Article 1. Poland and Rumania undertake to assist each other in the event of their being the object of an unprovoked attack on their present eastern frontiers.

Accordingly, if either State is the object of an unprovoked attack, the other shall consider itself in a state of war and shall render armed assistance.

Article 2. In order to coordinate their efforts to maintain peace, both Governments undertake to consult together on such questions of foreign policy as concern their relations with their eastern neighbours.

Article 3. A military Convention shall determine the manner in which either country shall render assistance to the other should the occasion arise.

This Convention shall be subject to the same conditions as the present Convention as regards duration and denunciation.

Article 4. If, in spite of their efforts to maintain peace, the two States are compelled to enter on a defensive war under the terms of Article 1, each undertakes not to negotiate nor to conclude an armistice or a peace without the participation of the other State.

Article 5. The duration of the present Convention shall be five years from the date of its signature, but either Government shall be at liberty to denounce it after two years, on giving the other State six months' notice.

Article 6. Neither of the High Contracting Parties shall be at liberty to conclude an alliance with a third Power without having previously obtained the assent of the other party.

Alliances with a view to the maintenance of treaties already signed jointly by both Poland and Rumania are excepted from this provision.

Such alliances must, however, be notified.

The Polish Government hereby declares that it is acquainted with the agreements entered into by Rumania with other States with a view to upholding the Treaties of Trianon and Neuilly, which agreements may be transformed into treaties of alliance.

The Rumanian Government hereby declares that it is acquainted with the agreements entered into by Poland with the French Republic.

Treaty of Guarantee between Poland and Rumania, 26 March 1926

The President of the Polish Republic and His Majesty the King of Rumania, noting with satisfaction the consolidation of the guarantees for the general peace of Europe, and anxious to satisfy the desire for peace by which the peoples are animated, desirous of seeing their country spared from war, and animated also with the sincere desire of giving to their peoples supplementary guarantees within the framework of the Covenant of the League of Nations and of the treaties of which they are signatories, have determined to conclude a Treaty with this object. . . .

Article 1. Poland and Rumania undertake each to respect and preserve against external aggression the territorial integrity and existing political independence of the other.

Article 2. In the event of Poland or Rumania, contrary to the undertakings imposed by Articles 12, 13, and 15 of the Covenant of the League of Nations, being attacked without provocation, Poland and reciprocally Rumania, acting in application of Article 16 of the Covenant of the League of Nations, undertake to lend each other immediately aid and assistance.

In the event of the Council of the League of Nations, when dealing with a question brought before it in accordance with the provisions of the Covenant of the League of Nations, being unable to secure the acceptance of its report by all its Members other than the representatives of the parties to the dispute, and in the event of Poland or Rumania being attacked without provocation, Poland or reciprocally Rumania, acting in application of Article 15, paragraph 7, of the Covenant of the League of Nations, will immediately lend aid and assistance to the other country.

Should a dispute of the kind provided for in Article 17 of the Covenant of the League of Nations arise, and Poland or Rumania be attacked without provocation, Poland and reciprocally Rumania undertake to lend each other immediately aid and assistance.

The details of application of the above provisions shall be settled by technical agreements.

Article 3. If, in spite of their efforts to maintain peace, the two States are compelled to enter on a defensive war under the terms of Articles 1 and 2, each undertakes not to negotiate or conclude an armistice or a peace without the participation of the other State.

Article 4. In order to coordinate their efforts to maintain peace, both Governments undertake to consult together on such questions of foreign policy as concern both Contracting Parties.

Article 5. Neither of the High Contracting Parties shall be at liberty to conclude an alliance with a third Power without having previously consulted the other party.

Alliances with a view to the maintenance of treaties already signed jointly by both Poland and Rumania are excepted from this provision.

Such alliances must, however, be notified.

Article 6. The High Contracting Parties undertake to submit all disputes which may arise between them or which it may not have been possible to settle by the ordinary methods of diplomacy, to conciliation or arbitration. The details of this procedure of pacific settlement shall be laid down in a special convention to be concluded as soon as possible.

Article 7. The present Treaty shall remain in force for five years from the date of its signature, but either of the two Governments shall be entitled to denounce it after two years, upon giving six months' notice.

[*Article 8*. Ratification.]

Protocol

The Convention of Defensive Alliance which expires on April 3, 1926, being recognized to have had results beneficial to the cause of peace, the undersigned plenipotentiaries, holding full powers, found in good and due form, from the President of the Polish Republic and from His Majesty the King of Rumania, respectively, have agreed to conclude a Treaty of Guarantee for a further period of five years. . . .

[The Treaty of Guarantee was concluded again on 15 January 1931.]

Supplementary Agreement to the Treaties of Friendship and Alliance between the States of the Little Entente, 27 June 1930

[Czechoslovakia, Rumania and Yugoslavia . . .]

Being desirous of strengthening still further the ties of friendship and alliance which exist between the States of the Little Entente,

Wishing to supplement the organization of the political cooperation and of the defence of the common interests of their three States by means of a fixed procedure,

Have resolved to confirm the present practice and the present procedure of close cooperation between their States by defining them with greater precision. . . .

Article I. The Ministers for Foreign Affairs of the Little Entente shall meet whenever circumstances make it necessary. They shall in any case meet at least once a year. Compulsory ordinary meetings shall be held, in turn, in each of the three States at a place selected beforehand. There shall also be an optional ordinary meeting at Geneva during the Assemblies of the League of Nations.

Article II. The compulsory meeting shall be presided over by the Minister for Foreign Affairs of the State in which it is held. That Minister is responsible for fixing the date and selecting the place of the meeting. He draws up its agenda and is responsible for the preparatory work connected with the decisions to be taken.

Until the regular meeting of the following year he is considered as President for the time being.

Article III. In all the questions which are discussed and in all the measures which are taken in regard to the relations of the States of the Little Entente between themselves, the principle of the absolute equality of the three States shall be rigorously respected. That principle shall also be respected more particularly in the relations of these States with other States or with a group of States, or with the League of Nations.

Article IV. According to the necessities of the situation, the three Ministers for Foreign Affairs may decide, by common agreement, that in regard to any particular question the representation or the defence of the point of view of the States of the Little Entente shall be entrusted to a single delegate or to the delegation of a single State.

Article V. An extraordinary meeting may be convened by the President for the time being when the international situation or an international event requires it.

Article VI. The present Agreement shall enter into force immediately. It shall be ratified and the exchange of ratifications shall take place at Prague as soon as possible. . . .

Pact of Organization of the Little Entente, 16 February 1933

. . . Desirous of maintaining and organizing peace;

Firmly determined to strengthen economic relations with all States without distinction and with the Central European States in particular,

Anxious that peace shall be safeguarded in all circumstances, that progress in the direction of the real stabilization of conditions in Central Europe shall be assured and that the common interests of their three countries shall be respected,

Determined, with this object, to give an organic and stable basis to the relations of friendship and alliance existing between the three States of the Little Entente, and,

Convinced of the necessity of bringing about such stability on the one hand by the complete unification of their general policy and on the other by the creation of a directing organ of this common policy, namely, the group of the three States of the Little Entente, thus forming a higher international unit, open to other States under conditions to be agreed upon in each particular case . . .

Article 1. A Permanent Council of the States of the Little Entente, composed of the Ministers for Foreign Affairs of the three respective countries or of the special delegates appointed for the purpose, shall be constituted as the directing organ of the common policy of the group of the three States. Decisions of the Permanent Council shall be unanimous.

Article 2. The Permanent Council, apart from its normal intercourse through the diplomatic channel, shall be required to meet at least three times a year. One obligatory annual meeting shall be held in the three States in turn, and another shall be held at Geneva during the Assembly of the League of Nations.

Article 3. The President of the Permanent Council shall be the Minister for Foreign Affairs of the State in which the obligatory annual meeting is held. He shall take the initiative in fixing the date and the place of meeting, shall arrange its agenda and shall draw up the questions to be decided. He shall continue to be President of the Permanent Council until the first obligatory meeting of the following year.

Article 4. In all questions that may be discussed, as in all decisions that may be reached, whether in regard to the relations of the States of the Little Entente among themselves or in regard to their relations with other States, the principle of the absolute equality of the three States of the Little Entente shall be rigorously respected.

Article 5. According to the exigencies of the situation, the Permanent Council may decide that in any given question the representation or the defence of the point of view of the States of the Little Entente shall be entrusted to a single delegate or to the delegation of a single State.

Article 6. Every political treaty of any one State of the Little Entente, every unilateral act changing the existing political situation of one of the States of the Little Entente in relation to an outside State, and every economic agreement involving important political consequences shall henceforth require the unanimous consent of the Council of the Little Entente.

The existing political treaties of each State of the Little Entente with outside States shall be progressively unified as far as possible.

Article 7. An Economic Council of the States of the Little Entente shall be constituted for the progressive coordination of the economic interests of the three States, whether among themselves or in their relations with other States. It shall be composed of specialists and experts in economic, commercial and financial matters and shall act as an auxiliary advisory organ of the Permanent Council in regard to its general policy.

Article 8. The Permanent Council shall be empowered to establish other stable or temporary organs, commissions or committees for the purpose of studying and preparing the solution of special questions or groups of questions for the Permanent Council.

Article 9. A Secretariat of the Permanent Council shall be created. Its headquarters shall be established in each case for one year in the capital of the President in office of the Permanent Council. A section of the Secretariat shall function permanently at the seat of the League of Nations at Geneva.

Article 10. The common policy of the Permanent Council shall be inspired by the general principles embodied in all the great international instruments relating to post-war policy, such as the Covenant of the League of Nations, the Pact of Paris, the General Act of Arbitration, any Conventions concluded in regard to disarmament, and the Locarno Pacts. Furthermore, nothing in the present Pact shall be construed as contrary to the principles or provisions of the Covenant of the League of Nations.

Article 11. The Conventions of Alliance between Roumania and Czechoslovakia of April 23, 1921, between Roumania and Yugoslavia of June 7, 1921, and between Czechoslovakia and Yugoslavia of August 31, 1922, which were extended on May 21, 1929, and are supplemented by the provisions of the present Pact, as well as the Act of Conciliation, Arbitration and Judicial Settlement signed by the three States of the Little Entente at Belgrade on May 21, 1929, are hereby renewed for an indefinite period.

Article 12. The present Pact shall be ratified and the exchange of ratifications shall take place at Prague not later than the next obligatory meeting. . . .

Pact of Balkan Entente between Turkey, Greece, Rumania and Yugoslavia, 9 February 1934

Article 1. Greece, Roumania, Turkey and Yugoslavia mutually guarantee the security of each and all of their Balkan frontiers.

Article 2. The High Contracting Parties undertake to concert together in regard to the measures to be taken in contingencies liable to affect their interests as defined by the present Agreement. They undertake not to embark upon any political action in relation to any other Balkan country not a signatory of the present Agreement without previous mutual consultation, nor to incur any political obligation to any other Balkan country without the consent of the other Contracting Parties.

Article 3. The present Agreement shall come into force on the date of its signature by the Contracting Parties . . .

Protocol: Annex of the Pact, 9 February 1954

In proceeding to sign the Pact of Balkan Entente, the four Ministers for Foreign Affairs of Greece, Roumania, Yugoslavia, and Turkey have seen fit to define as follows the nature of the undertakings assumed by their respective countries, and to stipulate explicitly that the said definitions form an integral part of the Pact.

1. Any country committing one of the acts of aggression to which Article 2 of the London Conventions of July 3rd and 4th, 1933, relates shall be treated as an aggressor.

2. The Pact of Balkan Entente is not directed against any Power. Its object is to guarantee the security of the several Balkan frontiers against any aggression on the part of any Balkan State.

3. Nevertheless, if one of the High Contracting Parties is the victim of aggression on the part of any other non-Balkan Power, and a Balkan State associates itself with such aggression, whether at the time or subsequently, the Pact of Balkan Entente shall be applicable in its entirety in relation to such Balkan State.

4. The High Contracting Parties undertake to conclude appropriate Conven-

tions for the furtherance of the objects pursued by the Pact of Balkan Entente. The negotiation of such Conventions shall begin within six months.

5. As the Pact of Balkan Entente does not conflict with previous undertakings, all previous undertakings and all Conventions based on previous treaties shall be applicable in their entirety, the said undertakings and the said treaties having all been published.

6. The words 'Firmly resolved to ensure the observance of the contractual obligations already in existence', in the Preamble to the Pact, shall cover the observance by the High Contracting Parties of existing treaties between Balkan States, to which one or more of the High Contracting Parties is a signatory party.

7. The Pact of Balkan Entente is a defensive instrument; accordingly, the obligations on the High Contracting Parties which arise out of the said Pact shall cease to exist in relation to a High Contracting Party becoming an aggressor against any other country within the meaning of Article 2 of the London Conventions.

8. The maintenance of the territorial situation in the Balkans as at present established is binding definitively on the High Contracting Parties. The duration of the obligations under the Pact shall be fixed by the High Contracting Parties in the course of the two years following the signature of the Pact, or afterwards. During the two years in question the Pact cannot be denounced. The duration of the Pact shall be fixed at not less than five years, and may be longer. If, two years after the signature of the same, no duration has been fixed, the Pact of Balkan Entente shall *ipso facto* remain in force for five years from the expiry of the two years after the signature thereof. On the expiry of the said five years, or of the period on which the High Contracting Parties have agreed for its duration, the Pact of Balkan Entente shall be renewed automatically by tacit agreement for the period for which it was previously in force, failing denunciation by any one of the High Contracting Parties one year before the date of its expiry; provided always that no denunciation or notice of denunciation shall be admissible, whether in the first period of the Pact's validity (namely, seven or more than seven years) or in any subsequent period fixed automatically by tacit agreement, before the year preceding the date on which the Pact expires.

9. The High Contracting Parties shall inform each other as soon as the Pact of Balkan Entente is ratified in accordance with their respective laws.

Balkan Entente between Turkey, Greece, Rumania and Yugoslavia, 9 February 1934, and Bulgaria, 31 July 1938

Whereas Bulgaria is an adherent of the policy of consolidation of peace in the Balkans, and is desirous of maintaining relations of good neighbourhood and full and frank collaboration with the Balkan States, and

Whereas the States of the Balkan Entente are animated by the same pacific spirit in relation to Bulgaria and the same desire of cooperation,

Now therefore the undersigned:

His Excellency Monsieur Georges KIOSSÉIVANOV, President of the Council of Ministers, Bulgarian Minister for Foreign Affairs and Public Worship, of the one part, and

His Excellency Monsieur Jean METAXAS, President of the Council of Ministers, Greek Minister for Foreign Affairs, acting in his capacity as President in Office of the Permanent Council of the Balkan Entente, in the name of all the Members of the Balkan Entente, of the other part,

Hereby declare, on behalf of the States which they represent, that the said States undertake to abstain in their relations with one another from any resort to force, in accordance with the agreements to which they have severally subscribed in respect of non-aggression, and are agreed to waive the application in so far as they are concerned of the provisions contained in Part IV (Military, Naval and Air clauses) of the Treaty of Neuilly, as also of the provisions contained in the Convention respecting the Thracian Frontier, signed at Lausanne, July 24th, 1923.

V · The Soviet Union and her neighbours, 1919–37

The years from 1918 to 1921 saw an astonishing transformation of Bolshevik Russia's fortunes. In the spring of 1918 the control of the Bolsheviks over Russia's territory had shrunk to only a shadow of the former empire. Russia was occupied on the one hand by the Germans who could still advance at will, and also by Allied 'intervention'. But even after Germany's collapse in November 1918, Soviet Russia's troubles were far from over. Allied 'intervention' continued; Soviet Russia simultaneously fought and survived both the Civil War and the Polish War.

The first task facing the Soviet leaders was to achieve settled frontiers and to secure Soviet power within them. Taking advantage of Russia's weakness, the Poles early in 1919 had occupied as much territory eastwards as they could, whilst from Siberia, Admiral Kolchak's anti-Bolshevik forces were pushing into European Russia. Kolchak was defeated but the Poles could not be simultaneously resisted. That autumn of 1919 Yudenich advanced from his Baltic base and threatened Moscow. But early in 1920 the Red Army defeated the White Russian forces and Wrangel's last stand in the Crimea during 1920–1 proved but an epilogue to the Civil War. Allied intervention, never effective, ceased for all practical purposes. During the spring of 1920 the Poles, led by Marshal Joseph Pilsudski, posed the greatest threat to Russia. In April 1920 Pilsudski negotiated an agreement with the hard pressed anti-Bolshevik régime of what remained of the independent State of the Ukraine. The Poles advanced and reached Kiev in May 1920. The Russian counter-attack came within reach of Warsaw in August, but Pilsudski was able to counter-attack in turn and to force the Red Army to withdraw. In October 1920 an armistice brought the war to an end, and the *Treaty of Riga, 18 March 1921* (p. 137), settled the frontiers of the two States until 1939. That same year,

1920, Soviet Russia recognized the independence of the three Baltic Republics, Estonia, Latvia and Lithuania, and also of Finland. With Finland Russia concluded the *Treaty of Dorpat, 14 October 1920* (p. 136). Not until the spring of 1921 did Soviet Russia win a measure of international recognition with the signature of the *Anglo-Soviet Trade Agreement, 16 March 1921* (p. 140). Soviet foreign policy was designed to achieve two complementary objectives: to strengthen and broaden the Soviet base and to weaken the 'capitalist' opposition.

Soviet treaties, 1921–7

Soviet treaties fall into distinctive groups: treaties of peace with Russia's neighbours, Poland, the Baltic Republics and Finland, all formerly part of the Russian Tsarist Empire and now recognized as independent States with mutually agreed and delimited frontiers.

The need for recognition and trade led Soviet Russia to make a number of treaties and agreements with the West. The first breakthrough came with the signature of the *Anglo-Soviet Trade Agreement, 16 March 1921* (p. 140), whereby Soviet Russia secured *de facto* recognition from the world's most important 'capitalist State'. Soviet Russia gradually gained international recognition throughout the world including the United States (1933). While the Russian Soviet Government on the one hand signed treaties in which conditions were to be created for normalizing relations between the Soviet Union and its neighbours, the Russian Communist Party on the other sought to organize world revolution with the help of the Comintern.

The First Congress of the Third International held in Moscow in March 1919 served Lenin's purpose in that it created an organization around which could be grouped a worldwide international socialist movement under the control of the Russian Communist Party. Its aim was to promote revolution abroad. The Second Congress met in July 1920, and during its course Lenin laid down the conditions which had to be met before a communist group could be admitted to the Third International. By the time of the meeting of the Third Congress (June–July 1921) it had become evident that world revolution was no longer imminent, but the efforts to promote it were not abandoned: revolution was merely delayed.

Alliances and treaties with anti-colonial and nationalist movements were concluded by *Soviet Russia and Iran on 26 February 1921* which, as one Soviet historian recently wrote, 'struck a powerful blow at imperialism and its colonial system'. Two days later came the signature of a *Soviet Treaty with Afghanistan, 28 February 1921*, whereby the Soviets intended to weaken the British position in India; and a month later the remarkable Soviet coup was completed with the signature of the *Soviet–Turkish Treaty of Friendship, 16 March 1921* (p. 77). These treaties were confirmed by the signatures of the *Soviet–Turkish Treaty of Non-Aggression and Neutrality, 17 December 1925*, and similar treaties with *Afghanistan, 31 August 1926*, and *Iran, 1 October 1927*.

Relations between the Soviet Union and Germany

Germany and Russia, once in the relationship of victor and vanquished when Brest-Litovsk was signed, had both become defeated Powers after November 1918. The war had gravely weakened the two countries. Nevertheless Russia and Germany remained potentially Great Powers. Thus despite their entirely different political complexions there was a community of interest which brought Russia and Germany together in the 1920s. Their collaboration involved some limited secret military cooperation and limited economic assistance for Russia; joint enmity towards Poland within its post-war frontiers was the basis. In 1922 the *Genoa Conference* of major European Powers met to reconstruct the economy of Europe and to revive world trade. It proved abortive. The most important result was that two of the participants, Soviet Russia and Germany, unable to persuade the Western Powers to make sufficient concessions, signed a treaty with each other at the neighbouring resort of Rapallo. The significance of the *Treaty of Rapallo, 16 April 1922* (p. 139) lay in the fact that both Soviet Russia and Germany broke out of diplomatic isolation. Their cooperation was based not on an identity of views or genuine friendship but on self-interest. The Locarno reconciliation with the West and Germany's entry into the League of Nations in 1926 was carefully dovetailed by Stresemann to harmonize with Germany's undertakings to Soviet Russia. Thus Germany would not be automatically obliged to join in any action against Russia under Article 16, because it need only do so to an extent that was compatible with its military situation and geographical location, a phrase that left Germany the decision. Weimar Germany reaffirmed its relationship with Soviet Russia by the *Treaty of Berlin, 24 April 1926* (p. 142); but the relative position of the two countries had changed. Locarno meant that Germany was no longer exclusively reliant on the Soviet Union for support (p. 96). The Soviet Union attempted to extend the principle of neutrality and non-aggression treaties to the Baltic States. All these efforts failed except for a *treaty with Lithuania, 28 September 1926*. On *25 January 1929, Germany and the Soviet Union concluded a Conciliation Convention* (pp. 144, 145).

The consequences of the world depression of 1929 ended the collaboration between the Weimar Republic and Soviet Russia. From 1930 to 1933 the German Communists combined with the Nazis to undermine the Weimar Republic. In this they succeeded.

A NOTE ON SECRET GERMAN–SOVIET MILITARY COOPERATION

Several secret military agreements were concluded between the German industrialists, the German army (with the knowledge of some ministers of the Weimar Government) and the Soviet Union. The first of these was a provisional agreement, 15 March 1922, which provided the finance for Junkers to build an aeroplane factory in the Soviet Union. German troops were sent for training to the Soviet Union in 1922; munitions and poison gas were manufactured in Russia. The agreements were not formal treaties, but nevertheless were concrete arrangements to further what were then regarded by the German military as the mutual and parallel interests of Germany and the Soviet Union; they both looked on post-Versailles Poland as the enemy. By 1926 relatively little was actually achieved in providing Germany with armaments. The most important advantage for Germany was the provision of training facilities for German pilots. After 1929 a tank school trained some German troops in the Soviet Union; there were some joint German–Soviet poison gas experiments, and a number of German officers participated in Soviet manœuvres. These agreements broke the military terms of the Versailles treaty. They were, however, much more limited than the rumoured 'secret treaties' of extensive military cooperation, which did not exist.

Treaties of non-aggression and mutual assistance in Europe, 1926–36

The years after 1926 mark a new stage in Soviet policy. Within the Soviet Union, Stalin emerged as sole dictator and the organs of the State were transformed to a fully totalitarian system. Stalin embarked on a policy of industrialization, on collectivization of agriculture regardless of human life, and on a policy of terror against all probable and improbable opponents. Internationally the Soviet Union, despite its recognition and entry into the League of Nations in 1934, felt itself increasingly isolated and in danger. All was now subordinated to the security of the State. The virulent hatred of the Nazis for the Bolsheviks cut the links between the Soviet Union and Germany. These had been weakening since Locarno.

The Soviet Union engaged in vigorous diplomatic activity to assure its safety from attack and to prevent a hostile coalition of Powers coming into being. From 1926 to 1937 the Soviet Union concluded a large number of non-aggression treaties. Stalin acquiesced for the time being in the existence of the 'Buffer States', Poland, the Baltic States and Finland. The most important *non-aggression treaty was that concluded with Poland, 25 July 1932* (p. 145); similar treaties were concluded with *France, 29 November 1932* (p. 148), and *Finland, 21 January 1932* (p. 149), *Latvia, 5 February 1932, Estonia, 4 May 1932, and Lithuania in 1926* (p. 144).

The failure to obtain an Eastern Locarno, whereby France and Russia would have guaranteed the independence of the Buffer States, led the Russians to sign with France a *Treaty of Mutual Assistance, 2 May 1935* (p. 152). Although the clauses of the treaty suggest a complete and effective alliance, appearances are misleading. The obligation to go to war was not automatic; the League of Nations had first to recognize the fact of aggression under Article 16 of the Covenant. There were no detailed military provisions; geography ensured that since Russia and Germany lacked a common frontier, Russia could not help France as long as Germany and Russia respected Polish and Baltic neutrality; similarly France could not 'attack' Germany without a breach of Locarno. The treaty was not ratified for almost a year and entered into force on 27 March 1936. The *Soviet Union also signed a Mutual Assistance Treaty with Czechoslovakia, 16 May 1935* (p. 154), but it contained the provision that it would only become operative if France first came to the help of the Czechs. Once more geography denied Soviet Russia the possibility of giving direct military help without passing through hostile Poland or Rumania. Despite these agreements Czechoslovakia was sacrificed to Hitler at Munich in September 1938 (without Soviet participation at the conference but also without any real chance of Soviet help for Czechoslovakia during the crisis).

Soviet treaties in eastern Asia

In 1919 in the Far East, Soviet Russia felt itself threatened by Allied and Japanese intervention, by occupation and by support given to anti-Bolshevik forces. Attempts to win over China by denouncing Tsarist imperialism were not very successful. The Chinese, taking advantage of Russian impotence, had regained control of the Chinese Eastern Railway and over autonomous Outer Mongolia. By April 1920 the Soviet position improved. Only the Japanese remained a strong foreign force on Russian soil. A Soviet-supported revolution brought Outer Mongolia back under Soviet protection. Russo-Chinese relations in the 1920s varied from normalization, advanced by the *Agreement of 31 May 1924 concerning the Chinese Eastern Railway*, to the all but declared war in 1929 as a result of Soviet attempts to establish Soviet influence in China. In the 1920s good relations were established between Russia and Japan, marked especially by the *Convention between Japan and the Soviet Union concerning their general relationship, 20 January 1925* (p. 156).

But the 1930s saw a reversal of Russia's Far Eastern policies. With Japanese aggression in China and Japan's growing expansionism, the Soviet Union gave support to China. The change in this relationship with China is marked by the signature of a *Treaty of Non-Aggression between the U.S.S.R. and the Republic of China, 21 August 1937* (p. 160). Despite the agreement reached between the Soviet Union with Japan's puppet state of Manchukuo for the sale of the *Chinese Eastern Railway, 23 March 1935* (p. 159), Soviet–Japanese relations remained very strained. With the *Mongolian People's Republic the Soviet Union concluded a Mutual Assistance Treaty, 12 March 1936* (p. 159).

Treaty of Peace between Latvia and Soviet Russia, 11 August 1920

[Similar treaties were concluded with the other Baltic States.]

Russia on the one hand, and Latvia on the other, being strongly desirous of bringing to an end the present state of war between them, and of bringing about a final settlement of all the questions arising from the former subjection of Latvia to Russia, have decided to commence negotiations for peace and to conclude as soon as possible a lasting, honourable and just peace ... and have agreed on the following terms:

Article I. The state of war between the Contracting Parties shall cease from the date of the coming into force of the present Treaty.

Article II. By virtue of the principle proclaimed by the Federal Socialist Republic of the Russian Soviets, which establishes the right of self-determination for all nations, even to the point of total separation from the States with which they have been incorporated, and in view of the desire expressed by the Latvian people to possess an independent national existence, Russia unreservedly recognizes the independence and sovereignty of the Latvian State and voluntarily and irrevocably renounces all sovereign rights over the Latvian people and territory which formerly belonged to Russia under the then existing constitutional law as well as under international treaties, which, in the sense here indicated, shall in future cease to be valid. The previous status of subjection of Latvia to Russia shall not entail any obligation towards Russia on the part of the Latvian people or territory.

Article III. The State frontier between Russia and Latvia shall be fixed as follows: ... [for details of frontiers, see map on p. 39].

Article IV. The two Contracting Parties undertake:

1. To forbid any army to remain on either territory except their own army or that of friendly States with which one of the Contracting Parties has concluded a military convention, but which are not in a *de facto* state of war with either Contracting Party; and also to forbid, within the limits of their respective territory, the mobilization and recruiting of any personnel intended for the armies of States, organizations or groups, for purposes of armed conflict against the other Contracting Party....

2. Not to permit the formation or residence in their territory of organizations or groups of any kind claiming to represent the Government of all or part of the territory of the other Contracting Party; or of representatives or officials of organizations or groups having as their object the overthrow of the Government of the other Contracting Party.

3. To forbid Governments in a *de facto* state of war with the other party, and organizations and groups having as their object military action against the other Contracting Party, to transport through their ports or their territory anything which might be used for military purposes against the other Contracting Party, in particular, military forces belonging to these States, organizations or groups; material of war; technical military stores belonging to artillery, supply services, engineers or air services.

4. To forbid, except in cases provided for by international law, passage through or navigation in their territorial waters of all warships, gunboats, torpedo boats, etc., belonging either to organizations and groups whose object is military action against the other Contracting Party, or to Governments which are in state of war with the other Contracting Party and which aim at military action against the other Contracting Party. This provision shall come into force as soon as such intentions are known to the Contracting Party to whom the said territorial waters and ports belong.

Article V. The two parties mutually undertake not to claim the expenses of the war from each other. By this is understood the expenses incurred by ,the State for the conduct of the war, and likewise any compensations for losses occasioned by the war, that is, losses occasioned to themselves or to their subjects by military operations, including all kinds of requisitions made by one of the Contracting Parties in the territory of the other.

Article VI. In view of the fact that it is necessary to apportion in an equitable manner among the States of the world the obligation to make good the damages caused by the World War of 1914–17 to States that have been ruined, or to portions of States on whose territory military operations have taken place, the two Contracting Parties undertake to do all in their power to secure an agreement among all States in order to establish an international fund, which would be used to cover the sums intended for the reparation of damages due to the war.

Independently of the creation of this international fund, the Contracting Parties consider it necessary that Russia and all new States constituting independent Republics in what was formerly Russian territory should render each other, as far as possible, mutual support to make good from their own resources the damage caused by the World War, and undertake to do all in their power to secure this agreement between the above-mentioned Republics.

Article VII. Prisoners of war of both parties shall be repatriated as soon as possible. The method of exchange of prisoners is laid down in the Annex to this present Article.
Note: All captives who are not serving voluntarily in the army of the Government which has made them prisoners shall be considered as prisoners of war.

ANNEX TO ARTICLE VII

1. Prisoners of the two Contracting Parties shall be repatriated unless, with the consent of the Government on whose territory they are, they express the desire to remain in the country in which they are or to proceed to any other country. . . .

Treaty of Peace between Finland and Soviet Russia (Treaty of Dorpat), 14 October 1920

Whereas Finland declared its independence in 1917, and Russia has recognized the independence and the sovereignty of Finland within the frontiers of the Grand Duchy of Finland,

The Government of the Republic of Finland, and the Government of the Federal Socialist Republic of Soviet Russia,

Actuated by a desire to put an end to the war which has arisen between their States, to establish mutual and lasting peace relations and to confirm the situation which springs from the ancient political union of Finland and Russia,

Have resolved to conclude a Treaty with this object in view, and have agreed on the following provisions:

Article I. From the date upon which this Treaty shall come into force, a state of war shall cease to exist between the Contracting Powers, and the two Powers shall mutually undertake to maintain, for the future, an attitude of peace and goodwill towards one another.

Article II. The frontier between the States of Russia and of Finland shall be as follows ... [for frontier details see map on p. 4].

. . .

Article VI. 1. Finland guarantees that she will not maintain, in the waters contiguous to her seaboard in the Arctic Ocean, warships or other armed vessels, other than armed vessels of less than 100 tons displacement, which Finland may keep in these waters in any number, and of a maximum number of fifteen warships and other armed vessels, each with a maximum displacement of 400 tons.

Finland also guarantees that she will not maintain, in the above-mentioned waters, submarines or armed airplanes.

2. Finland also guarantees that she will not establish on the coast in question naval ports, bases or repairing stations of greater size than are necessary for the vessels mentioned in the preceding paragraph and for their armament.

. . .

Article VIII. 1. The right of free transit to and from Norway through the territory of Pechenga shall be guaranteed to the State of Russia and to its nationals. . . .

. . .

Article XII. The two Contracting Powers shall on principle support the neutralization of the Gulf of Finland and of the whole Baltic Sea, and shall undertake to cooperate in the realization of this object.

Article XIII. Finland shall militarily neutralize the following of her islands in the Gulf of Finland: Sommaro (Someri), Nervo (Narvi), Seitskar (Seiskari), Peninsaari, Lavansaari, Stora Tyterskar (Suuri Tytarsaari), Lilla Tyterskar (pieni Tytarsaari) and Rodskar. . . .

Article XIV. As soon as this Treaty comes into force, Finland shall take measures for the military neutralization of Hogland under an international guarantee. . . .

. . .

Article XVI. . . . Russia shall, however, have the right to send Russian war vessels into the navigable waterways of the interior by the canals along the southern bank of Ladoga and even, should the navigation of these canals be impeded, by the southern part of Ladoga.

2. Should the Gulf of Finland and the Baltic Sea be neutralized, the Contracting Powers mutually undertake to neutralize Ladoga also.

. . .

Article XXIV. The Contracting Powers will exact no indemnity whatsoever from one another for war expenses.

Finland will take no share in the expenses incurred by Russia in the World War of 1914–1918.

Article XXV. Neither of the Contracting Powers is responsible for the public debts and other obligations of the other Power.

Article XXVI. The debts and other obligations of the Russian State and of Russian governmental institutions towards the State of Finland and the Bank of Finland, and, similarly, the debts and obligations of the State of Finland and Finnish governmental institutions towards the Russian State and its governmental institutions, shall be regarded as mutually liquidated. . . .

Treaty of Peace between Poland and Soviet Russia (Treaty of Riga), 18 March 1921

Poland of the one hand and Russia and the Ukraine of the other, being desirous of putting an end to the war and of concluding a final, lasting and honourable peace based on a mutual understanding and in accordance with the peace preliminaries signed at Riga on October 12, 1920, have decided to enter into negotiations and have appointed for this purpose as plenipotentiaries . . . and have agreed to the following provisions:

Article I. The two Contracting Parties declare that a state of war has ceased to exist between them.

Article II. The two Contracting Parties, in accordance with the principle of national self-determination, recognize the independence of the Ukraine and of White Ruthenia and agree and decide that the eastern frontier of Poland, that is to say, the frontier between Poland on the one hand, and Russia, White Ruthenia and the Ukraine on the other, shall be as follows . . . [details].

Article III. Russia and the Ukraine abandon all rights and claims to the territories situated to the west of the frontier laid down by Article II of the present Treaty. Poland, on the other hand, abandons in favour of the Ukraine and of White Ruthenia all rights and claims to the territory situated to the east of this frontier. The two Contracting Parties agree that, in so far as the territory situated to the west of the frontier fixed in Article II of the present Treaty includes districts which form the subject of a dispute between Poland and Lithuania, the question of the attribution of these districts to one of those two States is a matter which exclusively concerns Poland and Lithuania.

Article IV. Poland shall not, in view of the fact that a part of the territories of the Polish Republic formerly belonged to the Russian Empire, be held to have incurred any debt or obligation towards Russia, except as provided in the present Treaty.

Similarly, no debt or obligation shall be regarded as incurred by Poland towards White Ruthenia or the Ukraine and vice versa except as provided in the present Treaty, owing to the fact that these countries formerly belonged to the Russian Empire.

Article V. Each of the Contracting Parties mutually undertakes to respect in every way the political sovereignty of the other party, to abstain from interference in its internal affairs, and particularly to refrain from all agitation, propaganda or interference of any kind, and not to encourage any such movement.

Each of the Contracting Parties undertakes not to create or protect organizations which are formed with the object of encouraging armed conflict against the other Contracting Party or of undermining its territorial integrity, or of subverting by force its political or social institutions, nor yet such organizations as claim to be the Government of the other party or of a part of the territories of the other party. The Contracting Parties therefore, undertake to prevent such organizations, their official representatives and other persons connected therewith, from establishing themselves on their territory, and to prohibit military recruiting and the entry into their territory and transport across it of armed forces, arms, munitions and war material of any kind destined for such organizations.

Article VI. 1. All persons above the age of 18 who, at the date of the ratification of the present Treaty are within the territory of Poland and on August 1, 1914 were nationals of the Russian Empire and are, or have the right to be, included in the registers of the permanent population of the former Kingdom of Poland, or have been included in the registers of an urban or rural commune, or of one of the class organizations in the territories of the former Russian Empire which formed part of Poland, shall have the right of opting for Russian or Ukrainian nationality. A similar declaration by nationals of the former Russian Empire of all other categories who are within Polish territory at the date of the ratification of the present Treaty shall not be necessary.

2. Nationals of the former Russian Empire above the age of 18 who at the date of the ratification of the present Treaty are within the territory of Russia and of the Ukraine and are, or have the right to be, included in the register of the permanent population of the former Kingdom of Poland, or have been included in the registers of an urban or rural commune, or of one of the class organizations in the territories of the former Russian Empire which formed part of Poland, shall be considered as Polish citizens if they express such a desire in accordance with the system of opting laid down in this Article. Persons above the age of 18 who are within the territory of Russia and of the Ukraine shall also be considered as Polish citizens if they express such a desire, in accordance with the system of opting laid down in this Article, and if they provide proofs that they are descendants of those who took part in the Polish struggle for independence between 1830 and 1865, or that they are descendants of persons who have for at least three generations been continuously established in the territory of the former Polish Republic, or if they show that they have by their actions, by the habitual use of the Polish language and by their method of educating their children, given effective proof of their attachment to Polish nationality. . . .

Article VII. 1. Russia and the Ukraine undertake that persons of Polish nationality in Russia, the Ukraine and White Ruthenia shall, in conformity with the principles of the equality of peoples, enjoy full guarantees of free intellectual development, the use of their national language and the exercise of their religion. Poland undertakes to recognize the same rights in the case of persons of Russian, Ukrainian and White Ruthenian nationality in Poland. . . .

. . .

3. The churches and religious associations in Russia, the Ukraine and White Ruthenia, of which Polish nationals are members, shall, so far as is in conformity with the domestic legislation of these countries, have the right of independent self-administration in domestic matters. . . .

Article VIII. The two Contracting Parties mutually abandon all claims to the repayment of war expenses, that is to say all the expenses incurred by the State during the war, and of the indemnities for damages caused by the war, that is to say, for damages caused to them or to their nationals in the theatre of war as a result of the war or of military measures taken during the Polish-Russian-Ukrainian War.

Treaty between Germany and Soviet Russia (*Treaty of Rapallo*) regarding the solution of general problems, 16 April 1922

The German Government, represented by Reichsminister Dr Walther Rathenau, and the Government of R.S.F.S.R., represented by People's Commissar Chicherin, have agreed upon the following provisions:

Article I. The two Governments agree that all questions resulting from the state of war between Germany and Russia shall be settled in the following manner:

(a) Both Governments mutually renounce repayment for their war expenses and for damages arising out of the war, that is to say, damages caused to them and their nationals in the zone of the war operations by military measures, including all requisitions effected in a hostile country. They renounce in the same way repayment for civil damages inflicted on civilians, that is to say, damages caused to the nationals of the two countries by exceptional war legislation or by violent measures taken by any authority of the State of either side.

(b) All legal relations concerning questions of public or private law resulting from the state of war, including the question of the treatment of merchant ships which fell into the hands of the one side or the other during the war, shall be settled on the basis of reciprocity.

(c) Germany and Russia mutually renounce repayment of expenses incurred for prisoners of war. The German Government also renounces repayment of expenses for soldiers of the Red Army interned in Germany. The Russian Government, for its part, renounces repayment of the sums Germany has derived from the sale of Russian army material brought into Germany by these interned troops.

Article II. Germany renounces all claims resulting from the enforcement of the laws and measures of the Soviet Republic as it has affected German nationals or their private rights or the rights of the German State itself, as well as claims resulting from measures taken by the Soviet Republic or its authorities in any other way against subjects of the German State or their private rights, provided that the Soviet Republic shall not satisfy similar claims by any third State.

Article III. Consular and diplomatic relations between Germany and the Federal Soviet Republic shall be resumed immediately. The admission of consuls to both countries shall be arranged by special agreement.

Article IV. Both Governments agree, further, that the rights of the nationals of either of the two parties on the other's territory as well as the regulation of commercial relations shall be based on the most-favoured-nation principle. This principle does not include rights and facilities granted by the Soviet Government to another Soviet State or to any State that formerly formed part of the Russian Empire.

Article V. The two Governments undertake to give each other mutual assistance for the alleviation of their economic difficulties in the most benevolent spirit. In the event of a general settlement of this question on an international basis, they undertake to have a preliminary exchange of views. The German Government declares itself ready to facilitate, as far as possible, the conclusion and the execution of economic contracts between private enterprises in the two countries.

Article VI. Article I, paragraph (b), and Article IV of this agreement will come into force after the ratification of this document. The other Articles will come into force immediately.

Trade Agreement between Britain and the Soviet Union, London, 16 March 1921

Whereas it is desirable in the interests both of Russia and of the United Kingdom that peaceful trade and commerce should be resumed forthwith between these countries, and whereas for this purpose it is necessary pending the conclusion of a formal general Peace Treaty between the Governments of these countries by which their economic and political relations shall be regulated in the future that a preliminary Agreement should be arrived at between the Government of the United Kingdom and the Government of the Russian Socialist Federal Soviet Republic, hereinafter referred to as the Russian Soviet Government.

The aforesaid parties have accordingly entered into the present Agreement for the resumption of trade and commerce between the countries.

The present Agreement is subject to the fulfilment of the following conditions, namely:

(a) That each party refrains from hostile action or undertakings against the other and from conducting outside of its own borders any official propaganda direct or indirect against the institutions of the British Empire or the Russian Soviet Republic respectively, and more particularly that the Russian Soviet Government refrains from any attempt by military or diplomatic or any other form of action or propaganda to encourage any of the peoples of Asia in any form of hostile action against British interests or the British Empire, especially in India and in the Independent State of Afghanistan. The British Government gives a similar particular undertaking to the Russian Soviet Government in respect of the countries which formed part of the former Russian Empire and which have now become independent.

(b) That all British subjects in Russia are immediately permitted to return home, and that all Russian citizens in Great Britain or other parts of the British Empire who desire to return to Russia are similarly released.

It is understood that the term 'conducting any official propaganda' includes the giving by either party of assistance or encouragement to any propaganda conducted outside its own borders.

The parties undertake to give forthwith all necessary instructions to their agents and to all persons under their authority to conform to the stipulations undertaken above.

Article I. Both parties agree not to impose or maintain any form of blockade against each other and to remove forthwith all obstacles hitherto placed in the way of the resumption of trade between the United Kingdom and Russia in any commodities which may be legally exported from or imported into their respective territories to or from any other foreign country, and do not exercise any discrimination against such trade, as compared with that carried on with any other foreign country or to place any impediments in the way of banking, credit and financial operations for the purpose of such trade, but subject always to legislation generally applicable in the respective countries. It is understood that nothing in this Article shall prevent either party from regulating the trade in arms and ammunition under general provisions of law which are applicable to the import of arms and ammunition from, or their export to foreign countries. . . .

. . .

Article IV. Each party may nominate such number of its nationals as may be agreed from time to time as being reasonably necessary to enable proper effect to be given to this Agreement, having regard to the conditions under which trade is carried on in its territories, and the other party shall permit such persons to enter its territories, and to sojourn and carry on trade there, provided that either party may restrict the admittance of any such persons into any specified areas, and may refuse admittance to or sojourn in its territories to any individual who is *persona non grata* to itself, or who does not comply with this Agreement or with the conditions precedent thereto. . . .

. . .

Article XIII. The present Agreement shall come into force immediately and both parties shall at once take all necessary measures to give effect to it. It shall continue in force unless and until replaced by the Treaty contemplated in the preamble so long as the conditions laid down both in the Articles of the Agreement and in the preamble are observed by both sides. Provided that at any time after the expiration of twelve months from the date on which the Agreement comes into force either party may give notice to terminate the provisions of the preceding Articles, and on the expiration of six months from the date of such notice those Articles shall terminate accordingly. . . .

Provided also that in the event of the infringement by either party at any time of any of the provisions of this Agreement or of the conditions referred to in the preamble, the other party shall immediately be free from the obligations of the Agreement. Nevertheless it is agreed that before taking any action inconsistent with the Agreement the aggrieved party shall give the other party a reasonable opportunity of furnishing an explanation or remedying the default. . . .

Declaration of Recognition of Claims

At the moment of signature of the preceding Trade Agreement both parties declare that all claims of either party or of its nationals against the other party in respect of property or rights or in respect of obligations incurred by the existing or former Governments of either country shall be equitably dealt with in the formal general Peace Treaty referred to in the preamble.

In the meantime and without prejudice to the generality of the above stipulation the Russian Soviet Government declares that it recognizes in principle that it is liable to pay compensation to private persons who have supplied goods or services to Russia for which they have not been paid. The detailed mode of discharging this liability shall be regulated by the Treaty referred to in the preamble.

The British Government hereby makes a corresponding declaration.

It is clearly understood that the above declarations in no way imply that the claims referred to therein will have preferential treatment in the aforesaid Treaty as compared with any other classes of claims which are to be dealt with in that Treaty.

Treaty of Berlin between the Soviet Union and Germany, Berlin, 24 April 1926

The German Government and the Government of the Union of Socialist Soviet Republics, being desirous of doing all in their power to promote the maintenance of general peace,

And being convinced that the interests of the German people and of the peoples of the Union of Socialist Soviet Republics demand constant and trustful cooperation,

Having agreed to strengthen the friendly relations existing between them by means of a special Treaty ... have agreed upon the following provisions:

Article 1. The relations between Germany and the Union of Socialist Soviet Republics shall continue to be based on the Treaty of Rapallo.

The German Government and the Government of the Union of Socialist Soviet Republics will maintain friendly contact in order to promote an understanding with regard to all political and economic questions jointly affecting their two countries.

Article 2. Should one of the Contracting Parties, despite its peaceful attitude, be attacked by one or more third Powers, the other Contracting Party shall observe neutrality for the whole duration of the conflict.

Article 3. If on the occasion of a conflict of the nature mentioned in Article 2, or at a time when neither of the Contracting Parties is engaged in warlike operations, a coalition is formed between third Powers with a view to the economic or financial boycott of either of the Contracting Parties, the other Contracting Party undertakes not to adhere to such coalition.

Article 4. The present Treaty shall be ratified and the instruments of ratification shall be exchanged at Berlin.

It shall enter into force on the date of the exchange of the instruments of ratification and shall remain in force for five years. The two Contracting Parties shall confer in good time before the expiration of this period with regard to the future development of their political relations.

In faith whereof the plenipotentiaries have signed the present Treaty.

Exchange of Notes, 24 April 1926

(a) HERR STRESEMANN TO M. KRESTINSKI

With reference to the negotiations upon the Treaty signed this day between the German Government and the Government of the Union of Socialist Soviet Republics, I have the honour, on behalf of the German Government, to make the following observations:

(1) In the negotiation and signature of the Treaty, both Governments have taken the view that the principle laid down by them in Article 1, paragraph 2, of the Treaty, of reaching an understanding on all political and economic questions affecting the two countries, will contribute considerably to the maintenance of peace. In any case the two Governments will in their deliberations be guided by the need for the maintenance of the general peace.

(2) In this spirit also the two Governments have approached the fundamental questions which are bound up with the entry of Germany into the League of Nations. The German Government is convinced that Germany's membership of the League cannot constitute an obstacle to the friendly development of the relations between Germany and the Union of Socialist Soviet Republics. According to its basic idea, the League of Nations is designed for the peaceful and equitable settlement of international disputes. The German Government is determined to cooperate to the best of its ability in the realization of this idea. If, however, though the German Government does

not anticipate this, there should at any time take shape within the League, contrary to that fundamental idea of peace, any efforts directed exclusively against the Union of Socialist Soviet Republics, Germany would most energetically oppose such efforts.

(3) The German Government also proceeds upon the assumption that this fundamental attitude of German policy towards the Union of Socialist Soviet Republics cannot be adversely influenced by the loyal observance of the obligations, arising out of Articles 16 and 17 of the Covenant of the League and relating to the application of sanctions, which would devolve upon Germany as a consequence of her entry into the League of Nations. By the terms of these Articles, the application of sanctions against the Union of Socialist Soviet Republics would come into consideration, in the absence of other causes, only if the Union of Socialist Soviet Republics entered upon a war of aggression against a third State. It is to be borne in mind that the question whether the Union of Socialist Soviet Republics is the aggressor in the event of a conflict with a third State could only be determined with binding force for Germany with her own consent; and that, therefore, an accusation to this effect levelled by other Powers against the Union of Socialist Soviet Republics and regarded by Germany as unjustified, would not oblige Germany to take part in measures of any kind instituted on the authority of Article 16. With regard to the question whether, in a concrete case, Germany would be in a position to take part in the application of sanctions at all, and to what extent, the German Government refers to the Note of December 1, 1925, on the interpretation of Article 16 addressed to the German Delegation on the occasion of the signing of the Treaties of Locarno.

(4) In order to create a secure basis for disposing without friction of all questions arising between them, the two Governments regard it as desirable that they should immediately embark upon negotiations for the conclusion of a general treaty for the peaceful solution of any conflicts that may arise between them, when special attention shall be given to the possibilities of the procedure of arbitration and conciliation.

I avail myself of this opportunity to renew to Your Excellency the assurance of my highest consideration.

(b) M. Krestinski to Herr Stresemann

. . . I have the honour, on behalf of the Union of Socialist Soviet Republics, to make the following reply :

(1) In the negotiation and signature of the Treaty, both Governments have taken the view that the principle laid down by them in Article 1, paragraph 2, of the Treaty, of reaching an understanding on all political and economic questions jointly affecting the two countries, will contribute considerably to the maintenance of peace. In any case the two Governments will in their deliberations be guided by the need for the maintenance of the general peace.

(2) The Government of the Union of Socialist Soviet Republics takes note of the explanation contained in Sections 2 and 3 of your Note concerning the fundamental questions connected with Germany's entry into the League of Nations.

(3) In order to create a secure basis for disposing without friction of all questions arising between them, the two Governments regard it as desirable that they should immediately embark upon negotiations for the conclusion of a general treaty for the peaceful solution of any conflicts that may arise between them, when special attention shall be given to the possibilities of the procedure of arbitration and conciliation . . .

Treaty of Non-Aggression concluded between the Soviet Union and Lithuania, 28 September 1926

...

Article 1. The relations between the Union of Socialist Soviet Republics and the Lithuanian Republic shall continue to be based on the Treaty of Peace between Lithuania and Russia, concluded at Moscow on July 12, 1920, all provisions of which shall retain their force and inviolability.

Article 2. The Lithuanian Republic and the Union of Socialist Soviet Republics undertake to respect in all circumstances each other's sovereignty and territorial integrity and inviolability.

Article 3. Each of the two Contracting Parties undertakes to refrain from any act of aggression whatsoever against the other party.

Should one of the Contracting Parties, despite its peaceful attitude, be attacked by one or several third Powers, the other Contracting Party undertakes not to support the said third Power or Powers against the Contracting Party attacked.

Article 4. If, on the occasion of a conflict of the type mentioned in Article 3, second paragraph, or at a time when neither of the Contracting Parties is engaged in warlike operations, a political agreement directed against one of the Contracting Parties is concluded between third Powers, or a coalition is formed between third Powers with a view to the economic or financial boycott of either of the Contracting Parties, the other Contracting Party undertakes not to adhere to such agreement or coalition.

Article 5. Should a dispute arise between them, the Contracting Parties undertake to appoint conciliation commissions if it should not prove possible to settle the dispute by diplomatic means.

The composition of the said commissions, their rights and the procedure they shall observe shall be settled in virtue of a separate agreement to be concluded between the two parties.

...

Conciliation Convention between Germany and the Soviet Union, 25 January 1929

The Central Executive Committee of U.S.S.R. and the President of the German Reich, animated by a desire further to strengthen the friendly relations which exist between the two countries, have decided, in execution of the Agreement reached in the Exchange of Notes of April 24, 1926, to conclude an Agreement for a procedure of conciliation, and ... have agreed upon the following terms:

Article I. Disputes of all kinds, particularly differences of opinion which arise regarding the interpretation of the bilateral treaties which exist between the two Contracting Parties or regarding past or future agreements concerning their elucidation or execution, shall, in the event of difficulties arising over their solution through diplomatic channels, be submitted to a procedure of conciliation in accordance with the following provisions.

Article II. The procedure of conciliation shall be before a Conciliation Commission.

The Conciliation Commission shall not be permanent, but shall be formed expressly for each meeting. It shall meet once a year in the middle of the year, in ordinary session, the exact date of which shall be arranged each year by agreement between the two Governments.

There shall be extraordinary sessions whenever in the opinion of the two Governments special need arises.

The meetings of the Conciliation Commission shall be held alternately in Moscow and Berlin. The place of the first meeting shall be decided by lot.

A session shall ordinarily last not longer than fourteen days.

...

Article V. The task of the Conciliation Commission shall be to submit to the two Governments a solution of the questions laid before it which shall be fair and acceptable to both parties, with special regard to the avoidance of possible future differences of opinion between the two parties on the same question.

Should the Conciliation Commission in the course of a session fail to agree upon a recommendation regarding any

question on the agenda, the question shall be laid before an extraordinary session of the Conciliation Commission, which must, however, meet not later than four months after the first meeting. Otherwise the matter shall be dealt with through diplomatic channels.

The results of each session of the Conciliation Commission shall be submitted to the two Governments for approval in the form of a report.

The report, or parts of it, shall be published only by agreement between the two Governments.

...

[In an additional Protocol, it was stated that the Soviet Union could not accept any provision for the appointment of a Chairman; the possibility was not excluded in special cases.]

[NOTE: This Convention and the Agreement of Neutrality and Non-Aggression of 24 April 1926 were prolonged by a Protocol concluded 24 June 1931.]

Pact of Non-Aggression between the Soviet Union and Poland, 25 July 1932

The President of the Polish Republic of the one part, and the Central Executive Committee of U.S.S.R. of the other part; desirous of maintaining the present state of peace between their countries and convinced that the maintenance of peace between them constitutes an important factor in the work of preserving universal peace; considering that the Treaty of Peace of March 18, 1921 constitutes, now as in the past, the basis of their reciprocal relations and undertakings; convinced that the peaceful settlement of international disputes and the exclusion of all that might be contrary to the normal condition of relations between States are the surest means of arriving at the goal desired; declaring that none of the obligations hitherto assumed by either of the parties stands in the way of peaceful de-

velopment of their mutual relations or is incompatible with the present Pact; have decided to conclude the present Pact with the object of amplifying and completing the Pact for the Renunciation of War signed at Paris on August 27, 1928, and put into force by the Protocol signed at Moscow on February 9, 1929; ... and have agreed on the following provisions:

Article I. The two Contracting Parties, recording the fact that they have renounced war as an instrument of national policy in their mutual relations, reciprocally undertake to refrain from taking any aggressive action against or invading the territory of the other party, either alone or in conjunction with other Powers.

Any act of violence attacking the integrity and inviolability of the territory or the political independence of the other Contracting Party shall be regarded as contrary to the undertakings contained in the present Article, even if such acts are committed without declaration of war and avoid all warlike manifestations as far as possible.

Article II. Should one of the Contracting Parties be attacked by a third State or by a group of other States, the other Contracting Party undertakes not to give aid or assistance, either directly or indirectly, to the aggressor State during the whole period of the conflict.

Should one of the Contracting Parties commit an act of aggression against a third State, the other Contracting Party shall have the right to denounce the present Pact without notice.

Article III. Each of the Contracting Parties undertakes not to be a party to any agreement openly hostile to the other party from the point of view of aggression.

Article IV. The undertakings provided for in Articles I and II of the present Pact shall in no case limit or modify the international rights and obligations of each Contracting Party under agreements concluded by it before the coming into force of the present Pact, so far as the said agreements contain no aggressive elements.

Article V. The two Contracting Parties, desirous of settling and solving, exclusively by peaceful means, any disputes and differences, of whatever nature or origin, which may arise between them, undertake to submit questions at issue, which it has not been possible to settle within a reasonable period by diplomacy, to a procedure of conciliation, in accordance with the provisions of the Convention for the application of the procedure of conciliation which constitutes an integral part of the present Pact and shall be signed separately and ratified as soon as possible simultaneously with the Pact of Non-Aggression.

Article VI. The present Pact shall be ratified as soon as possible, and the instruments of ratification shall be exchanged at Warsaw within thirty days following the ratification by Poland and U.S.S.R., after which the Pact shall come into force immediately.

Article VII. The Pact is concluded for three years. If it is not denounced by one of the Contracting Parties, after previous notice of not less than six months before the expiry of that period, it shall be automatically renewed for a further period of two years.

Article VIII. The present Pact is drawn up in Polish and Russian, both texts being authentic.

Protocol of Signature (I)

The Contracting Parties declare that Article VII of the Pact of July 25, 1932 may not be interpreted as meaning that the expiry of the time limit of denunciation before the expiry of the time period under Article VII could have as a result the limitation or cancellation of the obligations arising out of the Pact of Paris of 1928.

Protocol of Signature (II)

On signing the Pact of Non-Aggression this day, the two parties, having exchanged their views on the draft Conciliation Convention submitted by the Soviet Party, declare that they are convinced that there is no essential difference of opinion between them.

Protocol prolonging the Pact of Non-Aggression, 25 July 1932, with Final Protocol, 5 May 1934

The Central Executive Committee of U.S.S.R. and the President of the Republic of Poland; being desirous of providing as firm a basis as possible for the development of the relations between their countries; being desirous of giving each other fresh proof of the unchangeable character and solidity of the pacific and friendly relations happily established between them; moved by the desire to contribute to the consolidation of world peace and to the stability and peaceful development of international relations in Eastern Europe; noting that the conclusion on July 25, 1932 at Moscow of the Treaty between U.S.S.R. and the Republic of Poland has had a beneficial influence on the development of their relations and on the solution of the above-mentioned problems; have decided to sign the present Protocol and have ... agreed on the following provisions:

Article I. In modification of the provisions of Article VII of the Treaty of Non-Aggression concluded at Moscow on July 25, 1932 between U.S.S.R. and the Republic of Poland concerning the date and manner in which that Treaty shall cease to have effect, the two Contracting Parties decide that it shall remain in force until December 31, 1945.

Each of the High Contracting Parties shall be entitled to denounce the Treaty by giving notice to that effect six months before the expiry of the above-mentioned period. If the Treaty is not denounced by either of the Contracting Parties, its period of validity shall be automatically prolonged for two years; similarly, the Treaty shall be regarded as prolonged on each occasion for a further period of two years, if it is not denounced by either of the Contracting Parties in the manner provided for in the present Article.

Article II. The present Protocol is drawn up in duplicate, each copy being in the Russian and Polish languages and both texts being equally authentic.

The present Protocol shall be ratified as soon as possible, and the instruments of ratification shall be exchanged between the Contracting Parties at Warsaw.

The present Protocol shall come into force on the date of the exchange of the instruments of ratification.

Final Protocol

In connection with the signature on this date of the Protocol prolonging the Treaty of Non-Aggression between the U.S.S.R. and the Republic of Poland of July 25, 1932, each of the High Contracting Parties, having again examined all the provisions of the Peace Treaty concluded at Riga on March 18, 1921, which constitutes the basis of their mutual relations, declares that it has no obligations and is not bound by any declarations inconsistent with the provisions of the said Peace Treaty in particular of Article III thereof.

Consequently, the Government of U.S.S.R. confirms that the Note from the People's Commissar, G. V. Chicherin, of September 28, 1926, to the Lithuanian Government cannot be interpreted to mean that that Note implied any intention on the part of the Soviet Socialist Government to interfere in the settlement of the territorial questions mentioned therein.

Joint Soviet–Polish Statement, 26 November 1938

A series of conversations recently held between the U.S.S.R. People's Commissar for Foreign Affairs, M. Litvinov, and the Polish Ambassador in Moscow, M. Grzybowski, has led to the following statement:

1. Relations between the Polish Republic and U.S.S.R. are and will continue to be based to the fullest extent on all the existing Agreements, including the Polish–Soviet Pact of Non-Aggression dated July 25, 1932. This Pact, concluded for five years and extended on May 5, 1934 for a further period ending December 31, 1945, has a basis wide enough to guarantee the inviolability of peaceful relations between the two States.

2. Both Governments are favourable to the extension of their commercial relations.

3. Both Governments agree that it is necessary to settle a number of current and longstanding matters that have arisen in connection with the various Agreements in force and, in particular, to dispose of the various frontier incidents that have recently been occurring.

Protocol of Signature

...

2. The High Contracting Parties declare that subsequent denunciation of the present Treaty before its termination or annulment shall neither cancel nor restrict the undertakings arising from the Pact for the Renunciation of War signed at Paris on August 27, 1928.

Pact of Non-Aggression between the Soviet Union and France, 29 November 1932

[A Conciliation Convention was signed at the same time.]

The President of the French Republic and the Central Executive Committee of U.S.S.R.; animated by the desire to consolidate peace; convinced that it is in the interests of both High Contracting Parties to improve and develop relations between the two countries; mindful of the international undertakings which they have previously assumed and none of which, they declare, constitutes an obstacle to the pacific development of their mutual relations or is inconsistent with the present Treaty; desirous of confirming and defining, so far as concerns their respective relations, the General Pact of August 27, 1928 for the renunciation of war; ... have agreed on the following provisions:

Article I. Each of the High Contracting Parties undertakes with regard to the other not to resort in any case, whether alone or jointly with one or more third Powers, either to war or to any aggression by land, sea or air against that other party, and to respect the inviolability of the territories which are placed under the party's sovereignty or which it represents in external relations or for whose administration it is responsible.

Article II. Should either High Contracting Party be the object of aggression by one or more third Powers, the other High Contracting Party undertakes not to give aid or assistance, either directly or indirectly, to the aggressor or aggressors during the period of the conflict.

Should either High Contracting Party resort to aggression against a third Power, the other High Contracting Party may denounce the present Treaty without notice.

Article III. The undertakings set forth in Articles I and II above shall in no way limit or modify the rights or obligations of each Contracting Party under agreements concluded by it before the coming into force of the present Treaty, each Party hereby declaring further that it is not bound by any agreement involving an obligation for it to participate in aggression by a third State.

Article IV. Each of the High Contracting Parties undertakes, for the duration of the present Treaty, not to become a party to any international agreement of which the effect in practice would be to prevent the purchase of goods from or the sale of goods or the granting of credits to the other party, and not to take any measure which would result in the exclusion of the other party from any participation in its foreign trade.

Article V. Each of the High Contracting Parties undertakes to respect in every connection the sovereignty or authority of the other party over the whole of that party's territories as defined in Article I of the present Treaty, not to interfere in any way in its internal affairs, and to abstain more particularly from action of any kind calculated to promote or encourage agitation, propaganda or attempted intervention designed to prejudice its territorial integrity or to transform by force the political or social régime of all or part of its territories.

Each of the High Contracting Parties undertakes in particular not to create, protect, equip, subsidize or admit in its territory either military organizations for the purpose of armed combat with the other party or organizations assuming the role of government or representing all or part of its territories.

Article VI. The High Contracting Parties having already recognized, in the General Pact of August 27, 1928 for the renunciation of war, that the settlement or solution of all disputes or conflicts, of whatever nature or of whatever origin they may be, which may arise among them, shall never be sought except by pacific means, confirm that provision, and, in order to give effect to it, annex to the present Treaty a Convention relating to conciliation procedure.

Article VII. The present Treaty, of which the French and Russian texts shall both be authentic, shall be ratified, and the ratifications thereof shall be exchanged at Moscow. It shall enter into effect on the date of the said exchange and shall remain in force for the period of one year as from the date on which either High Contracting Party shall have notified the other of its intention to denounce it. Such notification may not, however, be given before the expiry of a period of two years from the date of the entry into force of the present Treaty.

Treaty of Non-Aggression between the Soviet Union and Finland, 21 January 1932

The Central Executive Committee of U.S.S.R. on the one part, and the President of the Republic of Finland on the other part, actuated by the desire to contribute to the maintenance of general peace; being convinced that the conclusion of the undertakings mentioned below and the pacific settlement of any dispute whatsoever between U.S.S.R. and the Republic of Finland is in the interests of both High Contracting Parties and will contribute towards the development of friendly and neighbourly relations between the two countries; declaring that none of the international obligations which they have hitherto assumed debars the pacific development of their mutual relations or is incompatible with the present Treaty; being desirous of confirming and completing the General Pact of August 27, 1928 for the renunciation of war; have resolved to conclude the present Treaty ... and have agreed upon the following provisions:

Article I. 1. The High Contracting Parties mutually guarantee the inviolability of the frontiers existing between U.S.S.R. and the Republic of Finland, as fixed by the Treaty of Peace concluded at Dorpat on October 14, 1920, which shall remain the firm foundation of their relations, and reciprocally undertake to refrain from any act of aggression directed against each other.

2. Any act of violence attacking the integrity and inviolability of the territory or the political independence of the other High Contracting Party shall be regarded as an act of aggression, even if it is committed without declaration of war and avoids warlike manifestations.

PROTOCOL TO ARTICLE I. In conformity with the provisions of Article IV of the present Treaty, the Agreement of June 1, 1922 regarding measures ensuring the inviolability of the frontiers shall not be affected by the provisions of the present Treaty and shall continue to remain fully in force.

Article II. 1. Should either High Contracting Party be the object of aggression on the part of one or more third Powers, the other High Contracting Party undertakes to maintain neutrality throughout the duration of the conflict.

2. Should either High Contracting Party resort to aggression against a third Power, the other High Contracting Party may denounce the present Treaty without notice.

Article III. Each of the High Contracting Parties undertakes not to become a party to any treaty, agreement or convention which is openly hostile to the other party or contrary, whether formally or in substance, to the present Treaty.

Article IV. The obligations mentioned in the preceding Articles of the present Treaty may in no case affect or modify the international rights or obligations of the High Contracting Parties under agreements concluded or undertakings assumed before the coming into force of the present Treaty, in so far as such agreements contain no elements of aggression within the meaning of the present Treaty.

Article V. The High Contracting Parties declare that they will always endeavour to settle in a spirit of justice any disputes of whatever nature or origin which may arise between them, and will resort exclusively to pacific means of settling such disputes. For this purpose, the High Contracting Parties undertake to submit any disputes which may arise between them after the signature of the present Treaty, and which it may not have been possible to settle through diplomatic proceedings within a reasonable time, to a procedure of conciliation before a joint conciliation commission whose powers, composition and working shall be fixed by a special supplementary Convention, which shall form an integral part of the present Treaty and which the High Contracting Parties undertake to conclude as soon as possible and in any event before the present Treaty is ratified. Conciliation procedure shall also be applied in the event of any dispute as to the application or interpretation of a Convention concluded between the High Contracting Parties, and particularly the question whether the mutual undertaking as to non-aggression has or has not been violated.

[*Articles VI and VII*. Ratification.]

[*Article VIII*. Treaty concluded for three years, automatically renewed for a further two years unless six months' notice of termination is given.]

Convention concluded between the Soviet Union, Afghanistan, Estonia, Latvia, Persia, Poland and Rumania regarding the definition of aggression, 3 July 1933

[A similar Convention was concluded by the Soviet Union, Rumania, Turkey and Yugoslavia on 4 July 1933.]

...

Article II. Accordingly, the aggressor in an international conflict shall, subject to the agreement in force between the parties to the dispute, be considered to be that State which is the first to commit any of the following actions:

1. Declaration of war upon another State;

2. Invasion by its armed forces, with or without a declaration of war, of the territory of another State;

3. Attack by its land, naval or air forces, with or without a declaration of war, on the territory, vessels or aircraft of another State;

4. Naval blockade of the coasts or ports of another State;

5. Provision of support to armed bands formed in its territory which have invaded the territory of another State, or refusal, notwithstanding the request of the invaded State, to take in its own territory all the measures in its power to deprive those bands of all assistance or protection.

No political, military, economic or other considerations may serve as an excuse or justification for the aggression referred to in Article II. (For examples, see Annex.)

Annex

The High Contracting Parties signatories of the Convention relating to the definition of aggression; desiring, subject to the express reservation that the absolute validity of the rule laid down in Article III of that Convention shall be in no way restricted, to furnish certain indications for determining the aggressor; declare that no act of aggression within the meaning of Article II of that Convention can be justified on either of the following grounds, among others:

A. The internal condition of a State: e.g. its political, economic or social structure; alleged defects in its administration; disturbances due to strikes, revolutions, counter-revolutions or civil war.

B. The international conduct of a State: e.g. the violation or threatened violation of the material or moral rights or interests of a foreign State or its nationals; the rupture of diplomatic or economic relations; economic or financial boycotts; disputes relating to economic, financial or other obligations towards foreign States; frontier incidents not forming any of the cases of aggression specified in Article II.

The High Contracting Parties further agree to recognize that the present Convention can never make legitimate any violations of international law that may be implied in the circumstances comprised in the above list.

Baltic Entente between Lithuania, Estonia and Latvia, 3 November 1934

Article 1. In order to coordinate their efforts in the cause of peace, the three Governments undertake to confer together on questions of foreign policy which are of common concern and to afford one another mutual political and diplomatic assistance in their international relations.

Article 2. For the purpose set forth in Article 1, the High Contracting Parties hereby decide to institute periodical conferences of the Ministers for Foreign Affairs of the three countries, to take place at regular intervals, at least twice a year, in the territories of each of the three States in turn. At the request of one of the High Contracting Parties and by joint agreement, extraordinary conferences may be held in the territory of one of the three States or elsewhere. . . .

Article 3. The High Contracting Parties recognize the existence of the specific problems which might make a concerted attitude with regard to them difficult. They agree that such problems constitute an exception to the undertakings laid down in Article 1 of the present Treaty.

Article 4. The High Contracting Parties shall endeavour to settle amicably and in a spirit of justice and equity any questions in respect of which their interests may clash and also to do so in the shortest possible time. . . .

Treaty of Mutual Assistance between the Soviet Union and France, 2 May 1935

The Central Executive Committee of U.S.S.R. and the President of the French Republic, being desirous of strengthening peace in Europe and of guaranteeing its benefits to their respective countries by securing a fuller and stricter application of those provisions of the Covenant of the League of Nations which are designed to maintain the national security, territorial integrity and political independence of States; determined to devote their efforts to the preparation and conclusion of a European agreement for that purpose and in the meantime to promote, as far as lies in their power, the effective application of the provisions of the Covenant of the League of Nations; have resolved to conclude a Treaty to this end and have appointed as their pleni-potentiaries . . . and have agreed upon the following provisions:

Article I. In the event of France or U.S.S.R. being threatened with or in danger of aggression on the part of any European State, U.S.S.R. and reciprocally France undertake mutually to proceed to an immediate consultation as regards the measures to be taken for the observance of the provisions of Article X of the Covenant of the League of Nations.

Article II. Should, in the circumstances specified in Article XV, paragraph 7, of the Covenant of the League of Nations, France or U.S.S.R. be the object, notwithstanding the sincerely peaceful intentions of both countries, of an unprovoked aggression on the part of a European State, U.S.S.R. and reciprocally France shall immediately come to each other's aid and assistance.

Article III. In consideration of the fact that under Article XVI of the Covenant of the League of Nations any member of the League which resorts to war in disregard of its covenants under Articles XII, XIII or XV of the Covenant is *ipso facto* deemed to have committed an act of war against all other members of the League, France and reciprocally U.S.S.R. undertake, in the event of one of them being the object, in these conditions and notwithstanding the sincerely peaceful intentions of both countries, of an unprovoked aggression on the part of a European State, immediately to come to each other's aid and assistance in application of Article XVI of the Covenant.

The same obligation is assumed in the event of France or U.S.S.R. being the object of an aggression on the part of a European State in the circumstances specified in Article XVII, paragraphs 1 and 3, of the Covenant of the League of Nations.

Article IV. The undertakings stipulated above being consonant with the obligations of the High Contracting Parties as members of the League of Nations, nothing in the present Treaty shall be interpreted as restricting the duty of the latter to take any action that may be deemed wise and effectual to safeguard the peace of the world, or as restricting the obligations resulting for the High Contracting Parties from the Covenant of the League of Nations.

[*Article V*. Ratification to be exchanged as soon as possible. Treaty to remain in force for five years unless denounced by either party giving at least one year's notice; at end of five years the Treaty to continue indefinitely, each party being at liberty to terminate it with one year's notice.]

Protocol of Signature

Upon proceeding to the signature of the Franco-Soviet Treaty of Mutual Assistance of today's date the plenipotentiaries have signed the following Protocol, which shall be included in the exchange of ratifications of the Treaty.

1. It is agreed that the effect of Article III is to oblige each Contracting Party immediately to come to the assistance of the other by immediately complying with the recommendations of the Council of the League of Nations as soon as they have been issued in virtue of Article XVI of the Covenant. It is further agreed that the two Contracting Parties will act in concert to insure that the Council shall issue the said recommendations with all the speed required by the circumstances, and that should the Council nevertheless, for whatever reason, issue no recommendation or fail to reach a unanimous decision, effect shall none the less be given to the obligation to render assistance. It is also agreed that the undertakings to render assistance mentioned in the present Treaty refer only to the case of an aggression committed against either Contracting Party's own territory.

2. It being the common intention of the two Governments in no way to contradict, by the present Treaty, undertakings previously assumed toward third States by France and by U.S.S.R. in virtue of published treaties, it is agreed that effect shall not be given to the provisions of the said Treaty in a manner which, being incompatible with treaty obligations assumed by one of the Contracting Parties, would expose that party to sanctions of an international character.

3. The two Governments, deeming it desirable that a regional agreement should be concluded aiming at organizing security between Contracting States, and which might moreover embody or be accompanied by pledges of mutual assistance, recognize their right to become parties by mutual consent, should

occasion arise, to similar agreements in any form, direct or indirect, that may seem appropriate, the obligations under these various agreements to take the place of those assumed under the present Treaty.

4. The two Governments place on record the fact that the negotiations which have resulted in the signature of the present Treaty were originally undertaken with a view to supplementing a security agreement embracing the countries of north-eastern Europe, namely, U.S.S.R., Germany, Czechoslovakia, Poland and the Baltic States which are neighbours of U.S.S.R.; in addition to that agreement, there was to have been concluded a treaty of assistance between U.S.S.R. and France and Germany, by which each of those three States was to have undertaken to come to the assistance of any one of them which might be the object of aggression on the part of any other of those three States. Although circumstances have not hitherto permitted the conclusion of those agreements, which both parties continue to

regard as desirable, it is nonetheless the case that the undertakings stipulated in the Franco-Soviet Treaty of Assistance are to be understood as intended to apply only within the limits contemplated in the three-party agreement previously planned. Independently of the obligations assumed under the present Treaty, it is further recalled that, in accordance with the Franco-Soviet Pact of Non-Aggression signed on November 29, 1932, and moreover, without affecting the universal character of the undertakings assumed in the Pact, in the event of either party becoming the object of aggression by one or more third European Powers not referred to in the above-mentioned three-party agreement, the other Contracting Party is bound to abstain, during the period of the conflict, from giving any aid or assistance, either direct or indirect, to the aggressor or aggressors, each party declaring further that it is not bound by any assistance agreement which would be contrary to this undertaking.

Treaty of Mutual Assistance between the Soviet Union and Czechoslovakia, 16 May 1935

The President of the Czechoslovak Republic and the Central Executive Committee of the U.S.S.R.; being desirous of strengthening peace in Europe and of guaranteeing its benefits to their respective countries by securing a fuller and stricter application of those provisions of the Covenant of the League of Nations which are designed to maintain the national security, territorial integrity and political independence of States; determined to devote their efforts to the preparation and conclusion of a European agreement for that purpose, and in the meantime to promote, as far as lies in their power, the effective application

of the provisions of the Covenant of the League of Nations; have resolved to conclude a Treaty to this end and have appointed as their plenipotentiaries:

The President of the Czechoslovak Republic: Eduard Benes, Minister for Foreign Affairs;

The Central Executive Committee of U.S.S.R.: Sergei Alexandrovsky, Envoy Extraordinary and Minister Plenipotentiary of the U.S.S.R.;

. . . and have agreed upon the following provisions:

Article I. In the event of the Czechoslovak Republic or U.S.S.R. being threatened with, or in danger of, aggression on the part of any European State, U.S.S.R. and reciprocally the Czechoslovak Republic undertake mutually to proceed to an immediate consultation as regards the measures to be taken for the observance of the provisions of Article X of the Covenant of the League of Nations.

Article II. Should, in the circumstances specified in Article XV, paragraph 7, of the Covenant of the League of Nations, the Czechoslovak Republic or U.S.S.R. be the object, notwithstanding the sincerely peaceful intentions of both countries, of an unprovoked aggression on the part of a European State, U.S.S.R. and reciprocally the Czechoslovak Republic shall immediately come to each other's aid and assistance.

Article III. In consideration of the fact that under Article XVI of the Covenant of the League of Nations any member of the League which resorts to war in disregard of its covenants under Articles XII, XIII or XV of the Covenant is *ipso facto* deemed to have committed an act of war against all other members of the League, the Czechoslovak Republic and reciprocally U.S.S.R. undertake, in the event of one of them being the object, in these conditions and notwithstanding the sincerely peaceful intentions of both countries, of an unprovoked aggression on the part of a European State, immediately to come to each other's aid and assistance in application of Article XVI of the Covenant.

The same obligation is assumed in the event of the Czechoslovak Republic or U.S.S.R. being the object of an aggression on the part of a European State in the circumstances specified in Article XVII, paragraphs 1 and 3, of the Covenant of the League of Nations.

Article IV. Without prejudice to the preceding provisions of the present Treaty, it is stipulated that should either of the High Contracting Parties become the object of an aggression on the part of

one or more third Powers in conditions not giving ground for aid or assistance within the meaning of the present Treaty, the other High Contracting Party undertakes not to lend, for the duration of the conflict, aid or assistance, either directly or indirectly, to the aggressor or aggressors. Each High Contracting Party further declares that it is not bound by any other agreement for assistance which is incompatible with the present undertaking.

Article V. The undertakings stipulated above being consonant with the obligations of the High Contracting Parties as members of the League of Nations, nothing in the present Treaty shall be interpreted as restricting the duty of the latter to take any action that may be deemed wise and effectual to safeguard the peace of the world or as restricting the obligations resulting for the High Contracting Parties from the Covenant of the League of Nations.

Article VI. The present Treaty, both the Czechoslovak and the Russian texts whereof shall be equally authentic, shall be ratified and the instruments of ratification shall be exchanged at Moscow as soon as possible. It shall be registered with the Secretariat of the League of Nations.

It shall take effect as soon as the ratifications have been exchanged and shall remain in force for five years. If it is not denounced by either of the High Contracting Parties giving notice thereof at least one year before the expiry of that period, it shall remain in force indefinitely, each of the High Contracting Parties being at liberty to terminate it at a year's notice by a declaration to that effect.

Protocol of Signature

Upon proceeding to the signature of the Treaty of Mutual Assistance between the Czechoslovak Republic and U.S.S.R. of today's date, the plenipotentiaries have signed the following Protocol, which shall be included in the exchange of ratifications of the Treaty.

I. It is agreed that the effect of Article III is to oblige each Contracting Party immediately to come to the assistance of the other by immediately complying with the recommendations of the Council of the League of Nations as soon as they have been issued in virtue of Article XVI of the Covenant. It is further agreed that the two Contracting Parties will act in concert to ensure that the Council shall issue the said recommendations with all the speed required by the circumstances and that, should the Council nevertheless, for whatever reason, issue no recommendation or fail to reach a unanimous decision, effect shall none the less be given to the obligation to render assistance. It is also agreed that the undertakings to render assistance mentioned in the present Treaty refer only to the case of an aggression committed against either Contracting Party's own territory.

II. The two Governments declare that the undertakings laid down in Articles I, II and III of the present Treaty, concluded with a view to promoting the estab-lishment in Eastern Europe of a regional system of security, inaugurated by the Franco-Soviet Treaty of May 2, 1935, will be restricted within the same limits as were laid down in paragraph 4 of the Protocol of signature of the said Treaty. At the same time, the two Governments recognize that the undertakings to render mutual assistance will operate between them only in so far as the conditions laid down in the present Treaty may be fulfilled and in so far as assistance may be rendered by France to the party victim of the aggression.

III. The two Governments, deeming it desirable that a regional agreement should be concluded aiming at organizing security between Contracting States, and which might moreover embody or be accompanied by pledges of mutual assistance, recognize their right to become parties by mutual consent, should occasion arise, to similar agreements in any form, direct or indirect, that may seem appropriate; the obligations under these various agreements to take the place of those resulting from the present Treaty.

Convention between Japan and the Soviet Union, Peking, 20 January 1925

Japan and U.S.S.R., desiring to promote relations of good neighbourhood and economic cooperation between them, have resolved to conclude a Convention embodying basic rules in regulation of such relations and, to that end, have agreed as follows:

Article I. The High Contracting Parties agree that with the coming into force of the present Convention, diplomatic and consular relations shall be established between them.

Article II. U.S.S.R. agrees that the Treaty of Portsmouth of September 5, 1905, shall remain in force.

It is agreed that the treaties, conventions and agreements other than the said Treaty of Portsmouth, which were concluded between Japan and Russia prior to November 7, 1917, shall be re-examined at a conference to be subsequently held between the Governments of the High Contracting Parties and are liable to revision or annulment as altered circumstances may require.

Article III. The Governments of the High Contracting Parties agree that upon the coming into force of the present Convention, they shall proceed to the revision of the Fishery Convention of 1907, taking into consideration such changes as may have taken place in the general conditions since the conclusion of the said Fishery Convention.

Pending the conclusion of a convention so revised, the Government of U.S.S.R. shall maintain the practice established in 1924 relating to the lease of fishery lots to Japanese subjects.

Article IV. The Governments of the High Contracting Parties agree that upon the coming into force of the present Convention, they shall proceed to the conclusion of a treaty of commerce and navigation in conformity with the principles hereunder mentioned, and that, pending the conclusion of such a treaty, the general intercourse between the two countries shall be regulated by those principles. . . .

Article V. The High Contracting Parties solemnly affirm their desire and intention to live in peace and amity with each other, scrupulously to respect the undoubted right of a State to order its own life within its own jurisdiction in its own way, to refrain and to restrain all persons in any governmental service for them, and all organizations in receipt of any financial assistance from them, from any act overt or covert liable in any way whatsoever to endanger the order and security in any part of the territories of Japan or U.S.S.R.

It is further agreed that neither Contracting Party shall permit the presence in the territories under its jurisdiction: (a) of organizations or groups pretending to be the Government for any part of the territories of the other party, or (b) of alien subjects or citizens who may be found to be actually carrying on political activities for such organizations or groups.

Article VI. In the interest of promoting economic relations between the two countries, and taking into consideration the needs of Japan with regard to natural resources, the Government of U.S.S.R. is willing to grant to Japanese subjects, companies and associations, concessions for the exploitation of minerals, forests and other natural resources in all the territories of U.S.S.R.

[*Article VII.* Ratification.]

Protocol A

Japan and U.S.S.R., in proceeding this day to the signature of the Convention embodying basic rules of the relations between them, have deemed it advisable to regulate certain questions in relation to the said Convention, and have, through their respective plenipotentiaries, agreed upon the following stipulations:

Article I. Each of the High Contracting Parties undertakes to place in the possession of the other party the movable and immovable property belonging to the embassy under consulates of such other party and actually existing within its own territories. . . .

Article II. It is agreed that all questions of the debts due to the Government of subjects of Japan on account of public loans and treasury bills issued by the former Russian Governments, to wit, by the Imperial Government of Russia and the Provisional Government which succeeded it, are reserved for adjustment at subsequent negotiations between the Government of Japan and the Government of U.S.S.R.: provided that in the adjustment of such question, the Government or subjects of Japan shall not, all other conditions being equal, be placed in any position less favourable than that which the Government of U.S.S.R. may accord to the Government or nationals of any other country on similar questions.

It is also agreed that all questions relating to claims of the Government of either party to the Government of the other, or of the nationals of either party to the Government of the other, are reserved for adjustment at subsequent negotiations between the Government of Japan and the Government of U.S.S.R.

Article III. In view of climatic conditions in Northern Sakhalin preventing the immediate homeward transportation of

Japanese troops now stationed there, these troops shall be completely withdrawn from the said region by May 15, 1925.

Such withdrawal shall be commenced as soon as climatic conditions will permit, and any and all districts in Northern Sakhalin so evacuated by Japanese troops shall immediately thereupon be restored in full sovereignty to the proper authorities of U.S.S.R. . . .

Article IV. The High Contracting Parties mutually declare that there actually exists no treaty or agreement of military alliance nor any other secret agreement which either of them has entered into with any third party and which constitutes an infringement upon, or a menace to, the sovereignty, territorial rights or national safety of the other Contracting Party.

Article V. The present Protocol is to be considered as ratified with the ratification of the Convention embodying basic rules of the relations between Japan and U.S.S.R., signed under the same date.

Protocol B

The High Contracting Parties have agreed upon the following as the basis for the concession contracts to be concluded within five months from the date of the complete evacuation of Northern Sakhalin by Japanese troops, as provided for in Article III of Protocol A signed this day between the plenipotentiaries of Japan and of U.S.S.R.

Article 1. The Government of U.S.S.R. agrees to grant to Japanese concerns recommended by the Government of Japan the concession for the exploitation of 50 per cent, in area, of the oil fields in Northern Sakhalin which are mentioned in the Memorandum submitted to the representative of the Union by the Japanese representative on August 29, 1924. . . .

Article 2. The Government of U.S.S.R. also agrees to authorize Japanese concerns recommended by the Government of Japan to prospect oil fields, for a period of from five to ten years, on the eastern coast of Northern Sakhalin over an area of one thousand square versts to be selected within one year after the conclusion of the concession contracts, and in case oil fields shall have been established in consequence of such prospecting by the Japanese, the concession for the exploitation of 50 per cent, in area, of the oil fields so established shall be granted to the Japanese.

Article 3. The Government of U.S.S.R. agrees to grant to Japanese concerns recommended by the Government of Japan the concession for the exploitation of coal fields on the western coast of Northern Sakhalin over a specific area which shall be determined in the concession contracts.

The Government of U.S.S.R. further agrees to grant to such Japanese concerns the concession regarding coal fields in the Doue district over a specific area to be determined in the concession contracts.

With regard to the coal fields outside the specific areas mentioned in the preceding two paragraphs, it is also agreed that should the Government of U.S.S.R. decide to offer them for foreign concession, Japanese concerns shall be afforded equal opportunity in the matter of such concession.

Article 4. The period of the concession for the exploitation of oil and coal fields stipulated in the preceding paragraphs shall be from forty to fifty years.

Article 5. As royalty for the said concessions, the Japanese concessionaires shall make over annually to the Government of U.S.S.R., in case of coal fields, from 5 to 8 per cent of their gross output and, in case of oil fields, from 5 to 15 per cent of their gross output. . . .

Declaration

In proceeding this day to the signature of the Convention embodying basic rules of the relations between U.S.S.R. and Japan, the undersigned plenipotentiary of U.S.S.R. has the honour to declare that the recognition by the Government of

U.S.S.R. of the validity of the Treaty of Portsmouth of September 5, 1905 does not in any way signify that the Government of the Union shares with the former Tsarist Government the political responsibility for the conclusion of the said Treaty.

. . .

Agreement on the sale of Chinese Eastern Railway to Manchukuo, Tokyo, 23 March 1935

Manchukuo and U.S.S.R., being desirous of settling the question of the North Manchuria Railway (Chinese Eastern Railway) and thus to contribute to the safeguarding of peace in the Far East, have resolved to conclude an Agreement for the cession to Manchukuo of the rights of U.S.S.R. concerning the North Manchuria Railway (Chinese Eastern Railway), and have . . . agreed upon the following Articles:

Article I. The Government of U.S.S.R. will cede to the Government of Manchukuo all the rights it possesses over the North Manchuria Railway (Chinese Eastern Railway), in consideration of which the Government of Manchukuo will pay to the Government of U.S.S.R. the sum of one hundred and forty million (140,000,000) yen in Japanese currency.

Article II. All the rights of the Government of U.S.S.R. concerning the North Manchuria Railway (Chinese Eastern Railway) will pass to the Government of Manchukuo upon the coming into force of the present Agreement, and at the same time the North Manchuria Railway (Chinese Eastern Railway) will be placed under the complete occupation and the sole management of the Government of Manchukuo.

Article III. 1. Upon the coming into force of the present Agreement, the senior members of the administration of the North Manchuria Railway (Chinese Eastern Railway) who are citizens of U.S.S.R. will be released from their duties. The said senior members of the administration of the railway will hand over all the archives, records, papers and documents of whatever description in their charge to their respective successors in the new administration of the railway . . . [administrative and financial details].

Protocol of Mutual Assistance between the Mongolian People's Republic and the Soviet Union, Ulan Bator, 12 March 1936

The Governments of U.S.S.R. and the Mongolian People's Republic, taking into consideration the unalterable friendship that has existed between their countries since the liberation of the territory of the Mongolian People's Republic in 1921, with the support of the Red Army, from the White Guard detachments and the military forces with which the latter were connected and which invaded Soviet Territory, and desirous of supporting the cause of peace in the Far East and further strengthening the friendly relations between their countries, have decided to set forth in the form of the present Protocol the gentlemen's agreement existing between them since November 27, 1934, providing for mutual assistance in every possible manner in the matter of averting and preventing the danger of military attack and for support in the event of an attack by any third party on U.S.S.R. or the Mongolian People's Republic, and for these purposes have signed the present Protocol.

Article I. In the event of the threat of an attack on the territory of the Mongolian or Soviet Socialist Republics by a third country, the Governments of U.S.S.R. and the Mongolian People's Republic undertake to confer immediately regarding the situation and to adopt all measures that may be necessary for the protection and safety of their territories.

Article II. The Governments of U.S.S.R. and the Mongolian People's Republic undertake, in the event of a military attack on one of the Contracting Parties, to render each other every assistance, including military assistance.

Article III. The Governments of U.S.S.R. and the Mongolian People's Republic are in full understanding that the troops of either country will be sent into the territory of the other in accordance with a mutual agreement and in accordance with Articles I and II of this Protocol, and will immediately be withdrawn from that territory as soon as the period of necessity is over, as took place in 1925 when Soviet troops retired from the territory of the Mongolian People's Republic.

...

Treaty of Non-Aggression between China and the Soviet Union, Moscow, 21 August 1937

The National Government of the Republic of China and the Government of U.S.S.R., animated by the desire to contribute to the maintenance of general peace, to consolidate the amicable relations now existing between them on a firm and lasting basis, and to confirm in a more precise manner the obligations mutually undertaken under the Treaty for the Renunciation of War, signed in Paris on August 27, 1928, have resolved to conclude the present Treaty and have ... agreed on the following Articles:

Article I. The two High Contracting Parties solemnly reaffirm that they condemn recourse to war for the solution of international controversies, and that they renounce it as an instrument of national policy in their relations with each other, and, in pursuance of this pledge, they undertake to refrain from any aggression against each other either individually or jointly with one or more other Powers.

Article II. In the event that either of the High Contracting Parties should be subjected to aggression on the part of one or more third Powers, the other High Contracting Party obligates itself not to render assistance of any kind, either directly or indirectly to such third Power or Powers at any time during the entire conflict, and also to refrain from taking any action or

entering into any agreement which may be used by the aggressor or aggressors to the disadvantage of the parties subjected to aggression.

Article III. The provisions of the present Treaty shall not be so interpreted as to affect or modify the rights and obligations arising, in respect of the High Contracting Parties, out of bilateral or multilateral treaties or agreements to which the High Contracting Parties are signatories and which were concluded prior to the entering into force of the present Treaty,

Article IV. The present Treaty is drawn up in duplicate in English. It comes into force on the day of signature by the above-mentioned plenipotentiaries and shall remain in force for a period of five years. Either of the High Contracting Parties may inform the other six months before the expiration of the period of its desire to terminate the Treaty. In case both parties fail to do so in time, the Treaty shall be considered as being automatically extended for a period of two years after the expiration of the first period. Should neither of the High Contracting Parties inform the other six months before the expiration of the two-year period of its desire to terminate the Treaty, it shall continue in force for another period of two years, and so on successively.

VI · The collapse of the territorial settlements of Versailles, 1931–8

The security of post-Versailles Europe rested on certain assumptions: a military balance that favoured France and Britain, and the maintenance of the provisions of the Versailles treaty. The Germany of the Weimar Republic had already succeeded in weakening the control and constraints imposed by the Versailles treaty. By 1930, the Allies had evacuated the Rhineland ahead of time, German armaments were no longer closely controlled and Germany was no longer diplomatically isolated. But all this had been achieved by Governments which were determined to avoid another collision with France and Britain and which did not openly flout the provisions of the Versailles treaty. With the coming to power of Hitler, German policy was set on a revolutionary Nazi course. Hitler rejected pre-1914 concepts of the successful National State expanding through piecemeal territorial conquests. To re-establish Germany as an equal Great Power, to 'rectify' the eastern frontier – these were not just ends he had in view; for Hitler they were stepping stones to creating a new European order, and beyond that a new world order based on race with the German 'Aryan' race at its apex.

From 1933 to 1938 Hitler laid the foundation for his wars of conquest: he openly defied the disarmament restrictions of Versailles, he remilitarized the Rhineland in 1936, and prepared the way for undermining the independence of Austria and Czechoslovakia through support of local Nazi movements. The ambitions of Japan in Asia and Italy in Africa, and the international division caused by the Spanish Civil War, Italy's conquest of Abyssinia, Western suspicion of Soviet ideological policies, and the effect of economic depression, all provided Hitler with opportunities for ruthless exploitation. The creditability of the League of Nations was shattered in the 1930s: it could not check aggression by the adoption of 'procedures' when the European Powers and the

United States lacked either the will or the means to do so. Such was the case when Japan decided to dominate Manchuria by force.

War in Manchuria, 1931–3: the League, China and Japan

Manchuria played an important role in the Great Power rivalries of eastern Asia during the first half of the twentieth century. No Chinese Central Government was able to gain complete control over this great region before the 1950s. From 1900 to 1904 Russia exerted predominant control; after the Russo-Japanese war, Japan secured what were formerly Russian privileges in the south, whilst Russian influence remained in the north. Even when in 1925, after the death of Sun Yat-sen, Chiang Kai-shek successfully asserted control over the greater part of China, the warlord Chang Hsueh-liang was able to maintain his power and local autonomy in Manchuria. The warlord also tried to lessen Soviet and Japanese influence by regaining control over the railway lines (the Soviet, Chinese Eastern Railway and the Japanese South Manchurian railway) running through the province. The Japanese reacted forcefully. Japanese troops in Manchuria took matters into their own hands. During the night of *18–19 September 1931 the Mukden incident* marked the beginning of the Japanese military occupation of southern Manchuria and fighting spread to the north. In September 1932 Japan signed a treaty giving *de jure* recognition to a puppet state, Manchukuo, which had been set up the previous February.

The Chinese appealed on 21 September 1931 to the League under Article 11. But at the League Palace of Nations in Geneva, effective action, it was believed, would depend on securing the practical cooperation of the United States against Japan. This the United States would not contemplate. Secretary of State Stimson, in a Note of 7 January 1932, would go no further than enunciating an American doctrine of non-recognition of situations created in defiance of specific treaty engagements.

The conflict in China spread to Shanghai in January 1932. The Chinese now also invoked Articles 10 and 15 of the League Covenant, which in the event of a breach being found would bring the sanction article (19) into force (p. 59).

The League was unable to bring about a Japanese withdrawal in compliance with a League resolution and so break the deadlock, and on 21 November 1931 it accepted a Japanese proposal to send to Manchuria a Commission of Enquiry. Lord Lytton headed the commission, which left in February 1932. On 11 March 1932 the League issued a Declaration similar to the non-recognition doctrine first formulated by Stimson. But the League did not proceed to sanctions. Instead of sanctions, it postponed concrete action by deciding to wait for the report of the Lytton Commission. The Lytton Report, when finally laid before the League on 1 October 1932, found that Japan had no valid reason for invading Manchuria and envisaged as a solution some form of Manchurian autonomy under Chinese sovereignty. To achieve a solution Lytton recommended a League effort at conciliation. While the League attempted to find a way out along these lines, the Japanese in January 1933 extended their aggression against China. In February 1933 at Geneva, meantime, the principles of the Lytton Report were accepted. The only action the League took against Japanese aggression was juridical in that it refused to recognize the State of Manchukuo. In protest, on 27 March 1933 the Japanese announced their intention of leaving the League. Soon after, China, abandoning all hope of practical help, acknowledged defeat. *On 31 May 1933 the Chinese and Japanese concluded the Tangku Truce* which provided for Chinese withdrawal from a demilitarized zone of 5,000 square miles on the Chinese side of the Great Wall. The League had thus failed to preserve one of its members from aggression by another member, which was a Great Power. Collective security in the face of aggression had proved ineffective.

Japan in the 1930s moved away from her traditional alignment with Britain and began to turn to Nazi Germany. As a further step to gain ascendancy over China, and also in order to warn off the Soviet Union, Japan signed the German-inspired *Anti-Comintern Pact, 25 November 1936* (p. 168).

Germany's military revival, 1933–6

The coming to power of Hitler as Chancellor on 30 January 1933 marked the beginning of a German policy that destroyed the European territorial settlements of Versailles in the West, the East and Central Europe within the space of eight years, and substituted for these settlements the continental hegemony of Germany. The years from 1933 to the spring of 1939 are therefore more notable for the breach of treaties than for the conclusion of new ones. Hitler utilized the Disarmament Conference to further his plan to rearm while others disarmed and, unable to gain the approval of Britain and France, withdrew from the conference and the *League of Nations on 14 October 1933.* He followed this by proclaiming his peaceful intentions towards Poland and towards any frontier revisions in the East, and a *German–Polish Treaty was concluded on 26 January 1934* (p. 169) renouncing the use of force for ten years. An Austrian Nazi coup, involving the assassination of the Austrian Chancellor Dolfuss on 25 July 1934, failed. Mussolini was still acting as the protector of Austrian independence.

In January 1935 a plebiscite was held in the Saar which voted to return to Germany;

this was Germany's first, albeit legal, increase of territory since the peace settlements. In the spring of 1935 Hitler risked the open repudiation of the military clauses of the Versailles treaty, announcing on 9 March 1935 that a German air force was in existence, and a week later on 16 March he declared that Germany would resume complete freedom in establishing offensive forces and announced the introduction of conscription. At the *Stresa Conference, 11–14 April 1935*, Britain, France and Italy condemned Germany's unilateral repudiation of her Versailles obligations, and their resolution to this effect was carried unanimously by the League Council. But three months later Britain agreed to German naval rearmament, though the British Government hoped it would be limited by the terms of the *Anglo-German Naval Agreement, 18 June 1935* (p. 166). Meantime *France and the Soviet Union had signed the Pact of Mutual Assistance, 2 May 1935* (p. 152). The Franco-Soviet treaty was ratified by the French Chamber of Deputies almost a year later on 27 February 1936; this gave Hitler the pretext to make a crucial breach in the Versailles military limitations on Germany, and on 7 March 1936 he remilitarized the Rhineland. He justified his action by a *Note on 7 March 1936* denouncing the Locarno pact as incompatible with the Franco-Soviet pact; that denunciation was coupled with proposals for various new peace pacts.

The formation of the Rome–Berlin Axis: Abyssinia, Spain and Austria, 1935–8

Mussolini planned to dominate Abyssinia as a first step on the road to making Italy a World Power. The Duce prepared the way by seeking agreement with France. On *7 January 1935* Laval, the French Foreign Minister, and Mussolini signed a *secret agreement in Rome* intended to settle Italian–French colonial disputes and designed to facilitate the united front against Germany. The Stresa Conference in April 1935 was the public affirmation of this unity of purpose. It was shortlived. The Anglo-German Naval Agreement of 18 June 1935 (p. 166) shattered Anglo-French solidarity. The French paid a price: the Franco-Italian understanding of 7 January 1935 was interpreted by Mussolini as giving him practically a free hand in his dealings with Abyssinia as far as France was concerned. After months of tension, *Italy invaded Abyssinia on 3 October 1935*. The League Council on 7 October 1935 in its report condemned Italy for aggression. Member States were now obliged to apply the sanctions of Article 16. But the League followed a 'double policy': economic sanctions were gradually applied, but France and Britain were encouraged to seek a settlement of the Abyssinian–Italian conflict, it being understood this would involve the loss of some Abyssinian territory. In December 1935 the British

Foreign Secretary, Sir Samuel Hoare, and Pierre Laval agreed on a plan to end the conflict, to be put to the belligerents. The Hoare–Laval plan envisaged widespread concessions to Italy at Abyssinia's expense, but it was received with such disapproval by public opinion in Britain that Prime Minister Baldwin had to disavow it. Conciliation efforts were dead. Mussolini proceeded with the conquest of Abyssinia. On 5 May 1936 Addis Ababa fell and Italy proclaimed the annexation of Abyssinia. Meantime sanctions were not effectively applied by the League. A decision on oil sanctions was constantly postponed – the one sanction that might have hurt Italy's military effort – and the Suez Canal was not closed to Italy. Collective security through the adoption of sanctions in the face of aggression had completely failed.

The *de jure* recognition of Italy's conquest of Abyssinia by the most important of the Western democracies, Britain, followed some two years later when on 16 November 1938 the British Government brought into force an *Anglo-Italian Agreement, concluded on 16 April 1938* and concerned with Italian intervention in Spain where another war – the Civil War – was being fought. In accordance with the agreement, Italy promised to withdraw her troops from Spain, but only when the war was over; then the agreement would come into force.

The Civil War had begun in mid-July 1936 with a military revolt led by General Franco against the Spanish Government. The Italians provided substantial help for General Franco through 'volunteer' troops, planes and armaments, with the Germans supplying armaments and the fighters and bombers that formed the 'Condor Legion', which fought under German command. Russia sent arms and planes to Republican Spain. An International Brigade of some 18,000, including large volunteer contingents from France, Italy, Germany, Austria and Britain fought for the Republic. Officially, Britain, France, as well as Italy, Germany and Russia accepted a policy of neutrality and non-intervention in the Spanish Civil War by the end of August 1936. During the months it functioned, the ban was openly flouted by Italy, Germany and the Soviet Union. But two Anglo-Italian agreements were concluded: on 2 January 1937, in the so-called 'Gentleman's Agreement', Italy and Britain disclaimed any desire to see modified the *status quo* as regards national sovereignty of territories in the Mediterranean region; and an agreement in March 1937 provided for the withdrawal of volunteers and the setting-up of an international blockade to report on breaches of the agreements reached on non-intervention. The policy of non-intervention was a failure. But when 'pirate' submarines, actually Italian submarines aiding Franco, attacked neutral ships including British ones, a conference of Mediterranean and Black Sea Powers met at Nyon, and *on 14 September 1937 signed the Agreement of Nyon* (p. 171) to defend neutral ships by sinking at sight suspicious submarines. The Governments effectively defended their own ships and interests. The Italians were Franco's main ally and helped him to win the Civil War by the spring of 1939.

March 1938 marked the demise of Austria, a member of the League of Nations, as a result of a German military invasion and a German proclamation of Anschluss or union with Germany. The way to Nazi dominance had been prepared by the *Austro-German Agreement, 11 July 1936* (p. 172). It committed Germany to a promise of respecting Austrian independence, but the Austrian Government was gravely weakened by having to admit Nazi sympathizers into the Government itself, by opening Austria to Nazi propaganda, and by conceding that Austrian foreign policy would be based on the principle that Austria was a 'German State'.

Austrian independence had rested partly on Italian support. The growing intimacy of Germany and Italy, partly the consequence of Italy's Abyssinian and Spanish policies, undermined Austria's independence. Italian–German cooperation was first set out in the *October Protocol, 1936*, on a number of issues. On 1 November 1936 in a speech at Milan, Mussolini referred to the existence of a Rome–Berlin axis. The treaty ties between Italy and Germany were drawn closer when Italy *on 6 November 1937 joined the Anti-Comintern Pact signed a year earlier by Germany and Japan* (p. 174) and they culminated in an *Italian–German alliance, The Pact of Steel, 22 May 1939* (p. 193). Between the signatures by Italy of the Anti-Comintern Pact and the Pact of Steel occurred the loss of Austrian independence, and this time without Italian protest.

Anglo-German Naval Agreement, 18 June 1935 (Exchange of Notes)

Your Excellency,

1. During the last few days the representatives of the German Government and His Majesty's Government in the United Kingdom have been engaged in conversations, the primary purpose of which has been to prepare the way for the holding of a general conference on the subject of the limitation of naval armaments. I have now much pleasure in notifying your Excellency of the formal acceptance by His Majesty's Government in the United Kingdom of the proposal of the German Government discussed at those conversations that the future strength of the German navy in relation to the aggregate naval strength of the Members of the British Commonwealth of Nations should be in the proportion of 35:100. His Majesty's Government in the United Kingdom regard this proposal as a contribution of the greatest importance to the cause of future naval limitation. They further believe that the agreement which they have now reached with the German Government, and which they regard as a permanent and definite agreement as from today between the two Govern-

ments, will facilitate the conclusion of a general agreement on the subject of naval limitation between all the naval Powers of the world.

2. His Majesty's Government in the United Kingdom also agreed with the explanations which were furnished by the German representatives in the course of the recent discussions in London as to the method of application of this principle. These explanations may be summarized as follows:

(a) The ratio of 35:100 is to be a permanent relationship, i.e. the total tonnage of the German fleet shall never exceed a percentage of 35 of the aggregate tonnage of the naval forces, as defined by treaty, of the Members of the British Commonwealth of Nations, or, if there should in future be no treaty limitations of this tonnage, a percentage of 35 of the aggregate of the actual tonnages of the Members of the British Commonwealth of Nations.

(b) If any future general treaty of naval limitation should not adopt the method of limitation by agreed ratios between the fleets of different Powers, the German Government will not insist on the incorporation of the ratio mentioned in the preceding sub-paragraph in such future general treaty, provided that the method therein adopted for the future limitation of naval armaments is such as to give Germany full guarantees that this ratio can be maintained.

(c) Germany will adhere to the ratio 35:100 in all circumstances, e.g. the ratio will not be affected by the construction of other Powers. If the general equilibrium of naval armaments, as normally maintained in the past, should be violently upset by any abnormal and exceptional construction by other Powers, the German Government reserve the right to invite His Majesty's Government in the United Kingdom to examine the new situation thus created.

(d) The German Government favour, in the matter of limitation of naval armaments, that system which divides naval vessels into categories, fixing the maxi-

mum tonnage and/or armament for vessels in each category, and allocates the tonnage to be allowed to each Power by categories of vessels. Consequently, in principle, and subject to (f) below, the German Government are prepared to apply the 35 per cent ratio to the tonnage of each category of vessel to be maintained, and to make any variation of this ratio in a particular category or categories dependent on the arrangements to this end that may be arrived at in a future general treaty on naval limitation, such arrangements being based on the principle that any increase in one category would be compensated for by a corresponding reduction in others. If no general treaty on naval limitation should be concluded, or if the future general treaty should not contain provision creating limitation by categories, the manner and degree in which the German Government will have the right to vary the 35 per cent ratio in one or more categories will be a matter for settlement by agreement between the German Government and His Majesty's Government in the United Kingdom, in the light of the naval situation then existing.

(e) If, and for so long as, other important naval Powers retain a single category for cruisers and destroyers, Germany shall enjoy the right to have a single category for these two classes of vessel, although she would prefer to see these classes in two categories.

(f) In the matter of submarines, however, Germany, while not exceeding the ratio of 35:100 in respect of total tonnage, shall have the right to possess a submarine tonnage equal to the total submarine tonnage possessed by the Members of the British Commonwealth of Nations. The German Government, however, undertake that, except in the circumstances indicated in the immediately following sentence, Germany's submarine tonnage shall not exceed 45 per cent of the total of that possessed by the Members of the British Commonwealth of Nations. The German Government reserve the right, in the event of a situation arising which in their opinion makes it necessary for Germany to avail herself of her right to a percentage of submarine tonnage exceeding the 45 per cent above mentioned, to give notice to this effect to His Majesty's Government in the United Kingdom, and agree that the matter shall be the subject of friendly discussion before the German Government exercise that right.

(g) Since it is highly improbable that the calculation of the 35 per cent ratio should give for each category of vessels tonnage figures exactly divisible by the maximum individual tonnage permitted for ships in that category, it may be necessary that adjustments should be made in order that Germany shall not be debarred from utilizing her tonnage to the full. It has consequently been agreed that the German Government and His Majesty's Government in the United Kingdom will settle by common accord what adjustments are necessary for this purpose, and it is understood that this procedure shall not result in any substantial or permanent

departure from the ratio 35 : 100 in respect of total strengths.

3. With reference to sub-paragraph (c) of the explanations set out above, I have the honour to inform you that His Majesty's Government in the United Kingdom have taken note of the reservation and recognize the right therein set out, on the understanding that the 35 : 100 ratio will be maintained in default of agreement to the contrary between the two Governments.

4. I have the honour to request your Excellency to inform me that the German Government agree that the proposal of the German Government has been correctly set out in the preceding paragraphs of this note.

[On 10 December 1938 Germany formally exercised its option to build submarines up to the strength of the British and Commonwealth number, having in fact already laid down submarines in breach of the 1935 treaty. On 27 April 1939 Hitler denounced the treaty.]

Agreement (Anti-Comintern) between Japan and Germany, Berlin, 25 November 1936

The Imperial Government of Japan and the Government of Germany,

In cognizance of the fact that the object of the Communistic International (the so-called Komintern) is the disintegration of, and the commission of violence against, existing States by the exercise of all means at its command;

Believing that the toleration of interference by the Communistic International in the internal affairs of nations not only endangers their internal peace and social welfare, but threatens the general peace of the world;

Desiring to cooperate for defence against communistic disintegration, have agreed as follows:

Article I. The High Contracting States agree that they will mutually keep each other informed concerning the activities of the Communistic International, will confer upon the necessary measures of defence, and will carry out such measures in close cooperation.

Article II. The High Contracting States will jointly invite third States whose internal peace is menaced by the disintegrating work of the Communistic International, to adopt defensive measures in the spirit of the present Agreement or to participate in the present Agreement.

Article III. The Japanese and German texts are each valid as the original text of this Agreement. The Agreement shall come into force on the day of its signature and shall remain in force for the term of five years. The High Contracting States will, in a reasonable time before the expiration of the said term, come to an understanding upon the further manner of their cooperation. . . .

Supplementary Protocol to the Agreement guarding against the Communistic International

On the occasion of the signature this day of the Agreement guarding against the Communistic International the undersigned plenipotentiaries have agreed as follows:

(a) The competent authorities of both High Contracting States will closely cooperate in the exchange of reports on the activities of the Communistic International and on measures of information and defence against the Communistic International.

(b) The competent authorities of both High Contracting States will, within the framework of the existing law, take stringent measures against those who at home or abroad work on direct or indirect duty of the Communistic International or assist its disintegrating activities.

(c) To facilitate the cooperation of the competent authorities of the two High Contracting States as set out in (a) above, a standing committee shall be established. By this committee the further measures to be adopted in order to counter the disintegrating activities of the Communistic International shall be considered and conferred upon. . . .

Declaration of Non-Aggression between Germany and Poland, 26 January 1934

The Governments of Germany and Poland consider that the time has arrived to introduce a new phase in the political relations between Germany and Poland by a direct understanding between State and State. They have therefore decided to lay the foundation for the future development of these relations in the present Declaration.

Both Governments base their action on the fact that the maintenance and guarantee of a permanent peace between their countries is an essential condition for the general peace of Europe. They are therefore determined to base their mutual relations on the principles contained in the Pact of Paris of the 27th August 1928, and desire to define more precisely the application of these principles in so far as the relations between Germany and Poland are concerned.

In so doing each of the two Governments declares that the international obligations hitherto undertaken by it towards a third party do not hinder the peaceful development of their mutual relations, do not conflict with the present Declaration and are not affected by this Declaration. In addition both Governments state that the present Declaration does not extend to questions which, in accordance with international law, are to be regarded exclusively as internal concerns of either of the two States.

Both Governments announce their intention to reach direct understanding on questions of any nature whatsoever concerning their mutual relations. Should any disputes arise between them and agreement thereon not be reached by direct negotiations, they will in each particular case, on the basis of mutual agreement, seek a solution by other peaceful means, without prejudice to the possibility of applying, if necessary, such modes of procedure as are provided for such cases by other agreements in force between them. In no circumstances, however, will they proceed to use force in order to settle such disputes.

The guarantee of peace created by these principles will facilitate for both Governments the great task of finding for political, economic and cultural problems solutions based upon just and equitable adjustment of the interests of both parties.

Both Governments are convinced that the relations between their countries will in this manner fruitfully develop and will lead to the establishment of good neighbourly relations, contributing to the well-being not only of their two countries but also of the other nations of Europe.

The present Declaration shall be ratified and the instruments of ratification shall be exchanged at Warsaw as soon as possible. The Declaration is valid for a period of ten years, reckoned from the date of the exchange of the instruments of ratification. If it is not denounced by either of the two Governments six months before the expiration of this period, it will continue in force, but can then be denounced by either Government at any time on giving six months' notice.

Done in duplicate in the German and Polish languages.

Berlin, January 26, 1934

For the German Government:
C. FREIHERR VON NEURATH

For the Polish Government:
JÓZEF LIPSKI

Rome Protocol between Italy, Austria and Hungary, 17 March 1934

The Head of the Government of His Majesty the King of Italy,

The Federal Chancellor of the Republic of Austria,

The President of the Royal Council of Ministers of Hungary,

Being anxious to contribute to the maintenance of peace and to the economic reconstruction of Europe on the basis of respect for the independence and rights of every State;

Being convinced that cooperation in this direction between the three Governments is likely to create a genuine basis for wider cooperation with other States;

Undertake, with a view to achieving the above-mentioned purposes:

To confer together on all problems which particularly concern them, and on problems of a general character, with a view to pursuing, in the spirit of the existing treaties of friendship between Italy and Austria, Italy and Hungary and Austria and Hungary,

which are based on a recognition of the existence of numerous common interests, a concordant policy directed towards the promotion of effective cooperation between the States of Europe and particularly between Italy, Austria and Hungary.

To this end, the three Governments shall proceed to hold joint consultations whenever at least one of them deems it desirable.

[A further Protocol for the Development of Economic Relations was also concluded on 17 March 1934.]

Additional Protocol, 23 March 1936

[Reaffirmed Protocol of 17 March 1934 and specifically to consult with each other before undertaking any important negotiation on Danubian questions with any other State. A permanent organ composed of Foreign Ministers of three States was to be established for consultation.]

Nyon Agreement between Britain, Bulgaria, Egypt, France, Greece, Rumania, Turkey, U.S.S.R. and Yugoslavia, Nyon, 14 September 1937

Whereas arising out of the Spanish conflict attacks have been repeatedly committed in the Mediterranean by submarines against merchant ships not belonging to either of the conflicting Spanish parties; and

Whereas these attacks are violations of the rules of international law referred to in Part IV of the Treaty of London of April 22, 1930 with regard to the sinking of merchant ships and constitute acts contrary to the most elementary dictates of humanity, which should be justly treated as acts of piracy; and

Whereas without in any way admitting the right of either party to the conflict in Spain to exercise belligerent rights or to interfere with merchant ships on the high seas even if the laws of warfare at sea are observed and without prejudice to the right of any participating Power to take such action as may be proper to protect its merchant shipping from any kind of interference on the high seas or to the possibility of further collective measures being agreed upon subsequently, it is necessary in the first place to agree upon certain special collective measures against piratical acts by submarines:

In view thereof the undersigned, being authorized to this effect by their respective Governments, have met in conference at Nyon between the 9th and the 14th September 1937, and have agreed upon the following provisions which shall enter immediately into force:

I. The participating Powers will instruct their naval forces to take the action indicated in paragraphs II and III below with a view to the protection of all merchant ships not belonging to either of the conflicting Spanish parties.

II. Any submarine which attacks such a ship in a manner contrary to the rules of international law referred to in the International Treaty for the Limitation and Reduction of Naval Armaments signed in London on April 22, 1930, and confirmed in the Protocol signed in London on November 6, 1936, shall be counterattacked and, if possible, destroyed.

III. The instruction mentioned in the preceding paragraph shall extend to any submarine encountered in the vicinity of a position where a ship not belonging to either of the conflicting Spanish parties has recently been attacked in violation of the rules referred to in the preceding paragraph in circumstances which give valid grounds for the belief that the submarine was guilty of the attack.

IV. In order to facilitate the putting into force of the above arrangements in a practical manner, the participating Powers have agreed upon the following arrangements:

1. In the western Mediterranean and in the Malta Channel, with the exception of the Tyrrhenean Sea, which may form the subject of special arrangements, the British and French fleets will operate both on the high seas and in the territorial waters of the participating Powers, in accordance with the division of the area agreed upon between the two Governments.

2. In the eastern Mediterranean:

(a) Each of the participating Powers will operate in its own territorial waters;

(b) On the high seas with the exception of the Adriatic Sea, the British and French fleets will operate up to the entrance to the Dardanelles, in those areas where there is reason to apprehend danger to shipping in accordance with the division of the area agreed upon between the two Governments. The other participating Governments possessing a sea border on the Mediterranean, undertake, within the limit of their resources, to furnish these fleets any assistance that may be asked for; in particular, they will permit them to take action in their territorial waters and to use such of their ports as they shall indicate.

3. It is further understood that the limits of the zones referred to in subparagraphs 1 and 2 above, and their allocation shall be subject at any time to revision by the participating Powers in order to take account of any change in the situation.

V. The participating Powers agree that, in order to simplify the operation of the above-mentioned measures, they will for their part restrict the use of their submarines in the Mediterranean in the following manner:

(a) Except as stated in (b) and (c) below, no submarine will be sent to sea within the Mediterranean.

(b) Submarines may proceed on passage after notification to the other participating Powers, provided that they proceed on the surface and are accompanied by a surface ship.

(c) Each participating Power reserves for purposes of exercises certain areas defined in Annex I hereto in which its submarines are exempt from the restrictions mentioned in (a) or (b).

The participating Powers further undertake not to allow the presence in their respective territorial waters of any foreign submarines except in case of urgent distress, or where the conditions prescribed in sub-paragraph (b) above are fulfilled.

VI. The participating Powers also agree that, in order to simplify the problem involved in carrying out the measures above described, they may severally advise their merchant shipping to follow certain main routes in the Mediterranean agreed upon between them and defined in Annex II hereto.

VII. Nothing in the present Agreement restricts the right of any participating Power to send its surface vessels to any part of the Mediterranean. . . .

'Gentlemen's' Agreement between Austria and Germany, 11 July 1936

CONFIDENTIAL!

Convinced that the mutually expressed desire for the re-establishment of normal and friendly relations between the German Reich and the Federal State of Austria requires a series of preliminary stipulations on the part of the two Governments, both Governments approve the following confidential Gentlemen's Agreement:

I · REGULATION OF THE TREATMENT OF REICH-GERMANS IN AUSTRIA AND OF AUSTRIAN NATIONALS IN THE REICH

Associations of their nationals in either country shall not be hindered in their activities so long as they comply with the policies established in their bylaws in conformity with the laws in force and do not interfere in the internal political affairs of the other country, nor, in particular, endeavour to influence citizens of the other State by means of propaganda.

II · MUTUAL CULTURAL RELATIONS

All factors decisive for the formation of public opinion of both countries shall serve the purpose of re-establishing normal and friendly relations. With the thought that both countries belong within the German cultural orbit, both parties pledge themselves immediately to renounce any aggressive utilization of radio, motion picture, newspaper, and theatrical facilities against the other party. . . .

III · THE PRESS

Both parties shall influence their respective Press to the end that it refrain from exerting any political influence on conditions in the other country and limit its objective criticism of conditions in the other country to an extent not offensive to public opinion in the other country. This obligation also applies to the *émigré* Press in both countries.

The gradual elimination of prohibitions on the importation of newspapers and printed matter of the other party is envisaged by both parties, in relation to the gradual *détente* in mutual relations aimed at in this Agreement. Newspapers admitted shall, in any criticism of the internal political situation in the other country, adhere particularly strictly to the principle enunciated in paragraph I. . . .

IV · EMIGRÉ PROBLEMS

Both parties agree in their desire to contribute by reciprocal concessions to the speediest possible satisfactory solution of the problem of the Austrian National Socialist exiles in the Reich.

The Austrian Government will proceed to the examination of this problem as soon as possible and will announce the result to a joint commission to be composed of representatives of the competent Ministries so that an agreement may be put into effect.

V · NATIONAL INSIGNIA AND NATIONAL ANTHEMS

Each of the two Governments declares that within the scope of existing laws, it will place the nationals of the other party on an equal footing with nationals of third States in regard to the display of the national insignia of their country.

The singing of national anthems shall – in addition to official occasions – be permitted to nationals of the other party at closed meetings attended by these nationals exclusively.

VI · ECONOMIC RELATIONS

The Government of the German Reich, putting aside considerations of Party policy, is prepared to open the way for normal economic relations between the German Reich and Austria, and this readiness extends to the re-establishment of routine border crossing [*der Kleine Grenzverkehr*]. Discrimination against persons and areas, if not based upon purely economic considerations will not be undertaken.

VII · TOURIST TRAFFIC

The restrictions on tourist traffic imposed by both sides because of the tension which had arisen between the two States shall be lifted. This understanding shall not affect restrictions based on the legislation of both countries for the protection of foreign exchange. . . .

VIII · FOREIGN POLICY

The Austrian Government declares that it is prepared to conduct its foreign policy in the light of the peaceful endeavours of the German Government's foreign policy. It is agreed that the two Governments will from time to time enter into an exchange of views on the problems of foreign policy affecting both of them. The Rome Protocols of 1934 and the Supplementary Protocols of 1936, as well as the position of Austria with regard to Italy and Hungary as parties to these Protocols, are not affected thereby.

IX · AUSTRIAN DECLARATION ON DOMESTIC POLICY IN RELATION TO THIS *modus vivendi*

The Federal Chancellor declares that he is prepared:

(a) To grant a far-reaching political amnesty, from which persons who have committed serious public crimes shall be excluded.

Also covered by this amnesty shall be persons who have not yet been sentenced by judicial decree or penalized by administrative process.

These provisions shall also be duly applied to *émigrés*.

(b) For the purpose of promoting a real pacification, to appoint at the appropriate moment, contemplated for the near future, representatives of the so-called 'National Opposition in Austria' to participate in political responsibility; they shall be men who enjoy the personal confidence of the Federal Chancellor and whose selection he reserves to himself. It is agreed, in this connection, that persons trusted by the Federal Chancellor shall be charged with the task of arranging, in accordance with a plan worked out with the Federal Chancellor, for the internal pacification of the National Opposition and for its participation in the shaping of the political will in Austria.

X · PROCEDURE FOR OBJECTIONS AND COMPLAINTS

For the handling of objections and complaints which may arise in connection with the above Gentlemen's Agreement, as well as in order to guarantee a progressive *détente* within the framework of the preceding agreements, there shall be established a joint commission composed of three representatives of the Foreign Ministry of each country. Its task shall be to discuss at regular meetings the operation of the Agreement as well as any supplements thereto which may be required.

SCHUSCHNIGG
Federal Chancellor

VIENNA, 11 July 1936

Protocol concluded by Italy, Germany and Japan (Anti-Comintern Pact), Rome, 6 November 1937

The Italian Government, the Government of the German Reich, and the Imperial Government of Japan,

Considering that the Communist International continues constantly to imperil the civilized world in the Occident and Orient, disturbing and destroying peace and order,

Considering that only close collaboration looking to the maintenance of peace and order can limit and remove that peril,

Considering that Italy – who with the advent of the Fascist régime has with inflexible determination combated that peril and rid her territory of the Communist International – has decided to align herself against the common enemy along with Germany and Japan, who for their part are animated by like determination to defend themselves against the Communist International,

Have, in conformity with Article II of the Agreement against the Communist International concluded at Berlin on November 25, 1936, by Germany and Japan, agreed upon the following:

Article 1. Italy becomes a party to the Agreement against the Communist International and to the Supplementary Protocol concluded on November 25, 1936, between Germany and Japan, the text of which is included in the Annex to the present Protocol.

Article 2. The three Powers signatory to the present Protocol agree that Italy will be considered as an original signatory to the Agreement and Supplementary Protocol mentioned in the preceding Article, the signing of the present Protocol being equivalent to the signature of the original text of the aforesaid Agreement and Supplementary Protocol.

Article 3. The present Protocol shall constitute an integral part of the above-mentioned Agreement and Supplementary Protocol.

Article 4. The present Protocol is drawn up in Italian, Japanese, and German, each text being considered authentic. It shall enter into effect on the date of signature.

In testimony whereof, etc. . . .

[signed] CIANO, VON RIBBENTROPP, HOTTA.

VII · From peace to world war in Europe and Asia, 1937–41

During the short space of eighteen months, from March 1938 to September 1939, Hitler plunged Europe from one crisis to another, each time 'breaking his word' that he had made his last territorial demand. When each crisis is examined in isolation there seems some merit in Germany's arguments: why should the Austrians of the Sudeten German-speaking population of Czechoslovakia be denied the right of self-determination; the 'rectification' of Germany's eastern frontier was an objective followed by the 'European' Stresemann in the 1920s before Hitler made his demands concerning the Polish corridor and Danzig; was it not time to remove the last vestiges of discrimination against Germany imposed by the Versailles *Diktat*? Reasonable Western statesmen would surely prefer diplomatic adjustments, even some sacrifice on the part of the 'artificially' created post-Versailles States, to world war.

To begin with, Neville Chamberlain, leading the French Daladier Government, was prepared to follow the path of apparent reason in preference to the human and material destruction that another world war would entail. But the cumulative impact of Hitler's aggressions of 1938–9 and the realization that he was launched on a policy of aggression without foreseeable 'diplomatic' limits led to a fundamental change of British policy in 1939 which carried France with it. The door to diplomatic agreements for a settlement of all European questions would not be closed; Hitler should be offered all possible enticements to choose diplomacy rather than force; he would hopefully also be deterred by an alliance against Germany; but if neither inducements nor deterrents could influence him then Britain was prepared for war rather than allow Hitler the hegemony of continental Europe. But where would the Soviet Union fit into this new pattern of diplomacy? No one in Britain or Germany knew for certain until Stalin made his choice in August 1939.

In Asia, Japan had resumed fighting in China in July 1937 and an 'undeclared war' began. The sympathy of the Western democracies was with China, but the more immediate threat of Germany in Europe decided France and Britain to preserve a policy of limiting help to China to an extent that would allow peaceful relations to be preserved with Japan. The outbreak of war in Europe only strengthened this resolve. After the fall of France in June 1940, Britain agreed to the closure of the Burma supply route to China, but reopened it in October 1940. From then on, British policy followed in the wake of American policy in the Pacific. United States resistance to Japanese expansion in South-east Asia finally led to the Japanese decision to start war advantageously with the surprise attack on Pearl Harbor, 7 December 1941. For the U.S.S.R., fighting a war for survival since June 1941, the absolute need to avoid having to face a second front in Asia as well overrode all other considerations; and so it remained loyal to the Neutrality Pact it had concluded with Japan in April 1941.

Europe, 1938–9

GERMAN EXPANSION

The German proclamation of the *Austrian Anschluss on 13 March 1938* for the first time during the Nazi era extended German sovereignty by the threat and use of force. When the opportunity was offered, Hitler assumed control over the whole of Austria. With similar opportunism Hitler broke up Czechoslovakia in October 1938 by annexing the so-called mainly German-speaking Sudeten areas. In the following March he partitioned what was left of the country and created an 'independent' Puppet State of Slovakia.

The first transfer of Czech territory in October 1938 was given a semblance of international sanction at the *Four Power Conference at Munich, 29–30 September 1938*. Germany, Italy, France and Britain participated in this 'settlement'. The Czechoslovak Government was not represented and only acquiesced in the decisions of Munich in the face of the German threat of force, and since without the help of her Western ally, France, military resistance would have been hopeless. The extent of Soviet help too would have been uncertain and in any case probably ineffective. (See p. 117 for the terms of the Franco-Czech alliance and pp. 152–6 for the Franco-Soviet and Czech–Soviet treaties of 1935.) A number of documents were signed at Munich: *the Munich Four Power Agreement, 29–30 September 1938* (p. 187), which provided for the occupation of the Sudetenland in stages from 1–10 October 1938; a *conditional guarantee* for the remainder of Czechoslovakia after Polish and Hungarian claims had been settled; and an *Anglo-German Declaration* (p. 189) of pacific intent. Not to be outdone the Daladier Government concluded a *Franco-German Agreement on 6 December 1938*. It recognized mutual frontiers and thus the Germans appeared to abandon claims to Alsace-Lorraine; it promised consultations between France and Germany on questions of mutual interest, while their 'relations' with other States were not affected. The use of the word 'relations' in place of existing 'alliances' seemed to point to a French desire to play down the alliances without abandoning them.

The validity of the Four Power Agreement was challenged by the Czecho-slovak Government, in exile during the Second World War, on the grounds that Czech assent to the occupation had been obtained under duress. Of the original signatories which later declared the treaty to be invalid, the French National Committee did so in 1942 and the French Provisional Government reaffirmed this in 1944, and post-Fascist Italy declared the treaty invalid from the beginning in 1944. The wartime British Government would not repudiate the legality of the original Munich Agreements but only bound itself in 1942 to regard the treaty as no longer in force due to the Germans having broken it. The Federal German Government in 1973 is currently negotiating this question among several with the Czechoslovak Government. The Soviet Union, not a signatory of Munich, was the first Great Power to declare to the Czecho-slovak Government that it had not recognized the Munich settlement at the time or since.

The guarantee given at Munich never became operative as the British and French Governments decided that they would only honour it in the event of Hitler's aggression if Italy also did so. Despite a visit by Chamberlain to Mussolini in January 1939 there was not the slightest chance that Italy would work against her Axis partner. When a political crisis in autonomous Slovakia gave Hitler his next opportunity, he ordered German troops on 15 March 1939 to occupy the remnants of the Czech State, and set up the Protectorate of Bohemia and Moravia on 16 March 1939. *On 23 March 1939 a German–Slovak treaty* was signed which described Slovakia as an independent State but under the protection of Germany, with closely subservient Slovak policies in matters of the army, foreign policy and economic and financial affairs; Germany was given the right to station troops in Slovakia and undertook to protect the independence of its satellite.

Poland and Hungary also benefited from the break-up of Czechoslovakia (October 1938–March 1939). Poland secured the territory of Teschen, 1–2 October 1938, after the Czechoslovak Government accepted a peremptory demand for its cession. Hungary, by the *First Vienna Award, 2 November 1938*, an arbitral judgement given by Germany and Italy, re-acquired the ethnic strip of Magyar territory along the Hungarian borders with Slovakia and Ruthenia, which left the rest of Slovakia and Ruthenia autonomous. *Hungary* formally joined the Axis Powers when adhering *on 26 February 1939 to the Anti-Comintern Pact*, and two weeks later on 14–15 March 1939, with German encouragement, the Hungarians annexed Ruthenia (also known as 'Carpatho-Ukraine') at the same time as the Wehrmacht marched into Czechoslovakia.

Hitler made his first aggressive move in the Baltic the day after entering Czechoslovakia, by sending an ultimatum to Lithuania on 16 March 1939 demanding the cession of the Memelland. Lithuania accepted on 19 March 1939. Hitler entered Memel from the sea on 23 March 1939 when the treaty of cession was formally signed. His next objective was the Free City of Danzig together with an extra-territorial corridor linking East Prussia to the rest of Germany. Mussolini now sprang his surprise by *annexing Albania to Italy on 7 April 1939.*

The Anglo-French response

These sudden violent changes created great uncertainty throughout Europe. Rumania was already more in the German than Western orbit, having signed a number of economic agreements with Germany in December 1938 and on 23 March 1939; but Rumania also felt its territorial integrity threatened by Hungary, Bulgaria and Germany during the crisis of mid-March 1939. Poland was threatened by a Slovakia under German control and by Hitler's ambitions in the Baltic. Against the background of general diplomatic confusion, and fearing a complete collapse of Central and Eastern Europe to Nazi aggression, there began the British attempt, in association with France, to call a halt to further German territorial expansion by force. On *31 March 1939 Chamberlain announced a provisional Anglo-French guarantee of Poland* (p. 189). After Italy seized Albania on 7 April 1939, this guarantee was extended to the Balkans when on *13 April 1939 an Anglo-French guarantee of Greece and Rumania was announced.* Turkey was brought into the Anglo-French alignment when on 12 May 1939 the British and Turkish Governments issued a declaration that they would cooperate in the event of aggression leading to war in the Mediterranean; the two Governments also said that they would conclude a long-term treaty (for the Anglo-French-Turkish Treaty, 19 October 1939, see p. 197). The long drawn-out diplomatic exchanges and negotiations between France, Britain and the Soviet Union from March 1939 to August 1939 led to no result.

The refusal of the Polish Government to give in to the substance of German demands and Britain's determination to stand by Poland led to a more definitive alliance, the *Anglo-Polish Agreement of Mutual Assistance, 25 August 1939* (p. 190).

THE AXIS

Germany bound Italy more closely to its side when Hitler finally persuaded Mussolini to conclude a military alliance, the *Pact of Steel, 22 May 1939* (p. 193), but in a secret memorandum for Hitler a week later Mussolini stated that Italy would not be ready for war until after the end of 1942. On the eve of Germany's attack on Poland, on 25 August 1939, Mussolini replied to Hitler that he could not take military action before the end of 1942 unless sufficient arms and raw materials were provided for Italy. Hitler preferred to do without immediate Italian military help when he attacked Poland on 1 September 1939, having already purchased Soviet acquiescence. Secretly the Soviet Union negotiated with Germany in Berlin whilst simultaneously negotiating with France and Britain in Moscow. The *German–Soviet Non-Aggression Pact was signed on 23 August 1939* (p. 195), and a secret Protocol was signed the same day which outlined the German and Soviet spheres of interest and paved the way for Soviet annexations of territory in the Baltic and Central Europe (p. 199). The German invasion of Poland on 1 September 1939 was followed on 3 September 1939 by British and French ultimatums and declarations of war.

Allied diplomacy, 1939–41

In September 1939 war did not immediately engulf all of Europe. The countries which declared war on Germany were Britain and the Dominions (with the exception of Eire) and France; Poland had no choice as she was attacked by Germany without a declaration of war. But Germany's ally Italy, with Hitler's consent, remained neutral. Portugal, Britain's ally, with British consent declared its neutrality on the outbreak of war. On the Allied side the earliest effort at diplomacy in wartime was to win the support of Turkey.

TURKEY

On 19 October 1939 Britain, France and Turkey concluded a Tripartite Treaty (p. 197). Five months earlier (12 May 1939) an Anglo-Turkish declaration had foreshadowed a long-term treaty to meet aggression in the Mediterranean region. The treaty now concluded on 19 October 1939 provided for a promise of British and French help if Turkey was attacked by a European Power; the three Powers, France and Britain on the one hand and Turkey on the other, promised mutual assistance if a European Power committed an act of aggression leading to a war which involved the signatories; Turkey promised aid if Britain and France were at war in consequence of their guarantees to Greece and Rumania, but could remain benevolently neutral if a war involving Britain and France was the result of events outside the Mediterranean region, as was the case over Poland. Thus in practice the application of the alliance was limited to aggression by Germany or Italy in the Balkans; an important additional clause provided that the obligations Turkey undertook were not to have the effect of compelling her to go to war with the U.S.S.R. When Italy entered the war on 10 June 1940 during the final phase of the French collapse, Turkey disavowed the Tripartite Treaty, claiming that France could no longer fulfil it, and declared its intention to remain non-belligerent. The Italian and German attacks on Greece in 1941 did not alter Turkey's stand. After Germany's threat had lessened through military failure, Turkey broke off diplomatic relations on 2 August 1944 but did not declare war until 23 February 1945.

THE UNITED STATES AND THE EUROPEAN WAR

On 11 December 1941, four days after the Japanese attack on Pearl Harbor (7 December 1941, p. 187), Germany and Italy declared war on the United States. By a number of agreements made during the period of American neutrality (September 1939 to December 1941) the United States had provided crucial help for the Allied cause even before becoming an ally. On 4 November 1939 Roosevelt approved the revised *Neutrality Act* which repealed the embargo on the export of munitions to belligerents, though American supplies to the Allies before the fall of France were not large. The German conquests of Denmark, Norway, the Netherlands, Belgium, and France in the spring and summer of 1940 led to increasing American help and to a tremendous expansion of the American armaments industry. *The Anglo-American Destroyer–Naval Base Agreement, 2 September 1940*, gave Britain fifty American First World War destroyers in exchange for leasing to the United States naval bases in the British islands of the western Atlantic, in the Caribbean and in British Guiana. *The Lend–Lease Act, 11 March 1941*, passed Congress with the stated purpose of promoting the defence of the United States by providing all-out material aid to any country whose defence the President regarded as vital to the defence of the United States, on whatever terms the President regarded as proper. In August 1941 Churchill and Roosevelt met and set out their principles of present and future policy in the *Atlantic Charter, published on 14 August 1941* (p. 198). On 17 November 1941 Congress further revised the Neutrality Acts. American merchant ships could now carry arms to belligerent ports (British ports) and so be armed.

The German victories in Europe also raised the possibility that German aggression might expand to the Western hemisphere. Pan-American solidarity in the event of the war reaching the American Republics was strengthened at the *Panama Conference, 23 September–3 October 1939* (p. 301). This created a neutral belt of several hundred miles from the coastline of the American Republics, foreshadowed the United States revision of the neutrality legislation and affirmed the no-transfer principle. The Declaration of Panama said: In case any geographic region of America subject to the jurisdiction of a non-American State should be obliged to change its sovereignty and there should result therefrom a danger to the security of the American continent, a consultative meeting such as the one now being held will be convoked with the urgency that the case may require. With the German occupation of France, Belgium, the Netherlands, Norway and Denmark, the danger envisaged had come near and the United States Congress on 18 June 1940 affirmed that it would not acquiesce in any transfer of sovereignty from one non-American State to another of territory in the American hemisphere. The Pan-American Conference met again in Havana on 21 July 1940. The no-transfer principle was re-affirmed by resolution and the *Act of Havana, which came into force on 8 January 1942* (p. 324). It provided in case of necessity that the Republics in collective trusteeship would administer any such territory that was threatened. The Havana Conference also passed a resolution that an act of aggression against one Republic would be treated as an act of aggression against all, which would lead to consultation on measures of common defence.

NEW ALLIES AND THE COLLAPSE OF FRANCE

In 1940 Britain lost the war on the continent of Europe and gained new allies, not by their choice but because they became victims of German aggression. Germany extended the war in the West by attacking Denmark and Norway on 9 April 1940. Denmark was occupied virtually without resistance and Norway, despite Allied attempts to create a front in the central and northern regions of the country, fell a few weeks later.

Germany opened her military offensive against France a month later on 10 May 1940 by crossing three neutral frontiers, the Netherlands, Belgium and Luxembourg. All three Governments after the complete military collapse refused to sign an armistice with Germany, and transferred themselves to London to join there the Polish and Norwegian Governments in exile. After the defeat of the British and French armies Marshal Pétain formed a new

Government which sought an armistice from the Germans. The *Franco-German armistice was signed on 22 June 1940* and became effective three days later. It divided France into an occupied zone of northern France and the Atlantic coastline and an unoccupied zone. The 'Free French' under de Gaulle continued to fight on the Allied side but were not recognized as a fully-fledged Government in exile. Meantime Italy had declared war on France and Britain on 10 June 1940 during the closing stages of the German campaign in France. Italy's contribution to the growing number of Allied Powers was to follow up her short campaign in France by attacking *Greece on 28 October 1940.* Greece now joined the war against Italy. Italian military ineptitude brought about German intervention when *Germany attacked Greece on 6 April 1941.*

The Axis Powers and the Soviet Union, 1939–41: the Winter War

For Germany and Poland the Second World War began on 1 September 1939 when the Wehrmacht and the Luftwaffe crossed the Polish frontier. Just a week earlier the Soviet Union and Germany announced a *Treaty of Non-Aggression, 23 August 1939* (p. 195). After Hitler's virulent anti-Bolshevik tirades, such a treaty marked a reversal of what the public could have anticipated. Equally, communists throughout Europe were thrown into confusion. An additiona *secret protocol* marked out German and Soviet 'spheres of influence' and en-l visaged the partition of Poland and other territories within each sphere according to the convenience of each signatory. On 17 September 1939, seventeen days after Germany's attack on Poland, with the Polish armies routed but still fighting the Germans, Soviet troops crossed Poland's eastern frontier. The detailed division of Poland was laid down in the *German–Soviet Boundary and Friendship Treaty, 28 September 1939* (p. 199), to which were added one confidential and two secret Protocols. These political treaties were accompanied by German–Soviet economic agreements. The first economic agreement, the *German–Soviet Trade Agreement, was concluded on 19 August 1939* (p. 194). Six months later a comprehensive and extensive *German–Soviet Commercial Agreement was signed on 11 February 1940* (p. 200).

Having concluded these political and economic agreements which apparently ensured that Germany and the Soviet Union could count on the neutrality of one State towards the other, Germany and the Soviet Union pursued their separate expansionist policies. Germany attacked Denmark and Norway on 9 April 1940 and the Netherlands, Belgium and Luxembourg on 10 May 1940.

The Soviet Union, in accordance with the German–Soviet Boundary and Friendship Treaty on 28 September 1939, had secured German agreement that Lithuania fell within her sphere of interest. Stalin was now determined to assure Soviet predominance in the Baltic States of Lithuania, Estonia and Latvia as well as Finland. Under threat of force a *Soviet–Estonian Mutual Assistance Pact was concluded on 28 September 1939*, which, whilst formally preserving Estonian sovereignty, made military bases available to the Soviet Union in Estonia and permitted the Soviet Union to station troops in these bases. *Latvia signed a similar pact with the Soviet Union on 5 October 1939* (p. 201). *Lithuania* also was forced to sign a pact with the Soviet Union permitting the stationing of the Red Army in Lithuania, but on *10 October 1939* received a 'consolation prize': Vilna and its region was transferred from occupied Poland to Lithuania. The Soviet Government wished to control the foreign and military affairs of the Baltic to strengthen Soviet security. Independent Governments continued to function in the Baltic States until mid-June 1940. Then, after unremitting pressure and when already under Soviet control, the Baltic States 'requested' incorporation in the Soviet Union. Lithuania was accordingly 'admitted' to the Soviet Union on 1 August 1940, Latvia on 5 August 1940, Estonia on 8 August 1940, and these States became Republics of the Soviet Union. This marked the extinction of the three Baltic States as sovereign nations.

Finland in October 1939 refused Soviet demands which involved frontier changes and the abandonment of the Mannerheim line of fortifications across the Karelian isthmus. After fruitless negotiations the Soviet Union began the invasion of Finland on 30 November 1939. The Winter War lasted unexpectedly long with strong Finnish resistance, but after three months of fighting Finland was forced to sue for peace. *On 12 March 1940 a Finnish–Soviet Peace Treaty was signed* which accepted Soviet demands for frontier changes and bases.

The Soviet Union next moved to increase the security of her southern frontier by demanding from Rumania on 26 June 1940 Bessarabia and northern Bukovina. The Rumanians accepted, on German advice, and by 1 July 1940 this region had been completely occupied by Soviet troops. The Hungarians now also wished to recover territory lost after the First World War (p. 46) and threatened to use force if Rumania did not hand back Transylvania; the Bulgarians demanded from Rumania frontier concessions in the Dobruja. Hitler imposed a settlement by the *Second Vienna Award, 30 August 1940*, partitioning Transylvania, which left Rumania about three-fifths and gave Hungary the remainder. *Rumania ceded the southern Dobruja to Bulgaria on 7 September 1940*. In its new frontiers Hitler now gave a *German guarantee to Rumania* at the request of the Rumanians, who on 1 July 1940 had formally denounced the *Anglo-French guarantee of March 1939* (see p. 189). In September 1940 German troops began to occupy Rumania at 'Rumania's request', as

Hitler assured the Russians. Russo-German relations deteriorated. In November 1940 Hitler secretly prepared for war in the Balkans and an attack on Russia, Bulgaria and Greece. Meantime, not to be outdone by Germany in the Balkans Mussolini attacked Greece on 28 October 1940.

Faced with the hostile Great Powers, Italy, Germany and Russia, the still independent Balkan States attempted to strengthen their security by diplomacy and by appeasing Hitler. The Bulgarians in November 1940 promised to cooperate with the three Axis Powers, Germany, Italy and Japan who had concluded the *Tripartite Pact of 27 September 1940* (p. 202). Hungary signed a *Protocol of Adherence to the Tripartite Pact, 20 November 1940*, but according to its terms the Hungarians were left some freedom in choosing what action to take to help the Axis partners. *Rumania* adhered to the *Tripartite Pact on 23 November 1940 and Slovakia on 24 November 1940*. On *12 December 1940 the Hungarian–Yugoslav Pact* apparently reconciled these two States. On the following day, 13 December 1940, Hitler issued military directives for a German attack on Greece and on 18 December 1940 for an attack on the Soviet Union. Germany strengthened her position by securing Bulgarian acquiescence to a virtual German military occupation during February 1941. *Bulgaria* next concluded a *Non-Aggression Pact with Turkey on 17 February 1942*.

The aggressive policies of Germany and Italy had thrown the Balkan States (all of which, apart from Greece, had remained at peace) into such a state of great alarm that they vied for German friendship. On *1 March 1941 Bulgaria openly adhered to the Tripartite Pact*. Finally, *on 25 March 1941 Yugoslavia adhered to the Tripartite Pact* receiving assurances from Germany that her sovereignty and territorial integrity would be respected. This pro-Axis policy resulted in a popular uprising in Yugoslavia: the military leaders took charge, the Prince Regent was deposed, and a new Government was formed. To gain time the new Yugoslav Government forwarded to Berlin protestations of friendship for Italy and Germany. Hitler responded to the Yugoslav coup by ordering a German surprise attack on Yugoslavia and on Greece, which commenced on 6 April 1941. Three days later the Hungarians also crossed the Yugoslav frontier. On 17 April 1941 the Yugoslav army surrendered. The Government under King Peter left the country, while in Yugoslavia the struggle was continued in the mountains. By the end of May 1941 the Germans had conquered Greece and Crete.

Hitler could now dispose of the spoils of victory. Yugoslavia was partitioned between Germany, Italy, Hungary and Bulgaria; an 'independent kingdom' of Croatia was allowed to exist under Italian control; what was left of Serbia became another 'independent State' under German occupation.

Greece was deprived of western Thrace and eastern Macedonia, which was handed to Bulgaria; Italy took the Ionian Islands and enlarged Albania at the Greeks' expense. The remainder of Greece was placed under mainly Italian occupation after a formal Greek military surrender to the Germans had been signed on 23 April 1941.

Having gained complete dominance in the Balkans, Hitler was now ready to take his most momentous step in expanding the war in Europe by next launching an attack on the Soviet Union. But Yugoslavia's resistance had postponed the original time set for the attack: instead of in May, it could only begin on 22 June 1941. Hitler was joined by allies. Italy and Rumania declared war on Russia on 22 June 1941, Slovakia on 23 June 1941, Finland on 25 June 1941 and Hungary on 27 June 1941. Only Bulgaria (practically under German control) remained neutral, together with Turkey. With the onset of winter, the Soviet Union avoided the defeat predicted by the Allies and the Axis in 1941.

Asia: Japan, Russia and China, 1937–41

In July 1937 Japan resumed an 'undeclared war' against China. During the two years from the renewed invasion of China by Japan in the summer of 1937 until the outbreak of war in Europe in September 1939, fighting not only spread through China but the tension between Russia and Japan increased to the point of open fighting on the borders of Manchuria.

On 21 August 1937 the Soviet Union and China signed a Non-Aggression Pact (p. 160). But Japan's diplomatic position was strengthened when Italy in November 1937 joined the *German–Japanese Anti-Comintern Pact* (p. 168). China's appeal to the League resulted in no effective support. In 1938 the Soviet Union began to provide credit and send war supplies to free China. By the summer of 1938 fierce fighting broke out between Japanese and Soviet troops over the border, near the junction of Manchuria, Korea and the Soviet Union. Although a truce was concluded the tension continued. From May–September 1939 serious clashes occurred between Japanese and Soviet troops on the Mongolian–Manchurian border. The Soviet Union appeared encircled and threatened by two Axis Powers – Germany and Japan. The alignment of the Axis against the Soviet Union was suddenly broken by the signature of the *German–Soviet Non-Aggression Pact* in August 1939 (p. 195). The Soviet Union, while continuing in 1939 and 1940 to aid China with supplies, also sought some accommodation with Japan. Japan meanwhile strengthened her ties with Italy and Germany after Germany's military successes in France, and concluded the *Tripartite Pact on 27 September 1940* (p. 202). For Japan, Indo-China and the Dutch East Indies were assuming new importance in the autumn of 1940. This Japanese drive southwards, partly to ensure for herself the raw materials essential for war, brought her into conflict with the United States. For Japan a settlement with the Soviet Union thus became more desirable. It was achieved when *Japan and the Soviet Union concluded a Neutrality Pact on 13 April 1941*.

Asia: the United States, Britain and Japan, 1940–1

Japan extended her influence in Asia and the Pacific as Germany, the Axis partner, spread over the continent of Europe. After unrelenting Japanese military pressure the Japanese and Vichy Government reached a *Franco-Japanese Agreement on Indo-China by an exchange of notes, 30 August 1940*. France recognized Japan's predominance in the Far East, special economic privileges in Indo-China and, most important, special military facilities to enable Japan to bring the war with China to an end; Japan recognized French sovereignty over Indo-China and Indo-China's territorial integrity. After further tension leading to the brink of conflict, a *Franco-Japanese Military Agreement concerning Indo-China was signed on 22 September 1940* which permitted the Japanese the use of three airfields in Tongking and the right to station 6,000 troops on them, as well as the right to send up to 25,000 men through Tongking to attack China.

Japan also supported Thailand (Siam). Thailand began to acquire Cambodian territory in Indo-China. This local conflict was brought to a halt by Japan on terms favourable to Japanese interests. The *Thailand–Franco-Japanese treaties of 9 May 1941* gave to Thailand about one-third of Cambodia and part of Laos on the west bank of the Mekong; Japan guaranteed the French–Thailand settlement, and Thailand and the Vichy French Government in Indo-China undertook to conclude no agreements which could involve them in political, economic or military collaboration with another country against Japan. *On 29 July 1941 the Japanese extended their occupation over southern Indo-China* having extracted an agreement from Vichy France under threat of using force. Japan had further strengthened her position for moving southwards by signing the *Tripartite Pact of 27 September 1940 with Italy and Germany* (p. 202) and the *Japanese–Soviet Pact of Neutrality of 13 April 1941*. But Japanese efforts to bring the Dutch East Indies into her Greater East Asia sphere from February 1940 to December 1941 met with Dutch resistance. The Dutch authorities would not consent to allowing Japan a privileged economic position which she wanted so as to be able to assure her vital oil supplies and other minerals. Japan was also faced with strong American diplomatic and economic opposition. The extension of the Japanese occupation of southern Indo-China in July 1941 provided bases against Britain in Malaya and the

Dutch East Indies. But the alarm felt at Japanese expansion by the United States led to a number of American measures intended to hinder further Japanese expansion; the United States adopted what in practice amounted to a financial and oil embargo, and also increased military aid to China.

Though there were American–Japanese negotiations for a general settlement these were broken off by the Japanese attack at dawn on the American fleet at *Pearl Harbor on 7 December 1941*. About an hour and a half earlier, under cover of darkness, Japanese troops began landing on the British Malay coast. At 6 a.m. Japan declared war on Britain and the United States, but owing to the international dateline the day of Pearl Harbor was 8 December 1941 in Tokyo and Malaya. Japan's surprise attack was followed by a *German and Italian declaration of war on the United States on 11 December 1941*. The United States had now become a full ally of Britain and the Allied nations both in Asia and Europe.

The Munich Agreement between Germany, Britain, Italy and France, Munich, 29 September 1938

Germany, the United Kingdom, France and Italy, taking into consideration the agreement which has been already reached in principle for the cession to Germany of the Sudeten German territory, have agreed on the following terms and conditions governing the said cession and the measures consequent thereon, and by this Agreement they each hold themselves responsible for the steps necessary to secure its fulfilment:

1. The evacuation will begin on 1st October.

2. The United Kingdom, France and Italy agree that the evacuation of the territory shall be completed by 10th October without any existing installations having been destroyed, and that the Czechoslovak Government will be held responsible for carrying out the evacuation without damage to the said installations.

3. The conditions governing the evacuation will be laid down in detail by an international commission composed of representatives of Germany, the United Kingdom, France, Italy and Czechoslovakia.

4. The occupation by stages of the predominantly German territory by German troops will begin on 1st October. The four territories marked on the attached map will be occupied by German troops in the following order: the territory marked No. I on the 1st and 2nd October; the territory marked No. II on the 2nd and 3rd October; the territory marked No. III on the 3rd, 4th and 5th October; the territory marked No. IV on the 6th and 7th October. The remaining territory of preponderatingly German character will be ascertained by the aforesaid international commission forthwith and be occupied by German troops by the 10th October.

5. The international commission referred to in paragraph 3 will determine the territories in which a plebiscite is to be held. These territories will be occupied

by international bodies until the plebiscite has been completed. The same commission will fix the conditions in which the plebiscite is to be held, taking as a basis the conditions of the Saar plebiscite. The commission will also fix a date, not later than the end of November, on which the plebiscite will be held.

6. The final determination of the frontier will be carried out by the international commission. This commission will also be entitled to recommend to the four Powers – Germany, the United Kingdom, France and Italy – in certain exceptional cases minor modifications in the strictly ethnographical determination of the zones which are to be transferred without plebiscite.

7. There will be a right of option into and out of the transferred territories, the option to be exercised within six months from the date of this Agreement. A German-Czechoslovak commission shall determine the details of the option, consider ways of facilitating the transfer of population and settle questions of principle arising out of the said transfer.

8. The Czech Government will, within a period of four weeks from the date of this Agreement, release from their military and police forces any Sudeten Germans who may wish to be released, and the Czech Government will, within the same period, release Sudeten German prisoners who are serving terms of imprisonment for political offences.

Munich, September 29, 1938

Annex

His Majesty's Government in the United Kingdom and the French Government have entered into the above agreement on the basis that they stand by the offer, contained in paragraph 6 of the Anglo-French proposals of 19th September, relating to an international guarantee of the new boundaries of the Czech State against unprovoked aggression.

When the question of the Polish and Hungarian minorities in Czechoslovakia has been settled, Germany and Italy, for their part, will give a guarantee to Czechoslovakia.

Munich, September 29, 1938

Declaration

The heads of the Governments of the four Powers declare that the problems of the Polish and Hungarian minorities in Czechoslovakia, if not settled within three months by agreement between the respective Governments, shall form the subject of another meeting of the heads of the Governments of the four Powers here present.

Munich, September 29, 1938

Supplementary Declaration

All questions which may arise out of the transfer of the territory shall be considered as coming within the terms of reference of the international commission.

Munich, September 29, 1938

The four heads of Governments here present agree that the international commission provided for in the Agreement signed by them today shall consist of the Secretary of State in the German Foreign Office, the British, French and Italian Ambassadors accredited in Berlin, and a representative to be nominated by the Government of Czechoslovakia.

Munich, September 29, 1938

Anglo-German Declaration, Munich, 30 September 1938

We, the German Führer and Chancellor and the British Prime Minister, have had a further meeting today and are agreed in recognizing that the question of Anglo-German relations is of the first importance for the two countries and for Europe.

We regard the agreement signed last night and the Anglo-German Naval Agreement as symbolic of the desire of our two peoples never to go to war with one another again.

We are resolved that the method of consultation shall be the method adopted to deal with any other questions that may concern our two countries, and we are determined to continue our efforts to remove possible sources of difference and thus to contribute to assure the peace of Europe.

(Signed) A. HITLER
(Signed) NEVILLE CHAMBERLAIN

Statement by Chamberlain in the House of Commons concerning the guarantee to Poland, 31 March 1939

The Prime Minister [Mr Chamberlain]: The Right Hon. Gentleman the Leader of the Opposition asked me this morning whether I could make a statement as to the European situation. As I said this morning, His Majesty's Government have no official confirmation of the rumours of any projected attack and they must not, therefore, be taken as accepting them as true.

I am glad to take this opportunity of stating again. the general policy of His Majesty's Government. They have constantly advocated the adjustment, by way of free negotiation between the parties concerned, of any differences that may arise between them. They consider that this is the natural and proper course where differences exist. In their opinion there should be no question incapable of solution by peaceful means, and they would see no justification for the substi-

tution of force or threats of force for the method of negotiation.

As the House is aware, certain consultations are now proceeding with other Governments. In order to make perfectly clear the position of His Majesty's Government in the meantime before those consultations are concluded, I now have to inform the House that during that period, in the event of any action which clearly threatened Polish independence, and which the Polish Government accordingly considered it vital to resist with their national force, His Majesty's Government would feel themselves bound at once to lend the Polish Government all support in their power. They have given the Polish Government an assurance to this effect.

I may add that the French Government have authorized me to make it plain that they stand in the same position in this matter as do His Majesty's Government.

Agreement of Mutual Assistance between Britain and Poland, London, 25 August 1939

The Government of the United Kingdom of Great Britain and Northern Ireland and the Polish Government:

Desiring to place on a permanent basis the collaboration between their respective countries resulting from the assurances of mutual assistance of a defensive character which they have already exchanged;

Have resolved to conclude an Agreement for that purpose and have ... agreed on the following provisions:

Article 1. Should one of the Contracting Parties become engaged in hostilities with a European Power in consequence of aggression by the latter against that Contracting Party, the other Contracting Party will at once give the Contracting Party engaged in hostilities all the support and assistance in its power.

Article 2. 1. The provisions of Article 1 will also apply in the event of any action by a European Power which clearly threatened, directly or indirectly, the independence of one of the Contracting Parties, and was of such a nature that the party in question considered it vital to resist it with its armed forces.

2. Should one of the Contracting Parties become engaged in hostilities with a European Power in consequence of action by that Power which threatened the independence or neutrality of another European State in such a way as to constitute a clear menace to the security of that Contracting Party, the provisions of Article 1 will apply, without prejudice, however, to the rights of the other European State concerned.

Article 3. Should a European Power attempt to undermine the independence of one of the Contracting Parties by processes of economic penetration or in any other way, the Contracting Parties will support each other in resistance to such attempts. Should the European Power concerned thereupon embark on hostilities against one of the Contracting Parties, the provisions of Article 1 will apply.

Article 4. The methods of applying the undertakings of mutual assistance provided for by the present Agreement are established between the competent naval, military and air authorities of the Contracting Parties.

Article 5. Without prejudice to the foregoing undertakings of the Contracting Parties to give each other mutual support and assistance immediately on the outbreak of hostilities, they will exchange complete and speedy information concerning any development which might threaten their independence and, in particular, concerning any development which threatened to call the said undertakings into operation.

Article 6. 1. The Contracting Parties will communicate to each other the terms of any undertakings of assistance against aggression which they have already given or may in future give to other States.

2. Should either of the Contracting Parties intend to give such an undertaking after the coming into force of the present Agreement, the other Contracting Party shall, in order to ensure the proper functioning of the Agreement, be informed thereof.

3. Any new undertaking which the Contracting Parties may enter into in future shall neither limit their obligations under the present Agreement nor indirectly create new obligations between the Contracting Party not participating in these undertakings and the third State concerned.

Article 7. Should the Contracting Parties be engaged in hostilities in consequence of the application of the present Agreement, they will not conclude an armistice or treaty of peace except by mutual agreement.

Article 8. 1. The present Agreement shall remain in force for a period of five years.

2. Unless denounced six months before the expiry of this period it shall continue in force, each Contracting Party having thereafter the right to denounce it at any time by giving six months' notice to that effect.

3. The present Agreement shall come into force on signature.

In faith whereof the above-named plenipotentiaries have signed the present Agreement and have affixed thereto their seals.

Done in English in duplicate at London, the 25th August 1939. A Polish text shall subsequently be agreed upon between the Contracting Parties and both texts will then be authentic.

(L.S.)   HALIFAX
(L.S.)   EDWARD RACZYŃSKI

Secret Protocol

The Polish Government and the Government of the United Kingdom of Great Britain and Northern Ireland are agreed upon the following interpretation of the Agreement of Mutual Assistance signed this day as alone authentic and binding:

1. (a) By the expression 'a European Power' employed in the Agreement is to be understood Germany.

(b) In the event of action within the meaning of Articles 1 or 2 of the Agreement by a European Power other than Germany, the Contracting Parties will consult together on the measures to be taken in common.

2. (a) The two Governments will from time to time determine by mutual agreement the hypothetical cases of action by Germany coming within the ambit of Article 2 of the Agreement.

(b) Until such time as the two Governments have agreed to modify the following provisions of this paragraph, they will consider: that the case contemplated by paragraph 1 of Article 2 of the Agreement is that of the Free City of Danzig; and that the cases contemplated by paragraph 2 of Article 2 are Belgium, Holland, Lithuania.

(c) Latvia and Estonia shall be regarded by the two Governments as included in the list of countries contemplated by paragraph 2 of Article 2 from the moment that an undertaking of mutual assistance between the United Kingdom and a third State covering those two countries enters into force.

(d) As regards Roumania, the Government of the United Kingdom refers to the guarantee which it has given to that country; and the Polish Government refers to the reciprocal undertakings of the Roumano-Polish alliance which Poland has never regarded as incompatible with her traditional friendship for Hungary.

3. The undertakings mentioned in Article 6 of the Agreement, should they be entered into by one of the Contracting Parties with a third State, would of necessity be so framed that their execution should at no time prejudice either the sovereignty or territorial inviolability of the other Contracting Party.

4. The present Protocol constitutes an integral part of the Agreement signed this day, the scope of which it does not exceed.

In faith whereof the undersigned, being duly authorized, have signed the present Protocol.

Done in English in duplicate, at London, the 25th August 1939. A Polish text will subsequently be agreed upon between the Contracting Parties and both texts will then be authentic.

(Signed)   HALIFAX
(Signed)   EDWARD RACZYŃSKI

Protocol of Mutual Assistance between Poland and France, 4 September 1939

Article 1. The Polish Government and the French Government, desiring to assure the full efficacy of the Polish-French Alliance, and having especially in view the present situation of the League of Nations, agree to confirm that their mutual obligations of assistance in the event of aggression by a third Power continue to be founded on the Agreements of Alliance in force.

At the same time they declare that henceforth they interpret the said Agreements as embodying the following obligations: The undertaking of the two Contracting Parties mutually to render all aid and assistance in their power at once and from the outbreak of hostilities between one of the Contracting Parties and a European Power in consequence of that Power's aggression against the said Contracting Party, equally applies to the case of any action by a European Power which manifestly directly or indirectly threatens the independence of one of the Contracting Parties, and is of such a nature that the Party in question considers it vital to resist that aggression with its armed forces.

Should one of the Contracting Parties become engaged in hostilities with a European Power in consequence of action by that Power which threatened the independence or neutrality of another European State in such a way as to constitute a clear menace to the security of that Contracting Party, the provisions of Article 1 will apply, without prejudice, however, to the rights of the other European State concerned.

Article 2. The methods of applying the undertakings of mutual assistance provided for by the present Agreement are established between the competent military, naval, and air authorities of the Contracting Parties.

Article 3. 1. The Contracting Parties will communicate to each other the terms of any undertakings of assistance against aggression which they have already given or may in the future give to other States.

2. Should either of the Contracting Parties intend to give such an undertaking after the coming into force of the present Agreement, the other Contracting Party shall, in order to ensure proper functioning of the Agreement, be informed thereof.

3. Any new undertaking which the Contracting Parties may enter into in the future shall neither limit their obligations under the present Agreement nor indirectly create new obligations between the Contracting Party not participating in those undertakings and the third State concerned.

Article 4. Should the Contracting Parties be engaged in hostilities in consequence of the application of the present Agreement, they will not conclude an armistice or treaty of peace except by mutual agreement.

The present Protocol, constituting an integral part of the Polish-French Agreements of 1921 and 1925, shall remain in force as long as the said Agreements.

Alliance between Germany and Italy (Pact of Steel), 22 May 1939

The German Chancellor and His Majesty the King of Italy and Albania, Emperor of Ethiopia, deem that the time has come to strengthen the close relationship of friendship and homogeneity, existing between National Socialist Germany and Fascist Italy, by a solemn pact.

Now that a safe bridge for mutual aid and assistance has been established by the common frontier between Germany and Italy fixed for all time, both Governments reaffirm the policy, the principles and objectives of which have already been agreed upon by them, and which has proved successful, both for promoting the interests of the two countries and also for safeguarding peace in Europe.

Firmly united by the inner affinity between their ideologies and the comprehensive solidarity of their interests, the German and Italian nations are resolved in future also to act side by side and with united forces to secure their living space and to maintain peace.

Following this path, marked out for them by history, Germany and Italy intend, in the midst of a world of unrest and disintegration, to serve the task of safeguarding the foundations of European civilization.

In order to lay down these principles in a pact there have been appointed plenipotentiaries ... and they have agreed on the following terms.

Article I. The High Contracting Parties will remain in continuous contact with each other in order to reach an understanding on all questions affecting their common interests or the general European situation.

Article II. Should the common interests of the High Contracting Parties be endangered by international events of any kind whatsoever, they will immediately enter into consultations on the measures to be taken for the protection of these interests.

Should the security or other vital interests of one of the High Contracting Parties be threatened from without, the other High Contracting Party will afford the threatened party full political and diplomatic support in order to remove this threat.

Article III. If, contrary to the wishes and hopes of the High Contracting Parties, it should happen that one of them became involved in warlike complications with another Power or Powers, the other High Contracting Party would immediately come to its assistance as an ally and support it with all its military forces on land, at sea and in the air.

Article IV. In order to ensure in specific cases the speedy execution of the obligations of alliance undertaken under Article III, the Governments of the two High Contracting Parties will further intensify their collaboration in the military field, and in the field of war economy.

In the same way the two Governments will remain in continuous consultation also on other measures necessary for the practical execution of the provisions of this Pact.

For the purposes indicated in paragraphs 1 and 2 above, the two Governments will set up commissions which will be under the direction of the two Foreign Ministers.

Article V. The High Contracting Parties undertake even now that, in the event of war waged jointly, they will conclude an armistice and peace only in full agreement with each other.

Article VI. The two High Contracting Parties are aware of the significance that attaches to their common relations with Powers friendly to them. They are resolved to maintain these relations in the future also and together to shape them in accordance with the common interests which form the bonds between them and these Powers.

Article VII. This Pact shall enter into force immediately upon signature. The two High Contracting Parties are agreed in laying down that its first term of validity shall be for ten years. In good time before the expiry of this period, they will reach agreement on the extension of the validity of the Pact.

In witness whereof the plenipotentiaries have signed this Pact and affixed thereto their seals.

Done in duplicate in the German and the Italian languages, both texts being equally authoritative.

Berlin, May 22, 1939, in the XVIIth year of the Fascist Era.

JOACHIM V. RIBBENTROP
GALEAZZO CIANO

Trade Agreement between the Soviet Union and Germany, 19 August 1939

[The contents of this agreement can be derived from the German Foreign Ministry Memorandum of 29 August 1939 below.]

Memorandum

The German-Soviet Trade Agreement concluded on August 19 covers the following:

1. Germany grants the Soviet Union a merchandise credit of 200 million Reichsmarks. The financing will be done by the German Golddiskontbank ... [at an actual rate of interest of 4½ per cent].

2. The credit will be used to finance Soviet orders in Germany. The Soviet Union will make use of it to order the industrial products listed in schedule A of the Agreement. They consist of machinery and industrial installations. Machine tools up to the very largest dimensions form a considerable part of the deliveries. And armaments in the broader sense (such as optical supplies, armour plate and the like) will, subject to examination of every single item, be supplied in smaller proportion.

3. The credit will be liquidated by Soviet raw materials, which will be selected by agreement between the two Governments. The annual interest will

likewise be paid from the proceeds of Soviet merchandise, that is, from the special accounts kept in Berlin.

4. In order that we might secure an immediate benefit from the Credit Agreement, it was made a condition from the beginning that the Soviet Union bind itself to the delivery, starting immediately, of certain raw materials as current business. It was possible so to arrange these raw-material commitments of the Russians that our wishes were largely met. The Russian commitments of raw materials are contained in schedule C. They amount to 180 million Reichsmarks: half to be delivered in each of the first and second years following the conclusion of the Agreement. It is a question, in particular, of lumber, cotton, feed grain, oil cake, phosphate, platinum, raw furs, petroleum, and other goods which for us have a more or less gold value.

5. Since these Soviet deliveries made as current business are to be compensated by German counterdeliveries, certain German promises of delivery had to be made to the Russians. The German industrial products to be supplied in current business as counterdeliveries for Russian raw materials are listed in schedule B. This schedule totals 120 million Reichsmarks and comprises substantially the

same categories of merchandise as schedule A.

6. From the welter of difficult questions of detail which arose during the negotiations, the following might also be mentioned: guaranteeing of the rate of exchange of the Reichsmark. The complicated arrangement arrived at appears in the Confidential Protocol signed on August 26 of this year. In order not to jeopardize the conclusion of the Agreement on August 19 of this year, the question was laid aside and settled afterwards. The questions of the liquidation of the old credits, the shipping clause, an emergency clause for the event of inability to deliver of either party, the arbitration procedure, the price clause, etc., were settled satisfactorily despite the pressure of time.

7. The Agreement, which has come into being after extraordinary difficulties, will undoubtedly give a decided impetus to German–Russian trade. We must try to build anew on this foundation and, above all, try to settle a number of questions which could not heretofore be settled, because of the low ebb which had been reached in our trade relations. The framework now set up represents a minimum. Since the political climate is favourable, it may well be expected that it will be exceeded considerably in both directions, both in imports and exports.

8. Under the Agreement, the following movement of goods can be expected for the next few years:

Exports to the U.S.S.R.

200 million Reichsmarks credit deliveries, schedule 'A'.

120 mill. RM. deliveries as current business, schedule 'B'.

X mill. RM. unspecified deliveries on current business.

Imports from the U.S.S.R.

180 mill. RM. raw material deliveries, schedule 'C'.

200 mill. RM. repayment of 1935 credit.

approx. 100 mill. RM. capitalized interest from present and last credit.

X mill. RM. unspecified deliveries of Soviet goods under German–Soviet Trade Agreement of Dec. 19, 1938.

The movement of goods envisaged by the Agreement might therefore reach a total of more than 1 billion Reichsmarks for the next few years, not including liquidation of the present 200 million credit by deliveries of Russian raw materials beginning in 1946.

9. Apart from the economic imports of the Treaty, its significance lies in the fact that the negotiations also served to renew political contacts with Russia and that the Credit Agreement was considered by both sides as the first decisive step in the reshaping of political relations.

Treaty of Non-Aggression between Germany and the Soviet Union, Moscow, 23 August 1939

The Government of the German Reich and

The Government of the Union of Soviet Socialist Republics

Desirous of strengthening the cause of peace between Germany and the U.S.S.R., and proceeding from the fundamental provisions of the Neutrality Agreement concluded in April 1926 between Germany and the U.S.S.R., have reached the following Agreement:

Article I. Both High Contracting Parties obligate themselves to desist from any act of violence, any aggressive action, and any attack on each other, either individually or jointly with other Powers.

Article II. Should one of the High Contracting Parties become the object of belligerent action by a third Power, the other High Contracting Party shall in no manner lend its support to this third Power.

Article III. The Governments of the two High Contracting Parties shall in the future maintain continual contact with one another for the purpose of consultation in order to exchange information on problems affecting their common interests.

Article IV. Neither of the two High Contracting Parties shall participate in any grouping of Powers whatsoever that is directly or indirectly aimed at the other party.

Article V. Should disputes or conflicts arise between the High Contracting Parties over problems of one kind or another, both parties shall settle these disputes or conflicts exclusively through friendly exchange of opinion or, if necessary, through the establishment of arbitration commissions.

Article VI. The present Treaty is concluded for a period of ten years, with the proviso that, in so far as one of the High Contracting Parties does not denounce it one year prior to the expiration of this period, the validity of this Treaty shall automatically be extended for another five years.

Article VII. The present Treaty shall be ratified within the shortest possible time. The ratifications shall be exchanged in Berlin. The Agreement shall enter into force as soon as it is signed.

Secret Additional Protocol

On the occasion of the signature of the Non-Aggression Pact between the German Reich and the Union of Socialist Soviet Republics the undersigned plenipotentiaries of each of the two parties discussed in strictly confidential conversations the question of the boundary of their respective spheres of influence in Eastern Europe. These conversations led to the following conclusions:

Article 1. In the event of a territorial and political rearrangement in the areas belonging to the Baltic States (Finland, Estonia, Latvia, Lithuania), the northern boundary of Lithuania shall represent the boundary of the spheres of influence of Germany and the U.S.S.R. In this connection the interest of Lithuania in the Vilna area is recognized by each party.

Article 2. In the event of a territorial and political rearrangement of the areas belonging to the Polish State the spheres of influence of Germany and the U.S.S.R. shall be bounded approximately by the line of the rivers Narew, Vistula, and San.

The question of whether the interests of both parties make desirable the maintenance of an independent Polish State and how such a State should be bounded can only be definitely determined in the course of further political developments.

In any event both Governments will resolve this question by means of a friendly agreement.

Article 3. With regard to south-eastern Europe attention is called by the Soviet side to its interest in Bessarabia. The German side declares its complete political disinterestedness in these areas.

Article 4. This Protocol shall be treated by both parties as strictly secret.

Moscow, August 23, 1939

For the Government
of the German Reich:
v. Ribbentrop

Plenipotentiary of the
Government of the U.S.S.R.
V. Molotov

Treaty of Mutual Assistance between Britain, France and Turkey 19 October 1939

Article 1. In the event of Turkey being involved in hostilities with a European Power in consequence of aggression by that Power against Turkey, France and the United Kingdom will cooperate effectively with Turkey and will lend her all aid and assistance in their power.

Article 2. 1. In the event of an act of aggression by a European Power leading to war in the Mediterranean area in which France and the United Kingdom are involved, Turkey will collaborate effectively with France and the United Kingdom and will lend them all aid and assistance in her power.

2. In the event of an act of aggression by a European Power leading to war in the Mediterranean area in which Turkey is involved, France and the United Kingdom will collaborate effectively with Turkey and will lend her all aid and assistance in their power.

Article 3. So long as the guarantees given by France and the United Kingdom to Greece and Roumania by their respective Declarations of the 13th April 1939 remain in force, Turkey will cooperate effectively with France and the United Kingdom and will lend them all aid and assistance in her power, in the event of France and the United Kingdom being engaged in hostilities in virtue of either of the said guarantees.

Article 4. In the event of France and the United Kingdom being involved in hostilities with a European Power in consequence of aggression committed by that Power against either of those States without the provisions of Articles 2 or 3 being applicable, the High Contracting Parties will immediately consult together.

It is nevertheless agreed that in such an eventuality Turkey will observe at least a benevolent neutrality towards France and the United Kingdom.

Article 5. Without prejudice to the provisions of Article 3 above, in the event of either:

1. Aggression by a European Power against another European State which the Government of one of the High Contracting Parties had, with the approval of that State, undertaken to assist in maintaining its independence or neutrality against such aggression, or

2. Aggression by a European Power which while directed against another European State, constituted, in the opinion of the Government of one of the High Contracting Parties, a menace to its own security,

the High Contracting Parties will immediately consult together with a view to such common action as might be considered effective.

Article 6. The present Treaty is not directed against any country, but is designed to assure France, the United Kingdom and Turkey of mutual aid and assistance in resistance to aggression should the necessity arise.

Article 7. The provisions of the present Treaty are equally binding as bilateral obligations between Turkey and each of the two other High Contracting Parties.

Article 8. If the High Contracting Parties are engaged in hostilities in consequence of the operation of the present Treaty, they will not conclude an armistice or peace except by common agreement.

Article 9. The present Treaty shall be ratified and the instruments of ratification shall be deposited simultaneously at Angora as soon as possible. It shall enter into force on the date of this deposit.

The present Treaty is concluded for a period of fifteen year If none of the High Contracting Parties has notified the two others of its intention to terminate it six months before the expiration of the said period, the Treaty will be renewed by tacit consent for a further period of five years, and so on.

Protocol No. 1

The undersigned plenipotentiaries state that their respective Governments agree that the Treaty of today's date shall be put into force from the moment of its signature.

The present Protocol shall be considered as an integral part of the Treaty concluded today between France, the United Kingdom and Turkey.

Protocol No. 2

At the moment of signature of the Treaty between France, the United Kingdom and Turkey, the undersigned plenipotentiaries, duly authorized to this effect, have agreed as follows:

The obligations undertaken by Turkey in virtue of the above-mentioned Treaty cannot compel that country to take action having as its effect, or involving as its consequence, entry into armed conflict with the Soviet Union.

Declaration of Principles known as the Atlantic Charter, made public on 14 August 1941

Joint Declaration of the President of the United States of America and the Prime Minister, Mr Churchill, representing His Majesty's Government in the United Kingdom, being met together, deem it right to make known certain common principles in the national policies of their respective countries on which they base their hopes for a better future for the world.

First, their countries seek no aggrandizement, territorial or other;

Second, they desire to see no territorial changes that do not accord with the freely expressed wishes of the peoples concerned;

Third, they respect the right of all peoples to choose the form of government under which they will live; and they wish to see sovereign rights and self-government restored to those who have been forcibly deprived of them;

Fourth, they will endeavour, with due respect for their existing obligations, to further the enjoyment by all States, great or small, victor or vanquished, of access, on equal terms, to the trade and to the raw materials of the world which are needed for their economic prosperity;

Fifth, they desire to bring about the fullest collaboration between all nations in the economic field with the object of securing, for all, improved labour standards, economic advancement and social security;

Sixth, after the final destruction of the Nazi tyranny, they hope to see established a peace which will afford to all nations the means of dwelling in safety within their own boundaries, and which will afford assurance that all the men in all the lands may live out their lives in freedom from fear and want;

Seventh, such a peace should enable all men to traverse the high seas and oceans without hindrance;

Eighth, they believe that all of the nations of the world, for realistic as well as spiritual reasons must come to the abandonment of the use of force. Since no future peace can be maintained if land, sea or air armaments continue to be employed by nations which threaten, or may threaten, aggression outside of their frontiers, they believe, pending the establishment of a wider and permanent system of general security, that the dis-armament of such nations is essential. They will likewise aid and encourage all other practicable measures which will lighten for peace-loving peoples the crushing burden of armaments.

Boundary and Friendship Treaty between the Soviet Union and Germany, Moscow, 28 September 1939

The Government of the German Reich and the Government of the U.S.S.R. consider it as exclusively their task, after the collapse of the former Polish State, to re-establish peace and order in these territories and to assure to the peoples living there a peaceful life in keeping with their national character. To this end, they have agreed upon the following:

Article I. The Government of the German Reich and the Government of the U.S.S.R. determine as the boundary of their respective national interests in the territory of the former Polish State the line marked on the attached map, which shall be described in more detail in a Supplementary Protocol.

Article II. Both parties recognize the boundary of the respective national interests established in Article I as definitive and shall reject any interference of third Powers in this settlement.

Article III. The necessary reorganization of public administration will be effected in the areas west of the line specified in Article I by the Government of the German Reich, in the areas east of this line by the Government of the U.S.S.R.

Article IV. The Government of the German Reich and the Government of the U.S.S.R. regard this settlement as a firm foundation for a progressive development of the friendly relations between their peoples.

Article V. This Treaty shall be ratified and the ratifications shall be exchanged in Berlin as soon as possible. The Treaty becomes effective upon signature.

Confidential Protocol

[Provided that Germans and people of German descent may leave territories under Soviet jurisdiction for Germany, and Ukrainians and White Russians may leave German territories for Soviet Union.]

Secret Supplementary Protocol

The undersigned plenipotentiaries declare the agreement of the Government of the German Reich and the Government of U.S.S.R. on the following:

The Secret Supplementary Protocol signed on August 23, 1939 shall be amended in Item 1 to the effect that the territory of the Lithuanian State falls in the sphere of influence of U.S.S.R., while, on the other hand, the province of Lublin and parts of the province of Warsaw fall in the sphere of influence of Germany (cf. the map attached to the Frontier and Friendship Treaty signed today). As soon as the Government of U.S.S.R. takes special measures on Lithuanian territory to protect its interests, the present German–Lithuanian frontier, for the purpose of a natural and simple frontier delineation, will be rectified in such a way that the Lithuanian territory situated to the south-west of the line marked on the attached map will fall to Germany.

Further it is declared that the Economic Agreements now in force between Germany and Lithuania will not be affected by the measures of the Soviet Union referred to above.

Secret Supplementary Protocol

The undersigned plenipotentiaries, on concluding the German–Russian Frontier and Friendship Treaty, have declared their agreement on the following:

Neither party will tolerate in its territories Polish agitation that affects the territories of the other party. Both parties will suppress in their territories all beginnings of such agitation and will inform each other concerning suitable measures for this purpose.

Declaration

After the Government of the German Reich and the Government of U.S.S.R. have, by means of the Treaty signed today, definitively settled the problems arising from the collapse of the Polish State and have thereby created a sure foundation for a lasting peace in Eastern Europe, they mutually express their conviction that it would serve the true interests of all peoples to put an end to the state of war existing at present between Germany on the one side, and England and France on the other. Both Governments will therefore direct their common efforts, jointly with other friendly Powers if occasion arises, towards attaining this goal as soon as possible.

Should, however, the efforts of the two Governments remain fruitless, this would demonstrate the fact that England and France are responsible for the continuation of the war, whereupon, in case of the continuation of the war, the Governments of Germany and of U.S.S.R. will engage in mutual consultations with regard to necessary measures.

Commercial Agreement between the Soviet Union and Germany, 11 February 1940

[Information based on German Foreign Ministry Memorandum below.]

Memorandum

The Agreement is based on the correspondence—mentioned in the Preamble —between the Reich Minister for Foreign Affairs and the Chairman of the Council of People's Commissars, Molotov, dated September 28, 1939. The Agreement represents the first great step towards the economic programme envisaged by both sides and is to be followed by others.

1. The Agreement covers a period of twenty-seven months, i.e. the Soviet deliveries, which are to be made within eighteen months, will be compensated by German deliveries in turn within twenty-seven months. The most difficult point of the correspondence of September 28, 1939, namely, that the Soviet raw material deliveries are to be compensated by German industrial deliveries over a *longer period*, is thereby settled in accordance with our wishes. . . .

2. The Soviet deliveries. According to the Agreement, the Soviet Union shall within the first twelve months deliver raw materials in the amount of approximately 500 million Reichsmarks.

In addition, the Soviets will deliver raw materials, contemplated in the Credit Agreement of August 19, 1939, for the same period, in the amount of approximately 100 million Reichsmarks.

The most important raw materials are the following:

1,000,000 tons of grain for cattle, and of legumes, in the amount of 120 million Reichsmarks

900,000 tons of mineral oil in the amount of approximately 115 million Reichsmarks

100,000 tons of cotton in the amount of approximately 90 million Reichsmarks

500,000 tons of phosphates

100,000 tons of chrome ores

500,000 tons of iron ore

300,000 tons of scrap iron and pig iron

2,400 kg of platinum

Manganese ore metals, lumber, and numerous other raw materials.

... [Stalin also promised to purchase raw materials in third countries for Germany.]

Pact of Mutual Assistance between the Soviet Union and Latvia, Moscow, 5 October 1939

[Pacts of Mutual Assistance were also concluded with Estonia, 28 September 1939, and Lithuania, 10 October 1939.]

The Presidium of the Supreme Soviet of U.S.S.R. on the one hand, and the President of the Latvian Republic on the other, for the purpose of developing the friendly relations created by the Peace Treaty of August 11, 1920, which were based on the recognition of the independent statehood and non-interference in the internal affairs of the other party; recognizing that the Peace Treaty of August 11, 1920 and the Agreement of February 5, 1932 concerning non-aggression and the amicable settlement of conflicts, continue to be the firm basis of their mutual relations and obligations; convinced that a definition of the precise conditions ensuring mutual safety is in accordance with the interests of both Contracting Parties; have considered it necessary to conclude between them the following Mutual Assistance Pact ...

Article I. Both Contracting Parties undertake to render each other every assistance, including military, in the event of a direct attack, or threat of attack, on the part of any European Great Power, with respect to the sea borders of the Contracting Parties on the Baltic Sea, or their land borders through the territory of the Estonian or Latvian Republics, or also the bases referred to in Article III.

Article II. The Soviet Union undertakes to render assistance on preferential conditions to the Latvian army in the form of armaments and other war materials.

Article III. In order to ensure the safety of U.S.S.R. and to consolidate her own independence, the Latvian Republic grants to the Union the right to maintain in the cities of Liapaja (Libava) and Ventspils (Vindava) naval bases and several airfields for aviation purposes on leasehold at a reasonable rental. The locations of the bases and airfields shall be exactly specified and their boundaries determined by mutual agreement.

For the purpose of protecting the Straits of Irbe, the Soviet Union is given the right to establish on the same conditions a coast artillery base between Ventspils and Pitrags.

For the purpose of protecting the naval bases, the airfields and the coast artillery base, the Soviet Union has the right to maintain at its own expense on the areas set aside for bases and airfields a strictly limited number of Soviet land and air forces, the maximum number of which is to be fixed by special agreement.

Article IV. Both Contracting Parties undertake not to enter into any alliances or to participate in any coalitions directed against one of the Contracting Parties.

Article V. The entry into force of the present Pact must in no way affect the sovereign rights of the Contracting Parties, in particular their political structure, their economic and social system, and their military measures.

The areas set aside for the bases and airfields (Article III) remain in the territory of the Latvian Republic.

Article VI. The present Pact goes into force with the exchange of documents of ratification. The exchange of documents will take place in the City of Riga within six days after the signing of the present Pact.

The present Pact shall remain in force for a period of ten years, and in the event that one of the Contracting Parties does not consider it necessary to denounce it prior to the expiration of such period, it will automatically remain in force for the following ten years.

Treaty of Non-Aggression between Germany and Turkey, 18 June 1941

Article 1. The Turkish Republic and the German Reich undertake to respect mutually the inviolability and integrity of their territories, and to abstain from all action aimed directly or indirectly against one another.

Article 2. The Turkish Republic and the German Reich undertake to enter into friendly contact in the future in regard to all matters involving their mutual

interests with a view to reaching an agreement for their solution.

Article 3. The present Treaty which shall enter into force on the date of its signature shall be valid for a period of ten years. The High Contracting Parties shall in due time reach an agreement on the matter of its prolongation.

The present Treaty shall be ratified and the ratifications shall be exchanged in Berlin as soon as possible. . . .

Three Powers Pact between Germany, Italy and Japan, Berlin, 27 September 1940

The Governments of Germany, Italy and Japan, considering it as the condition precedent of any lasting peace that all nations of the world be given each its own proper place, have decided to stand by and cooperate with one another in regard to their efforts in Greater East Asia and the regions of Europe respectively wherein it

is their prime purpose to establish and maintain a new order of things calculated to promote mutual prosperity and welfare of the peoples concerned.

Furthermore it is the desire of the three Governments to extend cooperation to such nations in other spheres of the world as may be inclined to put forth endeavours along lines similar to their own, in order that their ultimate aspirations for world peace may thus be realized. Accordingly the Governments of Germany, Italy and Japan have agreed as follows:

Article 1. Japan recognizes and respects the leadership of Germany and Italy in the establishment of a new order in Europe.

Article 2. Germany and Italy recognize and respect the leadership of Japan in the establishment of a new order in Greater East Asia.

Article 3. Germany, Italy and Japan agree to cooperate in their efforts on the aforesaid lines. They further undertake to assist one another with all political, economic and military means when one of the three Contracting Parties is attacked by a Power at present not involved in the European War or in the Sino-Japanese Conflict.

Article 4. With a view to implementing the present Pact, joint technical commissions the members of which are to be appointed by the respective Governments of Germany, Italy and Japan will meet without delay.

Article 5. Germany, Italy and Japan affirm that the aforesaid terms do not in any way affect the political status which exists at present as between each of the three Contracting Parties and Soviet Russia.

Article 6. The present Pact shall come into effect immediately upon signature and shall remain in force for ten years from the date of its coming into force.

At proper time before the expiration of the said term the High Contracting Parties shall, at the request of any one of them, enter into negotiations for its renewal....

Agreement between Germany, Italy and Japan on the joint prosecution of the war, Berlin, 11 December 1941

In their unshakeable determination not to lay down arms until the common war against the United States of America and Britain has been brought to a successful conclusion, the German Government, the Italian Government, and the Japanese Government have agreed upon the following provisions:

Article 1. Germany, Italy and Japan jointly and with every means at their disposal will pursue the war forced upon them by the United States of America and Britain to a victorious conclusion.

Article 2. Germany, Italy, and Japan undertake not to conclude an armistice or peace with the United States of America or Britain except in complete mutual agreement.

Article 3. After victory has been achieved Germany, Italy, and Japan will continue in closest cooperation with a view to establishing a new and just order along the lines of the Tripartite Agreement concluded by them on September 27, 1940.

Article 4. The present Agreement will come into force with its signature, and will remain valid as long as the Tripartite Pact of September 27, 1940.

The High Contracting Parties will in good time before the expiry of this term of validity enter into consultation with each other as to the future development of their cooperation, as provided under Article 3 of the present Agreement.

VIII · The Grand Alliance: Britain, the United States and the Soviet Union, 1941–5

Britain, the United States and the Soviet Union, June 1941–June 1942

In a broadcast on the evening of 22 June 1941, Winston Churchill promised help to Russians fighting for their homeland in the cause of 'free men and free people' everywhere. Military supplies from Britain and America began to reach the Soviet Union in appreciable quantities in the autumn of 1941. The Anglo-Soviet alliance against Germany was first placed on a formal basis by the brief *Anglo-Soviet Agreement of 12 July 1941*, in which the two Powers undertook to render each other assistance and support in the war against 'Hitlerite Germany', and not to negotiate an armistice or peace treaty except by mutual agreement. From the first, relations between the Soviet Union and Britain, and later the United States, were made difficult by Stalin's insistent demand that Russia's allies should engage the Germans on the continent of Europe. His call for a second front was not fully satisfied until the Allied landings in France in June 1944. As a result of Russian pressure, however, *Britain declared war on Finland, Hungary and Rumania on 6 December 1941*. Bulgaria had not joined in the German war against the Soviet Union, but to show a theoretical loyalty to the Axis declared war on Britain and the United States on 13 December 1941.

An *Anglo-Soviet–Iranian Treaty was concluded on 29 January 1942* (p. 210) which promised Britain and Russia all facilities to defend Iran from aggression, and Britain and Russia promised to respect Persian independence and integrity and to withdraw not later than six months after the war. Negotiations for a full Anglo-Soviet alliance were long drawn-out. Stalin's suspicions of Britain's resolution to relieve German military pressure in Russia, and Russian territorial demands in the post-war European settlement, were the major obstacles. Russia wished recognition of her right to the Baltic States and to

Poland up to the Curzon line, with possible minor frontier readjustments. But Britain, and later the United States, had agreed to postpone all questions of the new frontiers until after the war. Finally the Russian denial of, and Poland's insistence on, her claim to the right of restoration within her pre-1939 frontiers could not be reconciled; Britain gave support to Poland in 1941 declaring in a *Note to the Polish Government, 30 July 1941* (p. 211), that it recognized none of the changes of territory brought about in Poland by the Soviet Union or Germany since August 1939. The fundamental differences between the Allies are reflected in the difficulties the negotiators faced in attempting to reach agreement and to conclude treaties.

With Japan's attack on Pearl Harbor on 7 December 1941, and Germany's and Italy's declaration of war on the United States on 11 December 1941, Britain, the United States and Russia became allies in the war against Germany and Italy, but only Britain and the United States were allies in the war against Japan. In the drafting of a comprehensive alliance between the Powers at war this was a further cause of difficulty. Such a comprehensive alliance was first set out in negotiations in Washington and took the form of the *United Nations Declaration of 1 January 1942* (p. 212). The 'United Nations' declaration, a phrase originating with Roosevelt, was intended to circumvent the right of the United States Senate to pass by a two-thirds majority treaties of alliance negotiated with foreign Powers. The Free French did not sign despite the loophole which would have allowed 'appropriate authorities which are not Governments' to adhere. The Joint Declaration listed the Allied nations in alphabetical order but placed at the head were the United States, Britain, the U.S.S.R. and China. In this way these four nations were treated differently from the rest thus setting out their status as 'Great Powers'.

In the spring of 1942, Britain and the Soviet Union concluded the negotiation of an alliance treaty begun the previous autumn. The Soviet Union agreed to the omission of a clause defining specific frontiers, such as her rights to all territory included in Soviet Russia on 22 June 1941. The Russians at the time were anxious to hasten the opening of a 'second front' against Germany in France.

The *Anglo-Soviet Alliance of 26 May 1942* (p. 212) appeared momentous at the time because it provided a bond between the Soviet Union and Britain, a great 'capitalistic' imperial Power. The treaty was intended to outlast the German war for it was given a duration of twenty years. It repeated the undertakings of the agreement of 12 July 1941 (mutual assistance, no separate peace), but went further in a second part which set out some of the principles of post-war cooperation. The signatories envisaged an organization of States for the preservation of peace; Britain and the Soviet Union also declared that they would 'take into account' the interests of the United Nations and not seek 'territorial aggrandizement for themselves'. Stalin, of course, did not regard the incorporation in the Soviet Union of eastern Poland in 1939 and the Baltic States in 1940 as 'aggrandizement', since he claimed the populations concerned had opted for the Soviet Union. Churchill had been ready in March 1942 to go further and to breach the principle of no frontier discussions by accepting Russia's claim to her 1940 frontiers (including the Baltic States, Bessarabia, Bukovina and Finnish conquests), except for territories which had been Polish in 1939. In the event the Soviet Union accepted the treaty without territorial clauses.

Poland, Czechoslovakia and the Soviet Union, 1941-4

The Polish Government in exile in London, headed by General Wladislav Sikorski, fought uncompromisingly for Poland's pre-war frontiers. With the entry of the U.S.S.R. into the war the Polish Government with equal urgency wished to secure the release of Polish prisoners placed into camps by the Russians. Polish–Soviet diplomatic relations were resumed with the signature of the *Polish–Soviet Treaty of 30 July 1941*. Though the Soviet Union in this treaty declared that the German–Soviet treaties of 1939 relating to Polish territory had 'lost their validity' Stalin did not abandon his claim to the Polish territory then seized.

The *Anglo-Soviet Agreement of 12 July 1941* had been accompanied by a *British Note to the Polish Government of 30 July 1941* (p. 211) in which the British Government declared that, in conformity with the Anglo-Polish alliance of 1939, it had entered into no undertaking towards the U.S.S.R. affecting Polish–Soviet relations, and that His Majesty's Government did not recognize any territorial changes which had been effected in Poland since August 1939.

On *14 August 1941 a Polish–Soviet Military Agreement* was concluded providing for the organization of a Polish army in the U.S.S.R. Poles kept in camps in Russia were to be released. The U.S.S.R. was to assist in the arming of Polish units who would fight in the Soviet Union under Polish command, but this would be subordinated operationally under the High Command of the U.S.S.R. In December 1941 General Sikorski visited Moscow, and a *Polish–Soviet Declaration of Friendship and Mutual Assistance was signed on 4 December 1941*. But from 1941 to 1943 Polish–Soviet relations were embittered by Russia's claim to have irrevocably annexed the region of pre-war Poland occupied in 1939, and by Russian insistence that according to Soviet law the permanent inhabitants of those lands were Soviet citizens. The Poles were also dissatisfied with the treatment of Poles released from Russian camps, and individual cases of maltreatment. Polish officers and men continued to be missing. Soviet–Polish relations were close to breaking point when the Germans broadcast on 13 April 1943 that they had discovered a mass grave of some 10,000 Polish officers in Katyn, near Smolensk, and accused the Russians of their murder. The Polish Government requested the International Red Cross to investigate, and the Russians on 25 April 1943 severed relations with the Polish Government, declaring that the Germans had massacred the missing Polish officers and that in accusing the Russians the Polish Government in London was acting in collusion with Hitler. The problem of Poland continued to present a major difficulty in the way of Allied cooperation to the end of the war.

The Czechoslovak Government in exile chose a different course from the Polish Government in dealing with the Soviet Union. Soviet–Czech military cooperation against Germany was provided for in the *Czechoslovak–Soviet Agreement of 18 July 1941*. Benes had been disillusioned by the Munich settlement in 1938 (p. 176) and would no longer rely solely on the friendship of the Western Powers. He was determined to win Russia's friendship and to secure from all the Allies a declaration that since the Munich settlement had been imposed by threat of force on Czechoslovakia it was invalid. The British Government would only agree to declare that since the Germans had subsequently broken it, the Munich treaty was no longer binding. The Soviet Government, on the other hand, recognized the Czechoslovak Government in exile and Czechoslovakia in its 1937 frontiers, and also declared the Munich settlement as illegal and void. A *Soviet–Czechoslovak Treaty of Friendship and Alliance was signed on 12 December 1943* (p. 215). Benes, in Moscow for the signature of the treaty, was also confronted with Russian demands for aligning the post-war Czech economy with the Soviet economy, which he consented to in an additional agreement. *On 8 May 1944 a further Soviet–Czechoslovak Agreement regarding the administration of liberated Czechoslovak territories* was concluded. The Soviet advance into Czechoslovakia began in the autumn of 1944, but too late to prevent the Germans crushing a national uprising in Slovakia. Czech administrators were only permitted to function with Soviet consent and the Czechoslovak Government had to accept the 'wish' of the Ruthenians to accede to the Soviet Union. With the acquisition of this strategically vital territory together with the eastern Polish territories, the Soviet Union gained a common frontier with Hungary and Czechoslovakia.

The Allies and France, 1941-5

France and Germany signed an *armistice on 22 June 1940*. On 28 June 1940 the British Government recognized General de Gaulle as the 'Leader of all Free

Frenchmen, wherever they may be, who rally to him in support of the Allied cause'. The future of the French fleet, still in the control of the new French Government of Marshal Pétain, and of the French Colonial Empire remained in doubt, though Britain received French assurances that the fleet would not be allowed to fall into the hands of the Germans. But the British Government was not prepared to trust these assurances and there resulted the British bombardment on French warships at Mers-el-Kebir on 3 July 1940. Britain and Vichy France broke direct diplomatic links, but avoided a complete breach. The United States and Vichy France remained in complete and normal diplomatic relations after the armistice which precluded the recognition of de Gaulle's movement as the Government of France in exile. By the end of August 1940 the French African colonial territories of Chad and the Cameroons rallied to de Gaulle and became the nucleus of 'Free France'. The French Empire in North Africa and Indo-China remained loyal to Vichy France. On 8 June 1941 an Anglo-French force was sent to the French mandated territory of Syria, which remained loyal to Vichy. The Free French issued a proclamation declaring Syria and the Lebanon 'sovereign and independent peoples'. After heavy fighting *Syria* passed into Anglo-Free French wartime control with the *armistice of 14 July 1941*. In the autumn of 1941, the Free French movement was strengthened by the creation and British recognition of a Free French National Committee. But the United States continued to remain in full diplomatic relations with Vichy France after entering the war in December 1941. In July 1942 it recognized the French National Committee without breaking with Vichy, and by Allied agreement the Free French movement called itself the 'Fighting French', implying leadership of all Frenchmen fighting the Germans whether in 'Free' French territories or in metropolitan Vichy France.

Throughout 1942 the United States and Britain continued, for what appeared to be compelling military reasons, to treat Vichy France as a legitimate Government to ensure that the French fleet should remain in French hands and to avoid driving the Vichy North African territory into open opposition. In May 1942 British troops began the occupation of Vichy France Madagascar, without prior reference to General de Gaulle for fear of driving the Vichy colonial authorities into active opposition. Madagascar was a curtain raiser for North Africa where the Anglo-American allies were prepared to negotiate with the Vichy French authorities, ignoring the claims of the Free French National Committee to represent all French interests. Operation Torch was the name given to the Anglo-American invasion of French North Africa which had remained loyal to Vichy. General de Gaulle and the Free French did not participate in the landings, and the operation was kept secret from them. The

Allies pinned their hopes on General Giraud, who had escaped from a German prisoner-of-war camp in April 1942, to rally French North Africa to the Allied cause. The Allied landings began on 8 November 1942 near Algiers, Oran and Casablanca. Three days later, on 11 November, the Germans militarily occupied 'Unoccupied France', but the Vichy French commanders succeeded in scuttling the French fleet at Toulon. Contrary to expectations General Giraud had little influence. Admiral Darlan, who was visiting Algiers, as the highest ranking representative of Vichy commanded the French forces. *It was with the Vichy French administration under Darlan that the Allies reached agreement on 17 November 1942*, accepting Darlan's authority and securing the ending of French military resistance to the Allied operations. With the assassination of Darlan on 23 December 1942, Giraud assumed political leadership. Although General de Gaulle met General Giraud at the Casablanca conference in January 1943, Giraud maintained Vichy legality; *not until 3 June 1943 was an agreement signed fixing Giraud's and de Gaulle's authorities in a new French Committee of National Liberation* under their joint presidency. With the exception of the Soviet Government, Britain and the United States refused to recognize the National Committee as legitimately representing the interests of all France. The French Committee of National Liberation began to change its composition in November 1943, admitting French political parties and representatives of the Resistance and dropping Giraud step by step. On 15 May 1944 the French Committee of National Liberation changed its name to Provisional Government of the Republic of France under de Gaulle's leadership, General Giraud having resigned on 14 April 1944. But General Eisenhower, the Supreme Allied Commander, refused to recognize de Gaulle's authority before D-Day, 6 June 1944, when the Allies began their assault on German occupied France. Only on 11 July 1944 were the Americans prepared to recognize de Gaulle and his committee as the *de facto* representatives of the French people. Full recognition was awarded by Great Britain, the United States and the Soviet Union to General de Gaulle as the head of the Provisional Government of France on 23 October 1944. *An Alliance Treaty between the Soviet Union and France was concluded on 10 December 1944* (p. 216). France was invited to become a member of the European Advisory Commission and the fifth permanent member of the proposed Security Council of the United Nations organization (p. 242).

The Allies and Italy, 1943-5

The Allies landed in Sicily on 10 July 1943; on 25 July 1943 Mussolini fell from power and was replaced by Marshal Pietro Badoglio, who secretly negotiated a military armistice accepting the Allied terms of surrender on 3 September 1943. The *Italian armistice* required Italy to withdraw her armed forces from the war, established an Allied Military Government under the Allied Commander-in-Chief over all parts of Italy, and bound the Italian Government at a later time to accept the political and economic conditions demanded by the Allies. The armistice was publicly announced on *8 September 1943* to coincide with the Allied seaborne invasion of Italy at Salerno. More detailed armistice conditions were signed on *29 September 1943*. On 13 October 1943 the King of Italy declared war on Germany, and Italy was granted the status of co-belligerency. Italy became a battleground of the Allied forces and the Germans, who militarily occupied central and northern Italy over which Mussolini's Republic of Salo claimed legal control. The Italian Peace Treaty was eventually signed in February 1947, nearly two years after the German surrender in May 1945.

Alliance Treaty between Britain, the Soviet Union and Iran, 29 January 1942

Article 1. His Majesty The King of Great Britain, Ireland and the British Dominions beyond the Seas, Emperor of India, and the Union of Soviet Socialist Republics (hereinafter referred to as the Allied Powers) jointly and severally undertake to respect the territorial integrity, sovereignty and political independence of Iran.

Article 2. An alliance is established between the Allied Powers on the one hand and His Imperial Majesty The Shahinshah of Iran on the other.

Article 3. (i) The Allied Powers jointly and severally undertake to defend Iran by all means at their command from all aggression on the part of Germany or any other Power.

(ii) His Imperial Majesty The Shahinshah undertakes:

(a) To cooperate with the Allied Powers with all the means at his command and in every way possible, in order that they may be able to fulfil the above undertaking. The assistance of the Iranian forces shall, however, be limited to the mainten-

ance of internal security on Iranian territory;

(b) To secure to the Allied Powers, for the passage of troops or supplies from one Allied Power to the other or for other similar purposes, the unrestricted right to use, maintain, guard and, in case of military necessity, control in any way that they may require, all means of communication throughout Iran, including railways, roads, rivers, aerodromes, ports, pipelines and telephone, telegraph and wireless installations. . . .

Article 4. (i) The Allied Powers may maintain in Iranian territory land, sea and air forces in such number as they consider necessary. The location of such forces shall be decided in agreement with the Iranian Government so long as the strategic situation allows. . . .

Article 5. The forces of the Allied Powers shall be withdrawn from Iranian territory not later than six months after all hostilities between the Allied Powers and Germany and her associates have been suspended by the conclusion of an armistice or armistices, or on the conclusion of peace between them, whichever date is the earlier. The expression 'associates' of Germany means all other Powers which have engaged or may in the future engage in hostilities against either of the Allied Powers.

Article 6 (i) The Allied Powers undertake in their relations with foreign countries not to adopt an attitude which is prejudicial to the territorial integrity, sovereignty or political independence of Iran, nor to conclude treaties inconsistent with the provisions of the present Treaty. They undertake to consult the Government of His Imperial Majesty the Shahinshah in all matters affecting the direct interests of Iran.

(ii) His Imperial Majesty the Shahinshah undertakes not to adopt in his relations with foreign countries an attitude which is inconsistent with the alliance . . .

Note issued by the Foreign Office in London on non-recognition of any territorial changes in Poland since August 1939

London, 30 July 1941

1. An agreement between the Republic of Poland and the Soviet Union was signed in the Secretary of State's room at the Foreign Office on July 30. General Sikorski, Polish Prime Minister, signed for Poland; M. Maisky, Soviet Ambassador, signed for the Soviet Union. Mr Churchill and Mr Eden were present.

2. The agreement is being published.

3. After the signature of the agreement, Mr Eden handed to General Sikorski an official Note in the following terms:

On the occasion of the signature of the Polish–Soviet Agreement of today, I desire to take this opportunity of informing you that in conformity with the provision of the Agreement of Mutual Assistance between the United Kingdom and Poland of the 25th August 1939, His Majesty's Government in the United Kingdom have entered into no undertakings towards the Union of Socialist Soviet Republics which affect the relations between that country and Poland. I also desire to assure you that His Majesty's Government do not recognize any territorial changes which have been effected in Poland since August 1939.

General Sikorski handed to Mr Eden the following reply:

The Polish Government take note of your letter dated July 30 and desire to express sincere satisfaction at the statement that His Majesty's Government in the United Kingdom do not recognize any territorial changes which have been effected in Poland since August 1939. This corresponds with the view of the Polish Government which, as they have previously informed His Majesty's Government, have never recognized any territorial changes effected in Poland since the outbreak of the war.

Declaration by the United Nations, 1 January 1942

The Governments signatory hereto,

Having subscribed to a common programme of purposes and principals embodied in the Joint Declaration of the President of the United States of America and the Prime Minister of the United Kingdom of Great Britain and Northern Ireland dated August 14, 1941, known as the Atlantic Charter,

Being convinced that complete victory over their enemies is essential to defend life, liberty, independence and religious freedom, and to preserve human rights and justice in their own lands as well as in other lands, and that they are now engaged in a common struggle against savage and brutal forces seeking to subjugate the world,

Declare:

(i) Each Government pledges itself to employ its full resources, military or economic, against those members of the Tripartite Pact and its adherents with which such Government is at war.

(ii) Each Government pledges itself to cooperate with the Governments signatory hereto and not to make a separate armistice or peace with the enemies.

The foregoing Declaration may be adhered to by other nations which are, or may be, rendering material assistance and contributions in the struggle for victory over Hitlerism.

Alliance between Britain and the Soviet Union, London, 26 May 1942

His Majesty The King of Great Britain, Ireland, and the British Dominions beyond the Seas, Emperor of India, and the Presidium of the Supreme Council of the Union of Soviet Socialist Republics;

Desiring to confirm the stipulations of the Agreement between His Majesty's Government in the United Kingdom and the Government of the Union of Soviet Socialist Republics for joint action in the war against Germany, signed at Moscow on the 12th July 1941, and to replace them by a formal treaty;

Desiring to contribute after the war to the maintenance of peace and to the prevention of further aggression by Germany or the States associated with her in acts of aggression in Europe;

Desiring, moreover, to give expression to their intention to collaborate closely with one another as well as with the other United Nations at the peace settlement and during the ensuing period of reconstruction on the basis of the principles enunciated in the declaration made on the 14th August 1941 by the President of the United States of America and the Prime Minister of Great Britain to which the Government of the Union of Soviet Socialist Republics has adhered;

Desiring, finally, to provide for mutual assistance in the event of an attack upon either High Contracting Party by Germany or any of the States associated with her in acts of aggression in Europe....

Have decided to conclude a Treaty for that purpose and have appointed as their plenipotentiaries:

His Majesty The King of Great Britain, Ireland, and the British Dominions beyond the Seas, Emperor of India,

For the United Kingdom of Great Britain and Northern Ireland:

The Right Honourable Anthony Eden, M.P., His Majesty's Principal Secretary of State for Foreign Affairs,

The Presidium of the Supreme Council of the Union of Soviet Socialist Republics:

M. Vyacheslav Mikhailovich Molotov, People's Commissar for Foreign Affairs,

Who, having communicated their full powers, found in good and due form, have agreed as follows:

Part I

Article I. In virtue of the alliance established between the United Kingdom and the Union of Soviet Socialist Republics the High Contracting Parties mutually undertake to afford one another military and other assistance and support of all kinds in the war against Germany and all those States which are associated with her in acts of aggression in Europe.

Article II. The High Contracting Parties undertake not to enter into any negotiations with the Hitlerite Government or any other Government in Germany that does not clearly renounce all aggressive intentions, and not to negotiate or conclude except by mutual consent any armistice or peace treaty with Germany or any other State associated with her in acts of aggression in Europe.

Part II

Article III. (1) The High Contracting Parties declare their desire to unite with other like-minded States in adopting proposals for common action to preserve peace and resist aggression in the post-war period.

(2) Pending the adoption of such proposals, they will after the termination of hostilities take all the measures in their power to render impossible a repetition of aggression and violation of the peace by Germany or any of the States associated with her in acts of aggression in Europe.

Article IV. Should one of the High Contracting Parties during the post-war period become involved in hostilities with Germany or any of the States mentioned in Article III (2) in consequence of an attack by that State against that party, the other High Contracting Party will at once give to the Contracting Party so involved in hostilities all the military and other support and assistance in his power.

This Article shall remain in force until the High Contracting Parties, by mutual agreement, shall recognize that it is superseded by the adoption of the proposals contemplated in Article III (1). In default of the adoption of such proposals, it shall remain in force for a period of twenty years, and thereafter until terminated by either High Contracting Party, as provided in Article VIII.

Article V. The High Contracting Parties, having regard to the interests of the security of each of them, agree to work together in close and friendly collaboration after the re-establishment of peace for the organization of security and economic prosperity in Europe. They will take into account the interests of the United Nations in these objects, and they will act in accordance with the two principles of not seeking territorial aggrandizement for themselves and of non-interference in the internal affairs of other States.

Article VI. The High Contracting Parties agree to render one another all possible economic assistance after the war.

Article VII. Each High Contracting Party undertakes not to conclude any alliance and not to take part in any coalition directed against the other High Contracting Party.

Article VIII. The present Treaty is subject to ratification in the shortest possible time and the instruments of ratification shall be exchanged in Moscow as soon as possible.

It comes into force immediately on the exchange of the instruments of ratification and shall thereupon replace the Agreement between the Government of the Union of Soviet Socialist Republics and His Majesty's Government in the United Kingdom, signed at Moscow on the 12th July 1941.

Part I of the present Treaty shall remain in force until the re-establishment of peace between the High Contracting Parties and Germany and the Powers associated with her in acts of aggression in Europe.

Part II of the present Treaty shall remain in force for a period of twenty years. Thereafter, unless twelve months' notice has been given by either party to terminate the Treaty at the end of the said period of twenty years, it shall continue in force until twelve months after either High Contracting Party shall have given notice to the other in writing of his intention to terminate it.

In witness whereof the above-named plenipotentiaries have signed the present Treaty and have affixed thereto their seals.

Done in duplicate in London on the 26th day of May, 1942, in the English and Russian languages, both texts being equally authentic.

(L.S.) ANTHONY EDEN
(L.S.) V. MOLOTOV

Agreement between Poland and the Soviet Union, 30 July 1941

The Government of the Republic of Poland and the Government of the Union of Soviet Socialist Republics have concluded the present Agreement and decided as follows:

1. The Government of the Union of Soviet Socialist Republics recognizes that the Soviet-German treaties of 1939 relative to territorial changes in Poland have lost their validity. The Government of the Republic of Poland declares that Poland is not bound by any Agreement with any third State directed against the U.S.S.R.

2. Diplomatic relations will be restored between the two Governments upon the signature of this Agreement and an exchange of Ambassadors will follow immediately.

3. The two Governments mutually undertake to render one another aid and support of all kinds in the present war against Hitlerite Germany.

4. The Government of the Union of Soviet Socialist Republics expresses its consent to the formation on the territory of the Union of Soviet Socialist Republics of a Polish army under a commander appointed by the Government of the Republic of Poland, in agreement with the Government of the Union of Soviet Socialist Republics. The Polish army on the territory of the Union of Soviet Socialist Republics will be subordinated in operational matters to the Supreme Command of the U.S.S.R. on which there will be a representative of the Polish army. All details as to command, organization and employment of this force will be settled in a subsequent agreement.

5. This Agreement will come into force immediately upon its signature and without ratification. The present Agreement is drawn up in two copies, each of them in the Russian and Polish languages. Both texts have equal force.

Secret Protocol

1. Various claims both of public and private nature will be dealt with in the course of further negotiations between the two Governments.

2. This Protocol enters into force simul-

taneously with the Agreement of the 30th of July, 1941.

Protocol

1. As soon as diplomatic relations are re-established the Government of the Union of Soviet Socialist Republics will grant amnesty to all Polish citizens who are at present deprived of their freedom on the territory of the U.S.S.R. either as prisoners of war or on other adequate grounds.

2. The present Protocol comes into force simultaneously with the Agreement of July 30, 1941.

Treaty of Friendship and Mutual Assistance and Post-War Cooperation between the Soviet Union and Czechoslovakia, Moscow, 12 December 1943

The Presidium of the Supreme Soviet of the Union of Soviet Socialist Republics and the President of the Czechoslovakian Republic, desiring to modify and supplement the Treaty of Mutual Assistance existing between the Union of Soviet Socialist Republics and the Czechoslovakian Republic and signed in Prague on May 16, 1935, and to confirm the terms of the Agreement between the Government of the Union of Soviet Socialist Republics and the Government of the Czechoslovakian Republic concerning joint action in the war against Germany, signed July 18, 1941, in London; desiring to cooperate after the war to maintain peace and to prevent further aggression on the part of Germany and to assure permanent friendship and peaceful post-war cooperation between them, have resolved to conclude for this purpose a Treaty and ... have agreed to the following:

Article 1. The High Contracting Parties, having agreed mutually to join in a policy of permanent friendship and friendly post-war cooperation, as well as of mutual assistance, engage to extend to each other military and other assistance and support of all kinds in the present war against Germany and against all those States which are associated with it in acts of aggression in Europe.

Article 2. The High Contracting Parties engage not to enter during the period of the present war into any negotiations with the Hitler Government or with any other Government in Germany which does not clearly renounce all aggressive intentions, and not to carry on negotiations and not to conclude without mutual agreement any armistice or other treaty of peace with Germany or with any other State associated with it in acts of aggression in Europe.

Article 3. Affirming their pre-war policy of peace and mutual assistance, expressed in the treaty signed at Prague on May 16, 1935, the High Contracting Parties, in case one of them in the period after the war should become involved in military action with Germany, which might resume its policy of 'Drang nach Osten', or with any other State which might join with Germany directly or in any other form in such a war, engage to extend immediately to the other Contracting Party thus involved in military action all manner of military and other support and assistance at its disposal.

Article 4. The High Contracting Parties, having regard to the security interests of each of them, agree to close and friendly cooperation in the period after the restoration of peace and agree to act in accordance with the principles of mutual respect for their independence and sovereignty, as well as of non-interference in the internal affairs of the other State. They agree to develop their economic relations to the fullest possible extent and to extend to each other all possible economic assistance after the war.

Article 5. Each of the High Contracting Parties engages not to conclude any alliance and not to take part in any coalition directed against the other High Contracting Party.

Article 6. The present Treaty shall come into force immediately after signature and shall be ratified within the shortest possible time; the exchange of ratifications will take place in Moscow as soon as possible.

The present Treaty shall remain in force for a period of twenty years from the date of signature, and if one of the High Contracting Parties at the end of this period of twenty years does not give notice of its desire to terminate the Treaty twelve months before its expiration, it will continue to remain in force for the following five years and for each ensuing five-year period unless one of the High Contracting Parties gives notice in writing twelve months before the expiration of the current five-year period of its intention to terminate it.

Protocol

On the conclusion of the Treaty of Friendship, Mutual Assistance and Post-War Cooperation between the Union of Soviet Socialist Republics and the Czechoslovakian Republic the High Contracting Parties undertake that, in the event that any third country bordering on the U.S.S.R. or the Czechoslovakian Republic and constituting in this war an object of German aggression desires to subscribe to this Treaty, it will be given the opportunity, upon the joint agreement of the Governments of the U.S.S.R. and the Czechoslovakian Republic, to adhere to this Treaty, which will thus acquire the character of a tripartite agreement.

By Authority of the Presidium of the Supreme Council of the U.S.S.R.
V. MOLOTOV

By Authority of the President of the Czechoslovakian Republic
Z. FIERLINGER

Treaty of Alliance and Mutual Assistance between the Soviet Union and the French Republic, Moscow, 10 December 1944

The Presidium of the Supreme Soviet of the Union of Soviet Socialist Republics and the Provisional Government of the French Republic, determined to prosecute jointly and to the end the war against Germany, convinced that once victory is achieved, the re-establishment of peace on a stable basis and its prolonged maintenance in the future will be conditioned upon the existence of close collaboration between them and with all the United Nations; having resolved to collaborate in the cause of the creation of an international system of security for the effective maintenance of general peace and for ensuring the harmonious development of relations between nations; desirous of confirming the mutual obligations resulting from the exchange of letters of September 20, 1941, concerning joint actions in the war against Germany; convinced that the conclusion of an alliance between the U.S.S.R. and France corresponds to the sentiments and interests of both peoples, the demands of war, and the requirements of peace and economic reconstruction in full conformity with the aims which the United Nations have set themselves, have decided to conclude a Treaty to this effect and appointed as their plenipotentiaries . . .

Article I. Each of the High Contracting Parties shall continue the struggle on the side of the other party and on the side of the United Nations until final victory over Germany. Each of the High Contracting Parties undertakes to render the other party aid and assistance in this struggle with all the means at its disposal.

Article II. The High Contracting Parties shall not agree to enter into separate negotiations with Germany or to conclude without mutual consent any armistice or peace treaty either with the Hitler Government or with any other Government or authority set up in Germany for the purpose of the continuation or support of the policy of German aggression.

Article III. The High Contracting Parties undertake also, after the termination of the present war with Germany, to take jointly all necessary measures for the elimination of any new threat coming from Germany, and to obstruct such actions as would make possible any new attempt at aggression on her part.

Article IV. In the event either of the High Contracting Parties finds itself involved in military operations against Germany, whether as a result of aggression committed by the latter or as a result of the operation of the above Article III, the other party shall at once render it every aid and assistance within its power.

Article V. The High Contracting Parties undertake not to conclude any alliance and not to take part in any coalition directed against either of the High Contracting Parties.

Article VI. The High Contracting Parties agree to render each other every possible economic assistance after the war, with a view to facilitating and accelerating reconstruction of both countries, and in order to contribute to the cause of world prosperity.

Article VII. The present Treaty does not in any way affect obligations undertaken previously by the High Contracting Parties in regard to third States in virtue of published treaties.

Article VIII. The present Treaty, whose Russian and French texts are equally valid, shall be ratified and ratification instruments shall be exchanged in Paris as early as possible. It comes into force from the moment of the exchange of ratification instruments and shall be valid for twenty years. If the Treaty is not denounced by either of the High Contracting Parties at least one year before the expiration of this term, it shall remain valid for an unlimited time; each of the Contracting Parties will be able to terminate its operation by giving notice to that effect one year in advance. . . .

On the authorization of the Presidium of the Supreme Soviet of the U.S.S.R.

MOLOTOV

On the authorization of the Provisional Government of the French Republic

BIDAULT

IX · The Allied conferences and the political settlement of Europe, 1943–5

The conferences

The Allied conferences from 1943 to 1945 attempted to reconcile the wartime military policies of the Allies with an agreed programme of post-war settlements in Europe and Asia. For the sake of the maximum possible degree of military cooperation which was necessary to defeat the powerful and fanatically tenacious German war effort, fundamental Allied differences were not allowed to develop into major rifts. At the Yalta Conference the 'Great Power' interests of Britain, the United States and the Soviet Union largely determined the post-war settlements not only of defeated enemies but also of the smaller Allies. At Yalta, the Big Three displayed at least an outward show of unanimity of purpose and wartime comradeship. By the time of the Potsdam Conference a few months later the Allied differences which developed into the 'cold war' were already strongly in evidence.

The ten major Allied conferences of this period fall into two divisions: (1) predominantly Anglo-American, and (2) Three Power conferences between Russia, Britain and the United States, sometimes with other countries present. The table illustrated on pages 220–1 summarizes their sequence.

The first two important conferences of 1943 endeavoured to coordinate British and United States diplomacy and did not involve the Russians. From a political point of view the *Conference of Casablanca* (Churchill, Roosevelt, Combined Chiefs of Staff) *14–25 January 1943* was notable for the attempt made to bring together Generals Giraud and de Gaulle; also for the 'unconditional surrender' call as the only terms the Allies would offer their enemies. The phrase 'unconditional surrender' had been under discussion, but was omitted from the final communiqué, though publicly announced in a press conference given by President Roosevelt.

Research which was to lead to the making of the atomic bomb was the subject of a secret Anglo-American agreement at the *Quebec Conference of August 1943*, not disclosed until 1954. The exclusive possession of the bomb with its secrets, and the unknown possible application of atomic energy after the war, made the knowledge of the secrets one of the most prized assets of power in the war and in the post-war world. These secrets were not shared with the Soviet Union. *The Agreement on Anglo-American–Canadian collaboration and development of atomic research was signed on 19 August 1943* by Churchill and Roosevelt. It set out the policy of pooling in the United States the scientists and resources to speed the project. The two countries undertook not to use the atomic bomb against each other; they also agreed not to use it against another country without each others' consent; they agreed not to communicate any information to another country without their mutual consent. Britain disclaimed any 'post-war advantages of an industrial or commercial character' beyond what the President of the United States considered fair and just and for the welfare of the world. Allocation of materials, all policy, and interchange of information was to be the function of a Combined Policy Committee of the three American, two British and one Canadian officials. Information about large-scale plants was to become the subject of later agreements. The first atomic bomb was dropped on Hiroshima on 6 August 1945 and the second on Nagasaki on 9 August 1945. The post-war operation of this secret executive agreement caused Anglo-American differences of opinion in 1945 and 1946 after Roosevelt's death; its existence was unknown to Congress. The American desire to preserve secrecy and military nuclear monopoly led to the passing of the McMahon Act in 1946 which made the wartime agreement in practice inoperative (p. 510).

At the *Conference of Foreign Ministers at Moscow* (Molotov, Eden, Hull, Deane) *18–30 October 1943*, agreement was reached on a *Four Power Declaration of General Security* whereby the United States, Great Britain, the Soviet Union and China agreed to help establish a general international organization for the maintenance of peace and security, and to continue their collaboration in peace as in war. The conference also agreed to set up a *European Advisory Commission* with headquarters in London to consider all specific questions concerning the surrender terms and their execution; the commission was empowered to make recommendations but could exercise no mandatory authority. An *Advisory Council for Italy* was also established but exercised little influence. The Foreign Ministers agreed that Austria should be re-established as an independent State after the war. A decision on cooperating in the punishment of individuals

Date	Subjects discussed
14–25 January 1943	Reconciling 'Free French'; 'unconditional surrender' call; Far Eastern and European strategy.
August 1943	Atomic research and use of atomic bomb; 'second front' in Europe; Far Eastern strategy; Italian surrender.
18–30 October 1943	U.N.; Austria; surrender terms; war criminals.
22–26 November 1943	Japanese surrender terms; Far Eastern settlement; Far Eastern military strategy.
28 November–1 December 1943	European and Far Eastern strategy; Russia and Japan; U.N.; Turkey; Italy; Russia's eastern frontiers; Poland; Germany's eastern frontier.
21 August–28 September and 29 September–7 October 1944	U.N.
11–19 September 1944	Germany; military strategy in Europe and in war against Japan.
9–20 October 1944	Balkan 'spheres of influence'; Poland; Soviet entry into war against Japan.
30 January–3 February 1945	Military strategy; occupation zones in Germany; Italy and China.
4–11 February 1945	Post-war policies: Germany, U.N., Poland, liberated Europe, Russia, Japan and China.
25 April–26 June 1945	U.N.
1–22 July 1945	International finance and trade.
17 July–2 August 1945	Draft peace treaties; Germany; Poland; Japan.

Anglo-American and others	Three Powers: Britain, U.S. and U.S.S.R.
Casablanca	
Quebec (with Canada) Quadrant	
	Moscow Conference of Foreign Ministers
Cairo (with China)	
	Teheran
	Dumbarton Oaks (second part with China)
Quebec (with Canada) Octagon	
	Anglo-Soviet discussion in Moscow, Churchill, Eden and Stalin with Harriman as 'observer'
Malta	
	Yalta
	San Francisco (together with delegations of countries at war with Germany)
	Bretton Woods (U.N. conference)
	Potsdam

responsible for atrocities was also reached. At the end of the conference an official communiqué was issued together with four *Declarations on General Security, Italy, Austria, and German Atrocities, 30 October 1943.*

The Cairo Conference took place on 22–26 November 1943 (Roosevelt, Churchill, Chiang Kai-shek). The Russians would not attend since they were not at war with Japan. Besides military strategy in the Far East, the post-war settlement there was discussed. The final communiqué outlined the territorial peace terms the three Allies would impose on Japan, and promised Korea independence in due course.

Roosevelt and Churchill next flew to Persia to participate with the Russians in the *Teheran Conference* (Churchill, Roosevelt, Stalin, Eden, Hopkins, Combined Chiefs of Staff) *28 November–1 December 1943.* The military situation in Europe and the Far East was discussed. Stalin declared Russia would join in the war against Japan after victory over Germany. There were exploratory discussions concerning the future of France, Germany and Poland. Roosevelt initiated a discussion on the establishment of a post-war international organization to preserve peace and security. It was agreed that 'Overlord', the Anglo-American invasion of northern France, would take place on 1 May 1944. Turkey and Italy were discussed. No formal written agreement was reached on Russia's and Poland's western frontiers, though Churchill agreed to the Curzon line as a basis and to the acquisition by Poland of German territory east of the Oder river. A declaration promised to Iran independence and territorial integrity. A communiqué on the results of the conference was published on 6 December 1943.

More than a year elapsed after the conclusion of the Teheran Conference until Churchill, Roosevelt and Stalin met again at Yalta in February 1945. Meantime Roosevelt and Churchill and the Combined Chiefs of Staff had met at *Quebec, 11–19 September 1944* to discuss future policy towards Germany; Churchill flew to Moscow to discuss post-war spheres of influence, the Balkans and Poland, with Stalin; Harriman attended as an observer from 9–20 October 1944. Shortly before Yalta, the Combined Chiefs of Staff, Churchill, Eden and Stettinius met at *Malta, 30 January–3 February 1945*, to examine military strategy and the Anglo-American zones of occupation, and briefly discuss Italy and China.

The 'Big Three' meeting at *Yalta* (Churchill, Roosevelt, Stalin, Chiefs of Staff, Molotov, Stettinius, Eden, Hopkins) *4–11 February 1945* (p. 226) was the most crucial of the war in moulding the reconstruction of the post-war world. Roosevelt was anxious to secure a firm Russian undertaking to join in the war against Japan. He acceded to Stalin's condition that Russia should resume her old rights in China lost as a result of the Russo-Japanese war of 1904–5.

Despite the difficulties of China's rights, *a secret tripartite agreement was signed concerning Russia's participation in the war against Japan on 11 February 1945* (p. 230); this agreement was only published a year after its signature on 11 February 1946. Allied policy towards Germany led to discussions and agreements at Yalta. The European Advisory Commission had reached agreed recommendations which formed the basis of the awards at Yalta on the zones of occupation, on Berlin and on the form of Allied control. At Yalta agreement was also reached to allow the French a zone of occupation and to admit France as an equal member of the Allied Control Commission for Germany. A decision on reparations was referred to a Reparations Commission to be set up in Moscow. The decisions concerning Allied treatment of Germany reached at Yalta lacked precision and were vague, since practical details were not worked out. They were summarized in Protocols III, IV, V and VI of the Proceedings of the Conference. Protocol I set out the agreement reached on the setting up of a World Organization of the United Nations, and more especially on the voting formula for the Security Council; it was agreed to call a United Nations Conference at San Francisco on 25 April 1945 (p. 227).

The future of Poland was a most contentious and difficult issue at Yalta, and no precise conclusions were reached on post-war Polish boundaries (though the Curzon line with some small digressions in Poland's favour was referred to as Poland's eastern frontier). Nor was there agreement over the 'reconstruction' of the Polish Government. The ambiguous Declaration on Poland was embodied in Protocol VII. A number of other important post-war problems were set out in Protocols IX to XIV. Finally, the Declaration on Liberated Europe, Protocol II, is noteworthy as an attempt, on American initiative, to commit Russia to the restoration of democratic national self-government to the States occupied by the Russian armies at the close of the war.

By the time of the next Big Three meeting at Potsdam in July 1945 the war in Europe was over. Admiral Dönitz, who had succeeded Hitler, authorized the acceptance of Germany's unconditional surrender, and the instrument of surrender was signed at Eisenhower's headquarters in Rheims on 7 May 1945; Stalin insisted on a second capitulation in Berlin on 9 May 1945 a day after the fighting had ended. Before the Potsdam meeting the agreements reached at Yalta were being differently interpreted by the Allies. Russian pressure for the establishment of a communist Government on 6 March 1945 was regarded by the Western Allies as in breach of the Declaration of Liberated Europe. On 10 March 1945, Stalin assigned to Rumania the part of Transylvania which Hitler had awarded to Hungary. Allied disputes over the future Polish Government continued. On 12 April 1945 Roosevelt died and Truman was sworn in as President. Serious Allied differences over the control of Austria, deep suspicion of Russian intentions in Poland, problems in occupied Germany, hard-won agreement over the establishment of an international organization and the reparations question were all part of the diplomatic confrontation during the immediate aftermath of the end of the war in Europe. Some differences were patched up. The Charter of the United Nations was signed on 26 June 1945 (p. 247). The British and American Governments recognized a reorganized Soviet-sponsored Polish Provisional Government of National Unity on 5 July 1945. The machinery of Allied control over Germany was established, and the zones of occupation brought under the respective military control of the U.S.S.R., France, Britain and the United States. The Polish western frontier had not been finally settled at Yalta; the Russians handed over German territory as far as the rivers Oder and the western Neisse to Polish administration. The Potsdam Conference was to settle future Allied policies, to lay the foundation for definitive peace settlements and to reach agreed policies on the treatment of Germany.

The Potsdam Conference, 17 July–2 August 1945 (p. 231) – *Attlee, Churchill* (Prime Minister until 26 July when the General Election brought Attlee and the Labour Party to power), *Stalin, Truman, Bevin, Byrnes, Eden, Molotov* – appeared to get off to a good start with an agreement on an American proposal that a Council of Foreign Ministers should be set up to prepare drafts of peace treaties with the ex-enemy States in Europe and Asia (this body replaced the European Advisory Commission); London was chosen as the permanent seat of the council. The French had not been invited to Potsdam but were to be represented on the Council of Foreign Ministers. Germany's frontiers were not established with finality, though it was agreed that the frontiers of 1937 should be taken as the basis for discussion, which excluded Austria, the territory taken from Czechoslovakia at Munich, as well as German-occupied Poland. The Polish question led to acrimonious debate, particularly the extent of Polish expansion eastward at Germany's expense, the Russians and Britain and the United States differing later as to what had been settled. The agreement left under the Polish administration the territory assigned to them by the Russians, adding that it was not 'considered as part of the Soviet zone of occupation of Germany'; while the final delimitation of Poland's western frontier was reserved until the conclusion of a German peace treaty. Russian claims to about half of East Prussia including Königsberg were accepted, by Britain and the United States who undertook to support Russia when a peace conference assembled. Agreement was reached on the treatment of Austria. But Soviet insistence that immediate recognition be granted to the Soviet-sponsored Armistice Governments of Hungary, Bulgaria and Rumania proved unacceptable to the three Western Powers, as did Western insistence on supervised genuinely free elections. In practice these three countries were left in Soviet control. The Western interpretation of the Yalta Declaration on Liberated Europe could not be realized. Many questions remained unsettled, such as the Turkish Straits and the Italian colonies. On the central problem of the treatment of Germany, agreements were reached which reflected paper compromises. The idea of partitioning Germany into a number of States was dropped. Supreme authority in Germany was to be exercised by the Commanders-in-Chief of the British, French, American and Russian armed forces each in their own zones, whilst for Germany as a whole they were to act jointly as members of the Control Council. Principles governing the treatment of the whole of Germany leading to disarmament, de-Nazification and demilitarization were agreed. But policies in practice differed widely between the Russian and Western zones of occupation. Similarly, it was agreed that Germany was to be treated as a single economic unit with a living standard for the German people *not exceeding* the average of other Europeans, but again control of German industry was exercised differently in each zone, as was the collection of reparations despite agreement on general principles. The differing views of the Russians and Western Powers on reparations and the German frontiers proved amongst the most intractable problems of the conference. The decisions concerning Germany in practice undermined the general principle of treating occupied Germany as a whole, and confirmed the divisions of Germany especially as between the Russian and Western zones. A major problem was the settlement of German refugees, several million of whom were either fleeing or were being expelled from Polish-occupied Germany, from the Czech Sudetenland, East Prussia and Hungary. Their expulsion was accepted at Potsdam as necessary but it was to be carried out in an 'orderly and humane manner'.

The surrender of Japan, 14 August 1945

The British and American delegations at Potsdam agreed, on behalf of the nations at war with Japan, on a declaration calling upon Japan to submit to surrender 'unconditionally', and published the *Potsdam Declaration on 26 July 1945*. In practice this declaration outlined surrender conditions. On 6 and 9 August 1945 atomic bombs were dropped on Hiroshima and Nagasaki. On 8 August 1945 the Soviet Union declared war on Japan, to take effect the following day when the Russian armies began occupying Manchuria. On 10 August the Japanese acceptance of the conditions of the Potsdam Declaration was received by the Americans, but Japan's acceptance was conditional on the Allies agreeing that the prerogatives of the Emperor as a sovereign ruler were not prejudiced. The Americans replied on 11 August 1945 that the Emperor would be subject to the Supreme Commander and that the 'ultimate form of government of Japan shall, in accordance with the Potsdam Declaration, be established by the freely expressed will of the Japanese people'. On these conditions the Japanese surrendered on 14 August 1945. The formal instrument of surrender was signed on 2 September 1945 in Tokyo Bay. Japanese armies throughout Asia surrendered to the military Commander-in-Chief in each region. The Japanese armies in Manchuria, Korea north of the 38th parallel, the Kuriles and Sakhalin surrendered to the Russians. The Soviet Union regularized the hasty Russian invasion of Manchuria by concluding the *Sino-Soviet Treaty of Friendship on 14 August 1945* (p. 237).

Report of the Crimea Conference (*Yalta Conference*), *11 February 1945*

For the past eight days Winston S. Churchill, Prime Minister of Great Britain, Franklin D. Roosevelt, President of the United States of America, and Marshal J. V. Stalin, Chairman of the Council of People's Commissars of the Union of Soviet Socialist Republics, have met with the Foreign Secretaries, Chiefs of Staff and other advisers in the Crimea.

In addition to the three Heads of Government, the following took part in the Conference . . .

The following statement is made by the Prime Minister of Great Britain, the President of the United States of America, and the Chairman of the Council of People's Commissars of the Union of Soviet Socialist Republics, on the results of the Crimea Conference.

I · THE DEFEAT OF GERMANY

We have considered and determined the military plans of the three Allied Powers for the final defeat of the common enemy. The military staffs of the three Allied nations have met in daily meetings throughout the Conference. These meetings have been most satisfactory from every point of view and have resulted in closer coordination of the military effort of the three Allies than ever before. The fullest information has been interchanged. The timing, scope and coordination of new and even more powerful blows to be launched by our armies and air forces into the heart of Germany from the East, West, North and South have been fully agreed and planned in detail.

Our combined military plans will be made known only as we execute them, but we believe that the very close working partnership among the three staffs attained at this Conference will result in shortening the war. Meetings of the three staffs will be continued in the future whenever the need arises.

Nazi Germany is doomed. The German people will only make the cost of their defeat heavier to themselves by attempting to continue a hopeless resistance.

II · THE OCCUPATION AND CONTROL OF GERMANY

We have agreed on common policies and plans for enforcing the unconditional surrender terms which we shall impose together on Nazi Germany after German armed resistance has been finally crushed. These terms will not be made known until the final defeat of Germany has been accomplished. Under the agreed plan, the forces of the Three Powers will each occupy a separate zone of Germany. Coordinated administration and control has been provided for under the plan through a central Control Commission consisting of the Supreme Commanders of the Three Powers with headquarters in Berlin. It has been agreed that France should be invited by the Three Powers, if she should so desire, to take over a zone of occupation, and to participate as a fourth member of the Control Commission. The limits of the French zone will be agreed by the four Governments concerned through their representatives on the European Advisory Commission.

It is our inflexible purpose to destroy German militarism and Nazism and to ensure that Germany will never again be able to disturb the peace of the world. We are determined to disarm and disband all German armed forces; break up for all time the German General Staff that has repeatedly contrived the resurgence of German militarism; remove or destroy all German military equipment; eliminate or control all German industry that could be used for military production; bring all war criminals to just and swift punishment and exact reparation in kind for the destruction wrought by the Germans; wipe out the Nazi party, Nazi laws, organizations and institutions, remove all Nazi and militarist influences from public office and from the cultural and economic life of the German people; and take in harmony such other measures in Germany as may be necessary to the future peace and safety of the world. It is not our purpose to destroy the people of Germany, but only when Nazism and militarism have been extirpated, will there be hope for a decent life for Germans, and a place for them in the comity of nations.

III · REPARATION BY GERMANY

We have considered the question of the damage caused by Germany to the Allied nations in this war and recognized it as just that Germany be obliged to make compensation for this damage in kind to the greatest extent possible. A Commission for the Compensation of Damage will be established. The Commission will be instructed to consider the question of the extent and methods for compensating damage caused by Germany to the Allied countries. The Commission will work in Moscow.

IV · UNITED NATIONS CONFERENCE

We are resolved upon the earliest possible establishment with our Allies of a general international organization to maintain peace and security. We believe that this is essential, both to prevent aggression and to remove the political, economic and social causes of war through the close and continuing collaboration of all peace-loving peoples.

The foundations were laid at Dumbarton Oaks. On the important question of voting procedure, however, agreement was not there reached. The present Conference has been able to resolve this difficulty.

We have agreed that a Conference of United Nations should be called to meet at San Francisco in the United States on the 25th April 1945, to prepare the charter of such an organization, along the lines proposed in the informal conversations at Dumbarton Oaks.

The Government of China and the Provisional Government of France will be immediately consulted and invited to sponsor invitations to the Conference jointly with the Governments of the United States, Great Britain and the Union of Soviet Socialist Republics. As soon as the consultation with China and France has been completed, the text of the proposals on voting procedure will be made public.

V · DECLARATION ON LIBERATED EUROPE

We have drawn up and subscribed to a Declaration on Liberated Europe. This Declaration provides for concerting the policies of the Three Powers and for joint action by them in meeting the political and economic problems of liberated Europe in accordance with democratic principles. The text of the Declaration is as follows:

The Premier of the Union of Soviet Socialist Republics, the Prime Minister of the United Kingdom, and the President of the United States of America have consulted with each other in the common interests of the peoples of their countries and those of liberated Europe. They jointly declare their mutual agreement to concert during the temporary period of instability in liberated Europe the policies of their three Governments in assisting the peoples liberated from the domination of Nazi Germany and the peoples of the former Axis satellite States of Europe to solve by democratic means their pressing political and economic problems.

The establishment of order in Europe and the rebuilding of national economic life must be achieved by processes which will enable the liberated peoples to destroy the last vestiges of Nazism and Fascism and to create democratic institutions of their own choice. This is a principle of the Atlantic Charter – the right of all peoples to choose the form of government under which they will live – the restoration of sovereign rights and self-government to those peoples who have been forcibly deprived of them by the aggressor nations.

To foster the conditions in which the liberated peoples may exercise those rights, the three Governments will jointly assist the people in any European liberated State or former Axis satellite State in Europe where in their judgement conditions require: (a) to establish conditions of internal peace; (b) to carry out emergency measures for the relief of distressed peoples; (c) to form interim governmental authorities broadly representative of all democratic elements in the population and pledged to the earliest possible establishment through free elections of Governments responsive to the will of the people; and (d) to facilitate where necessary the holding of such elections.

The three Governments will consult the other United Nations and provisional authorities or other Governments in Europe when matters of direct interest to them are under consideration.

When, in the opinion of the three Governments, conditions in any European liberated State or any former Axis satellite State in Europe make such action necessary, they will immediately consult together on the measures necessary to discharge the joint responsibilities set forth in this Declaration.

By this Declaration we reaffirm our faith in the principles of the Atlantic Charter, our pledge in the Declaration by the United Nations, and our determination to build in cooperation with other peace-loving nations a world order under law, dedicated to peace, security, freedom and the general well-being of all mankind.

In issuing this Declaration, the Three Powers express the hope that the Provisional Government of the French Republic may be associated with them in the procedure suggested.

VI · POLAND

We came to the Crimea Conference resolved to settle our differences about Poland. We discussed fully all aspects of the question. We reaffirm our common desire to see established a strong, free independent and democratic Poland. As a result of our discussions we have agreed on the conditions in which a new Polish Provisional Government of National Unity may be formed in such a manner as to command recognition by the three major Powers.

The agreement reached is as follows:

A new situation has been created in Poland as a result of her complete liberation by the Red Army. This calls for the establishment of a Polish Provisional Government which can be more broadly based than was possible before the recent liberation of western Poland. The Provisional Government which is now functioning in Poland should therefore be reorganized on a broader democratic basis with the inclusion of democratic leaders from Poland itself and from Poles abroad. This new Government should then be called the Polish Provisional Government of National Unity.

M. Molotov, Mr Harriman and Sir A. Clark Kerr are authorized as a Commission to consult in the first instance in Moscow with members of the present Provisional Government and with other Polish democratic leaders from within Poland and from abroad, with a view to the reorganization of the present Government along the above lines. This Polish Provisional Government of National Unity shall be pledged to the holding of free and unfettered elections as soon as possible on the basis of universal suffrage and secret ballot. In these elections all democratic and anti-Nazi parties shall have the right to take part and to put forward candidates.

When a Polish Provisional Government of National Unity has been properly formed in conformity with the above, the Government of the Union of Soviet Socialist Republics, which now maintains diplomatic relations with the present Provisional Government of Poland, and the Government of the United Kingdom and the Government of the United States will establish diplomatic relations with the new Polish Government of National Unity, and will exchange Ambassadors by whose reports the respective Governments will be kept informed about the situation in Poland.

The three Heads of Government consider that the eastern frontier of Poland should follow the Curzon line with digressions from it in some regions of 5 to 8 kilometres in favour of Poland. They recognize that Poland must receive substantial accessions of territory in the north and west. They feel that the opinion of the new Polish Provisional Government of National Unity should be sought in due course on the extent of these accessions and that the final delimitation of the western frontier of Poland should thereafter await the Peace Conference.

VII · YUGOSLAVIA

We have agreed to recommend to Marshal Tito and Dr Subasić that the Agreement between them should be put into effect immediately, and that a new Government should be formed on the basis of that Agreement.

We also recommend that as soon as the new Government has been formed it should declare that:

(i) The Anti-Fascist Assembly of National Liberation (Avnoj) should be extended to include members of the last Yugoslav Parliament (Skupshtina) who have not compromised themselves by collaboration with the enemy, thus forming a body to be known as a temporary Parliament; and

(ii) Legislative acts passed by the Assembly of National Liberation will be subject to subsequent ratification by a Constituent Assembly.

There was also a general review of other Balkan questions.

VIII · MEETINGS OF FOREIGN SECRETARIES

Throughout the Conference, besides the daily meetings of the Heads of Governments, and the Foreign Secretaries, separate meetings of the three Foreign Secretaries, and their advisers, have also been held daily.

These meetings have proved of the utmost value and the Conference agreed that permanent machinery should be set up for regular consultation between the three Foreign Secretaries. They will, therefore, meet as often as may be necessary, probably about every three or four months. These meetings will be held in rotation in the three capitals, the first meeting being held in London, after the United Nations Conference on World Organization.

IX · UNITY FOR PEACE AS FOR WAR

Our meeting here in the Crimea has reaffirmed our common determination to maintain and strengthen in the peace to come that unity of purpose and of action which has made victory possible and certain for the United Nations in this war. We believe that this is a sacred obligation which our Governments owe to our peoples and to all the peoples of the world.

Only with continuing and growing co-operation and understanding among our three countries, and among all the peace-loving nations, can the highest aspiration of humanity be realized – a secure and lasting peace which will, in the words of the Atlantic Charter 'Afford assurance that all the men in all the lands may live out their lives in freedom from fear and want'.

Victory in this war and establishment of the proposed international organization will provide the greatest opportunity in all history to create in the years to come the essential conditions of such a peace.

(Signed)

WINSTON S. CHURCHILL
FRANKLIN D. ROOSEVELT
J. V. STALIN
11th February 1945

Yalta Agreement on the Kuriles and entry of the Soviet Union in the war against Japan, 11 February 1945 (released 11 February 1946)

The leaders of the three Great Powers – the Soviet Union, the United States of America and Great Britain – have agreed that in two or three months after Germany has surrendered and the war in Europe has terminated the Soviet Union shall enter into the war against Japan on the side of the Allies on condition that:

1. The *status quo* in Outer Mongolia (The Mongolian People's Republic) shall be preserved;

2. The former rights of Russia violated by the treacherous attack of Japan in 1904 shall be restored, viz:

(a) the southern part of Sakhalin as well as all the islands adjacent to it shall be returned to the Soviet Union,

(b) the commercial port of Dairen shall be internationalized, the pre-eminent interests of the Soviet Union in this port being safeguarded and the lease of Port Arthur as a naval base of the U.S.S.R. restored,

(c) the Chinese-Eastern Railroad and the South-Manchurian Railroad which provides an outlet to Dairen shall be jointly operated by the establishment of a joint Soviet-Chinese Company, it being understood that the pre-eminent interests of the Soviet Union shall be safeguarded and that China shall retain full sovereignty in Manchuria;

3. The Kuril islands shall be handed over to the Soviet Union.

It is understood that the agreement concerning Outer Mongolia and the ports and railroads referred to above will require concurrence of Generalissimo Chiang Kai-shek. The President will take measures in order to obtain this concurrence on advice from Marshal Stalin.

The Heads of the three Great Powers have agreed that these claims of the Soviet Union shall be unquestionably fulfilled after Japan has been defeated.

For its part the Soviet Union expresses its readiness to conclude with the National Government of China a pact of friendship and alliance between the U.S.S.R. and China in order to render assistance to China with its armed forces for the purpose of liberating China from the Japanese yoke.

February 11, 1945

J. STALIN
FRANKLIN D. ROOSEVELT
WINSTON S. CHURCHILL

Potsdam Conference Protocol, 2 August 1945

The Berlin Conference of the three Heads of Government of the U.S.S.R., U.S.A., and U.K., which took place from July 17 to August 2, 1945, came to the following conclusions:

I · Establishment of a Council of Foreign Ministers

A. The Conference reached the following agreement for the establishment of a Council of Foreign Ministers to do the necessary preparatory work for the peace settlements:

1. There shall be established a Council composed of the Foreign Ministers of the United Kingdom, the Union of Soviet Socialist Republics, China, France, and the United States.

2. (i) The Council shall normally meet in London which shall be the permanent seat of the joint Secretariat which the Council will form. . . .

3. (i) As its immediate important task, the Council shall be authorized to draw up, with a view to their submission to the United Nations, treaties of peace with Italy, Rumania, Bulgaria, Hungary and Finland, and to propose settlements of territorial questions outstanding on the termination of the war in Europe. The Council shall be utilized for the preparation of a peace settlement for Germany to be accepted by the Government of Germany when a Government adequate for the purpose is established.

(ii) For the discharge of each of these tasks the Council will be composed of the Members representing those States which were signatory to the terms of surrender imposed upon the enemy State concerned. For the purposes of the peace settlement for Italy, France shall be regarded as a signatory to the terms of surrender for Italy. Other Members will be invited to participate when matters directly concerning them are under discussion.

(iii) Other matters may from time to time be referred to the Council by agreement between the Member Governments.

4. (i) Whenever the Council is considering a question of direct interest to a State not represented thereon, such State should be invited to send representatives to participate in the discussion and study of that question.

(ii) The Council may adapt its procedure to the particular problems under consideration. In some cases it may hold its own preliminary discussions prior to the participation of other interested States. In other cases, the Council may convoke a formal conference of the States chiefly interested in seeking a solution of the particular problem.

B. It was agreed that the three Governments should each address an identical invitation to the Governments of China and France to adopt this text and to join in establishing the Council. . . .

[It was agreed to recommend that the European Advisory Commission be dissolved.]

II · The principles to govern the treatment of Germany in the initial control period

A · POLITICAL PRINCIPLES

1. In accordance with the Agreement on Control Machinery in Germany, supreme authority in Germany is exercised, on instructions from their respective Governments, by the Commanders-in-Chief of the armed forces of the United States of America, the United Kingdom, the Union of Soviet Socialist Republics, and the French Republic, each in his own zone of occupation, and also jointly, in matters affecting Germany as a whole, in their capacity as members of the Control Council.

2. So far as is practicable, there shall be uniformity of treatment of the German population throughout Germany.

3. The purposes of the occupation of Germany by which the Control Council shall be guided are:

(i) The complete disarmament and demilitarization of Germany and the elimination or control of all German industry that could be used for military production. . . .

(ii) To convince the German people that they have suffered a total military defeat and that they cannot escape responsibility for what they have brought upon themselves, since their own ruthless warfare and the fanatical Nazi resistance have destroyed German economy and made chaos and suffering inevitable.

(iii) To destroy the National Socialist Party and its affiliated and supervised organizations, to dissolve all Nazi institutions, to ensure that they are not revived in any form, and to prevent all Nazi and militarist activity or propaganda.

(iv) To prepare for the eventual reconstruction of German political life on a democratic basis and for eventual peaceful cooperation in international life by Germany.

4. All Nazi laws which provided the basis of the Hitler régime or established discriminations on grounds of race, creed, or political opinion shall be abolished. No such discriminations, whether legal, administrative or otherwise, shall be tolerated.

5. War criminals and those who have participated in planning or carrying out Nazi enterprises involving or resulting in atrocities or war crimes shall be arrested and brought to judgement. Nazi leaders, influential Nazi supporters and high officials of Nazi organizations and institutions and any other persons dangerous to the occupation or its objectives shall be arrested and interned.

6. All members of the Nazi Party who have been more than nominal participants in its activities and all other persons hostile to Allied purposes shall be removed from public and semi-public office, and from positions of responsibility in important private undertakings. Such persons shall be replaced by persons who, by their political and moral qualities, are deemed capable of assisting in developing genuine democratic institutions in Germany.

7. German education shall be so controlled as completely to eliminate Nazi and militarist doctrines and to make possible the successful development of democratic ideas.

8. The judicial system will be reorganized in accordance with the principles of democracy, of justice under law, and of equal rights for all citizens without distinction of race, nationality or religion.

9. The administration in Germany should be directed towards the decentralization of the political structure and the development of local responsibility. To this end:

(i) local self-government shall be restored throughout Germany on democratic principles and in particular through elective councils as rapidly as is consistent with military security and the purposes of military occupation;

(ii) all democratic political parties with rights of assembly and of public discussion shall be allowed and encouraged throughout Germany;

(iii) representative and elective principles shall be introduced into regional, provincial and State (*Land*) administration as rapidly as may be justified by the successful application of these principles in local self-government;

(iv) for the time being, no central German Government shall be established. Notwithstanding this, however, certain essential central German administrative departments, headed by State Secretaries, shall be established, particularly in the fields of finance, transport, communications, foreign trade and industry. Such departments will act under the direction of the Control Council.

10. Subject to the necessity for maintaining military security, freedom of speech, press and religion shall be permitted, and religious institutions shall be respected. Subject likewise to the maintenance of military security, the formation of free trade unions shall be permitted.

B · Economic principles

11. In order to eliminate Germany's war potential, the production of arms, ammunition and implements of war as well as all types of aircraft and sea-going ships shall be prohibited and prevented. Production of metals, chemicals, machinery and other items that are directly necessary to a war economy shall be rigidly controlled and restricted to Germany's approved post-war peacetime needs to meet the objectives stated in paragraph 15. Productive capacity not needed for permitted production shall be removed in accordance with the reparations plan recommended by the Allied Commission on Reparations and approved by the Governments concerned or if not removed shall be destroyed.

12. At the earliest practicable date, the German economy shall be decentralized for the purpose of eliminating the present excessive concentration of economic power as exemplified in particular by cartels, syndicates, trusts and other monopolistic arrangements.

13. In organizing the German economy, primary emphasis shall be given to the development of agriculture and peaceful domestic industries.

14. During the period of occupation Germany shall be treated as a single economic unit. To this end common policies shall be established in regard to:

(a) mining and industrial production and its allocation;

(b) agriculture, forestry and fishing;

(c) wages, prices and rationing;

(d) import and export programmes for Germany as a whole;

(e) currency and banking, central taxation and customs;

(f) reparation and removal of industrial war potential;

(g) transportation and communications.

In applying these policies account shall be taken, where appropriate, of varying local conditions.

15. Allied controls shall be imposed upon the German economy but only to the extent necessary....

16. In the imposition and maintenance of economic controls established by the Control Council, German administrative machinery shall be created and the German authorities shall be required to the fullest extent practicable to proclaim and assume administration of such controls....

17. Measures shall be promptly taken:

(a) to effect essential repair of transport;

(b) to enlarge coal production;

(c) to maximize agricultural output; and

(d) to effect emergency repair of housing and essential utilities.

18. Appropriate steps shall be taken by the Control Council to exercise control and the power of disposition over German-owned external assets not already under the control of United Nations which have taken part in the war against Germany.

19. Payment of reparations should leave enough resources to enable the German people to subsist without external assistance. In working out the economic balance of Germany the necessary means must be provided to pay for imports approved by the Control Council in Germany. The proceeds of exports from current production and stocks shall be available in the first place for payment for such imports....

III · Reparations from Germany

1. Reparation claims of the U.S.S.R. shall be met by removals from the zone of Germany occupied by the U.S.S.R., and from appropriate German external assets.

2. The U.S.S.R. undertakes to settle the reparation claims of Poland from its own share of reparations.

3. The reparation claims of the United States, the United Kingdom and other countries entitled to reparations shall be met from the Western zones and from appropriate German external assets.

4. In addition to the reparations to be taken by the U.S.S.R. from its own zone of occupation, the U.S.S.R. shall receive additionally from the Western zones:

(a) Fifteen per cent of such usable and complete industrial capital equipment, in the first place from the metallurgical, chemical and machine manufacturing industries as is unnecessary for the German peace economy and should be removed from the Western zones of Germany, in exchange for an equivalent value of food, coal, potash, zinc, timber, clay products, petroleum products, and such other commodities as may be agreed upon.

(b) Ten per cent of such industrial capital equipment as is unnecessary for the German peace economy and should be removed from the Western zones, to be transferred to the Soviet Government on reparations account without payment or exchange of any kind in return.

Removals of equipment as provided in (a) and (b) above shall be made simultaneously. . . .

8. The Soviet Government renounces all claims in respect of reparations to shares of German enterprises which are located in the Western zones of Germany as well as to German foreign assets in all countries except those specified in paragraph 9 below.

9. The Governments of the U.K. and U.S.A. renounce all claims in respect of reparations to shares of German enterprises which are located in the Eastern zone of occupation in Germany, as well as to German foreign assets in Bulgaria, Finland, Hungary, Rumania and Eastern Austria. . . .

IV · Disposal of the German Navy and Merchant Marine

A. The following principles for the distribution of the German Navy were agreed:

1. The total strength of the German Surface Navy, excluding ships sunk and those taken over from Allied Nations, but including ships under construction or repair, shall be divided equally among the U.S.S.R., U.K., and U.S.A. . . .

The German Merchant Marine, surrendered to the Three Powers and wherever located, shall be divided equally among the U.S.S.R., the U.K., and the U.S.A.

V · City of Koenigsberg and the adjacent area

The Conference examined a proposal by the Soviet Government to the effect that pending the final determination of territorial questions at the peace settlement, the section of the western frontier of the Union of Soviet Socialist Republics which is adjacent to the Baltic Sea should pass from a point on the eastern shore of the Bay of Danzig to the east, north of Braunsberg-Goldap, to the meeting point of the frontiers of Lithuania, the Polish Republic and East Prussia.

The Conference has agreed in principle to the proposal of the Soviet Government concerning the ultimate transfer to the Soviet Union of the City of Koenigsberg and the area adjacent to it as described above subject to expert examination of the actual frontier.

The President of the United States and the British Prime Minister have declared that they will support the proposal of the Conference at the forthcoming peace settlement.

VI · War criminals

[Trials to begin at earliest possible date.]

VII · Austria

The Conference examined a proposal by the Soviet Government on the extension of the authority of the Austrian Provisional Government to all of Austria.

The three Governments agreed that they were prepared to examine this question after the entry of the British and American forces into the city of Vienna.

It was agreed that reparations should not be exacted from Austria.

VIII · Poland

A · DECLARATION

We have taken note with pleasure of the agreement reached among representative Poles from Poland and abroad which has made possible the formation, in accordance with the decisions reached at the Crimea Conference, of a Polish Provisional Government of National Unity recognized by the Three Powers. The establishment by the British and United States Governments of diplomatic relations with the Polish Provisional Government of National Unity has resulted in the withdrawal of their recognition from the former Polish Government in London, which no longer exists.

The British and United States Governments have taken measures to protect the interest of the Polish Provisional Government of National Unity as the recognized Government of the Polish State in the property belonging to the Polish State located in their territories and under their control, whatever the form of this property may be. They have further taken measures to prevent alienation to third parties of such property. All proper facilities will be given to the Polish Provisional Government of National Unity for the exercise of the ordinary legal remedies for the recovery of any property belonging to the Polish State which may have been wrongfully alienated.

The Three Powers are anxious to assist the Polish Provisional Government of National Unity in facilitating the return to Poland as soon as practicable of all Poles abroad who wish to go, including members of the Polish armed forces and the Merchant Marine. They expect that those Poles who return home shall be accorded personal and property rights on the same basis as all Polish citizens.

The Three Powers note that the Polish Provisional Government of National Unity, in accordance with the decisions of the Crimea Conference, has agreed to the holding of free and unfettered elections as soon as possible on the basis of universal suffrage and secret ballot in which all democratic and anti-Nazi parties shall have the right to take part and to put forward candidates, and that representatives of the Allied press shall enjoy full freedom to report to the world upon developments in Poland before and during the elections.

B · WESTERN FRONTIER OF POLAND

In conformity with the agreement on Poland reached at the Crimea Conference the three Heads of Government have sought the opinion of the Polish Provisional Government of National Unity in regard to the accession of territory in the north and west which Poland should receive. The President of the National Council of Poland and members of the Polish Provisional Government of National Unity have been received at the Conference and have fully presented their views. The three Heads of Government reaffirm their opinion that the final delimitation of the western frontier of Poland should await the peace settlement.

The three Heads of Government agree that, pending the final determination of Poland's western frontier, the former German territories east of a line running from the Baltic Sea immediately west of Swinamunde, and thence along the Oder river to the confluence of the western Neisse river and along the western Neisse to the Czechoslovak frontier, including that portion of East Prussia not placed under the administration of the Union of Soviet Socialist Republics in accordance with the understanding reached at this Conference and including the area of the former Free City of Danzig, shall be under the administration of the Polish State and for such purposes should not be considered as part of the Soviet zone of occupation in Germany.

IX · Conclusion of peace treaties and admission to the United Nations Organization

The three Governments consider it desirable that the present anomalous position of Italy, Bulgaria, Finland, Hungary and

Rumania should be terminated by the conclusion of peace treaties. They trust that the other interested Allied Governments will share these views. . . .

As regards the admission of other States into the United Nations Organization, Article 4 of the Charter of the United Nations declares that:

1. Membership in the United Nations is open to all other peace-loving States who accept the obligations contained in the present Charter and, in the judgement of the Organization, are able and willing to carry out these obligations.

2. The admission of any such State to membership in the United Nations will be effected by a decision of the General Assembly upon the recommendation of the Security Council.

The three Governments, so far as they are concerned, will support applications for membership from those States which have remained neutral during the war and which fulfil the qualifications set out above.

The three Governments feel bound however to make it clear that they for their part would not favour any application for membership put forward by the present Spanish Government, which having been founded with the support of the Axis Powers, does not, in view of its origins, its nature, its record and its close association with the aggressor States, possess the qualifications necessary to justify such membership.

X · Territorial trusteeship

The Conference examined a proposal by the Soviet Government on the question of trusteeship territories as defined in the decision of the Crimea Conference and in the Charter of the United Nations Organization.

After an exchange of views on this question it was decided that the disposition of any former Italian colonial territories was one to be decided in connection with the preparation of a peace treaty for Italy and that the question of Italian colonial territory would be considered by the September Council of Ministers of Foreign Affairs.

XI · Revised Allied Control Commission procedure in Rumania, Bulgaria and Hungary

[Revision of procedures will be undertaken.]

XII · Orderly transfer of German populations

The three Governments, having considered the question in all its aspects, recognize that the transfer to Germany of German populations, or elements thereof, remaining in Poland, Czechoslovakia and Hungary, will have to be undertaken. They agree that any transfers that take place should be effected in an orderly and humane manner. . . .

XIII · Oil equipment in Rumania

[Commission of experts to investigate.]

XIV · Iran

It was agreed that Allied troops should be withdrawn immediately from Teheran, and that further stages of the withdrawal of troops from Iran should be considered at the meeting of the Council of Foreign Ministers to be held in London in September 1945.

XV · International zone of Tangier

[Agreement to be reached.]

XVI · The Black Sea Straits

The three Governments recognized that the Convention concluded at Montreux should be revised as failing to meet present-day conditions.

It was agreed that as the next step the matter should be the subject of direct conversations between each of the three Governments and the Turkish Government.

. . .

[Signed] Stalin, Truman, Attlee.

Treaty of Friendship and Alliance between China and the Soviet Union, Moscow, 14 August 1945

I · Treaty of Friendship and Alliance

The President of the National Government of the Republic of China and the Praesidium of the Supreme Soviet of the Union of Soviet Socialist Republics,

Being desirous of strengthening the friendly relations which have always prevailed between the Republic of China and the Soviet Union, by means of an alliance and by good neighbourly post-war collaboration;

Determined to assist each other in the struggle against aggression on the part of the enemies of the United Nations in this World War and to collaborate in the common war against Japan until that country's unconditional surrender;

Expressing their unswerving resolve to collaborate in maintaining peace and security for the benefit of the peoples of both countries and of all peace-loving nations . . . have agreed as follows:

Article 1. The High Contracting Parties undertake jointly with the other United Nations to prosecute the war against Japan until final victory is achieved. The High Contracting Parties mutually undertake to afford one another all necessary military and other assistance and support in this war.

Article 2. The High Contracting Parties undertake not to enter into separate negotiations with Japan or conclude, except by mutual consent, any armistice or peace treaty either with the present Japanese Government or any other Government or authority set up in Japan that does not clearly renounce all aggressive intentions.

Article 3. On the conclusion of the war against Japan, the High Contracting Parties undertake to carry out jointly all the measures in their power to render impossible a repetition of aggression and violation of the peace by Japan.

Should either of the High Contracting Parties become involved in hostilities with Japan in consequence of an attack by the latter against that party, the other High Contracting Party will at once render to the High Contracting Party so involved in hostility all the military and other support and assistance in its power.

This Article shall remain in force until such time as, at the request of both High Contracting Parties, responsibility for the prevention of further aggression by Japan is placed upon the 'United Nations' Organization.

Article 4. Each High Contracting Party undertakes not to conclude any alliance and not to take part in any coalition directed against the other Contracting Party.

Article 5. The High Contracting Parties, having regard to the interests of the security and economic development of each of them, agree to work together in close and friendly collaboration after the re-establishment of peace and to act in accordance with the principles of mutual respect for each other's sovereignty and territorial integrity and non-intervention in each other's internal affairs.

Article 6. The High Contracting Parties agree to afford one another all possible economic assistance in the post-war period in order to facilitate and expedite the rehabilitation of both countries and to make their contribution to the prosperity of the world.

Article 7. Nothing in this Treaty should be interpreted in such a way as to prejudice the rights and duties of the High Contracting Parties as Members of the Organization of the 'United Nations'.

Article 8. The present Treaty is subject to ratification in the shortest possible time. The instruments of ratification shall be exchanged in Chungking as soon as possible.

The Treaty comes into force immediately upon ratification, and shall remain in force for thirty years. Should neither of the High Contracting Parties make, one year before the date of the Treaty's expiry, a statement of its desire to denounce it, the Treaty will remain in force for an unlimited period, provided that each High Contracting Party may invalidate it by announcing its intention to do so to the other Contracting Party one year in advance.

...

Exchange of Notes

No. 1

In connection with the signing on this date of the Treaty of Friendship and Alliance between China and the Union of Soviet Socialist Republics, I have the honour to place on record that the following provisions are understood by both Contracting Parties as follows:

1. In accordance with the spirit of the above-mentioned Treaty and to implement its general idea and its purposes, the Soviet Government agrees to render China moral support and assist her with military supplies and other material resources, it being understood that this support and assistance will go exclusively to the National Government as the Central Government of China.

2. During the negotiations on the ports of Dairen and Port Arthur and on the joint operation of the Chinese Changchun Railway, the Soviet Government regarded the Three Eastern Provinces as part of China and again affirmed its respect for the complete sovereignty of China over the Three Eastern Provinces and recognition of their territorial and administrative integrity.

3. With regard to recent events in Sinkiang, the Soviet Government confirms that, as stated in Article 5 of the Treaty of Friendship and Alliance, it has no intention of interfering in the internal affairs of China.

...

No. 3

In view of the frequently manifested desire for independence of the people of Outer Mongolia, the Chinese Government states that, after the defeat of Japan, if this desire is confirmed by a plebiscite of the people of Outer Mongolia, the Chinese Government will recognize the independence of Outer Mongolia within her existing frontiers....

II · Agreement between the Chinese Republic and the Union of Soviet Socialist Republics on the Chinese Changchun Railway, signed at Moscow on 14 August 1945

The President of the National Government of the Republic of China and the Praesidium of the Supreme Soviet of the U.S.S.R. being desirous of strengthening, on the basis of complete regard for the rights and interests of each of the two parties, friendly relations and economic ties between the two countries, have agreed as follows:

Article 1. After the expulsion of the Japanese armed forces from the Three Eastern Provinces of China, the main trunk lines of the Chinese Eastern Railway and the South Manchurian Railway leading from the station of Manchouli to the station of Pogranichnaya and from Harbin to Dairen and Port Arthur, shall be combined to form a single railway system to be known as 'Chinese Changchun Railway', and shall become the joint property of the U.S.S.R. and the Chinese Republic and be jointly exploited by them. Only such lands and branch lines shall become joint property and be jointly exploited as were constructed by the Chinese Eastern Railway while it was under Russian and joint Soviet-Chinese management, and by the South Manchurian Railway while under Russian management, and which are intended to serve the direct needs of those railways. Ancillary undertakings directly serving the needs of those railways and constructed during the above-mentioned periods shall also be included. All other railway branch lines, ancillary undertakings and lands will be the exclusive property of the Chinese Government. The joint exploitation of the above-mentioned railways shall be effected by a single administration under Chinese sovereignty as a purely commercial transport undertaking.

[*Articles 2–18.* Details of administration.]

III · Agreement on the Port of Dairen, signed at Moscow on 14 August 1945

Whereas a Treaty of Friendship and Alliance has been concluded between the Chinese Republic and the Union of Soviet Socialist Republics, and whereas the U.S.S.R. has guaranteed to respect the sovereignty of China over the Three Eastern Provinces as an inalienable part of China, the Chinese Republic, in order to protect the interests of the Union of Soviet Socialist Republics in Dairen as a port for the import and export of goods, hereby agrees:

1. To proclaim Dairen a free port, open to the trade and shipping of all countries.

2. The Chinese Government agrees to allocate docks and warehouse accommodation in the said free port to be leased to the U.S.S.R. under a separate agreement.

Protocol

1. The Government of China when requested to do so by the Soviet Union shall grant the Soviet Union, freely and without consideration, a thirty years' lease of one-half of all harbour installations and equipment, the other half of the harbour installations and equipment remaining the property of China.

...

IV · Agreement on Port Arthur, signed at Moscow on 14 August 1945

In accordance with the Sino-Soviet Treaty of Friendship and Alliance and as an addition thereto, both Contracting Parties have agreed on the following:

1. In order to strengthen the security of China and the U.S.S.R. and prevent a repetition of aggression on the part of Japan, the Government of the Chinese Republic agrees to the joint use by both Contracting Parties of Port Arthur as a naval base....

V · Agreement on relations between the Soviet Commander-in-Chief and the Chinese administration following the entry of Soviet forces into the territory of the three Eastern Provinces of China in connection with the present joint war against Japan, signed at Moscow on 14 August 1945

The President of the National Government of the Chinese Republic and the Praesidium of the Supreme Soviet of the Union of Soviet Socialist Republics, being desirous that after the entry of Soviet forces into the territory of the Three Eastern Provinces of China in connection with the present joint war of China and the U.S.S.R. against Japan, relations between the Soviet Commander-in-Chief and the Chinese administration conform with the spirit of friendship and alliance existing between both countries, have agreed on the following:

1. After the entry, as a result of military operations, of Soviet troops into the territory of the Three Eastern Provinces of China, the supreme authority and responsibility in the zone of military activity in all matters relating to the conduct of the war shall, during the period necessary for conducting such operations, be vested in the Commander-in-Chief of the Soviet Armed Forces.

2. A representative of the National Government of the Chinese Republic and

a staff shall be appointed in any recaptured territory, who shall:

(a) Organize and control, in accordance with the laws of China, the administration on the territory freed from the enemy;

(b) Assist in establishing cooperation in restored territories between the Chinese armed forces, whether regular or irregular, and the Soviet armed forces;

(c) Ensure the active collaboration of the Chinese administration with the Soviet Commander-in-Chief and, in particular, issue corresponding instructions to the local authorities, being guided by the requirements and desires of the Soviet Commander-in-Chief.

3. A Chinese Military Mission shall be appointed to the Headquarters of the Soviet Commander-in-Chief for the purpose of maintaining contact between the Soviet Commander-in-Chief and the representative of the National Government of the Chinese Republic.

4. In zones that are under the supreme authority of the Soviet Commander-in-Chief, the administration of the National Government of the Chinese Republic for restored territories shall maintain contact with the Soviet Commander-in-Chief through a representative of the National Government of the Chinese Republic.

5. As soon as part of a recaptured territory ceases to be a zone of direct military operations, the National Government of the Chinese Republic shall assume complete power in respect of civil affairs and shall render the Soviet Commander-in-Chief all assistance and support through its civil and military organs.

6. All members of the Soviet armed forces on Chinese territory shall be under the jurisdiction of the Soviet Commander-in-Chief. All Chinese citizens whether civil or military, shall be under Chinese jurisdiction ...

Minutes

At the fifth meeting between Generalissimo Stalin and Mr T. V. Soong, President of the Executive Yuan, which took place on 11 July 1945, the question of the evacuation of Soviet forces from Chinese territory after participation of the U.S.S.R. in the war against Japan was discussed. Generalissimo Stalin declined to include in the Agreement on the Entry of Soviet Forces into the Territory of the Three Eastern Provinces any provision for the evacuation of Soviet troops within three months following the defeat of Japan. Generalissimo Stalin stated, however, that the Soviet forces would begin to be withdrawn within three weeks after the capitulation of Japan.

Mr T. V. Soong asked how much time would be required to complete the evacuation. Generalissimo Stalin stated that in his opinion the evacuation of troops could be completed within a period of not exceeding two months. Mr T. V. Soong again asked whether the evacuation would really be completed within three months. Generalissimo Stalin stated that three months would be a maximum period sufficient for the completion of the withdrawal of troops.

X·The alliances and alignments of the United States: from the League of Nations to the United Nations

The United Nations, the League of Nations and the United Nations

The traditional advice of the Founding Fathers against entangling alliances continued to influence United States policy until 1945. It was not decisively broken when the United States entered the war on the Allied side on 6 April 1917 against Germany, and on 7 December 1917 against Austria–Hungary. (There was no declaration of war, however, against Turkey or Bulgaria, Germany's other allies.) President Woodrow Wilson referred to Britain, France and Italy as 'associated powers'. In attempting to bring the war to an end, President Wilson also pursued independent initiatives after consultation with the Allied nations. While the President played a leading role in the founding of the *League of Nations*, its rejection by the Senate meant that the United States would not be bound in a comprehensive alliance with the other founding member nations.

During the years when the League proved itself viable and moderately successful in the early 1920s, the United States avoided even the slightest official contact with its work. But even then the United States could not 'isolate' herself from the rest of the world. On the contrary, the United States played a major role in naval disarmament and eastern Asian affairs in the complex of *Washington Treaties* in 1922 (pp. 87–92). During the latter part of the 1920s, however, the United States increasingly worked with various League organizations concerned with economic, health, social, judicial, financial, disarmament and intellectual questions, and although not a member of the Permanent Court of International Justice (the United States Senate in 1935 failed to approve membership by the required two-thirds majority vote) furnished a distinguished judge to its bench. In June 1930 a diplomatic representative of the United States was appointed to the League Headquarters at Geneva. Privately, Americans contributed substantially to the expenses of the League's work. The

United States, while not a member of the League did at times work in parallel with it; the *Briand–Kellogg Pact* or *Pact of Paris, 27 August 1928* (p. 108) associated the United States in the objectives of the League in keeping the peace. But with Japanese aggression in Manchuria in 1931 posing a serious challenge to the League, the United States administration retreated from close collaboration with the international body. Collaboration, it was feared, could have involved the United States in sanctions policies against Japan which the administration might not wish to adopt. As the international situation became increasingly threatening in the 1930s, it became clear that the administration, Congress and public opinion were overwhelmingly against making any political commitment which might have involved the United States in armed conflict. That is well illustrated by the *Neutrality Legislation* of 1935, 1936 and 1937 which was designed to prevent the United States being 'dragged' into war – a vain attempt by the isolationists to apply the lessons of the Great War of 1914–18.

With the outbreak of war in Europe in September 1939, Roosevelt secured a new *Neutrality Act* which repealed the embargo on arms and permitted belligerents and neutrals to buy arms for cash and and carry them away on their ships. The Allies, with their command of the surface of the oceans, would profit trom the 'cash and carry' basis of the act. Roosevelt and public opinion continued to hope that the United States would be kept out of the conflict by aiding the Allies in every way short of war. Such aid was provided by the *Destroyer–Naval Base Agreement, 2 September 1940*, and the *Lend-Lease Act, 11 March 1941* (p. 180). Roosevelt and Churchill set out the common aims of the two democratic nations for a peaceful future world in the *Atlantic Charter, 14 August 1941* (pp. 198–9). But opposition to a United States declaration of war against the Axis remained strong. Even when the Japanese attacked Pearl Harbour it was Germany that first declared war on the United States, though by 1941 polls indicated that the majority of Americans would have been ready for war on Britain's side if that alone could avert Britain's defeat.

Already in 1940 the State Department had begun to consider how peace might be maintained internationally once the war ended. From 1942 onwards detailed planning on the organization of peace and a persuasive campaign in favour of American participation in a new League, or a United Nations, paved the way for a fundamental change in American outlook. But isolationist feelings were only gradually overcome. The Anglo–American alliance became the core of the alliance fighting the Axis powers in the *Declaration by the United Nations, 1 January 1942* (p. 212); its twenty-six original signatories, including the U.S.S.R. and China, together with those nations joining later, became the participants in the San Francisco Conference and the founding members of the United Nations in 1945. The United States took the lead in preparing for the establishment of an international organization to preserve the peace once it had been attained. Point Four of *The Moscow Declaration, 1 November 1943*, signed by the Foreign Ministers of China, Britain and the Soviet Union, as well as by the United States Secretary of State, Cordell Hull, stated 'That they recognize the necessity of establishing at the earliest practicable date a general international organization, based on the principle of the sovereign equality of all peace-loving States, and open to membership by all such States, large and small, for the maintenance of international peace and security.' The bi-partisan support of the Senate was also assured when, on 5 November 1943, it approved the resolution introduced by Senator Tom Connally which called for American participation 'in the establishment and maintenance of international authority with power to prevent aggression and to preserve the peace of the world'. Any treaty made to implement this resolution would, however, still require the consent of two-thirds of the Senators present. Roosevelt continued to build on bi-partisan support for the establishment of an international organization in 1944 and before his death in 1945.

On the Dumbarton Oaks estate in the Georgetown section of Washington, from 21 August to 7 October 1944, agreement was reached on the main principles and many details of the United Nations Organization to be established and these were made public on 9 October 1944 as 'Proposals for the establishment of a General International Organization'. As the Soviet Union was not an ally of China, discussions had been divided into two parts: the United States, Britain and the Soviet Union first, and then the United States, Britain and China. But on the question of membership, and how the veto should be exercised at the Security Council, significant differences remained between the views of the Soviet Union and of Britain and the United States. At the *Yalta Conference, 4–11 February 1945* (pp. 226–30), further discussions and progress on voting procedures and membership questions led to the public declaration that the Big Three would call a conference at San Francisco of the signatories of the *United Nations Declaration*, on 25 April 1945. The full drafting conference for the U. N. Charter convened at San Francisco and lasted from 25 April to 26 June 1945. From it emerged the *United Nations Charter* (see *The Major International Treaties since 1945*, pp. 64–78). Public support had been mobilized in the United States and Senate approval had been carefully prepared so that the Wilsonian débâcle would not be repeated. The Senate approved *The Charter* and *The Court of International Justice* by a final vote of eighty-nine to two, on 28 July 1945.

The United States and Latin America

The United States maintained its tradition of claiming special rights and responsibilities in the Western hemisphere as embodied in the Monroe

4 The Americas

Doctrine (1823). In practice this has meant that the United States, whilst recognizing how varied the twenty Latin American Republics are, and how much of the time their interests have conflicted with each other, has also claimed that they form part of an American system. American Presidents have claimed the right to intervene unilaterally, if need be, if the vital interests of the United States were held to be endangered – vital interests which were declared to be equally in the interests of the American Republics as a whole. This might happen if a Latin American Republic developed close ties with a State potentially hostile to the United States and especially, as in Cuba, where foreign military bases or weapons were involved. Geographically, U.S. intervention has been confined in the main to the strategically vital Caribbean region; the United States possesses the Guántanamo naval base in Cuba and controlled the Panama Canal. Until Franklin D. Roosevelt proclaimed the Good Neighbor policy in 1933, United States armed intervention had been frequent, especially in Cuba, Panama, Nicaragua, Mexico, Haiti and the Dominican Republic, despite the attempts of inter-American conferences to prevent United States military action.

Eight international conferences of the American States met before the end of the Second World War: the first took place in Washington during 1889 and 1890, and since then numerous other special inter-American conferences have also been convened. They have produced many treaties, declarations and enunciations of principles, but the gap between these aspirations and practical achievements has been a wide one. Fervent expressions of faith in the principles of democracy have rung especially hollow when ascribed to by dictatorships that exist and continue to flourish in some of the Latin American Republics. Nor have the political, economic and international objectives of the Governments of the Latin American Republics always coincided with those of the much more powerful United States; the Republics are also divided on many issues among each other.

The International American Conferences have been concerned with four basic aspects of inter-American relations: (i) establishing the independence and sovereignty of each State; thus ensuring non-intervention by any other State especially by the United States; (ii) hemispheric security; (iii) inter-American cooperation in many fields, economic and social, which frequently entails attempting to secure favourable trading conditions and economic aid from the United States; (iv) establishing effective machinery for settling inter-American disputes peacefully.

Inter-American solidarity was not prominently in evidence during the First World War. After the war, *the Fifth International Conference of American States, meeting in Santiago, 25 March–3 May 1923*, was notable for the conclusion of a

Treaty to Avoid or Prevent Conflicts, generally known as the *Gondra Treaty*; this provided for a commission to investigate disputes and a six-months cooling-off period. At a special conference of American States, held in Washington, *10 December 1928–5 January 1929*, two treaties were adopted, the *General Convention of Inter-American Conciliation* and the *General Treaty of Inter-American Arbitration*; but the weakness of the latter treaty was that both parties to a dispute would have to agree to setting up arbitration machinery. A special commission of American jurists, appointed after the Sixth International Conference at Havana (1928), drew up a *Convention Defining the Rights and Duties of States* which was adopted by the *Seventh International Conference of American States at Montevideo, 3–26 December 1933*; according to Article 8 of this convention, no State had the right to intervene in the internal or external affairs of another. The United States ratified the convention in June 1934, but Franklin Roosevelt in practice interpreted Article 8 as referring only to armed intervention. On 29 May 1934 Roosevelt abrogated the *Platt Amendment* under which the United States enjoyed special rights in Cuba.

A large number of resolutions and conventions were agreed and signed at a special *Inter-American Conference for the Maintenance of Peace, held in Buenos Aires, December 1936*. This conference also led to the conclusion in treaty form of acceptance of the principle of non-intervention in the *Non-Intervention Additional Protocol between the United States and Other American Republics, 23 December 1936* (p. 253). Two years later, at the *Eighth International Conference of American States at Lima, December 1938*, one of many declarations (no. 109) provided for periodic consultations of the Foreign Ministers of the American Republics and affirmed the continental solidarity of the American Republics in case the peace, security or territorial integrity of any one of them was threatened. But despite the many treaties and convention resolutions from 1890 to 1938 the actual degree of inter-American cooperation and solidarity remained limited, and the machinery for settling disputes in the Americas peacefully was far from effective. The then twenty Republics had not succeeded in achieving complete security from undue United States influence in their affairs, although Roosevelt's Good Neighbor policy brought about a great improvement in their relationship. Nor had the United States secured complete security through the establishment of the kind of inter-American cooperation that would have induced all the Latin American Republics to give priority to relations with America as against relations with European States.

With the outbreak of war in Europe in September 1939, inter-American cooperation was strengthened. The first meeting of the Foreign Ministers of the Republics took place in *Panama, 23 September–3 October 1939*. This conference adopted the *Act of Panama*, a multilateral executive agreement, which included a general declaration of neutrality; an agreement on the setting-up of a committee of experts for the duration of the war to study and make recommendations on problems of neutrality; a declaration that a neutral zone was established on the high seas 300 miles from the shores of the Republics; and, most important of all, a resolution that if any region in the Americas belonging to a European State should change sovereignties, thereby endangering the security of the Americas, a consultive meeting should be called urgently. The German conquests of the Netherlands and of France brought about a danger of the kind contemplated at Panama, and the Foreign Ministers therefore met again in *Havana, 21–30 July 1940*, and adopted the *Act of Havana* (p. 254). It stated that should a change of sovereignty be threatened in the case of the European colonies, then the American Republics would create a committee to administer them; but should the emergency arise before a committee could act, then one State could take action alone, which in practice meant the United States. Another resolution declared that aggression against one of the Republics would be regarded as aggression against all, though they were only bound to consult in that event on measures of common defence. The United States concluded many bilateral agreements with individual American States during the Second World War, providing credit, purchasing raw materials and securing rights of bases.

When shortly after Pearl Harbour the *third consultive meeting of American Foreign Ministers took place in Rio de Janeiro, 15–28 January 1942*, nine Central American and Caribbean States had declared war on the Axis and eleven Latin American States either broke off diplomatic relations or declared non-belligerency. But inter-American military cooperation remained far from wholehearted, with the Argentine being sympathetic to the Axis, and only by the time war was drawing to a close in 1945 had all the American Republics declared war on Germany and Japan. The future relations of the American Republics and inter-American cooperation in the post-war world which would see established the United Nations was the principal subject of the *Inter-American Conference on Problems of War and Peace, in Mexico City, 21 February–8 March 1945*. The conference was more concerned with post-war problems, and especially with the United Nations organization, than with problems of wartime alliance. The *Dumbarton Oaks* proposals were generally endorsed, but resolutions were also passed urging adequate representation for Latin American States on the proposed Security Council; in general the Latin American Republics wished to reduce the dominant role of the Great Powers. Agreement was reached on the *Act of Chapultepec, 3 March 1945* (Resolution 8) which provided for sanctions and appropriate regional action in the event of an American or non-American State committing aggression against another

American State, but with the additional proviso that such action would need to be consistent with the purpose of the world international organization when established. The Act of Chapultepec only remained in force whilst the war continued; it was intended that a new treaty should replace it later in time of peace. Other resolutions called upon the next American conference to agree on measures to strengthen inter-American collaboration in the economic and other fields. At the *San Francisco Conference* establishing the United Nations, the United States and the Latin American States secured an important modification of the Dumbarton Oaks proposals. It emerged as Article 51 of the Charter, which permitted groups of States to make treaties for collective self-defence to meet an armed attack. But this right is limited to the point of time when the Security Council takes what action it deems appropriate. It is nevertheless an important safeguard where the Security Council is deadlocked or where one of the permanent members uses its veto against any enforcement action. Article 51 is further limited by Articles 53 to 54, which state that whilst the Security Council may authorize some regional action for 'enforcement action', no such action may be taken without the authorization of the Security Council; the Security Council also has to be kept fully informed of any action in contemplation. Thus Article 51 only confers a right of self-defence in case of armed attack, not of enforcement against a State that is more vaguely accused of aggression or aggressive intent before an armed attack has occurred.

The United States and Canada

By the end of the first decade of the twentieth century all territorial disputes between the United States and the Dominion of Canada had been settled. A Convention in 1909 between Britain and the United States provided for the regulation of boundary waters, and set up an International Joint Commission to conciliate and report by majority vote disputes involving the inhabitants of both countries along their common frontier: moreover, with the consent of the British Government and the Senate, the Commission could reach a decision by a majority vote and in the case of a deadlock, refer the dispute to an umpire. Thus treaty machinery was created for the peaceful resolution of disputes between these two North American neighbours whose frontier became the first militarily undefended frontier in the world.

But internationally, Canada and the United States adopted different global policies. Canada supported Britain in the two World Wars from the outset, as well as becoming a member of the League of Nations. During the 1930s relations between Canada and the United States suffered from mutually discriminating trade tariffs. The Second World War brought Canada and the

United States closer together. On 17 August 1940, President Roosevelt and the Canadian Prime Minister, Mackenzie King, concluded an agreement at Ogdensburg to establish a *Permanent Joint Board on Defence*. Two weeks later, the *Destroyer–Naval Base Agreement, 2 September 1940*, leased to the United States a naval and an air base in Newfoundland. In 1941, mutual agreements coordinated defence production and assistance to Britain in both countries. During the war from 1942 to 1945, Canadian-United States cooperation became close and after 1945 the defence of the North American continent led to even closer coordination between the two nations.

Convention between the United States of America and other American Republics concerning the fulfillment of existing treaties between the American States, Buenos Aires, 23 December 1936

The Governments represented at the Inter-American Conference for the Maintenance of Peace,

Animated by a desire to promote the maintenance of general peace in their mutual relations;

Appreciating the advantages derived and to be derived from the various agreements already entered into condemning war and providing methods for the pacific settlement of international disputes;

Recognizing the need for placing the greatest restrictions upon resort to war; and

Believing that for this purpose it is desirable to conclude a new convention to coordinate, extend, and assure the fulfillment of existing agreements, have ... agreed upon the following provisions:

Article 1. Taking into consideration that, by the Treaty to Avoid and Prevent Conflicts between the American States, signed at Santiago, May 3, 1923 (known as the Gondra Treaty), the High Contracting Parties agree that all controversies which it has been impossible to settle through diplomatic channels or to submit to arbitration in accordance with existing treaties shall be submitted for investigation and report to a Commission of Inquiry;

That by the Treaty for the Renunciation of War, signed at Paris on August 28, 1928 (known as the Kellogg–Briand Pact, or Pact of Paris), the High Contracting Parties solemnly declare in the names of their respective peoples that they condemn recourse to war for the solution of international controversies and renounce it as an instrument of national policy in their relations with one another;

That by the General Convention of Inter-American Conciliation, signed at Washington, January 5, 1929, the High Contracting Parties agree to submit to the procedure of conciliation all controversies between them, which it may not have been possible to settle through diplomatic channels, and to establish a 'Commission of Conciliation' to carry out the obligations assumed in the Convention;

That by the General Treaty of Inter-American Arbitration, signed at Washington, January 5, 1929, the High Contracting Parties bind themselves to submit to arbitration, subject to certain exceptions, all differences between them of an international character, which it has not been possible to adjust by diplomacy and which are juridical in their nature by reason of being susceptible of decision by the application of the principles of law, and moreover, to create a procedure of arbitration to be followed; and

That by the Treaty of Non-Aggression and Conciliation, signed at Rio de Janeiro, October 10, 1933 (known as the Saavedra Lamas Treaty), the High Contracting Parties solemnly declare that they condemn wars of aggression in their mutual relations or in those with other States and that the settlement of disputes or controversies between them shall be effected only by pacific means which have the sanction of international law, and also declare that as between them territorial questions must not be settled by violence, and that they will not recognize any territorial arrangement not obtained by pacific means, nor the validity of the occupation or acquisition of territories brought about by force of arms, and, moreover, in a case of non-compliance with these obligations, the Contracting States undertake to adopt, in their character as neutrals, a common and solidary attitude and to exercise the political, juridical, or economic means authorized by international law, and to bring the influence of public opinion to bear, without, however, resorting to intervention, either diplomatic or armed, subject nevertheless to the attitude that may be incumbent upon them by virtue of their collective treaties; and, furthermore, undertake to create a procedure of conciliation;

The High Contracting Parties reaffirm the obligations entered into to settle, by pacific means, controversies of an international character that may arise between them.

Article 2. The High Contracting Parties, convinced of the necessity for the cooperation and consultation provided for in the Convention for the Maintenance, Preservation and Re-establishment of Peace signed by them on this same day, agree that in all matters which affect peace on the continent, such consultation and cooperation shall have as their object to assist, through the tender of friendly good offices and of mediation, the fulfillment by the American Republics of existing obligations for pacific settlement, and to take counsel together, with full recognition of their juridical equality, as sovereign and independent States, and of their general right to individual liberty of action, when an emergency arises which affects their common interest in the maintenance of peace.

Article 3. In case of threat of war, the High Contracting Parties shall apply the provisions contained in Articles 1 and 2 of the Convention for the Maintenance, Preservation, and Re-establishment of Peace, above referred to, it being understood that, while such consultation is in progress and for a period of not more than six months, the parties in dispute will not have recourse to hostilities or take any military action whatever.

Article 4. The High Contracting Parties further agree that, in the event of a dispute between two or more of them, they will seek to settle it in a spirit of mutual regard for their respective rights, having recourse for this purpose to direct diplo-

matic negotiations or to the alternative procedures of mediation, commissions of inquiry, commissions of conciliation, tribunals of arbitration, and courts of justice, as provided in the treaties to which they may be parties; and they also agree that, should it be impossible to settle the dispute by diplomatic negotiation and should the States in dispute have recourse to the other procedures provided in the present Article, they will report this fact and the progress of the negotiations to the other signatory States. These provisions do not affect controversies already submitted to a diplomatic or juridical procedure by virtue of special agreements.

Article 5. The High Contracting Parties agree that, in the event that the methods provided by the present Convention or by agreements previously concluded should fail to bring about a pacific settlement of differences that may arise between any two or more of them, and hostilities should break out between two or more of them, they shall be governed by the following stipulations;

(a) They shall, in accordance with the terms of the Treaty of Non-Aggression and Conciliation (Saavedra Lamas Treaty), adopt in their character as neutrals a common and solidary attitude; and shall consult immediately with one another, and take cognizance of the outbreak of hostilities in order to determine, either jointly or individually, whether such hostilities shall be regarded as constituting a state of war so as to call into effect the provisions of the present Convention.

(b) It is understood that, in regard to the question whether hostilities actually in progress constitute a state of war, each of the High Contracting Parties shall reach a prompt decision. In any event, should hostilities be actually in progress between two or more of the Contracting Parties, or between two or more signatory States not at the time parties to this Convention by reason of failure to ratify it, each Contracting Party shall take notice of the situation and shall adopt such an attitude as would be consistent with other multilateral treaties to which it is a party or in accordance with its municipal legislation. Such action shall not be deemed an unfriendly act on the part of any State affected thereby.

Article 6. Without prejudice to the universal principles of neutrality provided for in the case of an international war outside of America and without affecting the duties contracted by those American States, members of the League of Nations, the High Contracting Parties reaffirm their loyalty to the principles enunciated in the five agreements referred to in Article 1, and they agree that in the case of an outbreak of hostilities or threat of an outbreak of hostilities between two or more of them, they shall, through consultation, immediately endeavor to adopt in their character as neutrals a common and solidary attitude, in order to discourage or prevent the spread or prolongation of hostilities.

With this object, and having in mind the diversity of cases and circumstances, they may consider the imposition of prohibitions or restrictions on the sale or shipment of arms, munitions and implements of war, loans or other financial help to the States in conflict, in accordance with the municipal legislation of the High Contracting Parties, and without detriment to their obligations derived from other treaties to which they are or may become parties.

Article 7. Nothing contained in the present Convention shall be understood as affecting the rights and duties of the High Contracting Parties which are at the same time members of the League of Nations.

Article 8. The present Convention shall be ratified by the High Contracting Parties in accordance with their constitutional procedures. The original Convention and the instruments of ratification shall be deposited with the Ministry of Foreign Affairs of the Argentine Republic, which shall communicate the ratifica-

tions to the other signatory States. It shall come into effect when ratifications have been deposited by not less than eleven signatory States.

The Convention shall remain in force indefinitely; but it may be denounced by any of the High Contracting Parties, such denunciation to be effective one year after the date upon which such notification has been given. Notices of denunciation shall be communicated to the Ministry of Foreign Affairs of the Argentine Republic which shall transmit copies thereof to the other signatory States. Denunciation shall not be regarded as valid if the party making such denunciation shall be actually in a state of war, or shall be engaged in hostilities without fulfilling the provisions established by this Convention.

In witness whereof, the plenipotentiaries above-mentioned have signed this Treaty in English, Spanish, Portuguese, and French, and have affixed thereto their respective seals, in the City of Buenos Aires, Capital of the Argentine Republic, this twenty-third day of December of the year 1936.

RESERVATIONS

Reservation of the Argentine Delegation: (1) In no case, under Article 6, can foodstuffs or raw materials destined for the civil populations of belligerent countries be considered as contraband of war, nor shall there exist any duty to prohibit credits for the acquisition of said foodstuffs or raw materials which have the destination indicated.

With reference to the embargo on arms, each nation may reserve freedom of action in the face of a war of aggression.

Reservation of the Delegation of Paraguay: (2) In no case, under Article 6, can foodstuffs or raw materials destined for the civil populations of belligerent countries be considered as contraband of war, nor shall there exist any duty to prohibit credits for the acquisition of said foodstuffs or raw materials which have the destination indicated.

With reference to the embargo on arms,

each nation may reserve freedom of action in the face of a war of aggression.

Reservation of the Delegation of El Salvador: (3) With reservation with respect to the idea of continental solidarity when confronted by foreign aggression.

Reservation of the Delegation of Colombia: (4) In signing this Convention, the Delegation of Colombia understands that the phrase 'in their character as neutrals', which appears in Articles 5 and 6, implies a new concept of international law which allows a distinction to be drawn between the aggressor and the attacked, and to treat them differently. At the same time, the Delegation of Colombia considers it necessary, in order to assure the full and effective application of this Pact, to set down in writing the following definition of the aggressor:

That State shall be considered as an aggressor which becomes responsible for one or several of the following acts:

(a) That its armed forces, to whatever branch they may belong, illegally cross the land, sea, or air frontiers of other States. When the violation of the territory of a State has been effected by irresponsible bands organized within or outside of its territory and which have received direct or indirect help from another State, such violation shall be considered equivalent, for the purposes of the present Article, to that effected by the regular forces of the State responsible for the aggression;

(b) That it has intervened in a unilateral or illegal way in the internal or external affairs of another State;

(c) That it has refused to fulfill a legally given arbitral decision or sentence of international justice.

No consideration of any kind, whether political, military, economic, or of any other kind, may serve as an excuse or justification for the aggression here anticipated.

. . .

United States Senate Resolution when ratifying the Convention, 29 June 1937

The United States of America holds that the reservations of this Convention do not constitute an amendment to the text, but that such reservations, interpretations, and definitions by separate Governments are solely for the benefit of such respective Governments and are not intended to be controlling upon the United States of America.

Additional Protocol between the United States of America and other American Republics concerning non-intervention, Buenos Aires, 23 December 1936

The Governments represented at the Inter-American Conference for the Maintenance of Peace,

Desiring to assure the benefits of peace in their mutual relations and in their relations with all the nations of the earth, and to abolish the practice of intervention; and

Taking into account that the Convention on Rights and Duties of States, signed at the Seventh International Conference of American States, December 26, 1933, solemnly affirmed the fundamental principle that 'no State has the right to intervene in the internal or external affairs of another',

Have resolved to reaffirm this principle through the negotiation of the following Additional Protocol ...

Article 1. The High Contracting Parties declare inadmissible the intervention of any one of them, directly or indirectly, and for whatever reason, in the internal or external affairs of any other of the parties.

The violation of the provisions of this Article shall give rise to mutual consultation, with the object of exchanging views and seeking methods of peaceful adjustment.

Article 2. It is agreed that every question concerning the interpretation of the present Additional Protocol, which it has not been possible to settle through diplomatic channels, shall be submitted to the procedure of conciliation provided for in the agreements in force, or to arbitration, or to judicial settlement.

Article 3. The present Additional Protocol shall be ratified by the High Contracting Parties in conformity with their respective constitutional procedures. The original instrument and the instruments of ratification shall be deposited in the Ministry of Foreign Affairs of the Argentine Republic which shall communicate the ratifications to the other signatories. The Additional Protocol shall come into effect between the High Contracting Parties in the order in which they shall have deposited their ratifications.

Article 4. The present Additional Protocol shall remain in effect indefinitely but may be denounced by means of one year's notice after the expiration of which period the Protocol shall cease in its effects as regards the party which denounces it, but shall remain in effect for the remaining signatory States....

Convention on the provisional administration of European colonies and possessions in the Americas, Havana, 30 July 1940

The Governments represented at the Second Meeting of Ministers of Foreign Affairs of the American Republics,

Considering ...

That as a result of the events which are taking place in the European continent situations may develop in the territories of the possessions which some of the belligerent nations have in the Americas which may extinguish or materially impair the sovereignty which they exercise over them, or leave their Government without a leader, thus creating a state of danger to the peace of the continent and a state of affairs in which the rule of law, order, and respect for life, liberty and the property of inhabitants may disappear ...

That any transfer, or attempted transfer, of the sovereignty, jurisdiction, possession of any interest in or control over any such region to another non-American State, would be regarded by the American Republics as against American sentiments and principles and the rights of American States to maintain their security and political independence ...

That the American Republics, through their respective Government agencies, reserve the right to judge whether any transfer or attempted transfer of sovereignty, jurisdiction, cession or incorporation of geographic regions in the Americas, possessed by European countries up to September 1, 1939, has the effect of impairing their political independence even though no formal transfer or change in the status of such region or regions shall have taken place;

... Being desirous of protecting their

peace and safety and of promoting the interests of any of the regions herein referred to which may fall within the purview of the foregoing recitations, have resolved to conclude the following convention:

Article I. If a non-American State shall directly or indirectly attempt to replace another non-American State in the sovereignty or control which it exercised over any territory located in the Americas, thus threatening the peace of the continent, such territory shall automatically come under the provisions of this Convention and shall be submitted to a provisional administrative régime.

Article II. The administration shall be exercised, as may be considered advisable in each case, by one or more American States, with their previous approval.

Article III. When the administration shall have been established for any region it shall be exercised in the interests of the security of the Americas and for the benefit of the region under administration, with a view to its welfare and progress, until such time as the region is in a position to govern itself or is restored to its former status, whenever the latter is compatible with the security of the American Republics.

. . .

Article XVI. A Commission to be known as the 'Inter-American Commission for Territorial Administration' is hereby established, to be composed of a representative from each one of the States which ratifies this Convention; it shall be the international organization to which this Convention refers. Once this Convention has become effective, any country which ratifies it may convoke the first meeting proposing the city in which it is to be held. The Commission shall elect its chairman, complete its organization and fix its definitive seat. Two-thirds of the members of the Commission shall constitute a quorum and two-thirds of the members present may adopt decisions.

Article XVII. The Commission is authorized to establish a provisional administration in the regions to which the present Convention refers; allow such administration to be exercised by the number of States which it may determine in each case, and supervise its exercise under the terms of the preceding Articles.

Source references for the principal treaties

Treaty texts are usually to be found in several collections. Apart from national treaty series, there are some specialized regional compilations as mentioned in the preface. The publication of Peter H. Rohn's *World Treaty Index and Treaty Profiles* in six volumes (Santa Barbara, Calif., Clio Press) provides the first comprehensive indexing reference guide to more than 20,000 treaties concluded during the period since 1920. For the publication of contemporary treaty texts, a reliable compilation is provided by *Current Documents*, published as *International Legal Materials* (Washington, D.C.). For the chronological listing of principal treaties below, one major source reference is given in each case; the first number after the abbreviation refers to the volume and the second to the page in the volume. Thus LNTS 19:247 is the reference to the League of Nations Treaty Series, volume 19, page 247. One number after a name refers to the page in the book. The treaty texts reproduced from the *British and Foreign State Papers* and the British and German *Documents on Foreign Policy* are published by kind permission of Her Majesty's Stationery Office.

Key to abbreviations

BDFP   *Documents on British Foreign Policy 1919–1939*, edited by E. I. Woodward, R. Butler and others (London, 1949–).

Bevans   *Treaties and Other International Agreements of the United States of America 1776–1949*, compiled by Charles I. Bevans (Washington, D.C., 1968–).

BFSP   *British and Foreign State Papers* (London).

GDFP   *Documents on German Foreign Policy 1918–1945* (Washington, D.C., 1954–   ).

Hurewitz   *Diplomacy in the Near and Middle East. A Documentary Record*, by J. C. Hurewitz (Princeton, N.J., 1956, 2 vols.).

LNTS   *League of Nations Treaty Series. Treaties and international engagements registered with the Secretariat of the League of Nations* (Lausanne, 205 vols.).

NS   *Nazi–Soviet Relations 1939–41* (Washington, D.C., U.S. Department of State, 1948).

Shapiro   *Soviet Treaties, 1917–1939. A collection of bilateral agreements and conventions etc., concluded between the Soviet Union and foreign Powers*, edited by Leonard Shapiro (Washington, D.C., 1950–5, 2 vols.).

UST   *United States Treaties and Other International Agreements* (Washington, D.C.).

Wandycz   *France and her Eastern Allies 1919–25*, by P. S. Wandycz (Minneapolis, 1962).

1914–18

Alliance between Germany and Turkey, 2 August 1914   Hurewitz 2:1
Allied exchange of telegrams concerning the Straits, 4 March–10 April 1915   BDFP (1st ser.) 4:635
Treaty of London, 26 April 1915   BFSP 112:973
Alliance between Bulgaria, Germany and Austria-Hungary, 6 September 1915   LNTS 5:223
McMahon–Hussayn correspondence, July 1915–March 1916   Cmd 5937
Sykes–Picot Agreement, April–October 1916   BDFP (1st ser.) 4:241
Treaty of Brest-Litovsk, 3 March 1918   BFSP 123:727

1919

Treaty of Versailles, 28 June 1919   BFSP 112:1
Minorities Treaty between Allies and Poland, 28 June 1919   BFSP 112:232
Treaty of St Germain, 10 September 1919   BFSP 112:317
Treaty of Neuilly, 27 November 1919   BFSP 112:781

1920

Treaty of Trianon, 4 June 1920   BFSP 113:486
Treaty of Sèvres, 10 August 1920   BFSP 119:502
Treaty of Dorpat, 14 October 1920   LNTS 2:5

1921

Alliance Treaty between France and Poland, 19 February 1921, and Secret
   Military Convention between France and Poland, 21 February 1921
   Wandycz   app.:394–5
Treaty between Soviet Russia and Iran, 26 February 1921   LNTS 9:383
Treaty between Soviet Russia and Afghanistan, 28 February 1921   Shapiro
   1:96
Polish–Rumanian Alliance, 3 March 1921   LNTS 18:13
Anglo-Soviet Trade Agreement, 16 March 1921   BFSP 118:990
Treaty of Riga, 18 March 1921   LNTS 6:51
Four Power Washington Treaty, 13 December 1921   LNTS 25:84

1922

Limitation of naval armaments, 6 February 1922   BFSP 117:453
Nine Power Treaty, 6 February 1922   LNTS 38:278
Treaty of Rapallo, 16 April 1922   LNTS 19:247

1923

Treaty of Lausanne, 24 July 1923   LNTS 28:11

1924

Alliance Treaty between France and Czechoslovakia, 25 January 1924
   Wandycz app.:394–5

1925

Treaty between Japan and Soviet Union, 20 January 1925   LNTS 34:31
Locarno Treaties, 16 October 1925   LNTS 54:289
Alliance Treaty between France and Poland, 16 October 1925   LNTS 54:354
Alliance Treaty between France and Czechoslovakia, 16 October 1925
   LNTS 54:361

1926

Treaty of Berlin, 24 April 1926   LNTS 53:387
Treaty between Soviet Union and Lithuania, 28 September 1926   LNTS
   60:145

1927

Jedda Treaty, 20 May 1927   BFSP 134:273

1928

Pact of Paris, 27 August 1928   BFSP 128:447

1929

Soviet–German Conciliation Convention, 25 January 1929   LNTS 90:219
Conciliation and Arbitration Convention between American Republics, January 1929   Bevans 2:737
Protocol between Soviet Union and her neighbours concerning Pact of Paris, 9 February 1929   LNTS 89:369

1930

London Naval Treaty, 22 April 1930   LNTS 112:65
Little Entente Treaties, 27 June 1930   LNTS 107:215
Anglo-Iraq Alliance, 30 June 1930   BFSP 134:273

1932

Treaty between Soviet Union and Finland, 21 January 1932   LNTS 157:393
Treaty between Soviet Union and Latvia, 5 February 1932   LNTS 148:114
Treaty between Soviet Union and Estonia, 4 May 1932   LNTS 131:297
Treaty between Soviet Union and Poland, 25 July 1932   LNTS 136:41
Treaty between Soviet Union and France, 29 November 1932   LNTS 157:393

1933

Pact of Organization of Little Entente, 16 February 1933   LNTS 139:235
Treaty between Soviet Union and others defining aggression, 3–4 July 1933   LNTS 147:67

1934

Balkan Entente between Turkey, Greece, Rumania and Yugoslavia, 9 February 1934   LNTS 153:155
Baltic Entente, 3 November 1934   LNTS 154:95

1935

Soviet–Japanese Railway Treaty, 23 March 1935   LNTS 139:622
Soviet–French Mutual Assistance Treaty, 2 May 1935   LNTS 167:395
Soviet–Czech Mutual Assistance Treaty, 16 May 1935   LNTS 159:347
Anglo-German Naval Agreement, 18 June 1935   BFSP 139:182

1936

Soviet–Mongolian Alliance Treaty, 12 March 1936   BFSP 138:666
Austro-German Agreement, 11 July 1936   GDFP 1:278,342
Montreux Convention, 20 July 1936   BFSP 140:288
Anglo-Egyptian Alliance, 26 August 1936   BFSP 140:198
Anti-Comintern Pact between Japan and Germany, 26 November 1936
   Papers relating to Foreign Relations of the U.S. and Japan 1934–1941 (Washington, D.C., U.S. Department of State) 2:153
Fulfillment of treaties between American States, 23 December 1936   Bevans 3:348

1937

Soviet–Chinese Non-Aggression Treaty, 21 August 1937   LNTS 181:101
Nyon Agreement, 14 September 1937   LNTS 181:135

1938

Anglo-Italian Agreement, 16 April 1938   BFSP 142:147
Munich Agreement, 29 September 1938   BDFP (3rd ser.) 3:627
Franco-German Agreement, 6 December 1938   BDFP (3rd ser.) 3:391

1939

Alliance Treaty between Italy and Germany, 22 May 1939   GDFP 6:563
German–Soviet Trade Agreement, 19 August 1939   NS 83
German–Soviet Non-Aggression Pact, 23 August 1939   NS 76
Anglo-Polish Alliance Treaty, 25 August 1939   BFSP 143:301 and 158:393
German–Soviet Boundary Treaty, 28 September 1939   NS 105
Soviet–Estonian Pact, 28 September 1939   GDFP 8:166
Treaty between Britain, France and Turkey, 19 October 1939
   BFSP 151:213
Act of Panama, October 1939   Bevans 3:604

1940

German–Soviet Agreement, 11 February 1940   NS 131
Soviet–Finnish Peace Treaty, 12 March 1940   BFSP 144:383
Armistice between France and Germany, 22 June 1940   GDFP 9:671
Act of Havana, 30 July 1940   Bevans 3:619
Destroyer–Naval Base Agreement, 2 September 1940   BFSP 144:180
Tripartite Pact, 27 September 1940   LNTS 204:381

1941

Soviet–Japanese Neutrality Pact, 13 April 1941   BFSP 144:839
German–Turkish Non-Aggression Treaty, 18 June 1941   BFSP 144:816
Polish–Soviet Treaty, 30 July 1941   BFSP 144:869
British–Polish Note, 30 July 1941   BFSP 144:642
Atlantic Charter, 14 August 1941   LNTS 204:384

1942

United Nations Declaration, 1 January 1942   BFSP 144:1070
Anglo-Soviet–Iranian Treaty, 29 January 1942   BFSP 144:1017
Anglo-Soviet Alliance, 26 May 1942   BFSP 144:1038

1943

Italian armistice, 8–29 September 1943   Bevans 3:769
Soviet–Czechoslovak Treaty, 12 December 1943   BFSP 145:238

1944

Franco-Soviet Alliance, 10 December 1944   BFSP 149:632

1945

Yalta Conference, 4–11 February 1945   Bevans 3:1005
Act of Chapultepec, 6 March 1945   Bevans 3:1024

Index

Page references in **bold** lettering refer to the texts of the treaties